Best Sellers

from
Reader's Digest
Condensed Books

Best Sellers

from
Reader's Digest
Condensed Books

The Reader's Digest Association
Pleasantville, New York

The condensations in this volume
have been created by
The Reader's Digest Association, Inc.,
and are used by permission of
and special arrangement with
the publishers and the holders
of the respective copyrights.

•

With the exception of
actual personages identified as such,
the characters and incidents
in the fictional selections in this volume
are entirely the product of
the authors' imagination
and have no relation to any person
or event in real life.

Contents

The Gift of the Deer

The Gift of the Deer

A condensation of the book by
Helen Hoover

Illustrations by Stanley W. Galli
Line drawings by Adrian Hoover

Helen and Adrian Hoover gave up successful careers in Chicago to follow a dream into the chill, beautiful border forest between Minnesota and Canada. Through hard work and courage, they found a good life there. They also found the unexpected: a view of the intricacy, excitement, tragedy and humor of wilderness life granted to very few.

With patience and understanding, they helped and observed a family of deer of wildly and amusingly different personalities. Above all, they made a trusting friend of the founder of this family, a deer neither they nor the reader can ever forget—a generous, great-hearted buck they called Peter.

This is a true, magical story of wildlife in a sheltering wilderness. But it is especially, and uniquely, the story of Peter.

The First Year

SOME fifteen feet from the door of the two-room log cabin where my husband, Ade, and I have lived every winter and some summers of the past eleven years there is a white cedar tree, one of many in the ancient forest that surrounds the cabin. This tree, damaged by years of scanty rainfall, is dying. Near its roots lies a little pile of bare branches which gives perching space to small birds and cover to timid deer mice and voles. Neither Ade nor I will ever move these branches or fell the tree, for this was Peter Whitetail's tree and the branches are all that remain of the green and fragrant cedar cut for him on the memorable day that brought him to our clearing near the lake.

Peter was a buck who came to us in the fullness of his maturity. To have the trust of any deer is a joy, but when a buck, reserved and cautious as these regal animals are, accepts you, it is a very special thing. And Peter was a special kind of buck—gentle, generous, great of heart.

IT ALL began on a Christmas Day when our friend Jacques Plessis had been sharing a turkey dinner with us. Jacques is an old-time lumberjack, slow and quiet of speech, with the size and strength of those now almost legendary men. He also has an appetite developed in the days when trees were cut with handsaws.

Today Jacques had brought us a box of chocolate-covered cherries and the largest buttercup squash I ever saw. I had actually crooned over that squash. We had no car in those days and brought staples by boat down the border lake which separates our Minnesota shore from Canada. When the lake froze over, supplies had to be gotten by mail, forty-five miles from the nearest village on a one-way road, and had to be carried in Ade's packsack for the last three miles along our side road. Fresh things were out. Even a squash would freeze after an hour at thirty below.

Now, between the three of us, we turned half of the twenty-six-pound turkey into a handsome ruin, and then considered whether any more mashed potatoes, beets, peas, cranberries, raw-carrot salad, watermelon-rind pickles, Anadama bread or chocolate-coconut pie could safely be consumed. But I was as stuffed as the turkey had been. I got up, went to the cabin window and looked out at our small span of virgin timber, somehow spared by both fire and the axes of early lumbermen. On the forest's edge was a great white pine that had been a sapling when the Declaration of Independence was signed. It stood aloof as though wrapped in its memories. As I looked, I heard branches snap, and to my surprise out of the forest, into the clearing, stepped a deer.

He headed straight for some Swiss chard seedstalks that protruded above the snow in our tiny garden plot and began to eat. He was so thin that every rib stood out. His legs trembled and his head shook as he pulled the seedstalks loose. I made gestures to Jacques, who had known deer well from boyhood. As he and Ade came quietly, the buck looked up at us. His face was gaunt, his right ear raggedly notched, and his eyes dull. He jerked as though to run away, then dropped his head again to the seeds.

Jacques gave his special grunt of suppressed fury. "Some damfool's hit his head with fine shot," he snapped. "Look at his left eye—it's blind. Maybe two months ago, in the grouse season. He's near starved. No wild buck would come this close to a house otherwise." His voice subsided to a growl. "Maybe he'd be better off if we killed him."

"No!" I said. "Can't we feed him?"

"You can try. He's still on his feet. Let him snoop 'round the place and see you in the windows. Don't make any sudden moves to startle him. Then give him cedar. Ade can cut some of those branches the poor critter can't reach. Cedar'll help deer when they're so far gone they can't stand up on all fours. If he can nibble it, he'll get well." Jacques looked sideways at me. "But if he fattens up he'll be a mighty big pet—around two fifty pounds. Sure you won't be afraid of him?"

I stared. "Heavens, no. With us the only people within miles, it's almost miraculous that he managed to stumble in here. He won't bother us. Maybe I'm superstitious—but I'd bet on it."

"I wouldn't take you," Jacques said. "Animals know when you don't mean 'em any harm. They can smell when you're scared or mad. Queer, that."

"Not so queer. Fear and anger send adrenaline into your system and make you sweat. Maybe that's what they smell."

The buck had nosed his way to the near side of the garden, only six feet from the window. He looked up, but this time he did not start, just dropped his head again and went on feeding.

"My tree pruner would be fine for cutting cedar," Ade said.

"Peter is a nice name," Jacques suggested.

"Yes. Peter Whitetail," Ade agreed.

Peter having been named and his future hopefully planned, we set about watching him, first from one window, then another.

He chewed some dead raspberry canes and snatched eagerly at a spindly asparagus stalk and at length moved to the front of the house, where he painfully tried to rise on his shaking hind legs to reach the green cedar branches a few inches above his head. Unable to lift himself, he stood panting for several minutes, then sniffed the bleached bones of a turkey carcass, nailed onto a cedar trunk at Thanksgiving as a source of calcium and phosphorus for the squirrels. Chewing desperately and pitifully, he finally wrenched the bones loose from the tree and crunched and swallowed most of them. He raised his head and followed the scent of suet to a wire-mesh feeder hung on a branch for the

15

birds. In a sort of tottering lunge, he managed to knock it to the ground with his nose and licked at the fat through the mesh.

Jacques reached for his jacket, warming on a chair near the stove. "I'd better hustle home. That poor critter'll run when I go out, but not far. The suet'll bring him back."

"I'll go up to the road with you," Ade said, turning down the fur-lined flaps of his cap. "I can help you get started and I'll take the pruner and cut some cedar branches on the way back."

Jacques looked at Peter, still licking the suet cage. "Tomorrow take out anything you can spare—potato skins, bread. Deer don't usually eat meat, but this guy goes for suet."

With a last "Merry Christmas," Jacques opened the door slowly and stepped out. Peter started and looked fixedly at him. With his front hoofs on the suet cage, he stood firm until Ade, too, appeared outside. Then he whirled and tried to run, but staggered and almost fell. Glancing fearfully back with his good eye, he walked into the brush as fast as he could.

While Ade was helping build a small fire under the pan of Jacques's truck to warm the oil, I lighted the lamps and considered food for Peter. I took the wrapped potato peelings from the trash and stole a little from our canned vegetables. There were ten pounds of suet in the fifty-five-gallon oil drum that serves as our winter freezer. The birds would not miss small rations of their suet, and Peter's should be very small at first. Too much fat on a starved digestive system might be harmful.

I dug out some suet and knelt in the snow, struggling to close the bolt-and-spring contraption that Ade had designed to prevent fishers, those latch-lifting big cousins of the weasels, from raiding our meat supply in the drum. Then Ade, so loaded with branches that he looked like a walking tree, skidded down the path and laid the rich-scented greenery, with the suet, under our largest white cedar. It was near the door but somewhat secluded by smaller cedars, maple brush, and the miniature house and run that sheltered Bedelia, our pet black hen.

The early northern dusk had darkened into night before Ade and I finished clearing away the remains of our Christmas feast.

We waited a long time by the window in the darkened kitchen, while aurora lights flickered in the sky, but Peter did not come.

If he understood that a man had injured him, he might not dare come near the cabin again after he had seen us outside. On the other hand, if he had been far away from the shooter, he would have experienced only shock and pain, while darkness spread from his left side where he had seen his familiar forest before.

Only?

Suddenly I was sickened and furious at the trigger-happy unknown who had fired such a senseless shot. He had brought reasonless brutality into our forest, where no wild animal would injure another except for food or in defense of its life or young. Because of this, Peter had wandered—confused, handicapped, starving—as he tried inadequately to adjust to the partial blindness he could not understand. I was very near tears, when Ade touched my arm and pointed up the path.

Halfway to the road, between two tree boles, Peter was sniffing the air. The aurora had changed from green to red and the snow before him glowed like a carpet of rose quartz. Still sniffing, his head high, he began to walk down the hill, faster and faster until he was almost trotting. Straight on the scent of the cedar he came until he buried his nose in it and began to eat.

As though he read my mind, Ade said, "Things aren't quite so bad when you can help undo them, are they?"

At midnight an unusual chill in the cabin woke me and I went out to check on the weather. The thermometer had dropped to an ominous thirty-seven degrees below zero and would drop more before morning. Gusts of wind brought needles of snow from the north. We would need a helper fire in the stove in the morning. As I turned from the woodpile with my arms loaded, Peter, who had curled up in the snow to sleep under the big cedar tree, lifted his head, then settled down again. Beside him a snowshoe hare nibbled bark from a cedar stump. On a branch above, no doubt hoping for a mouse, a little saw-whet owl peered at the ground.

17

In spite of the bitter cold, I watched for minutes, amazed and marveling. There is a legend—from Norway, I think—which says that all lost animals come home at Christmastime.

Peter was no longer lost.

December 26 to February 3

IN THE dimness of early morning I woke to the sounds of wood crackling inside and wind roaring outside in the trees. I wrapped my wool robe around me, grabbed my clothes, and scooted across the cold floor to toast myself by the stove. As I dressed, Ade came down the path with two five-gallon cans of fuel oil on the toboggan. A blast of icy air accompanied him and one of the cans inside.

"It's forty-three below," he said, pouring oil into the big space heater. "And the wind is almost a full gale. There isn't a sign of life outside."

As the coffee dripped, I looked out the window. The sky was a pale robin's-egg blue and perfectly clear, but visibility on the ground was cut to fifty feet by slanting veils of blowing, drifting snow. A beautiful day, but a savage one, hard on man and beast.

Then I saw Peter. His head down against the wind, he was making his way laboriously from the partial shelter he had found in the maples on the hillside toward the house. As Ade smothered a sound of pity, I fixed breakfast for Peter. To the potato skins and some suet, I added leftover canned peas, mashed potatoes, turkey gravy and some of the cracked corn we kept for our hen, Bedelia. Everything but the corn would freeze solid in minutes, but I did not think Peter would mind.

18

When I opened the door, Peter was almost within arm's reach. His blind eye was frosted shut, but he flinched. Then his nostrils quivered as he smelled the food. His breath came in heavy gasps as he pushed his head forward, mouth open and pink tongue partly out. I put the food on the step and backed inside. He cleaned it, to the last crumb. When he looked at Ade and me through the glass of the kitchen-door window, he hold his head up with something like confidence. Then he tapped on the step with a hoof, ducked his head several times, and waited.

"That's plain enough," Ade said. "He's telling us he wants more. How about carrots! I ground about three times too many yesterday."

Ade reached into our icebox. Peter ate the carrots with enthusiasm. Finished, he licked his lips, captured a small piece that adhered to his black nose, shook his ears, and turned eagerly toward the door. For the first time I realized that the slight changes of a wild animal's facial expression might convey meaning to a human. Unless I was greatly mistaken Peter *liked* carrots. And I'd been wondering what to do with the bushel and a half of them we had buried in boxes of sand under Ade's drawing table—the only large crop from our garden in the thin, poor soil of the forest.

With one of the rapid changes of our northern winter, the noontime temperature went up to zero and the bitter wind died. I was standing in the yard enjoying the dry, cold-freshened air and the turquoise zigzags of shadow across the miniature snow dunes when I heard Jacques whistling as he snowshoed down Ade's toboggan track. "I brought Peter a sack of corn," Jacques said. "This here"—he unwrapped a parcel—"is a leg off a little fawn I found frozen a week ago. Got into deep snow and couldn't get out."

I looked at the sawed-off end of the frozen limb. The marrow was blood-red. "What caused that?"

"Starved. The fat on their body goes, then the fat inside the bones. When they get like this . . ." He shook his head. "I was afraid your boy Peter was too far gone, but I knew you'd want to help him. Ade and I will fix him a real garden before I go."

The men stacked most of the cedar branches in the storage building and pushed the cut ends of the rest firmly into the level snow above the garden plot. Then they walked back and forth through the drifts to open a way from our hard-packed path to Peter's garden. "Anything that saves his energy, like that little trail, will help him," Jacques said as he turned to go. "And as long as it's this cold you can cut cedar ahead and it won't dry out."

Ade and I waved good-by. Jacques was off to a lumber camp and we would not see him again until spring.

In the morning my first sight from the window was of Peter, nipping cedar in his garden. When he had enough, he walked slowly but steadily toward the cabin. There he bumped heavily against the ladder, which Ade had left slanting from the edge of the roof. He trembled with fright. The ladder was on his blind side and he seemed not to know what had struck him, nor how to turn his head to find out. While he moved timidly away to eat, Ade shifted the ladder and I thought over Peter's problem. He could not be independent if he did not learn how to cope with his one-sided blindness. He had managed to tell us that he wanted more food, and that he liked carrots. Could I show him how to see to the left with an eye designed mainly for front and right-hand vision?

I walked outside, repeating his name over and over. He twisted his ears toward the strange sound but did not turn his head. I stopped just behind his left shoulder and waved my arm slowly past the blind side of his head and ahead of his nose. His right eye caught the movement and, as I drew my hand back, he turned his head until he was looking back at me with his right eye.

After four days of this, Peter followed the sound of my voice, twisting his head to the left, or over his back. It is not unusual for deer to do this. Apparently Peter, either from the shock of his injury or from the confusion caused by his blindness, was afraid to look back. It was not until years later, after I had watched other deer step away when I approached too near, that I was humbled by an understanding of his amazing trust.

Only once did we unintentionally frighten Peter. Deer are said to be color-blind and we gave no thought as to what we wore. Once I had the bright idea of buying a bargain assortment of men's shirts from a mail-order house. Among them was an affair with inch-wide bars of green, black, yellow and scarlet. Ade gave one look and said, "Burn it!" I finally persuaded him to wear it in the winter when we were unlikely to have visitors. But the first time he went out in the thing Peter snorted and bounded at once into the brush. The "deer-scarer" shirt is now in the bag where I keep scraps for a rag rug.

By the end of January Peter was no thinner than many deer at the end of a hard winter. The small wounds on his head had disappeared, but there was a permanent notch on his right ear. The alarm squalls of the blue jays, which are one of the most quickly heeded wilderness danger signals, always alerted him, but he soon learned to distinguish between true alarms and the false alarms, which are the jays' clear-the-deck technique to give them uncontested access to our feeding area. He had also adjusted to the sound of voices from the lake, where ice fishermen huddled against the wind, and he frequently stepped up to the cabin to listen and sniff our many odors.

One afternoon when Ade was out cutting cedar I heard the heavy thudding of approaching hoofs and opened the door to meet Peter's skidding arrival in front of the step. He snorted like a terrified horse and lifted his head, with widespread nostrils, toward the west. I turned that way and smelled woodsmoke.

Peter, still too weak for a run, stood panting. I followed our path westward down a slope and across the frozen brook. Just beyond, dangerously close to a deserted cabin, an ice fisherman had left an oversized campfire burning. As I scattered the blazing branches with a stick and covered them with snow, I wondered why Peter had come to tell me of the fire. Had this blaze been left on a breezy, snowless day, his warning could well have prevented a fire which would have burned us out.

I ground an extra portion of carrots for Peter, thinking it a pity that research on game animals is so largely directed toward producing them, and that study of them as individuals is neglected. Primitive men respected their wild neighbors and learned from them. Much is lost by moderns who look on them only as things or meat.

As Peter accepted our odors, so he also became accustomed to our sounds, though more selectively. The loud clang when I accidentally dropped the heavy lid of my dutch oven on the iron stove only made him twitch his ears, but any thump like a deer's stomp brought a quick alert. When the wind was strong, he came near the cabin and listened nervously, apparently unable to separate out the sounds which might mean danger. Perhaps he felt safer near the cabin and us. We like to think so.

The hubbub of a city passes over me as though it were not there because it is none of my business; but here, windy nights make me restless. My cure is to turn on the battery radio. I had no idea that Peter, lying under his tree, would pay any attention to music until I went outside one evening to put food out for my flying squirrels and saw him sitting up with his ears turned to catch the strains of "Mood Indigo." He listened attentively until the program changed to a Strauss waltz. Then he lowered his head, laid his ears back, stood up, and stalked into the woods.

THERE IS much talk of the "January thaw"; actually, it may arrive anytime from December on. During Peter's first winter with us it came on February 3, a glorious, sunny, forty-five-degree day. While we stood outside, soaking up warmth, Bedelia set up a loud cackling. "I'd better get her screen door or she'll yell all day," Ade said, and headed for the storage building.

Bedelia is a hen of character. She arrived along with twenty-three other month-old black chicks a year after we moved here and is still scratching around outside today at the ripe old age of ten years plus. We had planned to raise chickens for eggs and food but proper heating and housing for them in this climate turned out to be uneconomical. We did try to set Bedelia once, but she looked at the nestful of eggs, gave an outraged squawk, and settled herself on some bare boards. Eggs she would lay, but her responsibilities ended there.

The other chickens went the way of all flesh, but Bedelia's antics were so entertaining that we kept her as an egg supplier and pet. Ade remodeled a small storage shed into a private cottage for her and turned an old-fashioned oil lantern into a stove, screened so Bedelia could not catch her tail feathers on fire. Then he built her a little run with a gate through which I can just manage to reach in to feed her, usually catching my hair on the wire in the process.

Once settled in her small domain, Bedelia rapidly adjusted to woods life. Bears peer at her with interest and ermines scoot around her feet while she goes right on preening her feathers. She does not like foxes, but she never sets up an alarm unless a big owl perches nearby.

On this particular day, when Ade opened her wooden door and fitted in her screen to let her enjoy the view, Peter walked out of the woods. He hesitated, then walked over and lowered his head to peer closely at this feathered creature. This was too much for Bedelia. Squawking and flapping, she managed to push out the unhooked screen, and shot straight into Peter's face with only the wire between them. He jerked back, caught his rear hoofs in some way and sat down on his rump. Bedelia flew onto a branch, where she set up a wild clamor, soon added to by the jays and squirrels. Ade ran to get a length of wire to catch her. Peter, staring incredulously at her, slowly rolled to one side, got up, and walked away, with what dignity he had left. He never again showed the slightest interest in Bedelia or her domain.

February 6 to Mid-February

THE thaw was short-lived and three nights later we had wind-less, bitter cold. Ade was already asleep when, with the lamp glowing on my night table, I settled down to read *Dracula,* in a forest which might well have been the prototype of the dark fictional one which surrounded the vampire's castle. I read:

"I heard a sound in the courtyard without . . . the voice of the Count calling in his harsh, metallic whisper. His call seemed to be answered from far and wide by the howling of wolves . . ."

I dropped the book and jerked sharply upright. I must be dreaming—I could *hear* those wolves! A chorus of their voices, moaning in different pitches, blending into a chorded song—coming near, getting louder. My skin crawled. Then Ade sat up, yawned, and said, in a matter of fact way, "Wolves on the road, aren't there?" Dracula's werewolves vanished like popped bubbles as Ade turned over and went back to sleep.

We had heard no wolves that winter and I had forgotten all about them. Now as their voices died away, I thought anxiously of Peter. But the breeze was from the east; Peter would have scented the wolves, I knew; and indeed, the next day, he sniffed the wind and listened carefully in all directions as he ate.

A FEW NIGHTS LATER I was wakened by the most dreadful sound I had ever heard, a hoarse scream that had a human quality. Icy with sweat, shaking, I sat up in bed and tried to locate it, but it moved through the woods, so muffled and distorted by snow and air currents that it seemed to shift directions. Then I caught a bleating undertone. It was a deer screaming, and the thing that sounded human was the note of mortal terror, which is the same in any creature's shriek of desperation.

I shook Ade awake. "Something's wrong with Peter!"

The terrible sound came again, now from the lake. We reached the north window just as a giant timber wolf ran across the snow beneath the window, head out, tail flowing—death on silent feet. I whimpered and Ade caught my shaking hands. "Get hold of yourself. It isn't Peter. Look—there on the ice."

A very small deer was struggling to keep its footing on the slippery surface. A wolf sprang on it from the rear. The deer slipped and fell. A second wolf closed in. There was one more scream, then silence and a huddled movement on the ice.

"There's something wrong," I babbled. "It doesn't *look* right—they might be ghosts—"

"You're just scared silly," Ade said. "Let's have some tea."

Ten minutes later, feeling a complete fool for my lapse into superstition, I handed Ade his teacup and looked out the window again. The huddle was still there. And something still looked unnatural to me, although I refrained from saying so.

"Let's sit down," Ade said. "There isn't anything more to see."

"Or hear," I added, thankfully.

But hours later I was still awake, trying to figure out why I was so disturbed. It had been quick; no more than three minutes from the deer's first cry to the end. And such an end was far easier than that of a doe who had broken through spring ice on the lake the year before and climbed up again and again, only to have the ice break, until exhaustion let her slip under the water. Or that of another doe, who, rising on her hind feet to get cedar, had slipped and caught a foreleg between two small trees; her long struggle must have been agonizing before it ended.

25

Then I realized that the ruthless savagery of the wolf kill had temporarily stunned my reason. Savage as it had been, it was for the betterment of the group from which one deer was now gone. This was the natural way to prevent overpopulation, and starvation for many.

I was dropping off to sleep when I thought I heard a faint bleat, like that of a lamb. I jumped up and as I looked out into the pale light Ade, who had not been able to sleep either, joined me. The tremulous sound came again.

"Behind Peter's cedar tree," I whispered. "A fawn."

"It must be the twin of the one that was killed. But where's the mother? It's too little and scared to take care of itself. It needs help."

As if in answer, Peter moved into sight very slowly, as the fawn bleated and backed uncertainly away until its rump was against our woodpile. Peter came near, nosed its face gently, licked behind an ear, then stood quietly by its side. We scarcely breathed while the fawn lifted its head and timidly licked the side of his face. When he moved away, the fawn, now quiet, followed him.

We stepped outside and watched them walk into the forest.

Ade shook his head in amazement. "You could watch deer for a lifetime and they'd show you some new side of themselves every day. Do you suppose it's his fawn?"

"Very doubtful. Bucks are Casanovas. He's just baby-sitting. . . . Sometimes the things I see here give me a bewitched feeling."

"This is an enchanted night," Ade said. "It's even light under the trees. And look—*we* aren't casting any shadows."

The sky was so screened with swirling frost and the snow so thickly covered with it that the light of the moon was wholly and perfectly diffused. Under the thickly branched trees, on our faces turned to the sky, on the snow behind us, there was a silvery, even glow. "That's why I thought the wolf wasn't real," I said. "No shadow. Perhaps nights like this started the superstition that werewolves cast no shadows."

A howl drifted to me on the rising wind, to be joined almost at once by another, lighter voice. The same wolves? Perhaps. I imagined them, heads up, ears cocked, bushy tails flowing behind them as their long legs made light of the hilly miles, hunting, always hunting, in their phase of the struggle for existence.

Mid-February to April 7

In the morning, a long, pale beam of sunlight slanted through the east window of the living room. Not since early November had the sun's arc been high enough to send morning light through that window. Responding to this advance notice of spring, I carried a cup of coffee outside to watch Ade feeding the birds.

He coaxed the gray jays down to his fingers for crackers while the blue jays perched in the trees and conversed in their spring voices—clicks and buzzes and little flutelike notes. Two male downy woodpeckers, with ruby-bright headpatches, argued in spirited squeals for first place at a hanging suet feeder. I saw the wide-spaced, neatly pared tracks of a bounding ermine and watched a snowshoe hare scamper across the hill like a boisterous snowball. I thought of people who have said to me, "From Christmas until April in the woods is just a long drag." How much they miss, sitting inside with a murmuring radio for company!

"We've had a special visitor," I said to Ade and pointed to a line of tiny deer tracks spaced between larger ones. "I saw the doe come at first light for her little buck. The lower halves of his front legs are white. I've named him Snowboots. I saw Peter, too, under his cedar tree. I think he brought the little guy back and the doe may have been waiting."

We walked to Peter's tree. We had not seen his tracks before in snow that took a clean impression, but now we saw that he had a notched hoof, the result of some accident, and as distinguishing an identification mark as a fingerprint.

As the days brightened and lengthened the pattern of forest life began to change. The barred owls, who enlivened winter nights with their deep "Who-*who*-waaah! You-*you*-aaaall!" set up a lively cackling and grunting, with periods of weird and noisy hooting. This is their voice of tenderness. Before going to their nest in a tree hollow, one pair did their courting in a big pine west of the cabin, bobbing and bowing to each other, flapping their wings and filling the air with full-voiced hoots that surely could be heard for miles.

Peter stayed near the clearing, eating his cedar, corn, vegetable scraps and suet, and the carrots, which always set him shaking his ears and prancing like a fawn—incongruous and delightful behavior in a dignified buck now fattened up to around two hundred pounds. By the middle of March his body was strong and his face beautiful. He began to roam the forest, usually coming to the yard once each day for a good meal.

One evening, as he was nipping his cedar, another buck, slim and long-legged, leaped from the forest into the garden. He struck at the snow in front of Peter, who snorted, lifted a foreleg to stomp solidly, and walked over until they were almost touching noses. I wondered if they would fight, but this was not the rutting season. They stood unmoving for several minutes. Then Peter stepped back and they both began to eat. Apparently they had settled matters to their mutual satisfaction because Peter soon moved away into the woods with his new friend at his heels.

Just after sundown, I was surprised and pleased to see young Snowboots walk cautiously into the cedar garden. Peter and his Friend appeared at the edge of the clearing at the same time. Friend bounded into the cedar garden almost on top of Snowboots, who fled without getting a bite, Friend hard after him. Peter ran diagonally through the woods in magnificent leaps, cut in front of Friend, and blocked him long enough for Snowboots to get away. Then Peter returned to the cedar and Friend followed shortly after. Friend stomped and snorted and generally expressed displeasure at the whole proceeding. Peter finally whirled and struck in his direction and Friend subsided. I reflected that their personalities varied even more than their appearance.

The next afternoon, while Ade was out cutting cedar and the bucks were gone, I saw Snowboots deep in the woods with his mother close by. She had a distinctive stance, head lifted and thrust forward, ears so twisted to listen for sounds from both cabin and road that she looked vaguely as though she wore one of the gallantly tip-tilted Australian hats. She stomped—and stomped and stomped. At last convinced that there was no imminent danger, she reared on her hind legs to reach and break down a high cedar branch. Snowboots leaped forward and buried his nose in the fresh and fragrant green.

Deer do not rear up for browse unless they need it badly. Instinct seems to warn them that there is danger of a fall, even of impalement on sharp branches. When Ade came back with his cedar, I asked him how to help the two.

"Simple," he said. "I'll make another garden. Where were they?" I pointed out the rather open place, and soon a new little patch of upright branches looked very enticing there.

We had just finished dinner when Ade said, "What's that?"

I listened. Thump—thump—thump. "The doe—stomping," I said. "Blow out the lamp. There's a young moon."

She moved in the soft light, a pale and wary wraith, stomping, listening, sniffing the air, the snow. At length, she turned toward the trees and Snowboots leaped out. They were eating quietly, probably free of hunger for the first time in many days, when a cloud bank rolled up from the south like the smoke of a vast campfire and hid them under its shadow.

THE WIND that brought the clouds was warm. Next morning loosened snow dropped from the trees and a pair of red squirrels started an early courtship and chased each other round a balsam trunk. The great cycle of forest life was approaching full swing again.

Peter and Friend began to roam farther and sometimes did not come to the yard for days. Friend tolerated us from a distance, but never trusted us as Peter did. Occasionally Snowboots approached when Ade and I were outside, as though he wanted to see what we were doing. This was always nipped in the bud by his mother, who chased after him, whacked him soundly on the rump with a hoof, and herded him back into the forest. Plainly, a wise doe kept her child out of people's way.

One day Jacques came whistling down the path. The thaw had stopped the winter lumbering. While we were sitting over tea and cookies, Jacques looked out of the window and almost dropped his cup. "There's a big buck out there!"

"That," Ade said smugly, "is Peter."

"Watch," I said, and opened the door.

Peter walked sedately to the door and peered inside as I went for his grain. His ears twitched, the tip of his tongue showed pink against his black muzzle. He backed up a step to let me go out and pour the grain on the snow. When it was finished he looked up expectantly and I brought him carrots. Those eaten and his appreciation expressed by the usual toss of his head and bouncy little step, he walked over to stand under his tree and chew his cud.

Jacques was shaking his head when I rejoined the men. "I was born in the woods, but I never thought I'd see that—a grown buck taking to people! He comes to you like a horse! How'd you get him trained?"

"I didn't train him," I said. "I let him train me."

CARS MOVED on the road now, and Snowboots and his mother quietly vanished into the forest. Peter fed hastily, keeping his eye on Friend, who no longer came down from the hill. If Friend walked away, Peter trotted after him. The time was near for bucks to leave for the secret places where they spend the summer, and Peter did not seem to want to go alone. I wondered if he needed Friend to aid him, once he was away from his familiar wintering place. Perhaps he just wanted companionship.

One morning in early April, we heard Peter tapping on the step. I went out with grain, but he only licked off the top of it, then stood looking around and sniffing the air. Up on the hill, half-hidden by the budding maple, Friend was slowly moving toward the east. Peter walked up the path. He stopped at a place where an animal trail crosses our human trail, and stood motionless, looking back at us. Then he followed his companion into the forest.

The Second Year

December 1 to December 24

LATE ON SNOWY December first, there was a sharp rap on the door, near the top. It didn't sound like a knock. It came again and sent a prickling across the back of my neck. But mindful that fear of the unknown must have no place in lives in the wilderness, I opened the door, and looked straight into Peter's face.

With a deep breath, I stepped aside to let the lamplight flow over his strong, heavy body, his neck so thickened for the rutting season that his face looked disproportionately small. With his thirteen-point antlers, he was a forest king, perhaps nine years old, in full mating armament; but his face was still gentle. He tapped on the step with a hoof and showed the tip of his tongue.

31

He had come for supper. He ate, chewed his cud, and then explored the yard carefully, examining every little change. After the cabin was dark, I heard the tap of his antler against the logs as he completed his survey by nosing into the woodshed.

The annual renewal of a buck's antlers will never cease to astonish me. In April, dark gray bumps appear slightly in front of and between the ears, on the bony mounds called pedicels. The development of the antlers is so rapid that they may reach full size in less than five months. Soft, growing antlers are covered by the layer of thick, fuzzy velvet which carries their blood supply. Does need only threaten to strike at tender growing antlers to chase away bucks from nursing fawns.

When the antlers harden, bucks rub the velvet off against trees and brush. This may take several days, during which the antlers look as though they are draped with shreds of bark. When the last velvet is gone and the antlers are polished, the buck is the handsomest fellow in the woods. The number of points does not indicate a buck's age. Sometimes first antlers, fully developed at one and a half years, have six or more points.

On the eighth of December, when Peter was eating in the yard, a squirrel climbed one of his legs. He stomped and jolted off this trespasser, just as a black-capped chickadee settled on one of his antler beams, protesting Peter's consumption of corn in a strident bass. Peter, looking slightly astonished, raised his head. The chickadee, in front of his ear, appeared to be yelling into an old-fashioned ear trumpet. This was too much for Peter's sensitive hearing. He jerked his head and the antler dropped, with the little bird hanging on all the way down to the ground, complaining loudly. Peter, his head cocked to one side to balance the remaining antler, strolled into the woods. Four days later he came back without his second antler.

It is not surprising that one rarely finds fallen antlers, for mice, moles, hares, squirrels and chipmunks, I discovered, demolish them for their calcium and phosphorus.

Antlers have a heavy, musky fragrance, which is very tenacious. As I write, I have an antler on my desk, dropped months

ago by Starface, Peter's son. Its scent is still so strong that it transfers to my fingers at the slightest handling.

Bucks are said to be unpredictable as long as they carry their antlers. But I think Peter had finished his season of fighting for does when he came back to us this first time. He did not wander far and I often saw him slowly walking through the brush on the hill, pulling twigs from the maples. Once he stood near the shore looking toward Canada. Perhaps he was considering the potentialities of emigrating.

ONE NIGHT I went out to feed a flying squirrel which had glided to a noisy landing against the kitchen door. The beam of my flashlight struck into a world of fantasy. Snow was falling slowly, each flake so delicate and light that it drifted and turned in the air. The ground was covered by points of white fire with minute flares of red and green, purple and blue and gold, ever changing, separating rainbow colors from the light. The very air glittered. A barred owl rose soundlessly from the woodpile, its wings spanning four feet of air, to cross the clearing like a coruscating phoenix, outlined by diamond-bright sparks. Then, as I looked, a wind began to whistle from the northeast. The delicate stars shattered as they were blown along the ground. The snow began to come like white cornmeal. I thought of a Cree Indian saying: "Snow like meal, snow a great deal," and went to bed.

Next morning, the snow and wind had covered the clearing with a range of white, three-foot mountains. Under the trees, eighteen squirrels were squealing and fighting. Drops of blood spattered as those who customarily fed here fought to hold their territory against the invaders from the forest. Ade swept snow and squirrels together from our paths. I followed, dropping cracked corn, oatmeal and graham crackers in little heaps along the cleared space. By the time Ade had refilled the suet cages, our regular group of woodpeckers, chickadees, nuthatches and grouse were busily eating. Then Peter walked casually through the assemblage, looking as large as Gulliver in Lilliput.

He was waiting at the step when he suddenly tightened his

muscles as though to leap away, pulled back his head, spread his ears wide, and stared at the woodshed's foundation. A weasel, ermine white and stretching up to all of eight inches, was returning the stare from interested black eyes. Peter gave a little snort and the weasel, with a flick of its black tailtip, popped into a snow tunnel, poked its head out at various points in the yard as though to annoy the squirrels, and vanished into a mouse hole under some roots. Peter was eating his cedar when the weasel

emerged, a mouse in its jaws. It hopped to a big drift and sat up, wanting its catch to be properly admired. Then, head high to keep the dangling mouse out of the way of its pattering front feet, it bounded toward home.

Peter was walking away from his garden when he suddenly blew, reared, and slammed his front feet down. A gray-brown streak shot away—somebody's Siamese cat, from where I have no idea. With ears laid back, Peter trotted out of sight.

I found that a deer's noisy blowing sound, made by forcing air violently through the nostrils, was strictly an alarm or threat. It could mean the near presence of lynx, bobcat, bear, strange human, domestic cat or dog, or, sometimes, foxes. I have never heard it when wolves were in the area, possibly because the deer scented them and withdrew before they were near enough to create a need to spread an alarm.

Ade went to get our mail Christmas Eve. I was remembering the previous Christmas and Peter, when I looked out and saw a strange man standing on our path with his back to me. He wore woodsman's clothes and carried a rifle across his arms.

I went out. "Looking for someone?" I asked.

He whirled to face me. "I didn't know anybody was here—" he mumbled. "I—uh—heard you had a tame buck. Thought I'd like to take a look at him."

I was staring at his rifle—a .30-30 with the safety off. My heart began to thump. "With that thing? Get out!"

There was a silence. Then he pointed the rifle at me and, with some colorful obscenities, ordered me into the house.

I obeyed, but I got my pistol, and went out again, the gun behind my back. Peter, ears forward, was by the storage building, just out of the poacher's sight. With an effort I managed not to turn my head in that direction. I walked slowly toward the intruder. "Still here?" I asked in what I think was an ordinary tone.

The man smirked nastily and started to raise the rifle again. I snapped the pistol around in front of me and thumbed back the hammer. The smirk melted. "I was only kiddin', lady!" And he took off up the path with me at his heels.

Ordinarily it would have been quite impossible for me to run up that steep slope in deep snow. This time I seemed to fly. But I reached the top only as a pickup truck with no rear license plate rattled away.

I was halfway back to the house when my knees started to shake and I sat down in the snow. I looked up and saw Peter walking toward me. Mentally thanking my father for having taught me to handle guns when I was hardly big enough to lift one, I eased the pistol hammer down and stood up.

"Peter," I said, "I have just pulled off the year's most important bluff." He turned his ears and cocked his head. "Nobody will ever eat you for dinner if I can help it. That's a promise."

January

THE OIL stove mumbled softly inside the cabin. Outside, sporadic sharp reports, like distant shots, ripped the silence of the night as tree trunks burst under the pressure of the frost. The roof snapped as though the ridgepole were breaking, as logs contracted and expanded. This night was getting very cold.

I threw on a jacket and went out to make sure that Bedelia's lantern heater was functioning properly.

She merely gave me what seemed like an annoyed glance from her perch, and I turned away to see Peter walking down the path. Then I caught the white flashes of two tails diving into the brush and a doe turning on her hind legs to follow. Peter leaped halfway across the yard and landed directly in front of her, knees bent and body tense. She hesitated, looking uneasily at me, then turned to him, her ears in the same forward position. During thirty-five seconds they did not move. Then, as though communication had been completed, both relaxed and their ears went back to the ordinary position. While I moved to and from Peter's tree with extra corn, the doe stood her ground beside him, twitching occasionally as though about to run.

In the morning, beside the tracks of Peter and the doe, there were fawn tracks, no doubt made by the twins whose tails I had seen going into the brush. Peter had invited company to share his windfall of food.

Later that day, Ade spotted the doe in the brush. She had a way of standing all her own—front legs spread, head lifted, one ear forward, the other back. We remembered that stance from the year before. This was Snowboots' mother, with her new fawns.

Just before dusk Peter brought the doe down into his cedar garden. She was nervous, but finally followed him, while the two fawns, identifiable as little bucks by the tufts of hair on their foreheads, stood on the bank and sniffed the delicious cedar odor. Peter withdrew, leaving the doe alone. Only when it was almost dark did she signal to the fawns, who leaped down to feed beside her.

With four deer coming for cedar, Ade began to make long treks through the forest for it, so that he would not strip the trees near the house nor damage any tree by too much cutting. You would not think that wandering through the woods would offer much news, but Ade almost always had something to report, from the moose he glimpsed near a swamp to the geological surveyor who heard the snap of the pruner and took off at high speed, no doubt thinking it was a bolt-action rifle being cocked.

Peter spent much time roaming his woods these days, but we had fine company in the doe and her children, although she was still somewhat doubtful of our intentions and suspicious of any change in the yard. As is the case with most wild creatures, she inspired her own name and became Mama from her devoted care of her fawns. One was called Pig because he ate hugely and was strictly for himself. His twin became Brother as a matter of course.

One morning Ade put out suet and corn while Mama and her little bucks stood at the edge of the woods. Pig immediately rushed in to eat. Brother followed and joined him at a corn pile. Pig slashed out with his front hoofs, striking Brother's cheek and

side. Mama crossed the yard in one leap and Pig guiltily jerked back from the corn. But Mama went over to Brother, so Pig began to guzzle again.

Mama, after licking Brother's cheek and moving her nose gently along his side as though checking for injury, saw him settled at a corn pile some distance away. Then she approached Pig and bumped him away from the corn with her lowered head. He reared, forefeet ready to strike. Mama, looking as though she could not believe he had shown such disrespect, brought her hoof smartly down on his head. It reminded Ade of his grandmother, who had whacked similarly with her thimble. Pig backed off, shaking his head, then tried to approach the corn again, but Mama blocked his way with raised hoof. He withdrew to the woods' edge and stood watching the other two enjoy their meal.

When they went back to the woods, Mama acted as though Pig did not exist. When he walked toward her she moved away to eat some cedar leaves. He stood dejectedly by himself, head hanging. Mama's fluttering eyelashes told us that she was watching him, although from his point of view she seemed to be ignoring his occasional glances. Later she walked toward him as though by chance. He looked up quickly, but let his head droop when she gave no response. Then she faced him, head lifted. He moved toward her step by step, gradually raised his head, and reached his nose out to her. Mama affectionately washed his face.

Restored to his usual high spirits, Pig ran toward the corn, Brother following. Pig, with perfect deer manners, shared a corn pile quietly with Brother, while Mama, overseeing them from the edge of the woods, looked as though well satisfied with her exercise in discipline.

That day some friends brought us hundred-pound sacks of cracked corn, whole-grain oats and scratch feed and we put out separated piles of each kind.

The deer did not gorge as horses will if let into the oats bin but took relatively small portions, though the first section of their stomach can hold two gallons or more. The second, smaller section is simply another type of storage chamber, while digestion

39

takes place in the last two sections. This elaborate arrangement gives deer an advantage in time of danger, when they may hastily eat a large quantity of food, then go into hiding to rest, chew their cud, and digest the food.

WHITE-TAILED deer of numerous species are found all over temperate North America, except for parts of the Far West. Their food varies according to their particular habitat. Acorns and apples are favorites in the East and South, but in our immediate area I know of only one oak and one apple tree.

The magnificent forest of red and white pine that greeted Minnesota's early settlers supported moose and caribou, but supplied so little food for whitetails that they did not flourish in the interior of northern Minnesota until the forests were felled after 1890. Deer browse on the cutover land reached a peak between 1910 and 1940, until the youngest trees began to rise above the deer's reach. Now considerable acreage is being lumbered again

and the brush that will spring up to cover the soil will provide good deer food for another twenty years or so.

On our lakeshore winter deer browse has not been good for some time. New growth of maple along roads and power lines has been killed by spraying. White cedar, a staple for winter browsing, was trimmed up to a height of seven feet by the deer before we arrived and they had destroyed most of the cedar saplings.

Any such change in a habitat affects all its interconnected life. Our red squirrels, for instance, feed all during the winter on evergreen cones and mushrooms. An infestation of budworms defoliated the spruce and balsam trees for three years and left them too weak to produce cones for three more. For a while, the squirrels stored quantities of other kinds of cones and mushrooms. Then drought caused even these crops to fail, and in the winter squirrels came daily to beg food. When spring arrived, I had only to step outside to be almost attacked by patchy-looking squirrels—jumping, clawing, snapping at my hands.

One day I heard a pitiful whimper and found a squirrel on the feeding shelf by the door. I held out a cracker and he nibbled at it without raising his head. Then he sat up but slumped sideways. Finally I held him in my hand to feed him. He seemed to weigh no more than a mouse and, through his sparse coat, I could feel his bones. This was the bitter shape of starvation.

When the sad little creature had gained enough strength to wobble away and sprawl in the sun, I made a thick sauce of flour, vitamin-and-mineral-rich MPF (a multipurpose emergency food), dry milk solids and water, and flavored half with cheese, half with chocolate. When it was cold and solid, I cut it into squares. The squirrels sniffed, ate, and came for more. Three days later they stopped scratching and snapping. After a month, their ragged fur was becoming sleek, but their poor winter diet had so weakened them that their matings produced no young.

Except for diseased or insect-damaged trees, the forest recovered with next year's plentiful rain. There was no begging at the door that fall. The squirrels were deep in the woods, hiding pine and balsam cones and mushrooms in private hollows everywhere, zigzagging under cover when they crossed the yard to prevent their trails being followed to their caches.

During the first part of the winter they had black and sticky forepaws and faces from dining on their resin-covered stores. As the snow grew deeper, and their stores diminished, they began to cut the little cedar cones which look like wooden flowers. Many cedar leaves fell with them, and deer ambled along the trails, licking up the leaves. Those deer that came to us for grain took considerably less after that, and Ade even stopped cutting cedar branches.

As I watched the deer, I thought how unlikely it seemed that a large population of little red squirrels, dropping cedar leaves, might spell the difference between a fair winter and hunger, even death, for deer!

Out of our fondness for our own deer, our interest in their behavior, Ade and I, too, were contributing to a change in the natural sequence of events in our part of the forest. Were we doing the right thing?

If browse is good, deer winter well. But as the deer increase and browse is depleted, the situation worsens from year to year until mass starvation and regrowth of the browse bring the deer herds again in line with their food supply. In our area timber wolves, if they had not been interfered with, would have limited the number of deer. But when we moved here, northeastern Minnesota, with the largest wolf population in the United States, had only three to four hundred wolves. The situation arose because of maudlin affection for deer, reasonless fear or hatred of wolves, desire for bounty money, and a wish for deer to entertain tourists and to lure hunters. But deer withdraw to inaccessible places and wolves will go where men do not. Governor Rolvaag recently vetoed Minnesota's bounty law, but the future well-being of the white-tailed deer deep in our forest depends on less persecution of wolves.

I looked at the little deer family lying in the snow, Pig and Brother asleep side by side, Mama head up and watching. Quietly Peter stepped into the yard and ate a little. Then he and Mama stared at each other, motionless, for half a minute. Mama lowered her head and closed her eyes, as Peter moved to a hummock and took over the guard duty.

I thought once again of Peter as he had come starving from the shadows. It had not been wrong to help him, not for him or for us. To give food and security to animals who would otherwise face hunger and danger all their lives was a small return for what they brought to us, and it would not be wrong as long as we remembered we must help the forest, too. To offset the effect of feeding the deer, we must encourage wild deer browse by cutting tall maple so that it could spring anew from the roots and by protecting young white cedars until they grew large enough to survive the deer's feeding.

Late March

I LOOKED at my kettle boiling with a mixture of flour, canned meat and vegetable juices, and our last egg until we could get more from town. It would soon hold some of the best soup you could eat, full of odds and ends I would not have thought of saving before our values changed with our move to the woods. We no longer wasted useful things and we no longer wanted useless things, though our basic interests had not changed. Instead of designing billboards, Ade drew animal illustrations. Instead of writing technical reports, I did nature and children's stories.

As I timed the soup, I considered that thing called "escape."

Brother

Many friends, when they learned of our planned move from Chicago, said in shocked tones, "Escape!" But people *cannot* escape by running away, because most difficulties in ordinary living arise from inside—and no one can leave himself behind. Ade and I did not run away from Chicago. We still love the blustery, noisy city, but we felt that we could more readily build the kind of life we wanted in the North Woods. We moved *toward* something, not *away* from anything—and there is a world of difference.

I took off the soup, which was to be Ade's lunch when he returned with the mail. Then I went out and plowed through knee-deep fresh snow to the thermometer. Twenty above zero—and the calendar said spring had arrived the day before!

Down the path, heels flying, rumps bouncing, ears flopping, came Pig and Brother, full of visions of corn. Hastily I put out grain, and, almost on my heels, they jumped in to start eating. Mama stopped on the path, looked at me, and stomped, so obediently I went inside and took my place at the window. Pig and Brother were now so tall that from the back they looked very much like Mama. Antler bumps were lifting the tufts of reddish hair on their foreheads. Mama's little bucks were growing up.

Peter appeared, turned toward the road, and stood guard, only his ears moving as he followed sounds too faint for human hearing. After the others had made a good start in cleaning up the grain, he turned his head toward them and flipped his ears forward. Mama in turn looked toward him with her ears forward, then tapped Brother lightly on the neck with a hoof. He turned toward her and a long look with ears forward passed between them. Then Brother trotted up to take over the guard duty and Peter came in to feed.

Brother was not as relaxed at the job as Peter had been. His tail twitched and his rump jerked every time he adjusted his ears or tested the air with widespread nostrils, as though he knew that their lives might depend on his alertness when he stood guard. Soon Mama went over to lick his nose. Brother returned the lick enthusiastically and hopped back to the feeding area, while Peter nudged Pig up to the guard position.

Pig plainly thought little of this business. He stood with head down and spent more time looking back toward the remaining grain than he did in watching for possible enemies. When Peter and Brother both were turned away from him, he bypassed Mama and slunk quietly back to the grain. He had taken only one mouthful when Peter spun around and whacked both his front hoofs down on Pig's rump. Pig gave a snort and took off toward the woods. Peter went after him and reared in front of him. Pig skidded to a stop and went down in the snow. Peter, grunting and snorting, shook threatening front hoofs above the cringing Pig, who, crestfallen, rose and took over his neglected guard duty.

Ade and I have seen this silent—to our ears—communication between deer many times, most often when they are changing guard. They may make sounds too soft for human ears to hear, or may "speak" in frequencies above or below our range. It is even possible that they communicate in some way alien to man. Jacques once asked me if I had ever felt a deer's "startle," explaining that when he was back in the woods he sometimes felt an abrupt uneasiness. If he turned slowly he would usually spot a deer watching him. He thought his uneasy feeling was a projection of the deer's alarm at seeing him. I thought he was joking

until it happened to me a couple of times when strange deer on the hill saw me in the yard and paused to evaluate the situation. I have no idea what alerted me to their alarm. I only know that I sensed something when none of my ordinary five senses had indicated that any living thing was near me.

Wild deer react to the slightest movement and to any change in environment, and Mama was the most cautious of all the deer that have come to know us. She investigated every change in the yard—Ade's snowshoes stuck upright in a drift, a decrease of a few pieces in the size of the woodpile. The day we hung some washing out to freeze dry, Mama fled with her twins, all three blowing.

One March day, we had a heavy, wet snow, followed by warm sun. The woods were full of rumblings and thumps as big snowballs dropped from boughs. The deer stood restlessly under the trees, all of them alert and listening. Sometimes Mama stomped when she heard a heavy thud, as though she thought other deer were nearby. I wondered if the vibration in the earth might not be even more important to deer than a sound.

Next day, the temperature dropped rapidly and water froze on the surface of the lake ice. As the new ice thickened, its expansion caused it to break noisily, and sometimes with such violence that we could feel the shock wave in the cabin. This added to the deer's uncertainty and once, after a very heavy tremor, they ran wildly. It took Peter more than an hour to herd them back into the yard again.

Lights also confuse deer. Once when I turned a flashlight across the yard and its beam was made visible by a heavy fog, Pig lifted his head and tried to lick it. When his tongue could not feel what his eyes could see, he bleated and ran. I have seen similarly confused hares nibbling at the edge of a spot of light.

A deer may run in panic ahead of car lights on a narrow road, trying fruitlessly to scramble up high banks. If the driver will stop, the deer will realize that the car is no longer following and will leap with ease and grace up to safety on the opposite bank. A deer needs room to make those beautiful leaps that are its means of escape from danger.

By April 1964, Ade and I had a car. One day, when we drove along the shore of Lake Superior to Duluth, we counted six dead deer by the highway. When we came back at dusk, small groups of deer stood by the road, wanting to cross to get water, but hesitating and uncertain. We stopped for them and the majority crossed at once.

In 1963 game wardens received reports of 2399 deer killed on Minnesota highways by cars. Some of the cars were badly damaged and their occupants painfully injured. A little less hurry, a little more patience—that is a small price for a safe journey.

But in the days when Peter and Mama were educating Pig and Brother, we gave little thought to having no transportation except our feet. There was enough to entertain us in learning to know the deer as individuals. Their temperaments varied as much as do those of human beings and each had his own way of doing things.

Peter, from his second day with us, indicated that he wanted something to eat by tapping on the step with a front hoof. Mama's method was to stand some fifteen feet from the door and stare fixedly at it, ears forward, as she did when communicating with another deer. If we did not bring out feed, she went around the cabin, looked from window to window until she saw us, then again took up her ears-forward stance. We checked frequently to see if the deer needed food, so Mama may have thought that her system worked.

Pig was more direct and nosed at the glassed-in flower box Ade had built in the living-room window. He could see us, and we could see him and supply his grain at once. Brother finally began to stand outside the window by the table where I wrote. I checked the grain whenever he came, and he always followed me to look at it, but returned immediately to the window. Evidently his long waiting had to do with food, but I did not understand what it was. Then, in mid-March, we ran low on corn and eked it out with oatmeal. Brother dashed at it as though it were for his delight alone and I soon discovered that he came to the window only when there was no oatmeal. Remembering the flavor of oatmeal from our emergency feeding two months before, he had patiently and persistently "asked" for it every day!

Difficult as it is to understand so simple a thing as a deer's indicating that he wants a special kind of food, it is even more difficult to try to communicate, human to deer. Peter turned at the sound of his name, but none of the others paid the slightest attention to any particular human words. However, if they were alerted by some unusual noise that we knew to be harmless, we could sometimes stop them from bolting by whistling or speaking softly.

ONE DAY NEAR THE END OF MARCH, Ade and I heard Mama making a great fuss. We went out to see her standing just below the bank, snorting, blowing and stomping, her big fawns huddled uneasily together. I walked slowly toward her and she grew even more excited, finally striking violently at the ground with both forefeet and bleating. I stopped. Bedelia was moving back and forth in her screened doorway, open for the first time this spring. She was pretty excited herself, and I remembered how she had startled Peter.

How could I tell Mama there was no danger? Well, when she

was uncertain about anything, she stalked it. Feeling a little silly, I decided to stalk the hen house. I backed up and made a wide circle behind it, then cautiously approached from the far side, leaned down, and stared at Bedelia—who stared back. Then I straightened up and walked in front of the coop as though it were completely unimportant.

I looked at Mama, who watched quietly and tensely. She turned and looked at the fawns, then moved in her own wide circle until she, too, obliquely peered into the coop. Bedelia merely returned her scrutiny, so Mama went back to the bank, faced the hen house, and stomped twice, quickly and lightly. The fawns leaped from the bank, one on each side of her, and headed straight past Bedelia, with Mama following more slowly.

48

Later, I read Lois Crisler's *Arctic Wild* and learned that she had used a similar method to reassure a frightened wolf. It is a human trait to expect animals to understand people, but it is absurd even to hope for this unless people first try to understand animals.

Late April to June 1

ON AN afternoon some four weeks after Mama had been introduced to Bedelia I left my work to go outside and behold the miracle of spring. As I looked up and wondered if I really saw the faintest misting of mauve buds on top of our tallest birch, Pig leaped high across the path, sailing on air, with Brother following. They circled, raced, glided, with first one, then the other leading, their hoofs hardly skimming the ground, soaring like winged creatures through the exciting air of spring.

I am still not used to the ease with which whitetails, averaging little more than three feet high at the shoulder, can clear an obstacle seven or eight feet high. I once stood in the road, Peter a short distance ahead of me and about to cross, when a car roared over a blind hilltop. I had a moment of horror—then Peter cleared car, road, and far bank as though he had been shot from a bow. His leap was more than thirty feet long with a rise of at least six feet.

AS THE DAYS warmed and lengthened in May, Peter roamed alone. Pig and Brother tried to stay with Mama, but she, after licking their noses, struck at them with her front feet, making it plain that it was time for them to begin independent lives. Only occasionally did the four come together in the yard. Their ears were beginning to lose their cottony winter lining and their tails became thinner and narrower. They had tucked their tails close to their bodies for warmth in the winter. Now they let them hang down, except when they used them as mosquito and fly switches. Their winter coats looked straggly and I found bunches of hair lying about the yard. These winter hairs are really hollow bristles, air-filled and crinkled to provide insulation against the cold.

Pig seemed to be irritated by his loose bristles and licked and

49

yanked with his mouth until he was a patchwork of smooth summer russet and bushy winter gray. Brother lost the bristles on his face and brow so that his red summer head looked out as though from a high-collared, gray fur coat. I hoped to see how Peter looked during the summer, but before he started to shed, he was gone. I shall always wonder what secluded green place was his during the time when our forest lost its silence and became a vacationland.

By mid-May, Mama and the young bucks had plenty to eat and took only a little of the grain we put at the edge of the forest. Against the background of the maples and the earth-and-leaf-patterned ground, the deer's red-and-gray coats were an almost perfect camouflage. I had to look closely to see them in the dusk, and sometimes I did not locate them until they moved. Ade and I still marvel at the way a deer can be in plain view one minute and, in the blink of an eye, disappear. In the winter their gray coats match the dry stems and the gray snow shadows; in the summer their red coats blend with the color of the red-brown duff, and their bodies are so narrow across the rump and shoulders that they may step behind a not very large tree and be instantly hidden.

Near the end of May, the corn we put out decreased by only the small amounts eaten by hares and mice, so we decided that the last deer was gone for the summer. But on the evening of June first I heard a stomp. Mama stood at the edge of the forest, looking from me in the window to the ground where she was used to finding her corn. Her silky summer coat was almost strawberry blond. I brought out oatmeal and corn, and she ate, moving slowly and heavily, for her fawns would soon be born.

When she had finished, the rays of the setting sun fanned through the trees to silhouette her. Her ears were translucent pink in the light and her outline was picked out with gold. She stood quietly chewing her cud until the long twilight began to fade. Then, with a flip of her tail, she vanished along the trail she, and perhaps her mother before her, had marked out with shining black hoofs.

The Third Year

June 3 to Mid-September

As the days warmed, Ade and I had gone back and forth on the question of whether it would be worthwhile to plant a vegetable garden again. It involved hauling uncounted buckets of water uphill from the lake—and there was Gregory, our groundhog. We could foil him with a heavy fence, but this would surely cost more than the worth of any vegetables we might grow. . . . But then again Gregory might not return this summer.

On June 3 a vigorous scratching on the screen door decided the matter for us. Ade opened the door and Gregory strolled in, standing up to peer cautiously around at every third step. Ade sat down with a handful of molasses cookies. Gregory went to him at once and demolished the cookies systematically, standing up and clawing at Ade's pant legs to ask for more after he finished each one. For dessert Ade offered a saucer of canned sliced peaches. Gregory held the slippery fruit tightly between his hands and, with much slurping and spilling of juice down his fur, ate all the peaches before he put both forepaws into the dish and licked up the syrup. Then, without a backward glance, he turned and marched out the door, leaving a trail of sticky paw prints. We watched him making a furious assault on the young dandelions and Ade with, I am sure, a sigh of relief said, "No garden."

I was putting fencing around our scarce and fragile pine seedlings, often destroyed by hares and deer, when I heard a snort. Mama, head down, blowing and stomping, blocked the path into the woods. I backed away because she seemed in a fighting mood. As I retreated, she quieted, and with a last look as though to make sure I was not going to follow she turned away. I saw that she was no longer heavy with her fawns. Somewhere, in a hidden, tiny glade, she had given birth to her twins.

We put out salted corn near the place where she had warned me from the path, and she came in the late afternoon to feed. She

51

never moved far from cover, though, and she started a private war with a little red fox who found our yard a good mousing place. She had paid no attention to foxes before, but she probably felt this one was a danger to her fawns. Several times we saw the fox flashing across the yard and diving for cover just ahead of Mama's pounding hoofs. Then she began to watch his trails. One day she circled ahead of him and, when he passed in front of her, leaped up to come down with great force on her four bunched hoofs. The fox yelped and fled, alive by the very hairs of his tail, and did not return.

ONE JUNE morning a yearling black bear came into the yard, on his own in the forest for the first time. He sniffed, listened, and watched for danger. After looking at the cabin for a long time, he ambled lazily away. He went to a vacation lodge on the lake and made his way to a screened window through which drifted delicious odors. As he felt around the window frame, his claws hooked under the edge of the screen. He lifted it out, set it on the ground, and climbed inside. The vacationers had gone fishing. He pawed around the refrigerator, accidentally depressing the latch, and the door swung open. He removed a carton of eggs and set them on the floor without breaking them. He ate some sausage, removed the lid from a garbage can and spread its contents on a sofa in the next room, picking out meat and bread scraps. Then he found an apple which he took away with him.

Next day he found the window closed, but an apple lay by the cabin door. Encouraged, he looked further; a ladyfinger was on a step. Still cautious, he loped into the woods with his cake.

As time passed, the little bear lost all fear of people and stood patiently while tourists took his picture. He learned to climb a pole for food, even to walk a few steps on his hind legs. And when he had performed and eaten and posed, he stretched out on the step in front of the lodge to sleep in deep content, warmed by the sun and secure in his trust.

One evening, when the full moon flooded the yard with brightness, I saw the little bear waiting on a branch by the woodshed, where we feed our flying squirrels. I threw a light on him, and he looked down, saying, "Whah? Whah?" I walked away from the cabin to gaze at the pine tops against the cobalt sky and felt a gentle nudge. The bear had slid down the tree to follow me and was walking beside me like a dog, nosing my hand. He wanted something to eat, but I would not feed him or any other bear. I slid my fingers into the thick hair behind an ear and scratched. He liked this and sat down to be petted.

Then Mama stepped into the open some fifty feet from us. She whirled to face us and stared, ears wide and head forward. She did not move until I lifted my hand from the bear's fur and he stood up. Then she woke the night with a flurry of snorts and stomps and blowing. When neither bear nor human did more than look at her, she leaped into the forest. Her blowing grew fainter as she ran. I did not see her again that summer.

The next day, when the little bear was walking through the woods, he heard a loud noise and felt a blow. He fell down and could not get up. His chest filled with pain and terror closed over him like ice. There were two more loud noises, but he heard only the first of them—for the second bullet broke his neck. He had been "eliminated"; a common ending for tame bears.

In the beginning no one had intended to bring harm to this friendly young animal, and he had done no harm; but bears, even small ones, are very powerful. When they lose their fear of man they may be both dangerous and destructive, not only if they are angered, hurt or frightened, but even if they are encouraged to play. One cannot expect them to control their strength.

Every time I go outside, I pass the claw marks the little bear left on the cedar bole as he slid down to join me in the yard. I remember the thickness of his fur under my fingers, and I wish that no one had fed him, that he had never learned to like people, that he still might be roaming the hills where the blueberries grow.

OUR SUMMER was filled with visitors. Then, almost before I was used to the warm weather, September had come, summer residents were leaving, and I had to settle down with a wholesale catalogue and make up a list of winter groceries—cases of canned goods, sacks of flour and potatoes and sugar, a whole cheese, a slab of bacon, oatmeal, graham crackers, cracked corn, and scratch feed for the wild creatures.

When Ade went off to the mailbox with the order and check in his packsack, Gregory, who had been missing for a week, probably digging out his burrow and putting in a soft bed for winter sleeping, came for an afternoon snack. I took two molasses cookies out to him and he ate them, yawning prodigiously between bites, then flopped face down on the sunny path for a rest. When he dragged his fat self away, still yawning, he looked fit to stand anything the coldest and longest winter might bring.

As I stood there in the sun, a snowshoe hare leaped within two feet of me. Then I saw hares everywhere, crossing the clearing in leisurely bounds and vanishing into the woods to the east. I counted twenty-two, and I am sure I did not see them all. Why they were moving, where they went, I shall never know; but wherever they came from, they had had a strong effect on the vegetation. I went into the forest and looked closely at the twig ends. Deer twist off their browse and leave ragged stem ends, while twigs taken by snowshoe hares look as though they were pruned by a sharp knife. A few of the twig ends were ragged and freshly broken, but most were sharp-cut by hares. Before moving on, they had eaten much of the deer's winter browse.

Other animals were having an effect in our small domain. Groundhogs were scarce when we moved here but their numbers had increased as had those of the chipmunks and hares. The groundhogs gobbled large quantities of the greenery that was especially liked by the hares and, with a special liking for dandelions, interfered with the production of dandelion seeds, which were a chipmunk staple The hares, short of greens, ate more of the deer browse, while the chipmunks ate more of the wild berries the groundhogs were so fond of. This led the groundhogs to eat more greens and, in turn, the hares to take still more deer food. Meadow mice were also present in such numbers now that they were eating more than their normal portion of seeds, leaving fewer to sprout and supply green food for the others next spring. These small animals were well on the way to increasing beyond their wild food supply.

I looked up to see a barred owl float away like a brown-and-white-striped shadow. At least one predator was still in our woods. I had seen only one fox, and had not seen or heard a wolf, fisher, lynx, bobcat or mink in a year. Even weasels were not too plentiful. Bounty hunters and trappers had been too busy for the good of the forest. Without wolves to control the deer, without lynxes to keep the hares in balance, without foxes to catch the meadow mice, starvation waited for the deer in some long winter of deep snow yet to come.

Looking up through the reddening maples, I was conscious of the absence of the summer birds, who had quietly moved on. I heard no cars, outboards or human voices. The summer guests had gone, leaving behind the silence of the woods—which is rarely soundless. There were faint rustles from the leaves, a whir of wings in sudden flight. Then there was a heavy crash in the brush ahead of me. I jumped and my foot slipped. I looked at the path. There was a muddy patch in it, and in its center was a huge bear track, just made. Keeping a sharp watch, I backed up and came to a break in the thick brush. I emerged from the woods by a pool. The foliage that surrounded it moved and I saw Mama and her fawns drinking, but before I could more than glimpse their red coats and white uplifted tails they streaked away. I was surprised that Mama had been so alarmed at seeing me.

Suddenly I caught an acrid scent. I looked over my shoulder. The bear, walking behind me, had come out of the brush and reared, nostrils testing the air, a black basalt statue as timeless as the forest itself.

Then it moved away and its harsh odor faded. I thought of our earliest ancestors. No doubt their noses, never offended by the pungent byproducts of today's mechanized way of life, would have caught many interesting scents in this air which to me now smelled only of earth and resin and dying leaves. I went back to the cabin with its lamps and stoves, its clock and typewriter and

books, the markers of the generations of civilization behind me. And I knew, feeling a little sad, that by those generations I was forever set apart, an alien in this wild and ancient land.

Mid-October to December 31

By Mid-October we could leave the suet cages hanging out-side overnight without danger of their being stolen by some enterprising bear. It was a pleasure not to be awakened at dawn by woodpeckers whacking on the logs to remind us to bring out their suet breakfast. The oil truck pumped six hundred gallons into our storage tanks and the last freight delivery brought the winter groceries. Ade went from window to window, sealing and insulating them.

In one of the abandoned garden plots a mass of jewelweed had grown from scattered seeds. When the warm bronze-and-blue Indian summer came, the flowers were gone, but the four-foot-high plants still held many red-and-green seedpods. One day we saw a fawn standing at the edge of the patch, nosing forward, then arching head and neck back as its touch popped the pods and the seeds peppered its face. It was a comical-looking youngster, having an extra thick coat and a face so fuzzy that from some angles it looked a little like a buffalo calf.

Ade caught my arm. "I think it's playing."

And so it seemed. Over and over it pushed into the weeds, ducking back as though trying to move faster than the flying seeds. A pair of black-edged ears appeared beyond the tall plants, a slim beautiful face parted them, and a second fawn walked through the greenery to join the first. "Mama's twins," Ade whispered. "She's up on the bank there. Boys or girls, d'you think?"

I looked at the fawns, now munching jewelweed. "Well—their heads are smooth. I say they're both girls. Let's name them Pretty and Fuzzy. Fuzzy'll do for either sex, and if I'm wrong about Pretty we'll change it to Handsome."

The fawns were shaking their ears and switching their tails as the warm day brought the mosquitoes out. Then Fuzzy had an

57

idea. She moved to the spring and sat down in it, so that the water cooled the bites on her sensitive underparts.

I laughed and the two fawns, their eyes wide with alarm, stared at us before bolting onto the bank and away.

AFTER HEAVY frosts withered the last leaves, Mama and her twins came every afternoon for a ration of grain. Mama was unchanged, the same little swaybacked, alert doe, always testing her surroundings with eyes, ears, nose and hoofs. Pretty was long-legged, pearl gray of coat, graceful of body, and serene of face, while Fuzzy was short and chunky.

One day I heard a rasping sound and looked out to see a buck

polishing his antlers on the trunk of a willow tree. His antlers were very fine, with points almost as tall as Peter's of the previous year. The buck turned; it *was* Peter, and I wondered if the decrease in the size of his antlers meant that he was past his peak. I was puzzled by his coming here so early until I saw him go to the bank and sniff at a spot where Mama had been lying. She was probably approaching her short mating period and Peter, with a gleam in his eye, had followed her scent.

There was nothing of the gentle buck I knew in his behavior now. He stomped back and forth, snorting and whacking his antlers against tree trunks. He reared and whirled on his hind legs and struck down with his forefeet, lowering his head and swaying as though practicing for a fight. Then he rubbed the scent glands inside his hind legs together and walked in widening circles through the brush before he left, perhaps making sure that Mama would know he was in the vicinity when she returned.

An hour later Ade came in. "Guess who I saw in the woods?"

Before I could answer, there was a bump at the door. Standing at the step, forefoot tapping lightly, pink tongue out, was Peter, not at the moment a warrior ready to fight all comers for his lady, but simply a large, hungry fellow who knew where to ask for a handout.

After he ate his grain and carrots, he stayed in the yard, wandering around, occasionally sampling a twig. As evening approached he turned his ears toward the forest. Pretty and Fuzzy pranced down the path, stopped abruptly when they saw Peter, and fled into the woods. Mama came slowly into the yard, never taking her eyes from Peter, and the two stood motionless, looking at each other. Peter moved toward her and they faced each other, tilting their heads. After a moment, Mama walked away. Peter followed and with many starts and stops they moved around the clearing, Peter always looking at Mama, Mama holding her head high and staring off into some place known only to herself.

The twins had returned and were peeking from behind the big boulder on the bank, but the others gave no sign that they knew the fawns were there. Then a car horn sounded on the road. Peter was between Mama and the possible danger with one leap, standing with his head lowered in fighting position until the car had passed, while Mama waited, completely relaxed, as though leaving everything to Peter. When the car had gone, Mama led the twins to a secluded place in a stand of infant balsam trees. Without looking back, she turned away from them and headed into the forest with Peter walking close behind.

While Mama was gone, Pretty and Fuzzy came each evening for some grain, going back to rest where Mama had left them. While Pretty showed caution in approaching us, Fuzzy seemed to lack this self-protective instinct. If Ade went out with grain, she let him approach almost within touching distance. But Fuzzy lost her self-possession when I turned on the radio. She stiffened, turned her head and ears in a vain attempt to locate the first music she had ever heard, and, uncertain whether to run or not, compromised by hunching down behind a balsam tree so small that it came only to her shoulder.

On the fourth morning after Mama left with Peter, she rejoined her daughters. The fawns showed no excitement at her return and the three fell into their former routines.

One day a strange buck wandered into the yard. Mama kept herself and her fawns well out of his way, bringing them at a fast trot to snatch a few mouthfuls of grain before leaping away again. This went on for two days. Then the buck headed down the road and we waited for Mama to settle into her old routine.

Long after midnight that night, I heard a stomp and, picking

up a can of corn and one of scratch feed, I stepped out to give the little family a welcoming banquet. I did not take a flashlight because I could not carry it with the two cans. I was picking my way slowly by starlight to the big pine when there was a snort directly in front of me. I was face-to-face with the strange buck.

I am somewhat confused as to what followed. I did not throw the feed at the buck, but think I tossed both cans into the air. The buck reared, looking as large as a bull moose to me, then pounded away into the woods. I dashed for the cabin, having no trouble at all in finding my way in the dark this time. I stopped in the yard to get my breath and to shake off the grain, which was falling from my hair and sliding down my neck. I even had some in my mouth and was chewing on it.

Then I heard other pounding hoofs and ducked to stand against a tree as Peter thundered past me, hard on the trail of the intruder. I was just starting away from the tree when Mama came leaping by, with the two fawns after her.

It was clouding over and turning ink dark. I felt besieged by deer and was ready to yell for light when Ade flung open the cabin door and swept the lantern beam across the yard to me.

"What's going on now?" he asked, as we heard a bleating bellow and a crash somewhere to the west.

I ducked gratefully through the light to the doorway and we stood listening to sounds of what was surely a buck fight.

"Peter has caught up with a stranger," I said.

The uproar did not last long and soon we heard hoofs pounding away again. "I hope Peter won," I said.

"With those antlers? Don't be silly." He paused. "And while I'm thinking about it, don't blunder out into the dark in the rutting season again."

Justly and properly subdued, I went in and combed the grain out of my hair.

Early in November I saw two bucks browsing companionably together on the hill. I thought this strange until they walked into the yard and began to lick up grain we had scattered for the birds. Pig and Brother, a year and a half old, had come back to us.

They were tall, sleek, and still individual. Pig had his calculating look and six-point antlers; Brother, his gentle expression and a left antler beam, apparently injured in its formative stages, turned forward over his nose so that he looked like a caribou.

Pig, as might be expected from his childhood brashness, snorted and huffed and grunted and chased Pretty and Fuzzy away from the grain. Mama confronted him and, ignoring his antlers, butted his nose. He meekly stepped aside. After Mama and the fawns had eaten enough, she went over to him, licked behind his ear vigorously, as she had done when he only reached her shoulder. Truly we had named Mama well.

Pig nosed at the glassed-in flower box as he had done before when he wanted grain—and got immediate service. He was not a patient deer and Ade had no desire to reglaze the windows.

Brother was still his amiable self and I took food to him as confidently as I would to Peter. One day when the first snowfall was cutting down visibility I did this without first looking around. I had just dumped the corn when Ade yelled from the doorway, "Watch yourself!" Pig, head down and mischief-bent, rushed from behind a tree and I fled to the nearest shelter, our log biffy. The man who built this rudimentary convenience did not bother to chink it and snow filtered in with every storm, but the openings gave me an excellent view of Pig, looking pleased with himself, and of Ade, whooping with laughter in the kitchen window.

January 3 to Mid-April

ON JANUARY 3, a storm arrived without warning—a steady faint whisper of fine crystals, soft white by day and glittering gold by night as they passed through the lamplight from the windows. After thirty hours of this dim, hidden world, the sky cleared and the sun shone on a strange landscape. Bushes, little evergreens, the woodpile, were covered. From the cabin, smooth white stretched over the buried rocks of the shore and onto the frozen lake. The only sound was the muffled grinding of the ice, not yet thick enough to bear the great weight of snow without cracking.

I threw grain out for the birds and squirrels. Ade was shoveling around Bedelia's little house when the deer came floundering out of the maple, Peter in the lead, his chest acting as a snowplow. Mama, apparently very hungry, turned aside to pass him, making her way by laborious, straining lunges.

Once the deer were near the cabin, their hoofs soon trampled and packed the snow. They stayed in the yard for the next week and if Pretty or Fuzzy started toward the woods, the "baby-sitter" administered disciplinary whacks. I wondered if wolves, not in the vicinity for a year, might be near again.

The next morning I explored the trails in the woods. The deer had walked over and over the same routes, packing the snow into narrow tunnellike ways; crossing and curving and turning back on themselves. The trails were patterned with the dainty marks of hoofs. A white tail flashed ahead of me and I saw Mama start to bolt. I spoke softly and she stopped, turned, and watched me. Pretty, her tail spread like a fan, was just behind Mama in this secret world of white tunnels. When Mama relaxed, so did Pretty, and the hairs realigned themselves into the tails' ordinary shapes. Then Mama switched her tail and walked away, and Pretty switched her tail and followed. This is so regular an action that Ade says he has a feeling that it unlocks their hind legs so that they can move!

The deer usually ran with their tails down. I had wondered whether their white flag was as much of an alarm signal as I had heard, until a character in a twin-engined Cessna buzzed our cabin. The deer were used to an occasional small plane, but the roar of the swooping Cessna set them quivering and jerking, trying to locate the noise. As the plane came to the bottom of its foolhardy dive, barely missing our trees, the deer leaped away in six different directions, all of them with their tails up.

That night the air warmed and a light rain fell which turned into freezing drizzle. Ade and I followed its progress anxiously. All life in the wilderness, including ours, is ruled by the weather, and ice may bring disaster to the woods. Now the leaves of the cedars were slowly coated as though encased in clear plastic, and cones and buds were armored with ice. Small branches gave way with a tinkling crash.

Ade cut down cedar cones, which we thawed and dried, then shook for seeds. We added cornmeal, rice, crumbs, and the vitamin-and-mineral-rich MPF. The yard soon boiled with life. Ade brought the suet cages in to thaw out. The woodpeckers squealed their annoyance, then by experiment found that they could eat grain, picking it up with their sticky tongues and scooping it with the side of their beaks. Some forty pine siskins fluttered down to eat, though they usually feed in a treetop. By midafternoon the ice began to melt in the strong sunlight, the siskins returned to their treetops and we knew that the danger of a bird catastrophe was over.

The deer came the next afternoon, uneasily listening to the strange sounds of ice shattering in the breeze. As Peter led them carefully into the yard, something alarmed them and they leaped away, their hoofs crashing through the icy crust. When they returned later we saw abrasions on their legs. Fuzzy, with a bad gash, had great difficulty in keeping on her feet.

I was thinking most unkindly of the supercilious pilot who had thought to startle some backwoodsmen and had succeeded only in frightening these harmless animals away. Had they stayed and moved back and forth on their trails, they would have broken the ice as it formed.

Ade said, "If that fool had his wings ice up and made a forced landing, he could share the fun of fear and hunger."

I was trying unsuccessfully to make myself say something about the thought being uncharitable when Mama blew and the deer hurried away over the trail they had just broken. A long-legged, short-tailed animal crossed the path and disappeared into the woods before I could say "Bobcat!"

Ade was looking a little ahead of where it disappeared and said, almost at the same moment, "Lynx!"

This went on for most of the evening. I was sure the cat had the bobcat's short ear tufts and Ade was equally sure it had the lynx's long ones.

Ade shook me awake at dawn.

"Come quick. The lynx is in front of the kitchen window."

The night before I had set out a roasting pan so that birds might pick the bits of meat and grease. The lynx was licking it with such strength that the pan moved and the cat followed in little jumps. The lynx is usually nocturnal. This one had been driven into the dangerous daylight, and the even more dangerous presence of man, by hunger. His haunches were almost skin and bones.

At last he moved aside and sat to lick his paws. The sun broke

Fuzzy

through clouds and, as the warmth touched him, he lay down wearily in front of the window and dozed.

His fur was thick and gray with darker shadings. He had a reddish snub nose, faint black face stripings, luxuriant whiskers, and black ear tufts more than an inch and a half long, and oversized feet. His ruff met in a point below his mouth, like a white Vandyke beard. Suddenly he turned his head toward the woods.

"There's my bobcat," I murmured to Ade.

A striped cat stepped from behind a tree. We expected a fight, but the bobcat merely waited while the lynx rose and returned to attack the pan again. When he finally dragged himself away, Ade said, "Poor, hungry Big Cat!" and our visiting lynx was named.

The bobcat was busy with the pan now. This animal was thin, but in good physical condition. It had a typical tiger-cat face, with glowing yellow eyes and a reddish snub nose like the lynx's. Its rusty coat was richly spotted and marked. In a few minutes it left the pan, stretched and stared wide-eyed up the hill, and walked away on dainty paws.

"It moves like a tiger," I said, and Tiger the bobcat became.

Ade said, "Do you think they're traveling together?"

"I never heard of such a thing, but it looks like it," I said.

We put out equal portions of suet, one under Peter's tree and the other ten feet away. The two cats came from the brush as soon as we were back in the cabin. They ate separately and without any clash, and when the food was gone they disappeared together under our storage building. That they were companions we did not doubt now. Many old-timers believe that gray bobcats are produced by cross-matings of bobcat and lynx, so our feline traveling companions might have been a mated pair. They roamed, moused and hunted hares separately, but almost every night during the two months they made our yard their headquarters we could see the two pairs of eyes glowing green in a flashlight beam, watching from under the storage building until we brought out food for them.

On the evening of the cats' arrival, Ade put grain under the tree as usual, but the deer would not come in. So Ade took grain to an open space in the forest, a hundred feet or so from the cats' temporary den, and the deer, posting a guard, accepted the arrangement at once.

The cats did not approach the deer, but the deer, as if to test the cats, decided to use a trail only fifteen feet from the storage building. Peter and Mama led the way, walking tensely, heads low, and turned toward the building. When nothing happened, they hurried past with quick, nervous little steps, then stood watching while the fawns followed and Pig and Brother protected the rear. They did this every afternoon. On one occasion near the end of the cats' visit, Big Cat, no longer weak and thin, was approaching the building in the open when the deer family came into view. He hastily retreated, possibly having no desire to be trampled by all those sharp hoofs.

There is no question that bobcats and lynxes occasionally kill deer, probably by dropping from a branch or ledge. However, a cat clinging to the back of a terrified deer bounding through thick woods would be in great danger of being brained against a tree, and any deer large enough to run could outdistance one of these cats on the ground. Considering that deer populations expand while their browse does not, the herd would probably benefit if wildcats did take some of them.

Early in April, when south winds began to push the molting snow away from the first patches of bare ground, Peter, Pig and Brother left for their summering place. We had not seen the cats for a week when Mama disappeared, then Pretty and Fuzzy. The yard seemed strangely empty with only squirrels and chipmunks.

I went to the shore to look across the ice once more before its white covering was swallowed by the runoff from the hills. Fishermen had seen a bobcat and a lynx cross the ice from Canada in February. Big Cat and Tiger, surely. But where were they now? The slanting sunlight brought into shadowed relief some marks out from the shore. I waded through slush and looked at a double line of tracks, melting but still clear—the neat, four toed marks of a bobcat's foot and the big, snowshoe tracks of a lynx. Tiger and Big Cat, fat and rested, had gone home.

The Fourth Year

Mid-May to November 17

THE GREEN that marks the northward progress of spring flows around our north-facing slope and comes together again on the sun-washed Canadian shore across the lake. From the air, the two shores look much alike at this time. In the forested portions, new-leaved aspen and birch tops stretch like rolling meadows between the black-green of spruce and pine. Waves of shaded green cover the open spots. From the ground, the sunny shore is clear of snow, and the open green breaks into masses of bracken, clumps of raspberry canes, and new grass with violets in bloom. But our own shaded earth seems a month behind, with the fiddleheads of the ferns just venturing to uncoil.

In mid-May I was sitting on the doorstep watching for something springlike, when Pretty stepped from the softly leaved maple.

How can I tell you of such beauty? She tiptoed through the swirls of mist on hoofs of polished jet. Light covered her slimness with a brocade of red-gold and shone rosily through ears like the uplifted petals of some marvelous opening flower. The gentleness of her slender face was heightened by shadings of gray, faintly touched with violet. Her great dark eyes looked from under their peaked eyebrow markings with the shy innocence of a child. Youth and spring had come to me in the form of a yearling doe.

She drifted across the yard to the muddy hollow where we throw the water from the kitchen and began to lick the mud with long sweeps of her pink tongue.

When Ade came back with the mail an hour later she was still licking. "I think she wants salt," I said.

"Salt!" he said, whacking his palm against his forehead. "Jacques left us a salt block before he cleared out for Canada! I put it in the storage building and never thought of it again."

He got the fifty-pound white block and set it on a stump near Peter's tree. Sniffing and testing the air along the ground, Pretty moved thirty feet to find that block of salt. And I know people who are not convinced that an animal can smell something which to human nostrils is quite odorless!

The next day Fuzzy joined her sister. What a contrast! Her coat was ruffled, her upper lip overhung her lower one at the sides, and her chin line sagged. Her ears flapped without much purpose and she pottered around the yard, sometimes stumbling over a stone or a fallen branch, then looking at her feet as though she could not understand how they could be so clumsy. She simply loved people. She bumped around the cabin at night until one of us came out to feed her, then stood so near that we had to shoo her out of the way. Ade said she acted as though she took tranquilizers.

One night I went out to get corn from the storage can near Bedelia's house, and Fuzzy came right along. As I came abreast of Bedelia's coop, a big barred owl took flight from its top, almost touching Fuzzy's ears. Moving faster than I thought she could, she turned and bounded out of sight. Next day she treated Ade as usual, but backed off from me with her ears laid back. She did not forgive me for weeks for throwing the owl at her.

Fuzzy soon learned that if she stuck her nose forward Ade would let her eat out of the can in his hand. One afternoon, he was holding out the feed can and Fuzzy was sauntering over to it, when there was a loud blowing and a stomp. Fuzzy's ears flipped to attention and she turned to face Mama, unexpectedly returned and distributing her reprimands equally between Ade and Fuzzy. They backed away from each other, both keeping an eye on Mama, and Ade dumped the grain on the ground and ducked inside. Mama followed him to the door and blew once more as though to say she might have expected such foolishness from Fuzzy but that Ade should have had better sense.

THAT SUMMER, Pretty quietly went away when the voices of vacationers began to come from the road and outboards followed the shoreline. But Fuzzy took all human sounds as a matter of course and spent hours standing by the recording rain gauge which Ade tends for the U.S. Weather Bureau. She listened to the voice of its clockwork, and now and then gave it a companionable lick.

One day in June when we were working outside, Ade froze in a half-risen position, put a finger to his lips, and made little gestures toward the west. I turned my head very slowly.

Mama stood at the edge of the woods, forefoot lifted and ready to stomp, and, in some nearby ferns, the tips of two pairs of little ears moved between the fronds. Slowly Mama backed away and the ears moved toward her. As she came to the grassy spot where her favorite bluebead lilies grew, she stopped to nip off a plant and her new fawns moved shyly to her on still wobbly legs.

They were not much taller than the lilies, with dark eyes full of wonder. Either of them could have found room for all four hoofs on the palm of my hand. One of them, with a white star on its forehead, took shelter in the safest place it knew—under Mama's belly. It nudged her and she drew aside and led her twin miracles into seclusion.

Although Mama was an exceptional mother, all does are devoted to their fawns. Only the capture or death of the mother leaves her little ones alone. Sometimes well-meaning people find a fawn and take it away, thinking it is orphaned. If a young wild creature is reared by humans and then returned to its natural home, it is seriously handicapped by the lack of training that only its own kind can give, and it may be less healthy than it

Little Buck

would have been had it been nourished on its mother's milk. Deer milk is three times as rich in fat and protein as cow's milk. It is best not even to touch fawns, because this not only frightens them but also gives them the human scent, which may attract dogs or cats. Mother deer will bathe a youngster who carries the scent of man until it once again does not smell at all, as is proper for a baby deer.

THAT AUGUST is still as clear in my mind as yesterday. While Mama and Fuzzy ate and rested on the bank, the little twins took over our yard. They rolled in the tall grass, reared on their slim legs to box, rushed up to Fuzzy as she lay resting and pattered their front hoofs on her paunch, then were gone before she could more than lift a hoof to wave them away. We named the slightly smaller twin Little Buck and the one with a white blaze above his eyes Starface.

As October frosts brought down the leaves, the deer's coats began to thicken and take on the gray of winter. Little Buck and Starface were growing heavier. Sometimes they lowered their heads in fighting position, pressed the tops of their heads together, and shoved back and forth until one or the other rolled over, while Mama watched complacently, as though nothing could please her more than to have her little fellows growing up with the correct competitive instincts.

Starface's weakness was butterflies. He flicked his tongue at every one he saw. He did not, to my knowledge, ever get one. When a cloud of migrating butterflies fluttered into the yard, he almost went wild, leaping, jumping, licking frantically at the orange-and-black flowerlike insects. He had seen nothing like them, and neither had we. Perhaps they had been blown off course. I hoped that they would settle on our bushes, but Starface scattered them with his antics and they drifted on, leaving him to stare foolishly after them.

Ade and I kept a sharp watch for the rest of the small herd. Pretty arrived near the end of October, taller than the others and more graceful. Two weeks later Pig and Brother walked down the path. Pig still had that wicked gleam in his eye and Brother still looked gentle as a doe.

In spite of the bucks' size, Mama remained the boss. She kept order at the grain piles. Once Pig poked her not too gently in the rump with his antlers. She tucked in her rear as she jumped aside and turned to give him a resounding thump on the bridge of his nose. He seemed to pay not the slightest attention to this attempt at discipline, but I noticed that he did not use his antlers against her again.

Little Buck kept out of the way of his big brothers, but Starface developed an acute case of hero worship for Pig and trailed him around the yard, hopefully reaching out his nose for a friendly lick. Pig responded by chasing Starface round and round, never really trying to overtake him, but just being fractious. Starface only seemed delighted with all this attention.

Shortly after the bucks returned we had one of those stirring

late-fall days, when the high wind sings and your blood stirs in answer to its song. Knowing that winter was hanging heavy overhead, I could not stay indoors. I went for a long walk on the road, scenting the smoky richness of autumn and reveling in the sun on my face. When I came back to the edge of our clearing, Pretty and Fuzzy were lying side by side on the bank, chewing rhythmically. Pig and Brother were snoozing in the dry grass. Mama stood nearby with her youngest twins, Little Buck nuzzling her neck and Starface squinting away from having his face washed. Bedelia was taking the last dust bath of the season and Ade was standing, an empty feed pan in his hand, watching the deer.

As I walked on to become part of this scene of deep peace and content, I thought of the words of an ancient king:

> *He maketh me to lie down in green pastures:*
> *he leadeth me beside the still waters. . . .*

November 18 to December ?

I WOKE with a start the next morning, wide awake and listening for some unusual sound, but I heard nothing except the chittering of squirrels. Ade was still sleeping. I must have dreamed the sound. It was dawn, and I decided that a walk before breakfast would be perfect. I made the coffee while I dressed, gulped a cup, and followed the deer trail into the woods between the cabins just as the first rays of the sun touched the treetops.

Suddenly the crash of a heavy rifle racketed through the woods, and then another, not a hundred feet from me. The deer season was open—and someone had found the tame deer. I yelled but got no answer. I hurried along the trail, shouting.

"Listen! There's another one!" came a man's voice.

I turned cold. This man might shoot at the sound of crackling branches, and I was on a deer trail, in thick shrubbery, dressed in navy blue from head to foot. With the thought, I dropped flat and slithered along a side trail.

Then I heard a scuffling sound and knew that they were drag-

73

ging the dead deer to the road. If I hurried I could confront them in the open. They wouldn't hear me now. They were too occupied with moving the carcass. Carcass! An odd way to think of one of those deer who had rested so peacefully by the log cabin only a few hours before. I stood up and ran, but when I jumped onto the road, a car with an out-of-state license was disappearing around a curve. Shaking and sick, I glimpsed the deer, tossed hastily across the trunk, its antlers profiled to the right. Pig? Brother? I could not bear to think. I walked to the gate, left open by the hunters.

There were drops of blood at my feet. I closed the gate and turned away, to walk back to the log cabin by way of the road. I did not want to see the blood soaking into our green pastures.

After I had drunk the remainder of the breakfast coffee and got over the jitters, which always come on me after danger has passed, I managed to give Ade an account of my walk.

"We don't own the deer, of course," he said, "but this shooting around the house is deadly dangerous."

"I don't think there'll be any more hunters this season," I said, fervently hoping that I would prove right. "Mama's old enough to know what gunshots mean. The other deer were never frightened before in their lives. By people, that is. We made them vulnerable."

"Yes, but I'll bet the deer that are left are heading for far places right now. D'you think they'll come back?"

"Some of them will," I answered, and refused to think of which ones or how many.

Ade put out grain as usual that night. In the morning a light snow covered the ground but the only tracks were those of a snowshoe hare and mice. As I looked at the barely touched grain, a gray jay warbled from a branch. I held out a piece of bread and the bird dropped to my hand. The feathers around its beak were red with the blood of a deer it had been feeding on. As it flew away and I looked at the scarlet dots left on my fingers, I wondered again who would never lie contentedly in our yard. Mama, or the daughters she had reared so devotedly? Pig, with his fine rack and his snorty, touchy temper? I shall never learn whose blood came back to my hand, but I know that some essence of the dead stays with me in the soaring birds and their descendants.

TWO NIGHTS after the season closed I heard bleating outside. It came and went, came and went, like the crying of a lamb, lost and running in panic. It was a fawn, but whether one of Mama's or a stranger's I could not tell, because it fled into the brush if I so much as cracked the door. All night the pitiful bleating went on.

In the morning, Starface was lying near the untouched food Ade and I had hopefully left out. When I stepped outside, he jumped up, shivering and bleating, and leaped into the forest, where we could see him watching us.

"He's had a bad fright," I said. "He's come back to wait for Mama. If she doesn't come back soon, he'll starve."

I took him oatmeal and Ade cut cedar for him, but he would not eat. He finally drank a little warm milk from a bowl. Day and night he walked up and down in the clearing, listening and bleating, now and then leaping eagerly forward at some sound, only to come back, head hanging, and lie down. Ade and I were both eating with effort and losing sleep as we watched and waited with him. "There ought to be something we can do," Ade said.

"No. He's dying of loneliness and fear. He hasn't any of the bred-in tameness of a lost puppy. He's a wild animal—and right now we are the enemy." I walked to the west window and looked sadly into the woods where Starface and Little Buck had had such carefree romps during the summer—and, high on the hill, I saw a deer moving slowly and cautiously through the brush.

"Hey," Ade said. "He's standing up. He hears something."

Pretty limped into the yard. Starface backed away when he caught her scent, but kept his head forward and his ears cocked. She glanced at him, then settled to eat, blood trickling from an unhealed bullet wound in her right hindquarter. "She's not seriously hurt," Ade said. "She couldn't walk so well if a bone were broken or a tendon cut. It'll heal over."

"Look at Starface," I said.

Inch by inch, quivering as if with uncertainty and eagerness, neck stretching forward, he was approaching Pretty. He had known her for only a couple of weeks before the shooting. He would probably have run up to Fuzzy—but I didn't think we would see Fuzzy again. She had ambled up to the wrong human.

Pretty paid no attention to Starface until he was almost within touching distance. Then she looked up and turned her ears toward him. They stood so for perhaps three minutes. Then she turned her head to lick his face and eyelashes clean, then nudged him around so that she could lick behind his ears. He leaned against her side for a moment, then bent his head and began to clean up the oatmeal. Clearly, being adopted made all the difference in the world.

It seemed strange to see only two deer in the yard. I missed Fuzzy's friendly ways and found myself watching the brush for Pig and Brother, although I knew one was dead and felt sure the sound that had waked me on the first morning of the open season had signaled the shooting of the other. I still hoped that Mama might have escaped, and Ade believed she was alive but staying in hiding. Neither of us mentioned Peter.

On the second of December we had a snowstorm that blanketed the earth and bent the trees. In the midst of it we heard a deer blowing—once, again, and then a muffled stomp. We almost knocked each other down getting the door open. There, under Peter's tree, was Mama, striking furiously at a hare who had presumed to come for some grain. There was no sign of Little Buck, and Mama was now as cautious as she had been when Peter first introduced her to our yard.

She forgot the hare when Starface came running to her from the brush. She licked him on whatever part he displayed near her face as he bounced and leaped around her. He bounded to meet Pretty, who was making her beautiful, quiet entrance, jumped up and bumped her face with his head, whirled to sidle against Mama with such force that she had to sidestep to balance herself. Then he stood quietly, rubbing his chin on the back of her neck, while she curved her head around to nose his side.

Swaying white curtains of snow blotted out the forest again next morning. The temperature dropped slowly from the high twenties to below zero and, when the storm finally passed, we were isolated. The lake ice was too thin for walking, and land travel, even on snowshoes, would be hard because snow hollows alternated with high drifts.

Isolation like this, which our pioneering forefathers took for granted, can disrupt common sense. There is no greater chance of developing acute appendicitis then than at any other time, but some perverseness of mind makes it *seem* more likely to happen. If you let your thoughts run wild, the warm, safe cabin can become a trap, menaced by trees about to fall and stoves about to overheat and burn it down. Your anxiety makes you accident-prone and then you are faced with real danger: yourself out of control.

During our first winter here I had moments when I started to give way to this feeling of helplessness. Then it came to me that security which depends on something outside of yourself is one of the great modern illusions, that such security as one may have comes from a recognition of one's abilities and limitations, along with a willingness to face and make the best of uncontrollable happenings. Life in isolation would be impossible under other conditions.

During the two days the snow closed the road, the deer were as free of fear as they had been before the hunting. Even though Mama had lost four of her six children and Pretty's wounded leg was still stiff, they seemed to know that no harm would come to them from Ade and me. But when we heard the distant rumble and clank of the snowplow, the deer faded out of sight and stayed away two days.

"I was getting a little worried," Ade said. "I thought they had got over their fright. But they aren't going to have anything to do with strangers in the future."

Starface seemed to miss Little Buck. He listened and looked

into the brush, and sometimes he practiced fighting by himself, lowering his head and shoving dispiritedly at a stump. Mama and Pretty were watching this one afternoon, when their ears lifted and they thrust their heads forward, moving from side to side in excitement.

At the edge of the forest stood Peter. Antlered and unharmed, our beloved gentle buck had come back.

Ade began to grind carrots. I peeled potatoes for skins and

Starface

recklessly gave my last bit of lettuce to make Peter's homecoming dinner a bit festive.

"He's getting old, isn't he?" I asked, as we watched him eat. "His antlers are deteriorating. I'd guess he might be eleven, maybe twelve years next spring."

"He's lasted this long because he's wary," Ade said. "I'll bet he took off at the first shot."

Peter finished his meal and stood chewing his cud, watching Starface, who was again fighting his one-sided battle with the stump. Starface started when he noticed Peter and went over to lower his head. Peter reared straight up on his hind feet. Any adult whitetail in this position is taller than most men, and Peter, with his antlers adding more than a foot to his already considerable height, was spectacular.

Starface, after two stumbling attempts, stood up to face him, the top of his head not reaching to the other's jaw. Then Peter turned away from Starface, and gave a demonstration of pawing and striking, his front hoofs slashing the air too fast for my eye to follow. After Starface had attempted this, Peter reared again to strike with both front feet at once, dropping forward at the same time and delivering a heavy blow to his nonexistent adversary.

Starface learned rapidly and all went well until Peter dropped both antlers somewhere in the woods and stopped the fighting practice while his pedicels healed. From then on Starface had to practice by attacking a cedar trunk, whose bark still bears scars made by his flashing hoofs.

By the first of the year, the deer had settled into quiet ways and Pretty's wound had healed without a trace. But she bolted at any loud noise, and when a freezing tree burst with a sound like a rifle shot, all the deer were gone in a flash. When ice fishermen were in the area and cars moved on the road, we did not see the deer. We were glad they knew the dangers outsiders might bring, but regretted that neither Mama nor Pretty was likely to bear fawns here in the future.

NEAR THE end of January the deer became very restless, stomping, listening, testing the air. They slept in the clearing, their beds in the snow close together as though for protection, and, while the others rested, not one, but two guards kept watch.

One Saturday morning it was thirty below zero and lightly snowing. The deer stood under Peter's tree, ignoring the birds and squirrels that squabbled in the corn around their feet. When Ade and I went to the main road to get the mail, we crossed the trail of a timber wolf.

"He's a giant," I said. "His forepaws are bigger than my hands! And he's headed toward the cabin." I turned around and started back. "He's after the deer. They knew he was around!"

"If he kept straight on he reached our place a long time ago," Ade said. "The deer are downwind. They'll have moved out ahead of him."

When we reached the cabin, the deer were gone. Their feed was untouched next morning and tracks showed where the wolf had crisscrossed the yard before going away to the east.

Tuesday we sighed with relief as Mama stepped from the brush with Pretty and Starface. They did not seem nervous, so we assumed that the wolf had gone on. But Peter did not come that night. Nor the next, nor the next.

Friday morning Ade came in after getting oil and found me staring out of the window. "All you've done the last few days is look out the window and wonder what's happened to Peter," he said gently. "I went on up to the road just now. There're tracks—plain ones. Let's go see what we can see before fishermen's tires wreck the trail."

I welcomed the idea of action. "It's possible he might be hurt,"

I said, zipping my jacket. "There are wolf traps set around here, and if they aren't set right, they can catch deer."

After a steep climb through the deep snow of the path, we stared at the still-sharp marks of the wolf's big foot on the road. I shivered. The line of loping footmarks turned off along a deer trail. We followed and soon came to one small and two moderately large hollows in the snow, where Starface, Mama and Pretty had been sleeping, and from which they had sprung away ahead of the wolf.

"The wolf followed the road just downwind of them so they couldn't smell him," Ade guessed. "He must have got almighty close before they ran."

We lost the trail in thick brush, found a wolf track and confused deer tracks in the thin snow of a protected spot, and finally came out on the road again. The small heart-shaped marks of Starface's hoofs led east, with the big tracks of the running wolf sometimes superimposed, so that we knew he was following.

"The wolf cut him off from the others," Ade said.

"However did he get away? He couldn't outrun him."

Ade shook his head and we walked on. Even though I knew that Starface was safe, I began to be sorry I had come. I lagged behind, wanting to say, "Let's go home."

Suddenly Ade stopped, looking up the hill on one side of the road, then downhill on the other side toward the shore. "That's Peter's track," he said, a little too calmly, and my uneasiness clotted into ice in the pit of my stomach.

The mark of Peter's dented front hoof was plain, and ahead of us, the trail of the leaping fawn was still clear—but the wolf tracks no longer followed it. They turned north on Peter's trail. I started to follow them, but Ade pulled me back.

"It's no use," he said, and I think that he, as well as I, had known that from the start. "Peter was big and strong and he could lead the wolf for miles."

He did not add that Peter was old and that the tracks were headed for the slippery lake ice. Nor did he say that neither of us would want to find what probably lay at the end of that trail. He pointed to the tracks. Peter had run straight toward the wolf and Starface. "He was running into the wind," Ade said. "He should have smelled both of them. I think he came to help Starface—and he was successful."

I looked numbly at the story in the snow, tried to speak, and could not. Ade touched my shoulder and turned me toward home.

"Remember how he came to quiet Snowboots when the wolves killed his twin? And how he stood aside and let Pig and Brother eat all his cedar when they were small and hungry? Starface is small and he needed help, too." Ade looked into the shadows, where the tracks were lost. "Peter was brave and gentle—and generous. He not only shared, he gave."

EPILOGUE

The Gift

YEARS HAVE passed since the wolf followed Peter away from Starface. I watched, waited, hoping that the long road Peter had taken might have had a turning somewhere, but he did not return. One night a month after he had gone I thought I heard a tap on the step and slipped out of bed to look just once more.

It was very cold, with branches stirring slightly in a silent breeze. Moonlight poured across the open spaces in silver rivers and fell in pale, glimmering splotches between the branches. I looked at the place under the cedar tree where Peter had stood to chew his cud in comfort and in safety. The moon shadows moved and I could almost see him there. Then, from far away, the wild and beautiful howl of a wolf came to my ears.

The shadows under the tree were only shadows. I knew that Peter would not come again. But he was not lost to us. I could never be sure what had happened to him—you never can be when a wild creature goes back to its own world—but I felt that he still lived in the wolves on the hills, in the ravens and gray jays and foxes, in the soil their droppings fertilize, in the green things that grow there, in the waters that quench the thirst of the earth. Life and death rise, one from the other, as day follows night. Nothing can be lost, for nothing exists alone.

MAMA is still here, a matriarch, wary, wise, a firm disciplinarian in spite of her years, for she is very old. Her back is deeply swayed. Her teeth are so worn that her cheeks wrinkle out when she chews. She bears fawns no longer. Her work is almost done.

Last winter was a long and bitter one, with snow piling deep. And out of the forest, where the snow locked the browse away, came the deer—Mama's children, and Peter's, back to the place where they had wintered as fawns. They brought their children and their children's children, and strangers followed timidly.

Among them were two thin, motherless fawns, so weak that they lacked spirit and did not dare approach the grain. Pretty adopted the little doe, as she had once cared for Starface; and Starface hooked a foreleg across the little buck's shoulders and gave him a shove that sent him stumbling in to eat. One night I looked out to see Snowboots, a white-stockinged forest king as impressive as Peter, standing where the cedar garden once had been, perhaps dimly remembering that he had smelled cedar there years before. And Mama was always busy—licking behind young ears, keeping order around the grain piles, mothering all of them, down to her great-great-great-grandchildren.

TONIGHT, AS ANOTHER YEAR nears its end, it is very quiet. An hour ago I stood under a black sky abounding in stars. I had not known they could shine like that—diamond-bright, even their colors clear through the clean, dry air. I watched Orion, tall as Creation, crossing the sky with strides light-years long, wearing red Betelgeuse for an epaulet and blue-white Rigel for a shoe buckle. Then moonlight flooded between the trees as it had on the night when I last looked for Peter, and, gliding in and out of tonight's moonstreams, were Mama, Pretty and her latest fawns, with Starface in antlered majesty. I thought of man and his brothers in fur, of the stars—and of Peter. I felt the snow melting on my hand and knew that to touch a snowflake, to feed Peter, was to touch them all.

If we had not brought Peter back from the edge of death, he would not have led Mama to stay with us. Starface would not have been born. Most of the things I have been writing about would never have happened. And when these deer have gone on the long road that Peter, and so many others, have taken, there will be deer still, following the old trails through the forest, perhaps to come to us for help in another winter of bitter cold and deep snow.

Peter brought them to us, he left them for us, a gift priceless beyond all accounting. What can I say of him?

He was Peter, our buck with the generous heart.

HELEN HOOVER

Fourteen years ago, Helen and Adrian Hoover were engrossed in busy lives in Chicago. Mrs. Hoover had studied science at Ohio University and the University of Chicago, and was using this background as a prize-winning research metallurgist for the International Harvester Company. (She holds a patent on an agricultural disk.) Mr. Hoover was an art director for a textbook publishing company. When he became ill in 1954, they decided to spend two months in one of America's last great wildernesses, the Boundary Waters Area of northern Minnesota, where they had vacationed in the summer for several years.

It was during this time—when they were both forty-four—that they decided to postpone no longer a cherished dream. Mrs. Hoover had always wanted to write. Mr. Hoover loved to draw. Life by a forest lake, miles from the nearest neighbor, would give them their chance.

The first years in their two-room cabin were hard, and Mrs. Hoover warns against trying such a life without built-in financial support. It was four years before she sold her first article to *Audubon Magazine* ("It saved our lives," she says). Since then, she has published numerous articles for both children and adults. Her first adult book, *The Long-Shadowed Forest*, was hailed by Harrison Salisbury of the *New York Times* as "a classic of wilderness life... to put on the shelf next to Thoreau's *Walden*." Her first children's book, *Animals at My Doorstep*, was published in 1966.

There have been many changes during the Hoovers' years on the edge of the Superior National Forest. They are now fed, warmed, and lighted by gas and oil, drive the three miles to get their weekly mail, and share an eight-party telephone with their still-distant neighbors. Though they may someday have to give up their way of life ("My muscles are getting stiffer every winter," says Mrs. Hoover), they have never regretted their decision. "There is too much to do," Mrs. Hoover explains. "But at least we have the freedom to *choose* what we want to do." Mrs. Hoover loves languages and has studied Swahili—because she is fascinated by a language which can express complicated ideas so simply—and Polish, which she practiced with a Polish-born neighbor. If she can find a spare moment, she plays the piano and tries fancy cooking, needlepoint and lace-making.

At Ease: *Stories I Tell to Friends*

Painted from life by NORMAN ROCKWELL

At Ease:

stories I tell to friends

A CONDENSATION OF THE BOOK BY

DWIGHT D. EISENHOWER

WITH A 10-PAGE PHOTOGRAPHIC PORTFOLIO
BEGINNING ON PAGE 135

★

ILLUSTRATIONS BY HOMER HILL

In a publishing event of the first importance
General Dwight David Eisenhower recalls,
"for the pleasure of it," the personal incidents
that shaped and colored his life. From a
childhood encounter with an angry goose to an
amusing scene with the King of England, all
are stories that only General Eisenhower
himself could tell—and his warm, open personality
shines through in the telling.

The General of the Army and former President
has written the historical record of his career
in his two earlier books, *Crusade in Europe*
and *The White House Years*. But *At Ease* is like a
friendly chat in the General's living room. In it
he paints an unforgettable picture of a boy
growing up in a Kansas home where the Christian
virtues were prized. He remembers the high-spirited
pranks which enlivened his school days and
early Army service. And he tells anecdotes that
reveal the human foibles of some of the famous
figures of World War II. The General's observations
are fresh and spontaneous, and it is a privilege
to observe history-making events from his unique
viewpoint.

An engaging and endearing memoir, *At Ease* will
be treasured for its revealing insights into one of
the most likable heroes that any age has known.

FOREWORD

A man talking to himself

TALKING to oneself in Abilene, in the days of my youth, was common enough. Generally speaking, it was a sure sign of senility or of preoccupation with one's worries. Now, it is nationally advertised as the hallmark of the efficient executive. He dictates to multiply his effectiveness.

These days, as I direct these casual reminiscences to an electronic machine that faithfully tapes every word, every tone, every mistake, perhaps I should be immersed in wonder at the changes in life since I was a boy. Instead, the preponderant notion in my mind is one that occurs to all those in a certain age bracket when they find themselves meditating on the years, the events, the people of their past. So it was before the first pyramid was built; so it will be when man is an interplanetary commuter. The notion is, of course: Time flies.

There was a period when time behaved differently. In my case, the coming Friday and the weekend respite from school always seemed, on Monday morning, an age away. Holidays, finally reached, passed instantly. But their arrival was a prolonged, tedious, barely perceptible movement of clock and calendar. I can still recall vividly my first formal idea of time and its glacial passage.

Shortly after we moved from Second Street into a new home on Fourth Street in Abilene, Kansas—I was getting along in years, being by then almost eight years old—I heard for the first time mention made of my mother's age. In conversation with a neighbor, my mother said, as I recall, "I've been married almost fourteen years and I am thirty-six years old." She added, "For the first time we have a home where my children will have room to play. I am most thankful."

Now I was not especially impressed by her remark about the space we would enjoy because I hadn't been conscious of its lack. But I was so intrigued by the figure 36 that I soon worked out the year in which I would attain her venerability. The result was disheartening. Nineteen twenty-six was ridiculously far off, a whole lifetime in the future.

Possibly, like most boys, I was convinced that life was a flat plateau of assigned tasks, unchanging in monotony and injustice. I suppose, too, that the only peak on my personal horizon would have been something like entering the halls of higher learning (the eighth grade) or bathing in glory (becoming a full-fledged member of the high-school baseball team).

I daydreamed now and then about the highest and remotest peaks of all, fantastically difficult even to contemplate scaling: to be an engineer (there was only one kind), racing across the land, arriving in Abilene, steam engine hissing, bell ringing, once again breaking the record from St. Louis or some other distant, mythical place; or to set down the next three batters on nine pitches in the last half of the ninth, with the bases loaded (of course), to the thunderous applause of five hundred spectators. Certainly I never thought of myself or those about me as makers or participants in any other kind of history.

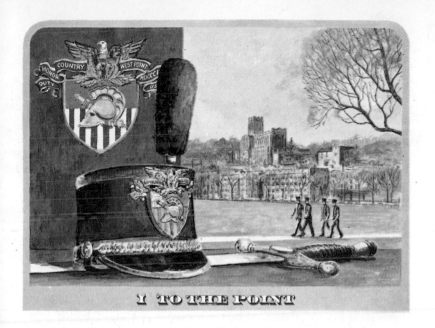

I TO THE POINT

Starting off for West Point in June 1911, I traveled light. No boy of my acquaintance had ever been overburdened with an extensive wardrobe, and since all civilian clothes were to be sent home or stored, there was no need for more than a single suitcase.

I took about a week for the trip, stopping off first in Chicago to see a girl named Ruby Norman, who was studying violin at the Chicago Conservatory; then in Ann Arbor, to visit my brother Ed. Ruby and I had been good friends in Abilene and I had been saddened when she went off to the city. We spent a couple of evenings going to the movies and seeing the sights.

Ed, a natural athlete, was just completing his second year at the University of Michigan. He had a job waiting on tables in a vast dining hall, which left him little time for athletics. What was worse, he had suffered a prolonged bout of appendicitis and had dropped from 170 pounds to 150. He did try track and baseball but he never got to play football at Michigan.

While he was finishing his exams, I walked around the campus and was much impressed. That evening Ed hired a canoe and we set out on the river with a couple of girls. We took along a phonograph and played popular songs. This was the most romantic evening I had ever known. I had a feeling that perhaps I had made a mistake in not joining Ed at Michigan.

THE NEW class of cadet candidates arrived at the Academy before noon on June 14, 1911. My impression of that first day was one of calculated chaos. All day we were shouted at by self-important upperclassmen telling us to pick up clothes, bring in bedding, put our shoulders back, keep our eyes up, and run, run, run. Everything was done on the double. I suppose that if we'd had time to sit down and think for a moment, most of the 285 of us would have taken the next train out. But no one was given much time to think—and when I did it was always, "Where else could you get a college education without cost?"

Toward evening we were sworn in as cadets of the United States Military Academy. When we raised our right hands and repeated the official oath, a feeling came over me that the expression "The United States of America" would henceforth mean something different from what it ever had before. Across half a century, I can look back and see a gawky Kansas boy earnestly repeating the words that would make him a cadet. It was a supreme moment.

THE FIRST three weeks were spent in what has been called, from time immemorial, Beast Barracks. During our three weeks as a Beast the cadet instructors were all over the place, their only mission to torment and persecute us. When we went to the cadet store for supplies, we would be handed a bundle of clothes and bedding that was almost unmanageable. When we went up and down stairs, we had to take the steps two at a time. And because the summer was a hot one, the experience was strenuous, and for those who weren't used to exercise it approached the unendurable. Previous years of working came to my rescue. So did my age—I was nearly twenty-one. At times the whole performance would strike me as funny, and in the semiprivacy of my room I could laugh a little at myself and at the system.

My roommate, a lad from the same state as myself, told me that when he had received his appointment a celebration had been held in his little town. He left the town a hero—and the contrast of Beast Barracks was too much. Part of his difficulty was that he had come to West Point quite young, only just past seventeen, and had had no experience of taking care of himself or earning any part of his living. My efforts at bucking him up were no help and he left the Academy. I liked him and I think it was only his youth and sheltered existence that defeated him.

Military drill was a problem for me. I had had no training in marching, and to keep in step with the music of the band was difficult. For days I was assigned to the Awkward Squad.

I knew little about the Army, but I did know we were required to salute all officers. I was double-timing down the street one of those first days when I heard a band coming. Before it turned the corner, I encountered the most decorated fellow I had ever seen, so I snapped to attention and presented arms. He did not return the salute. I did it again and a third time. I was mortified to find I had been saluting a drum major.

Beast period over, we were integrated into the corps of cadets, then living in summer camp almost on the banks of the Hudson. We were allowed a choice as to tentmates, and I was fortunate to find in our company Paul A. Hodgson from Wichita. P.A. was a fine athlete and a good student. He devoted every moment he could to improving his academic standing and urged me to do the same. But I was inclined to be easygoing about studies, attaching more importance to sports.

One of my reasons for going to West Point was the hope that I could pursue an athletic career. I was muscular and strong but very spare, five feet eleven and 152 pounds. It was dismaying to find that I was too light in comparison to men who were then on the football team. But the only thing to do was keep at it.

Perhaps in baseball I could hold my own. In high school I had had some reputation as a center fielder, and I was good at bat—

trained by my coach as a "chop hitter," to poke the ball at selected spots in the infield rather than to swing away freely. The West Point coach thought highly of my fielding, but not of this style of hitting. "Practice hitting my way for a year and you'll be on my squad next spring," he said.

THE LIFE of the cadet has been described many times by numerous and better writers. Its most unpleasant aspect during the Plebe, or first, year is the Plebe's awareness that he is considered to be awkward, clumsy, and of unequaled stupidity. But some of us were not above (or beneath) bedeviling superserious upperclassmen in their attempts to make us over. Once we learned that the punishment meted out was usually not of great moment, another Plebe, Tommy Atkins, and I found opportunities to needle our tormentors.

One day, having been found guilty—by a corporal named Adler—of a minor infraction of regulations, we were ordered to report to his room after tattoo that evening in "full-dress coats." This expression signified a complete uniform, but Tommy suggested that we obey the literal language of the order.

The full-dress coat has long tails in back, and is tailored straight across the waist in front. At the appointed time, each of us donned a full-dress coat and, with no other stitch of clothing, marched into the Corporal's room. We saluted and said solemnly, "Sir, Cadets Eisenhower and Atkins report as ordered."

Adler let out the cry of a cougar, while his roommate became convulsed with laughter. Predictably, all the upperclassmen of the Division rushed in to see what was going on. Some of them joined Corporal Adler in reading us out as arrogant, unruly Plebes. They forced us to strain our shoulders back, pull in our stomachs, and assume exaggerated positions of attention. Other visitors just howled with glee.

As time approached for taps everybody had to rush to his own room. As usual, the upperclassman had the last word. Dismissing us, he gave us a new order. "Immediately after taps you will report back in complete uniform including rifles and crossbelts, and if you miss a single item I'll have you down here every night for a week." After taps we went back, dressed as instructed, to be braced up against the wall until we left our bodily outlines on it in perspiration. But afterward we and the other Plebes had a lot of laughs—quiet ones—out of Adler's temporary discomfiture.

The discipline was not so much harsh as inexorable. Each offense had its prescribed demerits, and if in any month the total exceeded a certain level, the victim was required to "walk the area" during his free hours. Under the watchful eye of an officer or cadet officer, the offender would march up and down, one hour for each excess demerit. Ultimately I was discovered in an offense which caused a change in Academy regulations.

After I became an upperclassman, I went to cadet dances only now and then, preferring to devote my time to poker, in which the debts were recorded for payment after graduation. On one of the rare occasions when I did go to a dance, I met a girl, a professor's daughter, and we started dancing in a way that the authorities felt was not in accord with the sedate repertory of the time. We liked to whirl as rapidly as we could. I suppose this showed a little more of her ankles, possibly even her knees, than was thought seemly. I was warned not to dance that way anymore.

A few months later I met the same girl at a dance, and forgot the warning entirely. Hailed before the Commandant, I was informed that I had not only danced improperly, but had ignored a warning. I was demoted from sergeant to private; my punishment order read: ". . . and will be confined to the barracks for a month and will during this period walk punishment tours every Wednesday and Sunday afternoon."

At the same time a football injury put me into the hospital for a month, although I could go to classes on crutches. The result was that while I was indeed confined to barracks—the hospital—the injury prevented my walking the area "during this period."

The sharp-eyed Commandant of Cadets realized that I had in effect foiled the purposes of the punishment. Thereafter, such orders read simply: "Cadet _____ will be confined for one month to the barracks and will walk twenty-two punishment tours."

Even though an offender might have spent the entire month flat on his back, he would still have those tours to walk after he left the hospital. This is one of those unwilling contributions to the Academy for which no cadet can thank me.

I never fully reformed, and in matters of discipline I was far from a good cadet. I enjoyed life at the Academy, had a good time with my pals, and was undisturbed by a demerit or two, even though these had an effect on class standing.

Thirty or so years later, when I had become Chief of Staff of the Army—a post far higher than my loftiest cadet ambitions—an inquirer, unknown to me, thought that my West Point years might provide a clue to my later performance. Somehow he managed to get photostats of my disciplinary record. The offenses listed on sheet after sheet through four years must have appalled him by their multitude and variety. Eventually these photostats were sent to the White House after I became President, possibly as evidence, someone suggested charitably, that one cannot always read a man's future in the record of his younger days. Among about 162 men in my graduating class, I stood 125th in discipline.

My staggering catalogue of demerits was largely due to a lack of motivation in almost everything other than athletics. I didn't think of myself as a scholar or as a military figure whose career might be damaged by his disciplinary record. I suspect instead that I looked with disfavor on classmates whose days were haunted by fear of demerits and low grades.

In spite of a passion for athletics, my career as a player was short. I was, as mentioned, considered too light to make the football varsity. Although I was promoted to it several times in my first year, I always ended on the scrubs as "too small." During the summer, I practiced hitting the way the baseball coach had suggested, and I worked hard on the running track to improve my speed. I also set up a severe regimen of gymnastics to strengthen my leg and arm muscles. And I indulged my appetite to the limit.

When the 1912 football season started I weighed about 174 extremely solid pounds, and I played in West Point's first practice game. No player was more eager to prove himself and I showed up quite well. For the first time I attracted the attention of the varsity coaches, headed by Captain Ernest Graves. After the game, I was trotting toward the gymnasium when Captain Graves called sharply, "Eisenhower! Where did you get those pants?"

They were hanging around my ankles. "From the manager, Sir."

Turning to the cadet manager, Graves said, "Get this man completely outfitted with proper equipment."

I was as high as a kite. This was the first intimation that I might make the varsity. Thereafter, in no game or practice session could the coaches claim I lacked pugnacity and combativeness, assumed to offset my lack of tonnage. I tried to instill the fear of Eisenhower into every opponent. On one occasion an opposing player shouted to the referee, "Watch that man!" pointing at me.

With some astonishment, the referee asked, "Why? Has he slugged you or roughed you up?"

The man replied, "NO! But he's going to."

Until my injury, I was used that year consistently as a varsity player. In the Tufts game, when I was plunging through the line, a man got his hands on my foot. I twisted and threw my weight against it. Although my knee swelled rapidly, there was little pain. I was hospitalized for two or three days, then discharged, with no warning that the joint was permanently weakened and that I should be cautious in using it. A few days later, while taking part in "monkey drill," I leaped off my horse to vault over him as he jumped a low hurdle. The landing shock to my injured knee was more than it could take. I ended on the ground with my leg twisted behind me. Cartilages and tendons were badly torn.

The doctors spent four days straightening my leg, then put it in a cast. When I was released from the hospital and tried to use the leg, I learned to my dismay that rugged sports were denied to me from then on. To this day I have to be careful of that knee.

Homer and his legendary birthplaces cannot hold a candle to the number of Tufts men who say they caused the original injury. At public dinners and ceremonies, men of my own age have approached me, saying, "General, I was the man who inflicted that bad knee on you back in 1912. Wish I hadn't hit you so hard."

Over the years, I must have heard that sort of statement two or three dozen times. I wonder how many men Tufts had on the field when I was hurt?

The end of my career as a football player had a profound effect on me. My exercise was now limited to gymnastics, walking and calisthenics. I was almost despondent and several times had to be prevented from resigning by the persuasive efforts of classmates. I have often wondered why, at that moment, I did not give increased attention to studies. Instead I gave less. Life seemed to have little meaning; a need to excel was almost gone.

I learned to smoke and even in this I managed to be rebellious. Cadets were allowed to smoke pipes or cigars in their rooms, but cigarette smoking brought serious penalties. So I smoked cigarettes. Loose Bull Durham tobacco could be purchased at the cadet store, and I became a "roll your own" smoker.

One day I was asked by one of the better students in the class to come to his room to talk over some piece of business. When I arrived, he was properly uniformed and deep in study. I lounged in, sat down and began to roll a cigarette. Looking up, I saw a horror-stricken face. "Please, Ike, if you must smoke, do it in the hall and we'll talk there."

"Well, I didn't *ask* to come here. You wanted to see me."

"Yes," he said in distress, "but if the Tac (the tactical officer in charge) finds out, it could cost me a file in my class standing and I can't afford it." (A man's initial seniority in the Army follows his class standing at the time of commission.)

I obliged by stepping outside his room, and after listening to what he had to say, I left. I was so engrossed in thinking about his anxiety to avoid a single demerit that I walked out of the barracks with the cigarette lighted. It was a shock, then, to hear the Tac's voice say, "Mr. Eisenhower, put out that cigarette."

"Yes, Sir," I answered ruefully. This was a multiple-demerit offense and I would have to pay the penalty.

Things continued to run downhill. Vivid in my mind is an incident from which I learned the wickedness of arrogance and the embarrassment caused by lack of consideration for others.

There's probably no individual in the world more serenely arrogant than the cadet who has just left the ranks of Plebes to become a lordly Yearling. *He* now has the right to inflict on the incoming Plebes the verbal abuse that he has so much resented in the past year. Like other Yearlings, I did my part. There were standard questions which, voiced as roughly as possible, were intended to crush the Plebe deep into the mire of inferiority. One was, "Mr. Dumbguard (or Dumbjohn), what's your PCS?" (Previous Condition of Servitude or, What did you do before you came to West Point?)

I ran into a young fellow from my own state. Or to be precise, running down the street to carry out someone's orders, he ran into me. I reacted with a bellow of mock indignation. With all the scorn I could muster I demanded, "Mr. Dumbguard, what is your PCS?" And added, "You look like a barber."

He said softly, "I was a barber, Sir."

I didn't have enough sense to apologize on the spot and make a joke of the whole thing. I just turned on my heel and went to my tent where my roommate, P.A. Hodgson, was sitting. I said, "P.A., I'm never going to crawl (correct harshly) another Plebe as long as I live. I've just done something unforgivable. I made a man ashamed of the work he did to earn a living."

And never again, during the remaining three years at the U.S.M.A., did I take it upon myself to crawl a Plebe.

Every cadet looked forward to the few furloughs authorized during the four-year course. Neither in frequency nor in duration did the Academy provide the escape enjoyed by other college students. All things are relative, however, and every pressure, every restriction seemed more tolerable because ahead was the prospect of Christmas leave. Every cadet, except the Plebe, if he was not undergoing punishment, if he was completely proficient in his studies and physically fit, was allowed a few days off. In my second, or Yearling, year, there were two matters that prevented my taking Christmas leave. I was in the hospital with my knee, and my disciplinary record was not up to standard.

In 1913 and 1914 I was able to spend the eight-day Christmas leaves away from West Point. It was too short a time for me to go all the way home, so one year I went to Buffalo with a friend, and the next year to New York City. I couldn't have afforded to see the big city if it hadn't been for the Hotel Astor, the New York home of the Cadet Corps. For those who could not pay cash, the Astor carried all bills until graduation day. And then each of us got a twenty-five percent discount on everything except actual money advanced to us by the hotel cashier.

During this leave, I realized that I needed a few presentable civilian ties. I found two that I liked in a haberdashery near the hotel. Allowing for the high prices of New York City, I thought they would cost about $1.50 each. The salesman wrapped the package and calmly said, "That will be twenty-four dollars."

False pride would not let me say, "I can't afford them." The purchase took just about the last cent I had, and from then on I had to take all my meals in the hotel, where I could sign the bill.

At the end of the second year, West Pointers were given one furlough of about two and a half months. This aroused as much enthusiasm in us as the prospect of graduation. I went back to Abilene to see my family and friends.

During the year following my injury the football and medical authorities tried every experiment and exercise they could think of to get me back into condition, but nothing kept the knee from becoming dislocated under strain. Once he knew the struggle was hopeless, Captain Dailey, the new coach, suggested that I try coaching the junior varsity, the squad we called Cullum Hall. This was made up of men of all classes who were not quite good enough to make the first team. I got interested in this idea and did try it; and I was able to send on to the varsity a few performers who made the grade.

The knee that kept me from playing football came close to changing my whole life. As the time neared for graduation I was called to the office of the head of the medical department, Colonel Shaw. Because of my injury, he said, he might have to recommend that, while I be graduated and receive a diploma, I not be commissioned in the Army.

The Army was small in 1915, its total strength about 120,000, and the graduating class at West Point more than supplied the immediate demand for second lieutenants. The authorities were therefore very careful not to commission anyone with a serious physical difficulty, for his early retirement with disability pension would make him a drain on the government for life.

When Colonel Shaw had finished, I said this was all right with me. I remarked that I had always had a curious ambition to go to the Argentine (it sounded to me a little like the Old West) and I might go and see the place and maybe even live there for a few years. He was obviously surprised that I was not more upset. He said he would think over the matter of his recommendation.

Within a few days he sent for me again. He had been going over my record, he said, and had found that my injury had been aggravated by a riding accident. I confirmed this. He said, "Mr. Eisenhower, if you will not submit any requests for mounted service on your preference card, I will recommend to the Academic Board that you be commissioned."

The preference card required each cadet to put down which service of the Army he would like to join. Top-ranking students asked for the Engineers, for promotion came fast there, or for the Field Artillery. The Infantry, Coast Artillery and the Cavalry were available to the lower two-thirds of the class.

I told Colonel Shaw that my choice was the Infantry. "All right," he said, "I'll recommend you for a commission, but with the stipulation that you will ask for no other service in the Army."

In defense of Colonel Shaw and other officers who recommended me for commission, I should put in that my West Point record was not all bad. Perhaps I have overstressed my slight differences with the disciplinary code and the academic life. I had been a coach, a cheerleader, I gave talks to the Corps before games. One report on my early performance even said—it was shown to me years later—that I was "born to command." The man who wrote that was a reckless prophet.

II THE ABILENE YEARS

Sauce for the gander

My earliest memory involves an incident that occurred just before my fifth birthday. My mother's sister, Aunt Minnie, had been staying with us in Abilene—we lived in a cottage on Second Street then—and she took me back with her to Topeka for a visit. There was the train, and then a long horse-and-buggy ride to my relatives' farm. I remember looking down through the floorboards, watching the ground rush past under the horses' feet.

When we arrived, it seemed that there were dozens of grown-ups in the house. Even though they were, somehow, my family, I felt lonesome and lost among them and I began to wander around outside.

In the rear of the house was a pair of barnyard geese. The male had no intention of permitting me to penetrate his domain. Each time he saw me he would push along toward me with such a hideous hissing that my five-year-old courage couldn't stand the strain. I would race for the house, burst into the kitchen and tell any available elder about this awful old gander.

After several such skirmishes, Uncle Luther decided that something had to be done. He took an old broom and cut off all the straw, leaving a short, hard knob. He showed me how to swing the weapon, then took me out and announced that I was on my own. More frightened at the moment of my uncle's possible scolding than of the gander's aggression, I took what was meant to be a firm, but was really a trembling stand next time the fowl came close. Then I let out a yell and rushed toward him, swinging the club. He turned and I gave him a satisfying smack right on the fanny. He let out a squawk and ran off. From then on I was the proud boss of the backyard. I had learned never to negotiate with an adversary except from a position of strength.

Mother and Father maintained a genuine partnership in raising their six sons. Father was breadwinner, Supreme Court and Lord High Executioner. Mother was tutor and manager of our household. This may sound unbelievable, but I never heard a cross word pass between them. Before their children they were not demonstrative in their love for each other, but a quiet mutual devotion permeated our home. This had a lasting effect on us all.

Father had been given a sizable farm as a wedding present by his father, but he so disliked farming that he had sold it to buy a partnership in a store. For a time all went well, but one year drought and an invasion of grasshoppers ruined the crops of Dickinson County, Kansas. Father continued to extend credit; he carried the farmers to the end. Then his partner proved too weak to face the store's own creditors, so he took what little cash was left and departed one night for parts unknown. My parents never heard from him again.

Father set out at once to find any kind of job, and patiently started to pay off his former suppliers. He accomplished this in a relatively few years, but the experience left its mark. He had an obsession against owing anyone a nickel. He would allow the family no charge accounts—cash was paid or nothing was bought.

The first of these jobs was in Denison, Texas, where I was born. My brothers, older and younger, were all born in Dickinson County, to which we returned when I was less than two years old. There, Father was an engineer in a creamery, later manager of a gas plant, and finally director of employe savings for a group of public utilities. Usually, the work was hard, the pay meager. Father would work six days a week, leaving the house about 6:30 a.m. and returning about 5:00 p.m. Family life revolved around him. School, chores, meals and all other activities had to be adjusted to meet his requirements.

My mother, for all her gentleness, was outraged by the injustice of that early business catastrophe. For years she studied law at home, hoping someday to take legal action against the absconder, and she never ceased to warn her sons against embezzlers, chiselers and all kinds of crooks.

Her household problems were, I realize now, monumental. The least of them was to provide comfortable beds for six boys in three rooms. She skillfully assigned us to beds in such a pattern as to minimize the incidence of nightly fights. She rotated our duties so that each son learned all the responsibilities of running the house: helping with the cooking, dishwashing and laundry; pruning the orchard, harvesting the fruit and storing it for the winter; hoeing the corn and weeding the vegetable garden; putting up the hay; feeding the chickens and milking the cow. The task of making life happy and meaningful for a family of eight took insight, imagination and managerial skill.

Mother rarely resorted to corporal punishment, and when she did it was usually a slap on the hand with a ruler. She deeply believed in self-discipline. According to her, we should behave properly not through fear of punishment but because it was the right thing to do. Any serious infraction was passed along to Father, who was never one for sparing the rod. If the evidence showed that the culprit had offended deliberately, the application of stick to skin was a routine affair. Father had quick judicial instincts. Mother had insight into the fact that each son was a unique personality and she adapted her methods to each.

ARTHUR, THE FIRSTBORN, gave my parents little trouble. He was studious, ambitious and, to me, four years younger, he seemed a man-about-town. While he had his share of tussles with the rest of us, it is my impression that he was the best behaved. Following high school, he took a course in a local business college and went on to become a successful banker in Kansas City.

Edgar, second in line, was a natural athlete. He was two years older than I, and, though for years we were almost the same size, his superior qualities always made him the victor in our inevitable personal battles. Being a stubborn sort myself, I was determined to get even for his arm twists and toeholds. But not until I returned from West Point for my vacation in 1913 did I send him an all-inclusive challenge—anything he wanted, wrestling, boxing (bare-fisted or with gloves) or plain rough-and-tumble. Even then he got the best of me. In his reply from wherever his summer job had taken him, he wrote, "I would be glad to meet you with boxing gloves at forty paces." As he did not come home that season I was robbed of sweet revenge.

One of Ed's qualities I admired most was shown one day when we were digging a cistern together. I was using an adze and I brought it down neatly through the side of his foot. It had to hurt, but Ed's shouted exclamation was, "Oh Dwight! Clean through my new twenty-five-cent socks!"

Because Ed and I were constantly paired off, and Earl and Milton were much younger than he, Roy, the fourth son, was a bit of a lone wolf. Like Arthur, he had no interest in going to college. He began working in a drugstore even before he entered high school, and was soon the youngest registered pharmacist in Kansas. Eventually he purchased a drugstore in Junction City and did a thriving business.

Earl and Milton, only eighteen months apart, became the other set of natural partners. Earl, blind in his left eye because of an accident at the age of four, and Milton, left weakened by an attack of scarlet fever, did not enjoy as robust and disreputable a boyhood as Ed and I. Milton turned his energies more to studies and to the arts, particularly the piano. He organized a dance band which helped provide him with funds for college. One of his teachers headed him to newspaper work, which eventually led him to careers in government and higher education.

In appearance, we shared strong family characteristics but, since my father was dark and swarthy and my mother a golden blonde, there were predictable differences. Arthur and Roy were dark, Ed's and Milton's hair was chestnut-colored. I was so light that I was often dubbed "The Swede" by opponents in intercity athletics, while Earl was a fiery redhead.

Both parents were against quarreling and fighting, and deplored bad manners. However, I discovered that my father was far from being a turn-the-other-cheek type. One afternoon I came in from school on the run, chased by a belligerent boy of about my own size. My father called, "Why do you let that boy run you around like that?"

Instantly I shouted back, "Because if I fight him, you'll give me a whipping, whether I win or lose!"

"Chase that boy out of here."

This was enough for me. I turned around, and it was the suddenness of my counterattack rather than any fighting prowess that startled my tormentor, who took off at a rapid pace. I caught him, threw him down and promised to give him a thrashing every day unless he let me alone. I was rapidly learning that domination of others often comes about through bluff.

In spite of boyish frictions, the household and even life outside was exceptionally happy. Though our family was far from affluent, I never heard a word even distantly related to self-pity. If we were poor—and I'm not sure that we were by the standards of the day—we were unaware of it. We were always well fed and adequately clothed and housed. Each boy was permitted to earn his own money and to spend it according to his taste. One way to obtain cash was to raise and sell vegetables. Another was to get a summer job, or to work in a store after school.

From the beginning of our schooling, Mother and Father encouraged us to go to college. They said constantly, "Anyone who really wants an education can get it." But my father, remembering that he didn't become a farmer as his father had hoped, scrupulously refrained from suggesting courses of study.

His emphasis on college recalls one incident that I then looked on as almost tragic. Edgar decided, early in his high-school days, to follow Arthur's example and earn money rather than go on in school. For some months he pretended he was going to school while he worked, instead, for the town doctor. One day his continued absence was reported to Father. I never before or after saw Father so angry.

At noontime that day, Edgar and I had come home for lunch and Father, on a surprise visit from the creamery, found us in the barn. His face was black as thunder. With no pause for argument, he reached for a piece of harness, at the same time grabbing Ed by the collar. He started in.

A little over twelve at the time, I shouted to my father to stop. Finally I began to cry as loudly as I could, possibly hoping that Mother would arrive on the scene.

When I came up behind him and tried to catch hold of his arms, Father stopped his thrashing and turned on me. "Oh, do you want some of the same? What's the matter with you, anyway?"

"I don't think anyone ought to be whipped like that," I said, "not even a dog." Whatever his reason, I suffered no punishment.

Now I know, and I am sure Ed does too, that only through instant and drastic action could my father have persuaded him, a headstrong fellow, to change his attitude toward school. Had it not been for the application of leather, prolonged and unforgettable, my brother might well have become an unhappy handyman in Kansas.

In the end, Father's desire for his sons' education was fulfilled by four of them. Ed decided to go to Michigan to study law. All the younger brothers sent him funds on occasion, but he worked at the University and essentially financed his own education. My admission to West Point assured an education for me with no drain on household finances. Ed, remembering the help he had received, financed Earl at the University of Washington. Milton, by writing for magazines, correcting English papers, and, as I said, playing in a dance band, paid his costs at Kansas State University and later, in 1924, while an American Vice-Consul in Scotland, did graduate work at the University of Edinburgh.

This willingness of brothers to aid each other was one consequence of the guidance we received as youngsters. Years later, when Arthur was an authority on grain marketing, finance and banking, Edgar a successful lawyer and director of industrial companies, Earl a radio-station owner and public-relations director of the community newspaper, Milton the President of Johns Hopkins University and I a first-administration Republican President, friends often asked why there had not been a black sheep in the family.

The answer lies, I think, in the fact that our family life was free from parental quarreling and filled with genuine love. I never knew anyone from a divorced family until I went to West Point. Responsibility came as a part of maturing. Concern for others was natural in our small community. And ambition without arrogance was quietly instilled in us by both parents. Part of that ambition was self-dependence. Whenever any of us expressed a wish for something that seemed far beyond our reach, my mother often said, "Sink or swim," or "Survive or perish."

One other circumstance helped our character development: we were needed. I often think today of what a difference it would make if children believed they were *contributing* to a family's survival and happiness. In the transformation from a rural to an urban society, children are robbed of the opportunity to do genuinely responsible work.

The key to the closet

My first reading love was ancient history. At an early age, I developed an interest in the human record and I became particularly fond of Greek and Roman accounts. These subjects were so engrossing that I was frequently guilty of neglecting all others. My mother's annoyance at this indifference to the mundane life of chores and assigned homework grew until, despite her reverence for books, she locked my volumes of history in a closet. This had the desired effect for a while—until I found the key to the closet. Then, whenever Mother was somewhere else, I would sneak out the books. To this day, there are many unrelated bits of information about Greece and Rome that stick in my memory.

Among all the figures of antiquity, Hannibal was my favorite. This bias came about because I read one day that no account of Carthaginian history was ever written by a friendly hand. Everything we know about Carthage, about Hamilcar and his lion's brood—of which Hannibal was one—was written by an enemy. For a great man to come down through history with his only biographers in the opposite camp is a considerable achievement. Since those early years, history of all kinds, including historical novels if they are well documented, has always intrigued me mightily. And the campaigns of the more modern leaders—Frederick, Napoleon, Gustavus Adolphus, and all of our prominent American soldiers and statesmen—I have found absorbing.

Among the Americans, Washington was my hero. I never tired of reading about his exploits, particularly at Valley Forge, and I conceived an almost violent hatred of General Conway and his Cabal. I could not imagine anyone so stupid and so unpatriotic as to have wanted to remove Washington from command of the Army. His stamina and patience in adversity, first, and then his indomitable courage, daring, and capacity for self-sacrifice excited my admiration. While the cherry-tree story may be pure legend, Washington's Farewell Address, his counsels to his countrymen, like the speech at Newburgh to the rebellious officers of his Army, exemplified the human qualities I frankly idolized.

I know now that as a youngster I was concerned almost exclusively with the peaks and promontories of the historical terrain. Today I am interested too in what ordinary people, from age to age, moved by dissatisfaction with the inadequate, have done to accelerate the spiral of change.

But, as to the future, any predictions of mine might be as wrong as Cecelia Curry's, who wrote the class prophecy about her fellow Abilene High School graduates of 1909. My brother Edgar, she wrote—as though in a newspaper of the 1940s—is finishing his second term as President of the United States, might be elected to a third. And what, in 1940, has become of Dwight? "He's professor of history at Yale"!

For me, in Abilene days, the reading of history was an end in itself, not a source of lessons for the present or future. Nor was I aware that the richness of opportunity in this country would give me, like all of us, a chance to be joined, intimately and productively, with both the past and future of the Republic. Had one of Abilene's many Civil War veterans, for instance, suggested that not many years later I would visit Gettysburg to study the tactics of the great battlefield where he had fought, my reaction would have been—"Me?"

Yet so it came to pass in 1915. Three years later I was in Gettysburg again, as the commander of an Army camp. And in 1950 I bought property next to the fields where Pickett's men had assembled for the assault on Cemetery Ridge.

To the rapid reader or the hasty visitor, Gettysburg is Pickett's Charge, Little Round Top and Devil's Den, the Wheatfield and the Peach Orchard, plus a few names in high command. Everything else is a blur. This is understandable. To tell the whole story, in detail, has required enough books to fill a small library.

Nearly 170,000 men were engaged, from scores of regiments. Of course, major decisions were the responsibility of a few. But their execution depended on the initiative, the fidelity, the strength of many thousands of individuals known only to their immediate comrades in the battle, their names forgotten today.

Gettysburg, in fact, was a demonstration of what a small portion of a nation's number can accomplish in the shaping and the making of history. On the field, men found in themselves resources of courage, of leadership, of greatness they had not known before. Nor were they men of only physical courage. High moral courage marked them, too. Take one example.

George Gordon Meade was assigned command of the Army of the Potomac only three days before the Battle of Gettysburg commenced. No other officer in that war was given so little time to prepare himself and his troops for such a climactic engagement. As he rode toward the battle on July 1, 1863, he received reports throughout the afternoon and evening that his I Corps had been forced back, its commanding general killed, the XI Corps disastrously routed and thousands of its men taken prisoner. Meade must have been torn with anxiety about the future of his army and—for he was only human—occasionally must have worried about his own fate as its commander. For a year and a half, command of the Army of the Potomac had been an avenue to military disgrace: Meade's appointment was only one in a long succession of changes.

When he reached the field after midnight on the eve of the second day of battle, the prospect was far from heartening. The Confederates—except on the south—were ringing the Union lines, and all reports indicated that Lee would be ready in the morning for a heavy assault on the Union position. It might be late in the day before Meade would have enough troops on the field to balance Confederate strength.

The morning of July 2, after only a few hours' sleep, he was back on the lines. As he scrutinized from Cemetery Hill the terrain around him occupied by the enemy, he had to weigh the value of the ridges held by his men against the offensive capacity of Lee's victory-heartened veterans; to calculate the hours required to move in his reserves; to formulate in his mind moves that might thwart the plans of Lee.

For Meade, this was the moment when all within him had to bear tough and strong on the problem ahead. No council of war could be called. No delay for leisurely study would be permitted by Lee. And the decision was solely Meade's responsibility. He is quoted as saying, almost to himself, as he turned his horse: "We may fight it out here just as well as anywhere else."

In all this, there is neither visible drama nor glamour; only the loneliness of one man on whose mind weighed the fate of ninety thousand comrades and of the Republic they served. Meade's claim to greatness in that moment may be best evidenced by the total absence of the theatrical. When thousands of lives were at stake there was no time for postures or declamations.

And I plead for realization that the handful of heroes on a field such as Gettysburg merely symbolizes the courage or the daring or the high-spirited initiative of a multitude of men. Men such as these are worthy of every American's study. Thousands upon thousands of them, totally unknown to formal history, have performed as gloriously.

Those I came from

THE YEAR I was ten, my mother gave permission to Arthur and Edgar, my older brothers, to go out Halloween "trick-or-treating." It was upsetting when my father and mother said I was too young to go along. I argued and pleaded until the last minute. Finally, the two boys took off.

I have no exact memory of what happened immediately afterward, but suddenly my father was grabbing my shoulders to shock me into consciousness. Completely beside myself, I had been pounding an apple tree with my bleeding fists. My father legislated the matter with the traditional hickory switch and sent me off to bed.

Perhaps an hour later, my mother came into my room. I was still sobbing into the pillow, at odds with the entire world. Mother sat in the rocking chair by the bed and said nothing for a long time. Then she began to talk about temper and controlling it. As she often did, she drew on the Bible, paraphrasing, I suppose, "He that conquereth his own soul is greater than he who taketh a city." Hatred was a futile sort of thing, she said, and as she bandaged my injured hands, she did not fail to make the point that I had expressed resentment and damaged only myself. She added that among all her boys, I was the one who had most to learn.

I have always looked back on that conversation as one of the most valuable moments in my life. The incident was never mentioned again. But to this day I make it a practice to avoid hating anyone. If someone has acted despicably, especially toward me, I try to forget him. I used to follow a custom—somewhat contrived, I admit—of writing the man's name on a piece of scrap paper, dropping it into the lowest drawer of my desk, and saying to myself, That finishes the incident, and so far as I'm concerned, that fellow.

Eventually, out of my mother's talk grew my habit of not mentioning in public the name of anybody to whose actions or words I took violent exception. In private, of course, I have not always exercised tight control on temper or tongue. My staff has always held up under these bursts with an attitude of cheerful resignation. A quick explosion, as quickly forgotten, can sometimes be a necessary safety valve. I think my mother might have agreed.

My good fortune has been a lifetime of continuous association with widely different men and women who, sometimes in a few minutes by word of mouth, or sometimes over the years by their example, have given me encouragement or helped me to prepare My parents were first among them.

MY great-great-great-grandfather, Hans Nicholas Eisenhauer (Eisenhower)* was born in the Palatinate in 1691, and came to this country in 1741 with three sons. Peter was twenty-five, John and Martin were in their early teens. They settled in what is now Bethel Township, Lebanon County, Pennsylvania, where Hans farmed for the next twenty years.

During the Revolutionary War, the Susquehanna River territory where they lived was relatively free from armed conflict, though foraging parties undoubtedly made frequent requisitions on the farmers' barns and larders. Food for the troops and fodder for the horses often worried commanders more than the presence of the enemy. There is a small family sidelight on the supply problem. According to the New York Sons of the Revolution, two of

---

* The name Eisenhower translates roughly as "iron-hewer." Eisenschmidt could mean blacksmith, but an Eisenhower was something of an artist in iron, a man who literally hewed metal into useful and ornamental shapes, such as armor, weapons, etc.

the Eisenhowers, coming to camp to enlist, got special mention in a report because they brought with them "a supply of food."

I am directly descended from Hans Nicholas' oldest son, Peter, who was the father of seventeen children. A farmer, engaged in many land deals, he was also a blacksmith, a gunsmith, a merchant and, for a time at least, a constable. The raising of a large family, I suppose, required unusual efforts in moneymaking.

Peter's youngest son, Frederick, was my great-grandfather. He was a farmer and weaver who lived until 1884 and was the senior Eisenhower in the move from Pennsylvania to Kansas. His son, Jacob Frederick, my grandfather, was born September 19, 1826. In Jacob's person—he lived with us in Abilene from the time I was ten until I was almost sixteen—the long past of my family grew closer.

I never knew Rebecca Matter Eisenhower, my grandmother. Born in 1825, she was the great-granddaughter of a Revolutionary War soldier, and the daughter of a War of 1812 captain. She died four months before I was born. She and my grandfather had fourteen children, of whom five sons and one daughter died in infancy or childhood. A second daughter, who would have been my Aunt Lydia, was a little over seventeen when death took her. My grandparents' faith, in the face of repeated personal tragedy, is evident on the limestone marker they placed at the head of Lydia's grave:

> *She gave her heart to Jesus*
> *Who took her stains away*
> *And now in Christ Believ*
> *ing, the Father too can say*
>
> *I'm going home to glory*
> *A golden crown to wear*
> *O meet me meet me over there*

Everything I ever heard about them corroborates the sincerity of these chiseled words. The future life was of paramount importance. This life was only a preparation, the earth a place where heavenly reward might be earned. Frugal in worldly things, a minister who gave more than a tithe to the church, my grandfather nevertheless had his practical side. He was a good and farsighted steward of the land, and the valley farm he bought on the edge of Elizabethville in Pennsylvania's Lykens Valley was ideally situated for bountiful harvests. The house my grandfather built there, more than one hundred and ten years ago, still stands today.

Among the Plain People of Pennsylvania, a strong prejudice existed against any practice that implied a lack of trust in God, and I have read that insurance was barred among them. Grandfather evidently did not consider an insurance policy a reflection on Providence. Within a few weeks of completing his home, at the age of twenty-eight, he had it insured for $1367 (against an appraised value of $2050) with the Lykens Valley Mutual Fire Insurance Company. Still, Jacob Eisenhower was a cautious man. His was the forty-eighth policy issued by that company. He waited until the founder and the president of the company took out, respectively, policies forty-six and forty-seven.

In that house my father was born and lived until he was fifteen. He grew up to detest farming, despite the attractiveness of the homestead. But Grandfather prospered. By 1870, his farm was appraised at $13,000 and his personal property, including savings, at $6000. He could easily have spent his declining years in that comfortable house in the valley he knew so well. In the seventies, however, among the River Brethren of the Susquehanna Valley, tales were told of the richness of Kansas lands, of the bountiful wheat crops, of good acreage that could be bought at fairly low prices. Pennsylvania newspapers were full of stories about the success of Pennsylvanians who had gone west. The railroad vigorously pushed travel to Kansas by running excursion trains and cutting fares.

My family took the train and arrived in Abilene, county seat of Dickinson County, on April 12, 1878. There Grandfather bought land priced at $1200 a quarter section, or $7.50 an acre. (In Pennsylvania, his farm had sold for close to $175 an acre.) How much he took up, I do not know. It must have been a substantial amount because his customary wedding gift to his children was a quarter section from the land he owned and $2000 in cash. He himself, a year after arriving in Kansas, was farming 160 acres.

That was a bad crop year in Kansas, and worse were to come. Moreover, Grandfather had not yet learned how best to cultivate soil so different from his limestone valley in Pennsylvania. But unlike most of his neighbors, he had two strings to his farming bow—and the second was a dairy herd and poultry.

In 1879, his butter production was a full thousand pounds, more than six times the Dickinson County average. And Grandmother that year had gathered 300 dozen eggs, twice the county average. The estimated value of all production was $400. This was $85 less than average farm income in the county, but most of their neighbors had already been on their land five or six years.

In my memory, Grandfather is a patriarchal figure, dressed in black, wearing an underbeard with upper lip shaved clean. When I knew him he was retired and lived across the valley from our home. He kept a horse and buggy which, on occasion, he shared with us boys. His importance, in my mind then, rested on the beard and the buggy and the horse. Now I know otherwise.

My grandfather was more than fifty years old when he determined to take his family and leave the pleasant valley where he had lived a half century. This was, I would guess, the great adventure of his life—to risk all he possessed to start a new life on a new kind of ground.

For all his vision, he had no reason to think that a century and a quarter after he was born, his grandson would return to the Susquehanna Valley hoping to end his days on a Pennsylvania farm. Just that has come to pass. Only a few score miles separate my barn from his, still standing in the Lykens Valley.

Of my mother's family, I know less than of my father's, but if Ida Stover was representative of them all, they were a remarkable people. I may exhibit a son's prejudice, but my feeling reflects the affection and respect of all who knew her.

Mother's serenity, her open smile, her gentleness with all and her tolerance of their ways, despite an inflexible loyalty to her religious convictions and her own strict pattern of personal conduct, made a visit with her memorable even for a stranger. And for her sons, privileged to spend a boyhood in her company, the memories are indelible.

My mother was born close to the clamor of battle. Growing up, she could see its ravages in a devastated land and in broken bodies. If her hatred of war arose out of childhood memories, she had justification. She was born May 1, 1862, at Mount Sidney, Virginia, ten miles or so from Staunton in the Shenandoah Valley. Through the first three years of the Civil War, the valley above and below Mount Sidney was a secure highway for the movement of Confederate troops and supplies, and a rich granary that supported Lee's armies. To end all this became a fundamental purpose in Washington. When my mother was well into her third year, Sheridan, detached for the purpose from Grant's forces near Richmond, waged in the valley with fire and sword a campaign so devastating that "a crow flying over it would have to carry its own rations."

Mother grew up among the charred ruins of homes and barns, the decaying trees and blackened soil of uprooted orchards and burned fields, wrecked bridges and twisted railways. She was all her life a woman of peace.

Her mother died when Mother was not quite five. Because her father was unable to cope with eleven children, Mother lived in the home of her maternal grandfather, William Link, who became her guardian upon the death of her father. When she was about fifteen, two of her older brothers moved to Kansas, and she decided that eventually she would join them there.

In an age when, far more than now, most girls looked forward to careers as housewives, Mother was determined to get a good education before all else. This she did and very much on her own, using a small inheritance to see her through high school. To earn money for college, she taught school. In 1883 she left Virginia for Lecompton, Kansas, where she enrolled in Lane University.

Lane had several advantages. It was fairly new. It was lively. And, though she didn't know it, the man who was to be my father was enrolled there. And she could never have imagined that she would be staying in Kansas to help in the total education of this man's sons.

The "Gem" on the Plains

As it must to all small boys, there came a time when we began to comprehend that home was more than just our own backyard. Once in a while, news of the outside world crept in—a world beyond the limits of Kansas, even.

During the Spanish-American War, when I was seven, my uncle Abraham Lincoln Eisenhower was an avid seeker of news. Because he was busy in his veterinary practice, my job, at a penny a day, was to run uptown and get him the local paper, hot off the press. I can never forget his glee when the news came of Dewey's May Day victory over the Spanish fleet at Manila Bay; and he fairly danced with pleasure at word that the Spanish fleet in Cuba had been sunk to the last vessel—a somewhat bloodthirsty reaction for a man who would later become a minister.

But before I paid much attention to that distant, outside world, there was a lot to see and learn in the small world around me. Visually, Abilene was undistinguishable from scores of other rural towns that dotted the plains. It looked peaceful, pastoral, and was, at least in my childhood, happy. After all, the splendiferous C. W. Parker Circus made Abilene its home base. Merry-go-rounds were *built* there. Three decades earlier, though, as "the Cow Capital of the World," it was known as the toughest, meanest, most murderous town of the territory.

Texas cattlemen, after the Civil War, sought eastern markets. In 1869 they started to drive their herds into Abilene, then the western terminus of the Kansas Pacific (later the Union Pacific) Railway. Our national folk heroes were a fairly riotous breed in the best of times, and cowboys coming in off the long, lonely trails were starved for drink and excitement. It has been written that early Abilene's infamous Texas Street was "a glowing thoroughfare which led from the dreariness of the open prairies into the delight of hell itself." Whether or not the local hell was an unqualified delight, when the railroad moved on westward along about 1872, the citizens were pleased, and settled down into occupations that made for a slower but steadier growth. In many American towns of that period, civic pride was the most flourishing local industry, and when my dad and mother arrived, Abilene was enthusiastic about its future. On my desk lies a booklet printed in 1887, that proclaims Abilene, modestly:

A GEM

"The City of the Plains"

THE CENTER OF THE "GOLDEN BELT"

The unknown author writes in bountiful language about the wonders of Kansas, of the county, and of the county seat. That the reader may not think him extravagant in his appraisal, he submits in corroboration an extract from the Kansas City *Journal:*

> But whence this wealth . . . Whence these farms in Dickinson County, worth $10,000,000, and the wealth in stock, factories, business blocks, homes, railroads, salt wells, gypsum beds, etc., to the amount of $15,000,000—nearly $1,000 for every man, woman and child in the county? The answer is easy. They have industriously tilled this great garden of nature and its enormous product has been most widely disposed of by a progressive people.

In a final burst of civic puffery, the pamphlet's author, surely one of the progressive people to whom he refers, calls for ten thousand more citizens. "Abilene," he concludes, "is ready for any class of enterprising people to reap a rich reward from . . . a land favored of heaven and embellished by art." Whatever its endowments from heaven, and its cultural wonders, Abilene did not get ten thousand more citizens. Through my boyhood, it was definitely a small town.

It was located a mile or two north of the Smoky Hill River, and east of a slow-moving stream known as Mud Creek. Boys searching for fishing holes in the little waterway had to be content with a mud cat or an occasional channel cat, the latter always a prize. Our major amusements were baseball and football. When I grew older, we had a boxing club in the back of a printshop. Winter sports were skating and hooking a sled behind a horse; the rider, lying flat on his belly, took a fair amount of snow from the horses' hoofs. I remember seeing a tennis court but not seeing anyone play. I had never heard of golf.

Social life was centered in the churches. Church picnics, usually held on the riverbank, were an opportunity to gorge on fried chicken, potato salad and apple pie. The men pitched horseshoes, the women knitted and talked, and the youngsters fished.

High-school students formed little clubs, but Ed and I never joined. By the time I was old enough to be a member, I was gangly and awkward, with few of the social graces. Probably I was more than happy that I was never invited to membership. My brother and I referred with immense disdain to boys and girls who did belong.

The streets were unpaved, the sidewalks made of lumber, and the police force was one man, Henny Engle. He spent most nights watching trains go by or come in, inspecting the arriving passengers for dubious characters. There was also a town marshal, a daytime man. I never saw him do more than chase truant boys.

Shopping was not a recreation, as it has since become for me. Grocery stores, meat markets, "notion" stores, drugstores provided customers only with what they needed. Nothing was done to encourage the casual browser, the one who these days leaves a store freighted with things he had no intention of buying when he entered. That is just the sort of shopper I am, made for modern merchandising techniques. For me a supermarket is an oriental bazaar, a wonderland of bargains I cannot pass by.

My underground global reputation, I understand, is for the enthusiasm with which I storm a market. A few years ago when Mamie and I were at Culzean Castle, Scotland, a friend and I visited a clothing shop in Ayr. After we left, loaded down, a clerk went up to the proprietor. "You mean to tell me," he said, "that he was the man who used to be the American President? Why, mon, he acted like a lad from the hills!" Then he added, under his breath, "He's no a hard one to sell, that one. . . ."

No Abilene clerk or store owner would have radiated such pleasure when speaking of any of the Eisenhower boys. When it meant handing over hard-earned spending money, the canny Scots of Ayr could not hold a candle to us in our critical scrutiny of goods and prices. Not that we were taught to love money; far from it. We had a firm respect for it as a commodity hard to come by and quick to vanish unless one exercised vigilant care.

Prices were low but not low enough to suit us. The Abilene paper of October 14, 1890, the day I was born, offers a sample of the price structure. Eggs were five cents a dozen. Bread was three cents a loaf. A man could buy a suit for a few dollars. Boys, however, required bats, balls and mitts, powder and shot for muzzle-loading guns, footballs and helmets, and there was no money to spare for these.

Understanding our wants, Father allotted each boy a bit of ground where he was privileged to raise whatever he chose, to sell if possible to the neighbors. I chose sweet corn and cucumbers; I charged twenty-five cents a dozen for the earliest corn, and as the season advanced, the price went down. Having fixed my price, I would show the corn. If the customers said the price was too high, I would pick up my pack and go on my way.

Then I had another idea. In Texas, Mother had learned to make Mexican hot tamales. They were delicious, and I badgered her until she taught me the whole process, step by step. And I started making and selling tamales, three for five cents. It was a good off-season sales idea, and if there were leftovers, my brothers and I could consume them without strain.

THESE moneymaking ventures began only after we had moved from Second Street to our larger, permanent home on Fourth Street. The Second Street house was tiny, its yard large enough to swing a cat in if it were a small one. Mother must have wanted more room inside and out; and if ever she gave in to envy, it could have been inspired by the Fourth Street house of my Uncle Abraham, whose veterinary practice required a large barn and open acres around it.

In his boyhood on the family farm in Pennsylvania, Uncle Abe had loved horses more than the land. After his marriage, he had opened a veterinary office and hung out a shingle that read A. L. EISENHOWER, D.V.S. So far as anyone knows, the three letters after his name were self-conferred, although he had served an apprenticeship to a vet. But what he lacked in credentials, he made up for in energy and showmanship. Whenever his time was not occupied by animal care, he would hitch up his horse to a two-wheeled gig and drive hurriedly around the countryside, giving farmers the impression that he was rushing off to answer another emergency call. His practice increased gratifyingly, and he came to be known as the "genial veterinarian."

Then in 1898 he decided suddenly to follow the example of his father and be a preacher of the gospel. He made up his mind to go west, so Father offered to buy his house.

The move to Fourth Street was a step up in the world! There were two fairly large bedrooms upstairs with a miniature bedroom at the end of the hall. One large one was occupied by Father and Mother, with the baby, Earl, in a cradle. In the adjoining room, Roy and I slept in one bed, Edgar in the other. Arthur, the eldest, was awarded the little room—only six and a half feet square. He was the only person with a room of his own. Then Mother brought in a girl to help with the housework, and Arthur had to come in with the rest of us.

I don't know how my mother jammed us all in. A quick calculation reveals that her domain—for living, sleeping, working—totaled 818 square feet for a household of eight. Yet she used the space beautifully. Whenever, since, I've been given any choice of working quarters, my preference as to size may have reflected a subconscious effort to test my own capacity to use space against hers. But I haven't always been a free agent. As Chief of Staff after World War II, my office in the Pentagon was bigger than the whole house in Abilene. And in my last job, I had no say in the matter whatever.

The first addition to the house was a two-room wing, built when Grandfather Jacob came to live with us, and when the last baby, Milton, was born. With Grandfather's arrival, and without counting the baby, Mother never had less than eight people for breakfast and supper.

Dad carried a lunch or one of us took a hot midday meal to him. The creamery, where he was working then, was far enough

away to make it worthwhile to hitch old Dick to the buggy or ride him bareback. Either way, and for good reason, dispatch and promptness marked the deliveries. One day Ed dismounted to play a little baseball, and Father had to wait past the lunch hour for a meal that was lukewarm. Ed did not have to wait as long to get a very distinct physical reaction.

All in all, we were a cheerful and a vital family. Our pleasures were simple, but we had plenty of fresh air, exercise and companionship. And in that golden time I had my first experience in a political campaign. I know some people have always thought I wasn't much interested in politics, but my debut took place in 1896. Almost everybody in school had a bright yellow McKinley button, because there were few Democrats in the region.

One evening we learned that a big torchlight parade was to take place. Because I was only six, my mother was loath for me to go to it, but Arthur, now a lordly ten, and Ed, eight, assured her that they would take care of me, and we went up to the north end where the parade was to start. The torches were intriguing, each consisting of a rod with a can of liquid at the end, and a wick that threw a smoky flame into the evening air. It soon became clear that there were more torches than bearers, so, spying us standing there wide-eyed, the parade managers commanded us to come over. Each of us was handed a torch, and mine was exactly my own height. We were told to shoulder torches, somewhat like shouldering arms; then off we went.

The town band was supposed to keep us marching in cadence, but my short legs presented a problem and our group at the end of the parade was more like a cavorting crowd of lambs. There was a certain amount of disrespectful laughter, but we got through the parade with no singed hair and without undoing McKinley. That was not only my first appearance in parade formation but my first successful venture into politics. It was half a century later that I was drawn into my next campaign.

IN THE fall of that year, 1896, I entered the Lincoln School, unaware that I was starting a formal education which would not terminate until 1929 when I finished courses at the Army's War College in Washington, D.C. Into that third of a century was to be compressed a series of revolutions—political and economic, social and scientific—which were to transform the human environment of the entire globe. But nothing could have been more revolutionary to me than this new experience. Here I was, transported from the family circle into an immense brick building populated by strangers of varying ages. This upheaval was far more cataclysmic than any changes to follow.

They used a drum to rally us in ranks for reentering the school after playtime. The drummer could turn the tumult of a recess crowd into some semblance of orderly movement. I've always admired the drum since then, and despised the siren. The drum communicates a message and calms as it warns. The siren is an assault on the senses. In later years, when well-intentioned escorts elected to use a siren on my behalf, I asked—ordered—that it be stopped.

In 1898, during the Spanish-American War, there was talk about the possibility of the enemy bombarding American cities from the air. At a school recess one morning, a rumor spread that a Spanish airship was over Abilene. All the boys rushed uptown to see the sight, never questioning its feasibility, and classes went to pot. We quieted down when the object proved to be a huge box kite, used by merchants to advertise a sale of straw hats.

Memory of school is a blur of grades entered and grades passed. At one point a suggestion was made that I skip a grade. I may well have had some advantage over my classmates, for I lived in a home where learning was put into practice. The ability to read correctly in a good clear voice, for example, was necessary for a daily family rite, the reading of the Bible. The suggestion that I skip a grade was never put into effect. My conduct was not the equal of my reading ability.

Few of us at school in Abilene felt the classroom as important a center of learning as the office of Cecil Brooks, the telegrapher. He was the radio and television of our day, and to us most notable because during a World Series, he kept his wire open to the East until the games had ended. Nearby, in the "Smoke House," a poolroom, the scoreboard was set up and he relayed the results to the board at the end of each half inning. Those of us who crowded around him in his office could get even quicker results. In the 1906 series of hitless wonders, I remember that truancy rose to unusual peaks.

From time to time we heard news of our wandering Uncle Abraham. He and Aunt Anna, with another Brethren preacher, went off in a cumbersome covered wagon to the Cherokee Outlet country in Oklahoma Territory, an area newly opened to settlement, where they conducted what Aunt Anna described as a "highway-and-hedge call." When winter drove them home,

Uncle Abe designed them a better vehicle—fourteen feet long by seven wide, and six and one-half feet high from floor to canvas roof. It held a table and chairs, a stove, four cots, and a sliding curtain that divided it into sleeping compartments. This contrivance Uncle Abraham christened a "gospel wagon," and after a dedicatory ceremony, they set out again.

My uncle, whether as vet or preacher, had a streak of the carnival barker in him. He reached Herington, Kansas, on the Fourth of July, when a man with a large megaphone was directing the crowds toward the celebration at the edge of town. Uncle Abraham whipped his team and gospel wagon into the line of march. At the next intersection he turned down a side street, brandishing his whip as he stood upright, and shouting at the top of his voice, "This way to heaven!" The crowd followed Uncle Abraham to the other edge of town where, assembling them around his wagon, he delivered a soul-rousing sermon.

In an even smaller town, hard pressed to gather an audience, he lay on his back on the sidewalk, his feet elevated against a wall, and began to read his Bible. In no time at all, a crowd gathered and he sprang to his feet. He had his congregation and they got his sermon.

After their third highway-and-hedge season, my uncle and aunt returned to Pennsylvania where, for a short time, they lived at an orphanage conducted by the River Brethren. Childless themselves, they fell in love with the children, and got the idea of opening a similar home in the Oklahoma Territory.

With no qualms about where either money or orphans would come from, they filed a homestead claim near what is now Thomas, Oklahoma—then only a stopping place on a wagon trail. With his own funds and mainly with his own hands, Uncle Abraham built a frame house. On August 26, 1901, he and Aunt Anna were granted a charter and incorporated the Jabbok Faith Missionary Home and Orphanage. The children came to fill the house, and Uncle Abe farmed the 160 acres well enough to feed and clothe them, with something left over for cash sale. In 1906, the church formally took the orphanage over.

Among the River Brethren, Uncle Abraham came to be known as Mr. Jabbok. Today, on that site, a thriving school is a monument to the faith of two people who dared to dream and to do something about it.

My HERO was Bob Davis, a fisherman, hunter and guide. He was also a bachelor, a philosopher and, to me, a great teacher. Bob was in his fifties when I knew him, roughly from age eight to sixteen. He never seemed to mind my going along on his expeditions. In the Smoky Hill River, he caught channel cat illegally, using nets, and sold them to the markets for something like ten cents a pound, dressed. In fall and winter, he trapped muskrat, which abounded, and mink, which were scarce. For partially cured muskrat hides he got eleven cents; for mink, $1.50.

Bob had an old double-barreled shotgun. At the time it seemed perfectly natural that he should bring down two ducks, from high overhead, with two shots. Years later, when I began to try the same sport myself, I realized what a remarkable shot Bob Davis was.

We spent weekends together on the river with Mother's blessing. He taught me how to use a flatboat, with one paddle (you keep the paddle on one side and feather) and how to set and anchor a net, with the opening downstream. His favorite method of teaching was to ask questions. "In the woods, it's raining. How do you find north?" (The moss on the trees tends to be on the northern side.) "Bub, how do you catch a muskrat?" (You look for his slides, then put your trap on a short chain so he'll drown.)

One thing he taught me, without sanction, was the rudiments of poker. Bob knew poker percentages cold. He would deal me five cards and ask me whether I had a pair.

"Yes, nines."

"All right, how many nines are there out of the forty-seven cards that you have not yet seen?" (Two, of course.) "Well, then, the chance of your drawing a nine is two out of forty-seven with each card. Since you are drawing three cards you have six chances out of forty-seven of catching a third nine."

He dinned percentages into my head night after night around a campfire, using a greasy pack of nicked cards that must have been a dozen years old. So thoroughly did he drill me that I was never able to play the game carelessly or wide open. Since most tyros and many vets know nothing about probabilities, it was not remarkable that I should come to be a regular winner. In the Army, when I found I was playing with officers who were losing more than they could afford, I stopped playing the game.

My INTEREST in cooking has always caught the attention of the press. I have no idea how many miles of film have been wasted on me as I broiled fish or steaks over a fire. I suppose I began cooking when I made those tamales to sell. Then I acquired some rudiments of the art when Milton fell ill with scarlet fever. The doctor had quarantined certain rooms in the house, and my father and the rest of the boys lived downstairs while Mother and a neighbor woman remained with Milton the entire time. Arthur and Ed had part-time jobs, so the kitchen chores fell to me. Mother would call instructions from the sickroom and I would carry them out. It was a new experience and I felt very important indeed. I don't think the family lived too well during those weeks but I learned something about the preparation of simple dishes. My principal contribution was a hearty vegetable soup, always a family favorite.

While we were in high school, a group of us went camping out on Lyons Creek, about twenty miles south of town. We decided that each day two boys should do the cooking, and I paired off with Ames Rogers, a banker's son. I had asked Mother for help, and she had taught me to bake and boil potatoes, to handle steaks—which in those days were pan-grilled—and even to produce a satisfactory pie. The gang therefore wanted Ames and me to cook every day, and naturally we demanded our price: the others had to clean up, get the wood, build the fire. And we demanded first helpings of any scarce commodity.

In the last few days we ran short of money and the rations became meager. I took an old shotgun out, but all I got were two or three squirrels—very little to feed a sizable group of hungry boys. With a few potatoes and beans, I tried to build a good stew. When we saw that we were going to be short, Ames and I began to talk loudly about how we hoped that the crow we had shot would be edible.

The boys drifted over to the kettle, looked in and said they weren't hungry. Of course Ames and I ate heartily and then asked, "What's wrong with you people? Don't you like squirrel stew?"

The group, who had been looking at us with barely disguised distaste, now jumped up and began a rush. Ames and I took off as fast as we could, well knowing that they would stop to get a share of whatever was left.

These experiences gave me a continuing interest in cooking. When, as an officer in the Army, I had the usual chore of inspecting the enlisted men's mess, I knew that if we were to have a happy company, not only good food but decent preparation was essential. I volunteered for Cooks and Bakers School when I was at Fort Sam Houston, and though I didn't qualify as a cook, I did learn enough to say what was wrong with the food my men were getting.

THE MOST dramatic difference between high schools of today and those of my time is probably not in the curriculum but in the life expectancy of the students. Then, except for the common cold and chilblains, any illness might easily be fatal. It was taken for granted that a Fourth of July celebration would produce injuries ranging from powder burns to lockjaw. Quarantines were imposed for the more common ailments of diphtheria, scarlet fever and the like. Treatment consisted of a few simple medications and a nourishing diet while the victim and the family waited for cure or death. Diagnosis was hardly exact. "Blood poisoning" was a favorite phrase to cover a multitude of mishaps.

Racing down a wooden platform one evening with some of my friends, I slipped and fell. The damage seemed slight—just a raw, red spot on one knee. The next morning there were no ill effects and I went to school. On the evening of the second day, I did not feel well so I lay down on the sofa and dropped off, it seems, into delirium. There ensued a hectic couple of weeks. The doctor came two or three times a day and only occasionally was I conscious—usually when he had to explore the wound. Once, to my great alarm, I heard him mention the word "amputation."

When Ed got home that day, I made him promise to make sure that under no circumstances would they amputate my leg. "I'd rather be dead than crippled, and not be able to play ball." The doctors were frustrated by my attitude, but my parents agreed to accept my decision. Eventually the progress of the disease was stopped, but I was so ill that I remained out of school the rest of the spring and had to repeat that year.

This episode has often been told, and one story said that my parents prayed day and night, for two weeks. This is ridiculous. My parents were devout Christians and there is no doubt that they prayed for my recovery, but they did it in their morning and evening prayers. They did not believe in "faith healing."

EXCEPT for my extracurricular reading of history, no school subjects set me afire except geometry. I was more excited by my summer and after-hour jobs. I earned twenty-five cents a day picking apples, and fifty cents a day on a wheat-harvesting job. The binders were horse-drawn and for two seasons I rode the lead horse, until my employer told me I was getting too big.

A few days later I learned of a temporary job. A family moving from Abilene to Hutchinson had some livestock to take along. The animals were to ride in a boxcar, and railway regulations required that someone ride with them. I badgered the man for the job, but he said I was too small and turned me down flatly.

That evening I complained at length to my folks. In one week I had been told that I was too big for one job and too little for another.

High-school commencement, the high point of our lives, was in the Seelye Theatre, the largest gathering place in Abilene. There, on Sunday evening, May 23, 1909, baccalaureate was held. On Monday evening there were class-day exercises, on Wednesday evening the senior play, and on Friday evening the grand event, commencement itself.

The senior class play was our version of *The Merchant of Venice*. Edgar played the Duke of Venice and I was Launcelot Gobbo, servant to Shylock. According to the town's paper, Edgar "invested his character with dignity and art." For once in our school careers, however, I got more of the spotlight than Ed. My part was written for a blunderer and seemed to have been made to order for me. The review said:

> Dwight Eisenhower as Gobbo won plenty of applause and deserved it. He was the best amateur humorous character seen on the Abilene stage in this generation and gave an impression that many professionals fail to reach.

I have in later years been reviewed along similar lines, but never because I intended to be.

The commencement speaker, Henry J. Allen, editor of the Wichita *Beacon*, who would become Governor and United States Senator, said: "I would sooner begin life over again with one arm cut off than attempt to struggle without a college education."

For Edgar, whose plans to go to Michigan were far advanced, this statement was an endorsement. For me, determined to go, thinking to join Edgar in Michigan when we raised the money, such an emphatic pronouncement was iron in the spine of purpose.

Toward college

ED AND I had just one idea that summer: to get our hands on every cent we could earn. He started working at once for the Belle Springs Creamery Company, where Father was chief engineer.

My best chance seemed to be on a farm owned by a Mr. Bryan. We worked from dawn to dusk, the owner, his son and I. Then I was offered more by a small company making steel grain bins, so I worked there for some months, and became a sort of straw boss.

When the time came for Ed to go to the University, I found I could earn still more money as an iceman at the creamery, so I moved over there. The ice was frozen in three-hundred-pound cakes. Three or four of these had to be hauled up each hour on a windlass, and I had to manipulate them with a pair of tongs. The rest of the time I spent helping load the delivery wagons. Though far from intriguing, the job did develop muscles.

My last year in Abilene, I became the second engineer in the creamery's ice plant. The work week was eighty-four hours, from six p.m. until six a.m., and my agreement called for fifty-two weeks a year. (Three or four times a year I got a helper to take my place briefly.) But the salary was impressive—$90 per month.

THROUGH my early teens I had formed a friendship with Everett Hazlett, son of one of the town physicians, which endured to the day of his death in 1958. While I was in high school "Swede" Hazlett attended a private military school, where he acquired an interest in the service academies, particularly the Naval Academy at Annapolis. He applied for an appointment there, but he failed the mathematics examination. However, he got a reappointment and a chance to take the test again. Back in Abilene to study, he urged me to try it too.

I was not difficult to persuade—first, because of my long interest in military history, and second, because I realized that if I could make it, I would take the money burden entirely off my family. Swede wrote to the Navy Department for copies of past entrance examinations—which were, incidentally, almost identical to those for West Point—and we began to study together. We both had jobs, but we could meet for three or four hours a day. During these sessions we asked each other questions and then checked the answers against those given in the Navy exams. With the close of summer my friend went to what he called a "cram" school, and I went for a review course at my old high school, where my teachers were anxious to help.

My congressman had no additional vacancy in either military academy. So I wrote to Senator Joseph Bristow requesting an

Senior Class

EDGAR NEWTON EISENHOWER

♣

"Big Ike" is the greatest football player of the class. Also on his head there is a depression due to non-development of the conscious and over-development of the sub-conscious brain. Football teams '07, '08, '09. Base ball teams '07, '08, '09; captain '09.

DAVID DWIGHT EISENHOWER

♣

"Little Ike," now a couple inches taller than "big Ike," is our best historian and mathematician. President of Athletic Association, '09; Football, '07, '08; Baseball '08, '09.

Two "Ikes" graduate from Abilene High School, 1910.

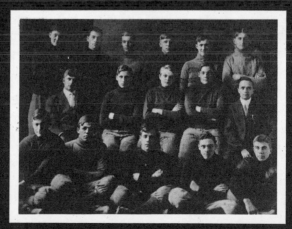

The Abilene High football team, 1909. I am third from left, back row.

Dwight (age about eight), Edgar, Earl, Arthur, Roy,
Father, Milton, Mother.

The family grown up. On the Fourth Street porch, 1926.

Our first house, on Second Street, was tiny.

Christmas 1952, New York. As President-elect with mother-in-law, wife, daughter-in-law Barbara, and grandchildren Susan, John, Jr., and Barbara Anne.

Mamie and I were married on July 1, 1916, in Denver.

In 1955 her wedding gown went on display in Washington.

We met at Fort Sam Houston, Texas, my first post.

With General MacArthur during the Army veterans'
bonus riots, Washington, D.C., 1932.

Honoring General de Gaulle and the Fighting French. London, July 14, 1942.

Signing the guest register at West Point, 1945, while Lieutenant John Eisenhower looks on.

Receiving the Legion of Merit from President Roosevelt, 1943.

Testing marksmanship with Prime Minister Churchill and General Omar Bradley in England, 1944.

As President, tossing out the ball to start the 1953 baseball season, Senators vs. Yankees. Future President Johnson is on the left.

A favorite sport—outdoor cooking in 1960.

appointment as either a cadet or a midshipman, and I asked various influential men in town to write him in support of my application. There must have been a score or more who wrote, and each one stressed the unimpeachable honesty of my father, David Eisenhower. I never ceased feeling grateful to my father.

Senator Bristow authorized me to participate in the preliminary examination which determines who is eligible for appointment. The examination would apply to both Annapolis and West Point, if the applicant so chose. Because Swede had been given a naval appointment, Annapolis was my first choice, and I came through as number one for the Naval Academy. Then came the blow. The entrance regulations for that academy specified an age limit of twenty, and I had assumed that meant until the twenty-first birthday. But because I would be almost twenty-one by the time the next class enlisted, I was ruled ineligible.

I had, however, come out as number two for West Point, so there was some hope there. Then I learned that the man who ranked above me had not met the physical requirements. I got the appointment from Senator Bristow in the spring of 1911.

This was a good day in my life. The only person truly disappointed was Mother. Courageous, sturdy, self-reliant, she was also the most honest and sincere pacifist I ever knew. It was difficult for her to approve the decision of one of her boys to embark upon military life. I told her not to worry because I hadn't yet passed the final examination. Most boys took special training for a full year to prepare for service-academy exams, and chances were that I would fail. This did not appease her, for she could hardly hope one of her boys would fail a tough examination. But, because she and my father always insisted that each boy should be the master of his own fate, she kept her own counsel.

So in the spring, I went to St. Louis to take the examination at Jefferson Barracks. The farm boy was completely unprepared for the sights of the river metropolis. One night, another applicant and I left the Barracks where we were quartered, and wandered around the city. We walked the streets for a while, then took a streetcar and rode it to the end of the line. We found ourselves at a carbarn in East St. Louis, on the eastern side of the Mississippi River. We thought we'd follow the tracks back to the river, but when the line branched we had no idea which one to take. No more streetcars were running on that side of the river, we saw no sign of any other kind of transportation and we were lost.

Then, in a nearby building, we saw a light. We knocked hopefully on the door and soon heard someone moving toward us. The door opened slowly and the first thing we saw was the muzzle of a revolver. A voice said, "Who are you?" We stammered that we just wanted help in getting back across the river. The man apparently decided we were harmless and gave us instructions.

We were only a block from the bridge. We crossed it at double time and just made the final car for the Barracks, which left at one a.m. But we had not solved the problem of how to get into the Barracks. We had violated instructions to be in bed by taps and were afraid we would be barred from completing the examination. Luck was with us. We found a spot where we could scale the wall, and sneaked safely into the building.

Back in Abilene, after an almost unbearable wait, I was informed that I had passed. I was directed to report to the United States Military Academy on June 14, 1911. I had ranked somewhat above the middle of all those admitted. Since many had undergone special training, I did not feel badly about my showing.

A financial deposit was required from the new cadet, to cover his initial clothing issue. I had been able to save this amount and had enough to pay my transportation costs. When I reached West Point, I would have about five dollars in my pocket. It was with such material wealth that I started a military career which, except for the interval of eight presidential years, still continues. It has been rewarding, in many more ways than monetary.

My mother saw me off, and then went back home. Milton told me later that for the first time in his life he heard her cry.

IN THE PEACETIME ARMY

Fort Sam Houston, Texas, 1916

BEFORE graduating from West Point, each cadet was to express his preference for duty station. I put down the Philippines, the only one in the class who did, I think, and it seemed logical that I would draw this assignment. The Philippines for years had been at the bottom of the preference list. Because of this, when the time came for purchasing uniforms, I ordered only tropicals. I figured a number of years would pass before I needed the olive drabs and the various dress blues. Since my tropicals cost far less than the average outfit, I was given, upon graduation, several hundred dollars from the forced savings deducted from my paycheck each month toward the purchase of my uniforms.

The President himself was required to sign every commission, and, when I graduated, Mr. Wilson was somewhat preoccupied with the Mexican troubles and with a war that had been going on in Europe since August 1914. I received no orders immediately.

Returning to my home, I set out to have a good time, and did. The money from my equipment-fund surplus was soon exhausted. I made an arrangement to borrow sums from my father, to be repaid after my commission. Then, with my own funds spent, and in debt to my father, I received orders to go to Texas.

Assignment to a continental station meant that all the uniforms necessary had to be in my possession. I was really up against it. In Leavenworth, Kansas, there was a uniformer named Springe, one of the best in the United States, also one of the most expensive. I told him I would have to buy on credit. He agreed and made all my necessary O.D. and blue uniforms, including full dress. So I reached my regiment in San Antonio properly uniformed and badly in debt. However, I soon received my delayed three months' pay and, what with this and some small checks I began receiving from participants in poker games of cadet days, I gradually started to pay off some of what I owed.

One Sunday afternoon after I'd been in Texas for some months, I walked out of the Bachelor Officer Quarters to make a guard-post inspection as Officer of the Day. On the sidewalk across the street was a small group of people, one of whom was Lulu Harris, the wife of a major.

"Ike," she called, "won't you come over here? I have some people I'd like you to meet."

"Sorry, Mrs. Harris," I called back, "I'm on guard and have to start an inspection trip."

She then turned to one young girl, as I discovered later, and said, "Humph! The woman hater of the post."

The girl said something to Mrs. Harris that caused her to call once more. "We didn't ask you to come over to *stay*. Just come and meet these friends of mine."

I walked stiffly across the street to say a polite greeting to the little family gathered around Mrs. Harris. Their name was Doud. They were from Denver and they spent each winter in San Antonio. My eye was instantly caught by a vivacious and attractive girl, smaller than average, with a saucy look about her. If she had been intrigued by my reputation as a woman hater, I was intrigued by her appearance. I asked her whether she would like to go along on my rounds of the guard posts. To my astonishment she said she would. Later I found that one of the things she was least fond of was walking. Possibly she went along just to take me down a peg. In any event, that was the entrance into my life of Mamie Geneva Doud.

While it soon became almost routine for me to call on her, I had more time than money to spend on courtship. When we went to dinner, it was usually to a Mexican restaurant called The Original, on the San Antonio River, where chili, tamales and enchiladas for two came to about $1.25, including tip. The old Majestic, a vaudeville house, was the Palace of San Antonio, and everybody went there once a week. These two places made up the largest item in my weekly budget.

When I was not out with Mamie I lived the life of a hermit. During that winter, however, I had one very fortunate evening in which there was more income than outgo. Two of my former classmates had come to San Antonio to take physical examinations for the Aviation Section of the Signal Corps, as our air force was then called. They were heroes: anyone who succeeded in getting into Aviation was assured of a fifty-percent rise in pay. The two young men had organized a little crap game to celebrate.

When I walked into the Infantry Club they greeted me joyfully, saying, "Come on, get in here. We're getting everyone's money because we want to give a party."

"I'm sorry," I said. "I've got two silver dollars in my pocket and that's all. You can't use me in that game."

They jeered good-naturedly and one said, "Come on, every little bit helps."

By dinnertime, I had run my two dollars up to a hundred.

I had warned my fellow players that I had a date and would have to leave at seven. When the time came the two new fliers, now flying low, protested that I couldn't go away and leave them losers.

"Well, I'll tell you what we will do. Both of you seem to be losers in about the same amount," I said. "I'll divide my winnings into two equal piles. Each of you can take one roll. You can either lose or win and it's O.K. with me."

They couldn't see themselves taking a shot at fifty dollars each on one turn of the dice; so they politely refused and the game was over. The following morning I completed my payments to Mr. Springe for uniforms. Now I was out of debt to everyone except my father.

The commanding officer of our regiment, the 19th U. S. Infantry, was Colonel Millard F. Waltz. My first encounter with him left me . . . well, a little up in the air. A small group of us happened to be standing one evening near the flagpole, which had strong supporting cables reaching from the ground to a point fifty or sixty feet up the pole. Just for fun I said that I could easily climb one of these, using hands only. Another second lieutenant said I was talking tommyrot.

I retorted, "What would you like to bet?" He produced five dollars. I had one lone five-dollar bill in my wallet, so I handed it to one of the other lieutenants, as stakeholder.

I stripped off my blouse and started up. I had no difficulty—rope climbing had been one of my favorite exercises at West Point—and was chuckling cockily about a windfall that would pay for an evening out with my girl when I heard a bellow from below. "Who are you up there?"

With a shock, I realized who was talking—it was Colonel Waltz. "Mr. Eisenhower, Sir."

"Come down here," he said.

"Sir," I called down, "I was bet five dollars that I couldn't overhand my way to the top of this cable. Could I please go on up and touch the pole and then come down?"

"DO AS I SAY AND DO IT RIGHT NOW, GET DOWN HERE!"

Sheepishly, I let myself down the cable and as quickly as my feet touched the ground came to a stiff salute. First he ordered me to don my blouse, and then began taking me over the coals. Finally he stalked off, and no sooner was he out of earshot than the man I'd had the bet with claimed he had won the five dollars.

I objected vigorously. The bet was, at the least, a draw, because it had been nullified by the intervention of the C.O. The argument got hot and heavy, until I suggested that we finish it with fists. However, the majority declared the bet to be a draw and the money was returned to each side.

As the winter wore on, I became more and more enamored of Mamie. On Valentine's Day, 1916, I gave her my class ring and shortly afterward went heart in mouth to ask her father for the hand of his daughter. She was nineteen. He said this was far earlier than he had expected her to marry, but he would approve, provided we waited a reasonable time. We tentatively agreed to the following November, when Mamie would be twenty.

Months earlier I had applied for transfer to the Aviation Section. Only a few nights after my talk with Mr. Doud, the application was approved. That night I went to the Douds' house walking on air. But the news of my good fortune was greeted by Mamie's family with a large chunk of chilly silence.

It was broken by Mr. Doud, who said that if I were so irresponsible as to want to go into flying, he and Mrs. Doud would have to withdraw their consent. For the next couple of days I pondered the matter in misery.

As anxious as I was to try it, the Aviation Section was just another branch of military service. Perhaps I should take a broader look at my future in the military. Possibly I had been too prone to lead a carefree debt-ridden life. Now I made a professional decision I have never regretted. It was to perform every duty given me to the best of my ability and to make a creditable record. In this way I would become the finest Army officer I could, it didn't matter in which branch of the service.

I went back to the Douds and announced that I was ready to give up aviation. My decision was an immense relief to them because Mamie, who understood how I felt about getting into flying, had been raising quite a fuss. Soon she went back to Denver with her family. As a symbol of my new seriousness and sacrifice, I stopped smoking ready-made cigarettes, which were then about a dollar a carton, and went back to rolling my own.

At about the same time, the troubles with Mexico became more intense and the National Guard was mobilized on the border area. I left the post to live in a camp where I became an Inspector Instructor of a Guard regiment. My duties were to help straighten out administrative snarls and to supervise training. I enjoyed the work, and it was one of the most valuable years of preparation in my early career. I began to devote more hours of study and reading to my profession, but I did not neglect my courting, which now had to be carried on by correspondence.

Throughout the winter of 1915-16 there was a rising clamor for the United States to act more vigorously against both German submarine warfare, in which many of our ships had been sunk, and against Mexico, whose depredations across the border seemed to us unconscionable. Many people became impatient with President Wilson. He was well aware that America was not militarily capable of joining immediately in any major war abroad and so he continued to apply reasonable arguments in an attempt to get the Kaiser to stop the inhuman submarine campaign.

All the trouble, of course, was reflected in the papers and in our letters. Finally, Mamie and I decided we should advance the date of our wedding. Mamie would contact her parents, then in the East, and I would try to get a short leave from the Army. I asked for twenty days. Although the War Department denied furloughs for any but emergency purposes, it seemed to me that imminent marriage was just that. This didn't impress the Colonel, but he did send my letter on to the department commander, General Funston. To my surprise, I was ordered to report to Department Headquarters. I marched over there, dressed in my best uniform, shoes polished and everything spick-and-span. I didn't want any sloppiness to create a bad impression.

"I understand you want to get married," the General said, and asked what the rush was all about.

I told him and he smiled. "You may have ten days. I am not sure that this is exactly what the War Department has in mind, but I'll take the responsibility."

Now I had to get to Denver. I had no wedding ring and it was

Sunday. Also, as usual, I was short of money. I looked up a friend who worked for the Lockwood National Bank of San Antonio, and told him my story. He laughed and said that any overdrafts that I might write during the wedding period would be honored. In those days the credit rating of an Army officer was of the highest order.

Next I went to find another friend who was the manager of Hertzberg's jewelry store. He opened the store and gave me a ring on credit. So with a new ring, new debts, ten days, and high hopes, I started on my journey.

We were married in the Denver Central Presbyterian Church. Our honeymoon was a couple of days at a nearby mountain resort, Eldorado Springs. We went back to Mamie's home for a day or two, then took the Union Pacific to Abilene, arriving about four in the morning.

We could stay only a few hours, but my mother was determined to give us at least one fine meal in her house. So instead of the normal breakfast that morning we had a monumental fried-chicken dinner. It was a warm and welcome banquet. Earl and Milton were excited to meet my bride, and became friends with her immediately.

We arrived back in San Antonio to be greeted by young Army friends laden with gifts. The post grapevine had given our wedding complete coverage. In my old bachelor quarters of two rooms and a bath, there were more packages. There was a chafing dish, a percolator, a toaster, a broiler and a tiny stove. We soon discovered we'd have use for them.

Mamie, young, attractive and full of life, was the pet of the post. She was showered with attention from officers and ladies of all ages, and thoroughly enjoyed the officers' mess, except for one detail—the food.

More unhappy each day with the menu, we began using our wedding presents to make coffee, candy and other minor dishes. My cooking experience was now some years in the past, and Mamie knew even less about cooking than I, but our table fare began to include pot roast, steaks and chicken—all of which were

153

plentiful and cheap—and the meals became so presentable that now and then we could invite a couple of friends.

Soon after we were married, I was made Provost Marshal of the post. We had trouble keeping order for a while, with untrained soldiers and conflict between the Regular Army and the National Guard. One evening I went out on a patrol with two men. We were checking on bars and other places of dim repute when suddenly there was a shot almost beside my ear. We looked around and there was a second shot. By then my corporal, a huge fellow, had located the shooter. He dragged him out of an alley.

"Hey, watch it," the man said harshly. "I'm an officer." And he was, a National Guard lieutenant.

"I don't care what you are," said the corporal. "You shot at my lieutenant."

We turned him in and a National Guard court fined him five dollars. Penalties were stiffer later, but there were times when I was frightened for Mamie, who often had to be alone. I had given her a .45 pistol and showed her how to use it. One morning I said, "Mamie, let's see you get your pistol out—as if there were somebody trying to break in through the front door."

She went to look for it. She had hidden it behind a piano, inside a bedding roll, under other possessions, and in general so far buried that she couldn't have gotten it out in a week. I decided to concentrate on trying to make the camp safer.

By early spring, 1917, the danger along our southern border had been reduced, but conditions between the United States and Germany had worsened. The Germans had resumed unrestricted submarine warfare, and in early April President Wilson went before the Congress and asked for a declaration of war. As usual, our country was unprepared. Intensive efforts were started to raise our strength and enable us to participate in a conflict that had been raging in Europe for more than two years. The great mobilization of 1917 was on.

One method of expanding the Army was drawing cadres of officers and men from the Regular regiments and forming them into new regiments together with recruits. The 19th Infantry was directed to form the 57th and I was chosen to go with the new group. My job was to be regimental supply officer, and my orders were enough to dismay a young man with less than two years of service. Within two or three days three thousand recruits, equipped only with clothing and barracks bags, would reach the now vacant Camp Wilson, just out of Fort Sam Houston. I was responsible for providing them with food, shelter, supplies, and anything else that men needed to subsist and train. For the next five days I was on the move almost around the clock.

Fortunately, I had with me one noncommissioned officer who had been in the supply business a long time. We borrowed trucks, found enough tents to shelter the men from the weather, and somehow appropriated enough food to give them at least a meager meal their first evening and the next morning.

Then it was decided that we would not stay at Camp Wilson but move twenty miles to a place called Leon Springs. Leon Springs boasted a large area for training movements, but nothing else. There was not a building on it

Competition for supplies was keen among the new regiments. I haunted the quartermaster, ordnance, engineer and medical services, pleading the case of our new Infantry regiment, now approaching full strength. And I kept hammering away at the War Department. But we were to remain critically short of supplies for a long time.

We were working so hard that the Colonel ordered that Sunday should definitely be a day of rest: except for religious services under the trees, we were free to do as we pleased. This was a limited privilege because there was no transportation to go into San Antonio. However, Mamie was determined not to let this situation defeat her. Although she had never driven a gasoline-powered vehicle, she decided to drive our own little car to the camp and spend some Sundays with us there. Her first venture was lively.

She did remember how to start the car and get it into forward gear, and so she began the twenty-mile trip, starting early in the morning to avoid traffic. She wanted the whole road to herself and I must say she needed it. She had telephoned in advance and asked me to meet her at the gate, so I walked the mile or so to the entrance and waited. I was finally rewarded by seeing Mamie coming down the hill. Then I heard her calling, "Ike! Get on, get on quickly—I don't know how to stop this thing!"

Cars in those days had broad running boards and it was no trick to hop aboard, get the door open and take over. She leaned back with a sigh of relief. She told me that when she'd reached a railroad crossing where she was supposed to stop and look, she had had to go straight across—fortunately without incident.

I spent part of that day giving her driving lessons. She became passably proficient; nevertheless, I induced her to make an early start back and to telephone me as soon as she arrived. Two hours later I got the welcome news that she was safely at home. From then on I arranged for an experienced driver to go along when Mamie visited the camp.

One day I assembled the regiment's junior supply officers for a lecture on supply in the field. We gathered just outside my tent, under a large tree. A drizzling rain started but we put on raincoats and kept on. Then there was a terrific bolt of lightning, and the next thing I knew I was lying on my back in the mud with an enlisted man pushing down on my ribs, trying to bring me back to consciousness. With a splitting headache and feeling a little woozy, I walked over to the tent of the adjutant, Captain Walton Walker, and found him in a state of upset. Walton had been telephoning when the lightning bolt came—the phone flew across the room and he had an arm that was rapidly turning black-and-blue. Colonel David J. Baker often remarked that he was the only regimental commander in the Army whose entire staff had been struck by lightning and lived to tell about it.

The Colonel was something of a dyspeptic and fussy about his meals. He complained constantly about the quality of the food and finally added the mess officer's job to my other duties of trying to supply a regiment of thirty-five hundred men with mules, transportation, weapons, shelter and all manner of hardware.

Supplying the Colonel was its own war. The meal of which he

was most sharply critical was breakfast. I had heard him talk often of his liking for game, and this gave me an idea. Walton Walker and I both liked to shoot. We began taking off each morning at about four a.m. for a field where doves were plentiful. By the time the Colonel was ready for breakfast, at about eight, he'd have a fine meal out of our morning shoot.

We learned to bring in at least half a dozen, because the Colonel would frequently say, "Any of these for lunch?" With the best cook we had, we tried broiled breast of dove with bacon, dove stews and dove pies. By giving him bacon and eggs about one morning a week, and lamb chops another, we seemed to keep him satisfied. The other officers got little attention, so preoccupied were we with the Colonel. But this helped everybody—we all enjoyed life more when he was in a good mood.

Anyhow, the regiment was in good shape. We were sure that we were one of the best outfits in the whole Army and were confident that we were destined for overseas duty. Then to my distress I got a special order detaching me from the 57th Infantry and assigning me to the training camp at Fort Oglethorpe, Georgia, to be an instructor of candidates for commission. I tried to get the order changed, but in vain. (The 57th, it turned out, never went to war.) Mamie couldn't go along because I was going to field duty, and the parting was particularly difficult as she was expecting our first child.

At Oglethorpe, a captain now, I went to work training candidates for commissions as second lieutenants. The training program was intensive and tough—designed as much for weeding out the weak and inept as to instruct. The work was fatiguing, but I enjoyed it. Luckily I had for months been reading everything I could find about infantry tactics on the Western Front, and it was paying off. We constructed dugouts, lived in trenches and put into practice what I had read.

Then on the twenty-sixth of September I came out of those trenches and found a telegram dated the twenty-fourth, saying that my son had been born. His name was Doud Dwight. Fortunately, when orders came shortly for me to proceed to another training assignment, at Fort Leavenworth, I was given time to go by way of San Antonio to visit my wife and our new son.

In San Antonio I reported in at the post and learned that a machine-gun battalion was being organized for overseas duty. It was to be commanded by my friend Colonel Gilbert M. Allen, who heartily endorsed my instant application to join it. I received a curt reply from the War Department, stating that I was considered to be a young officer with special qualities as an instructor. Disappointed, I trekked off to Leavenworth.

I had been on duty there for a few days when Colonel Miller, the post commandant, read me a letter from the Adjutant General which noted that I had several times applied for duty with troops headed overseas. The War Department did not approve of young officers applying for special duty; they were to obey orders and, in effect, let the War Department run the war.

This made me furious, and when the Colonel proceeded to add several reprimands of his own, I reverted to the old, red-necked cadet. I was asking nothing, after all, except to go to battle.

"Sir," I said, "this offense—if it is an offense—was committed before I came under your jurisdiction. If there is punishment to be given out, I think that it should be given by the War Department and not added to by yourself, with all due respect."

I was surprised to hear him say, "Well, I think you're right. I respect you for standing up to your convictions." I left in a friendly mood toward him, although my views of the War Department continued to be beyond easy conversion to parlor language.

Training for the invisible war

BY THIS time I knew enough about officer training and organizing new units—or thought I did—so that the prospect was a dull one. It was small comfort to tell myself that training young officers was a constructive contribution to the war. For one thing, all the West Point traditions that nourished élan and esprit centered on battlefield performance. My mastery of military paper work or of training methods hardly seemed a shining achievement after seven years of preparing to lead fighting men.

Some of my class were already in France. Others were ready to depart. I could see myself, years later, silent at class reunions while others reminisced of battle. For a man who likes to talk as much as I, that would have been intolerable punishment.

My elation, then, can well be imagined when I received orders in late winter to report to Camp Meade, Maryland, to join the 65th Engineers. This, I was told, was the parent group which was organizing tank-corps troops for *overseas* duty. That word put new spirit into me. I rushed back to San Antonio to see Mamie and our youngster, then took off for Camp Meade.

Our first job was to complete the organizing and equipping of the 301st Tank Battalion, Heavy. These troops were to man the big tanks, a rarity on World War I battlefields. Morale was high: as soldiers promised a new weapon always will, we convinced ourselves that we would have it in our power to clinch victory. All of us were itching to move. In mid-March, I was told that the 301st would soon be taking a ship at New York. I was to go along in *command!*

As a regular officer, I had to preserve the sedate demeanor of one for whom the summons to battle is no novelty. But my exuberance, I'm sure, was shown in every word and gesture to the battalion. I went to New York to plan the embarkation. Two days later I was back at Meade. The plan had been changed. My chief said he was impressed by my "organizational ability." I was to take the remnants of the troops who would not be going overseas, and proceed to an abandoned campsite in Gettysburg, Pennsylvania, of all places.

My mood was black. The new camp, called Colt, had to be established quickly, but I still had to complete all the details of shipping the 301st to New York. So I took a small detachment to Gettysburg, and left them in charge of a Captain Garner, who had been commissioned a year earlier from the ranks. I knew nothing about him, but he seemed quite capable.

We ran up the United States flag just before I started back to

159

Baltimore. I saw Garner watch it flap on top of the pole. "Captain," he said, "the last time I was on this ground I was standing before a general court-martial which sentenced me to six months in the guardhouse, and then suspended the sentence. Now I'm standing here as temporary commander of the camp in which I was disgraced." As I looked up, this gray-headed former noncom had tears streaming down his face.

All I could manage to say was, "Look, Garner, I know you'll do a splendid job. Good luck." And I got into the car and started off. To this day, whenever we stand to salute the flag, that memory is with me.

In place of the 65th Engineers the War Department set up an organization called the Tank Corps, under the direction of Colonel Ira C. Welborn. His office was located in Washington and I had to report to him twice a week. Otherwise, I was very much on my own at Camp Colt. As the only regular officer in the command, I really began to learn about responsibility. I was required to take in volunteers, equip, organize and instruct them, and have them ready for overseas shipment when called upon.

By the time the camp was at a strength of about five hundred men, I assumed they would be shipped out and replaced by a fresh lot. Once again I had not reckoned with the powers that be. Because of a crisis in troop strength along the Western Front, the British and American governments had made the "Abbeville Agreement," whereby the British were to provide all sea transport across the Atlantic, and the United States would, temporarily, move to ports of embarkation nothing but infantry troops and machine-gun battalions. This meant that, for an unpredictable period, we could not move tank troops overseas.

Our numbers at Colt began to grow rapidly. I could foresee that before summer several thousand men might be in camp. Once they were competent in basic drill, they would have little to do—we had no tanks as yet—and morale would deteriorate quickly.

I began to look around for ways to instruct the men in skills that would be valuable in combat and prevent the dry rot of tedious idleness. In earlier wars, crushing defeats had often been the product of lost or misunderstood messages. We realized that anyone who could learn telegraphy and master Morse code would be useful in the Tank Corps. In short order we had a telegraphic school in operation. Then we established a motor school, with secondhand motors of all kinds.

A number of machine guns came in, and we trained gunners until they could take them apart blindfolded and put them together again. Then someone had the notion of mounting the machine guns on truck trailers or on flatbed trucks, and so we were able to train the men to fire from mobile platforms. All this we took on without orders from Washington but with the approval of my chief, Colonel Welborn. It was just as well—the camp continued to expand, and toward the end of July we had ten thousand men and six hundred officers.

During the summer we saw our first tanks. Although we were part of the Tank Corps, we know about tanks only from hearsay and newspapers. With the cheerful cynicism of soldiers, we had not expected to see one until we reached Europe. However, someone in the war zone apparently thought that there might be virtue in letting the Tank Corps get a look at the machine we were to operate.

Three small French-manufactured Renault tanks were sent to us. Each weighed about seven tons, and each carried either a machine gun or a small one-pounder cannon, mounted in a revolving turret. Each *was* to carry, I should say; the tanks arrived without weapons. Again, we improvised.

I had been told that my command of Camp Colt would be only temporary, that, after I had the training operation organized, Colonel Welborn would consider my assignment overseas. Now that the camp was operating smoothly, the Colonel had a change of heart and said he could not possibly recommend my transfer to Europe until the camp closed for the winter.

He did, however, finally promise to put me in command of the November shipment of troops. After hearing this in late summer,

I began to assemble the troops I wanted to take overseas. Understandably I wanted to make certain that they were without any faults that I could eliminate.

It was one evening in September that we received our only group of inductees (or drafted men). The next morning, alarming reports started to reach me that some of the new men were registering high fevers and were obviously very ill. Before noon, Spanish flu was recognized. Because the men had not been confined to quarters, and some of them were obviously carriers, the whole camp had to be considered as exposed.

We put up every kind of tent with makeshift bedding, and any man with the slightest symptom was isolated from the others—if only by canvas partitions between the beds. Each man who had been directly exposed to the disease was, wherever possible, put in a tent by himself.

By the second day some of the men had died. The week was a nightmare and the toll was heavy. The little town had no facilities to take care of the dead—which were to number 175. Churches were taken over for hospital use as the numbers of sick mounted rapidly. The whole camp was on edge. No one knew who was going to be stricken, and death came suddenly.

In April, Mamie had arrived with our new baby, "Icky," and we found quarters in Gettysburg. While I could not be at home all night, whenever possible I would go there in the evening. It was fun to have the chance to see my son growing up and to spend the evenings with my wife. But now, of course, I was desperately worried about them. A doctor, Lieutenant Colonel Scott, who had been using a number of strong sprays on patients, told me he would like to experiment with my family and my headquarters staff. I told him to go ahead.

Each morning he would use two sprays on our throats and nostrils; one was intensely strong and pungent, and the other was, I think, a sort of soothing syrup to follow the first. We were fortunate—or he was smart. Not a single person in my headquarters command or my family contracted the flu.

The losses were heavy but because of the strict measures taken by the camp surgeon, one week after our first death the last one occurred, and the epidemic was under control. The flu experience in other and bigger camps was far less satisfactory than ours. I was ordered by the War Department to send thirty of our doctors to show what measures had been taken.

When the epidemic was over, Colonel Welborn offered to recommend me for full colonel if I would give up my plans for overseas service. I declined, saying, "I'm ready to take a reduction in rank to the average of my class—to major, that is—if the lieutenant colonelcy which I have now stands in the way of my going overseas." The November group was in good shape. Nothing was going to prevent my meeting the departure target date.

I had made no provision for imminent German defeat. In the first days of November, talk began about the weakening of German resistance. On the eleventh of November, 1918, the Armistice was signed. I had missed the boat in the war we had been told would end all wars.

For Mamie and me, the pleasure of the Armistice was qualified by the news that Mamie's younger sister was dead. This was a terrible blow for both of us. The girls had been close and I had loved "Buster" deeply. Mamie had to go alone to Denver for the funeral, taking Icky with her, because I could not leave. It was a difficult parting for us, the most trying we had encountered in our less than three years of married life.

At Colt, however, I had no time even for reflection. Nothing at West Point or in the forty months since graduation had prepared me for helping to collapse an Army from millions to a peacetime core. A trickle of applications for immediate discharge from every unit in the Army began flowing into our camp headquarters. The trickle became a small Niagara. Winter was coming on fast, and we had no proper shelter against cold. Fortunately, the War Department reached a fast decision.

As quickly as possible, we cleared the site we had occupied for nine months, and moved to Camp Dix in New Jersey. We had to be meticulous. Every soldier had to have a thorough physical. His financial records had to be checked to make sure that he had gotten all his final payments, and his transportation back home had to be arranged.

We arrived at Dix with more than five thousand people. We were left with between two and three hundred, plus three Renault tanks. We were ordered to Fort Benning, Georgia.

Through darkest America with truck and tank

OUR transfer to Fort Benning was only an interim move until the War Department found a permanent post for the remains of the infant Tank Corps. Mamie and I were impatient for a reunion. But we might be transferred to Texas, to California—or even to Colorado. It meant a brief spell of loneliness; brief, that is, meaning interminable.

As for my career, the prospects were none too bright. I was older than my classmates and was still bothered on occasion by a bad knee; I saw myself in the years ahead putting on weight in a chair-bound assignment, shuffling papers and filling out forms. At times I was tempted, at least faintly, to try my luck as a civilian. An Indiana businessman who had been a junior officer at Camp Colt offered me a position at considerably more pay than a lieutenant colonel and certainly more than a captain, the grade I would hold as soon as the inevitable demotions came. Staying in the Army meant years of trying to stretch dollars and merge dimes. No one can be a more fearful worrywart than a young man trying to read his future in a bleak moment.

There was, after all, a brighter side. I had been singularly fortunate in the scope of my first three and a half years of duty. How to take a cross section of Americans and convert them into first-rate fighting men had been learned by experience, not by textbook. Not to overstate the case, I had a feeling for the military potential, in human terms, of the United States.

At Benning I had far too much time on my hands. In March 1919, we moved back to Camp Meade—Meade to Meade within a year for me. But the Tank Corps was still marking time, its future uncertain. And Mamie, our son and I still had to be separated. Meade was a cantonment unsuitable for families. Tank officers were housed in Bachelor Officer Quarters. Because the cities were distant and the local recreation facilities were dismaying, there was every chance of going to seed, of filling the time at the card table or the bar.

But there were chances to reach out, to search for duty that was more than perfunctory. Major Sereno Brett and I heard about a truck convoy that was to cross the country from coast to coast, and we were immediately excited. Today such a trip might seem humdrum. In those days, we were not sure it could be accomplished at all. Nothing of the sort had ever been attempted. I wanted to go along, partly for a lark and partly to learn.

The trip would dramatize the need for better main highways. The use of Army vehicles of almost all types would offer an opportunity for comparative tests. And many Americans would be able to see samples of equipment used in the war just concluded: even a small Renault tank was to be carried along. Brett and I got our orders and joined the truck train the next day.

The convoy was directed to proceed overland from Washington to San Francisco without delay, via the Lincoln Highway. Delay, however, was to be the order of the day. The convoy had been literally thrown together. All drivers had claimed lengthy experience in driving trucks; most colored the air with expressions for starting and stopping that indicated a longer association with teams of horses. It took a week or ten days to achieve any kind of discipline. Roads varied from average to nonexistent. Even in the earliest stage of the trip, where the roads were paved, we were well supplied with trouble.

The convoy left Washington at 11:15 a.m. At 2:50 p.m. the Trailmobile Kitchen broke its coupling. A fan belt broke on a White Observation Car. And a Class B had to be towed into camp at the Frederick Fair Grounds with a broken magneto. The weather was fair and warm, the roads excellent. The convoy had traveled forty-six miles in seven and a quarter hours. The second day it made sixty-two miles in ten and a half hours.

In some places, the heavy trucks broke through the surface of the road and we had to tow them out with the caterpillar tractor. Some days when we had counted on sixty or seventy or a hundred miles, we would do three or four. Maintenance crews were constantly on the job to keep the vehicles running. They did good work, as I recall. We lost only two vehicles by accidents, and one was beyond their help—it rolled down a mountain.

One by-product of this trip was the nodding acquaintance that I acquired with the face and character of the country, east to west. We were always routed through the main streets of each community. Our snail's pace enabled me to observe anything different or unusual. At every overnight stop I tried to learn as much as I could about local interests.

Mamie and all the Douds met the truck train at South Platte in Nebraska and went along with us for the next three or four days, as far as Laramie, Wyoming. This was a fine interlude, and I decided that it would be nice, now that I was out there already, to apply for a leave with my family in the West at the end of the tour—if indeed we ever reached the end.

The trip wasn't all work. Once we got into a reasonably dependable pattern, for machines and men alike, there were effervescent spirits to take advantage of every lull—particularly after we had crossed the Missouri and were in more sparsely populated areas. In western Wyoming, we camped near a little settlement that boasted a restaurant, a post office, a telegraph station, two stores and a half dozen houses. Sereno Brett and I decided that one of the easterners in our group, a man who was more gullible than he should have been about conditions west of the Hudson River, should be given a taste of the authentic West.

On a visit to the little restaurant, Sereno made friends with several of the local people. After he talked to them, we took a table and waited for the arrival of the easterner and a few of the other boys. During dinner, the natives began to talk loudly about the possibility of Indian trouble. It appeared that an outbreak was imminent. They were terribly disappointed, we overheard, that the motor convoy had come into their region without arms.

As they went on, Sereno and several of us expressed our anxiety. Before we left for camp, we proclaimed our intention of mounting a guard. We borrowed an old shotgun from one of the townspeople and loaded it with shells (from which we had removed the shot). Then we arranged for sentinels.

Courageously, Sereno and I and a few others took the early duty, allotting the dreary small hours of the night to the officer for whom this episode was staged. Just before midnight Sereno let out an occasional shriek, in the manner of a carnival Indian. Then, as we came in off post, we took concealed positions to watch our man.

The recruit took his duties seriously, marching at attention around the camp as if on parade. Sereno and several others went off and from a distance let out weird and strident yelps. Finally, just as we had hoped, the sentry let go with both barrels—to arouse the camp, he explained later. We went back to bed, pleased with ourselves.

There had been no Indian trouble since 1890, of course, but another kind of threat loomed instantly. It happened that one of the duties of our victim was writing up daily progress reports to be telegraphed back to the War Department. We learned that he had drafted a telegram describing the local Indian trouble.

Faster than any vehicle in the convoy, we shot off to find the man who was carrying that message to the telegraph office. When we found him, we took the story to the commanding officer, and pointed out that if such news were to reach the Adjutant General he was unlikely to understand our brand of humor. The commanding officer went along with the gag, and the Indian story went no further.

We did get to San Francisco at long last, although even in California, where the highways were the best we had encountered, we averaged less than ten miles an hour. We were met at Oakland by city officials and the fire department and escorted through flag-festooned streets to dinner at the Hotel Oakland, fireworks, and a dance at the municipal auditorium. The next day we crossed San Francisco Bay on two ferries, paraded through the city, received our medals and listened as the Governor compared us to the "Immortal Forty-Niners."

The trip had been difficult, tiring and fun. I think that every officer on the convoy recommended in his report that efforts should be made to get our people interested in producing better roads. A third of a century later, after seeing the autobahns of modern Germany, I decided, as President, to put an emphasis on this kind of road building. When we finally secured the necessary congressional approval, we started the 41,000 miles of super-highways that are already proving their worth.

My request for leave was granted and I had four weeks with Mamie, our son and her family. The Douds were ready for their annual trip to San Antonio to spend the winter. Because there was still no place for Mamie and Icky near Camp Meade, she would go along with them, and I joined them for the early part of the trip.

It began to rain as we left Denver. In Oklahoma all the roads were mud. Finally, at Lawton, near Fort Sill, we bogged down and had to stay a full week in the hotel there. It was the week of the World Series when Cincinnati of the National League met Chicago of the American League. Mr. Doud and I watched every bulletin that came in, wondering why the great Chicago White Sox could not get going. We spent hours debating what was wrong with Chicago, plotting up every mistake of the Sox manager and coaches. We little dreamed we were second-guessing an event that was to stand in athletics as an all-time low for disloyalty and sellout of integrity.

Out of the "Black Sox" scandal, I learned a lesson and began to form a caution that, at least subconsciously, stayed with me. The stories after each game, narrating the play, were strictly objective. But stark facts and objective reports could not give the whole story. With the passage of years, I grew increasingly cautious about making judgments based solely on reports. Behind every human action, the truth may be hidden. Unless circumstances demanded an instant judgment, I learned to reserve mine until the last proper moment. This was not always popular.

During the White House years I found support from a distinguished American poet. At a time when I was being criticized by many people who thought I was moving too slowly, Robert Frost visited my office and gave me a book of his poetry. On the flyleaf he wrote: *The strong are saying nothing until they see.*

Colonel George Patton

When I returned to Camp Meade in the autumn, many changes had taken place. Senior officers of the Tank Corps were back from action in France. The one I learned to like best was a fellow named Patton. Colonel George S. Patton was tall, straight and soldierly looking. He had a high, squeaking voice, quite out of keeping with his bearing. His two passions were the military service and polo. From the beginning he and I got along famously. Both students of current military doctrine, we shared a belief in tanks—a belief derided by some experienced soldiers who thought tanks clumsy and slow, unreliable, expensive and tactically useless. On several counts they were right. On the last they were wrong.

Before I left on the transcontinental trip, we had started tactical and technical schools on this new weapon. Now we badgered George and the others who had been abroad for detailed accounts of battle operations. We began to evolve what we thought to be a new and better tank doctrine.

Because the tank was looked upon as a front-line infantry weapon, those who followed the accepted doctrine were not interested in any machine that moved faster than infantry could walk—some three miles an hour. George and I and a group of young officers believed that tanks should be speedy and should attack by surprise and in mass. They could cause the enemy confusion, and make actual breakthroughs in defensive positions.

Through a year or more of work, we refined our tactical ideas. We described in detail the tank we believed best for the American Army. We wanted speed, reliability and firepower. We wanted armor that would be proof against machine guns and light field guns, but not so heavy as to damage mobility.

We were constantly experimenting. The small tanks—the Renaults—bogged down much more easily than the big, clumsy American Mark VIIIs. The engine in the Mark VIII was the powerful Liberty, originally designed for airplanes. We devised a system of using Mark VIIIs to tow the Renaults through depressions and up slopes which they could not manage on their own.

One day we were working out an attack problem and testing our scheme through a deep, muddy ravine. We had hitched three light tanks to a big tank with inch-thick steel cables about twenty feet long. Patton and I were standing on the upslope as the big tank crawled painfully to the top of the ravine. The noise was almost deafening; but in the midst of it we heard a ripping sound and looked around just in time to see one of the cables part. The flying end whirled like a striking snake and snapped past our faces at machine-gun-bullet speed, cutting off saplings as if the ground had been shaved with a razor.

We looked at each other. I'm sure I was just as pale as George. That evening he said, "Ike, were you as scared as I was?"

"I was afraid to bring the subject up," I said. We were certainly not more than five or six inches from sudden death.

Immediately instructions were issued that when extra strain was put on cables, all personnel should be kept out of the way.

We were anxious to discover the best obtainable machine gun, and one day we took a .30 caliber Browning water-cooled gun into the field to test its endurance. We set up the targets in front of a backstop and shot away to our hearts' content.

Sustained firing does not improve a rifled weapon's accuracy. As a machine gun heats up and the barrel expands, the rifling begins to be ineffective and the bullets fly in a pattern called keyholing—that is, instead of rotating around their long axis, they fly helter-skelter through the air. While George operated the gun, I used a pair of strong field glasses to see how the bullets were behaving in the air. After an extra-long burst, they began acting strangely, and I said we should have a look at the target. We started forward from where we were standing, one on either side of the gun. As we converged to continue our conversation, the machine gun suddenly fired.

We jumped back in consternation. At the same time there was another burst of fire. "George," I shouted, "that gun's so hot it's just going to keep on shooting!" We raced off to one side, then back, and George twisted the belt so that no more rounds could feed into the piece. We looked at each other sheepishly. We had acted like a couple of recruits.

For some time, the War Department did not know exactly what George and I were up to, but we and our small group knew—we were pioneering with a weapon that could change completely the strategy and tactics of land warfare. In one respect, these circumstances were better than battle itself. We could experiment and test alternatives. Every mistake we made, every correction, every scrap of information about the exploitation of terrain was added to World War I's lessons, until we had the beginnings of a comprehensive tank doctrine that eventually would make George Patton a legend. Both of us began articles for the military journals; he for the Cavalry, I for the Infantry. Then I was called before the Chief of Infantry.

I was told that my ideas were not only wrong but dangerous, and that henceforth I would keep them to myself. Particularly, I was not to publish anything incompatible with solid infantry doctrine. If I did, I would be hauled before a court-martial.

George was given a similar message. The effect was to bring us even closer. With George's temper and my own capacity for something more than mild irritation, there was surely more steam around the officers' quarters than at the post laundry.

When the National Defense Act of 1920 was passed, the Tank Corps as such was abolished and was made part of Infantry. An impatient as well as a self-confident man, George applied for transfer back to Cavalry. This arm would, he hoped, display more receptiveness to ideas. I, a little less abrupt, began to hope for another assignment. In a new atmosphere, I might influence my superiors to take a look at the possibilities of the tank.

BEFORE GEORGE AND I were separated, my little family had been reunited. Permission was granted for post commanders to assign wartime barracks as quarters for officers and their families. All expenses of remodeling, renovating and furnishing were to be borne by the officer himself. I was allotted one set of barracks and George a neighboring one. In the early summer of 1920, Mamie and I began transforming the old building into a home. Much of the work was done with the help of soldiers who volunteered and whom I paid a nominal hourly sum. We tore down some partitions and put up others; we scrubbed and waxed floors and brushed buckets of paint onto fiberboard until we had a habitable three-bedroom house.

On an Army post the inhabitants know that their tenancy won't last long. They are unlikely ever to enjoy the trees or shrubs they plant. But they are tireless sowers of vegetables and annual flowers. In the barren surroundings of Camp Meade, we had a challenge to test any gardener's enthusiasm. There was scarcely a blade of grass in the entire encampment. But, with a few men who knew something about landscaping, we got busy. They plowed up our front yard and sowed it with a sturdy grass. They even built a low picket fence around it, which they painted white. At the end, we were proud of the place, which had cost us about seven or eight hundred dollars, not counting the labor Mamie and I had invested.

Perhaps it was the struggle to make it livable that made the place so attractive to us. Finally we felt able to send for Icky, who had been living with Mamie's aunt in Boone, Iowa. When he arrived, we settled down.

SOME of us managed to find time twice a week for a poker game. We normally insisted on playing only with bachelors or others who could afford to lose, but there were a number of men going through the camp who practically forced themselves into the games. One who appeared every night was a uniquely unskilled player. His style made me think of that old maxim of the Persian poet, Hafiz:

If he being young and unskillful
Plays for shekels of silver and gold,
Take his money, my son, praising Allah;
The fool was made to be sold.

This was my poker-playing philosophy until I was shocked into a different attitude. The young man came to me one morning and asked whether I would take government bonds to pay for his losses. "Okay," I said, "I'd be happy to."

Then it turned out that these were Baby Bonds, patiently saved by his wife during the years he had been away at war. I felt like a dog. I told the story to my other friends in the game and we agreed to find some way to return his money. Not wanting to hurt his pride by making him a charity case, we decided to let him win. This was not achieved easily. One of the hardest things known to man is to make a fellow win in poker when he plays as if bent on losing every nickel. It took until nearly midnight to get him back the amount he had lost.

The rest of us then divided our losses and I said I would go to Colonel Patton, the man's commanding officer, and suggest that he give an order that no one in his brigade be allowed to play cards for money. This would be easy because George was no enthusiast about card playing.

The next day the man dropped in and said, "You know what's happened? Old Patton has just stopped all card playing. Isn't that just my luck—just as I was started on a real winning streak?"

I decided that I had to quit playing poker. Most of us lived on our salaries, and most losers were bound to be spending not only their own money but their families'. From then on I did not play with anybody in the Army.

Social life among the married couples was rather thin in the postwar months at Meade, though occasionally a visitor would come up from Washington. One of the incalculable benefits I got from my friendship with George Patton was an invitation to meet a man who was to have a tremendous influence on my life.

Brigadier General Fox Conner had been the operations officer

173

at General Headquarters for General Pershing in France. When the Conners accepted an invitation from the Pattons to Sunday dinner, Mamie and I were among the guests. Apparently, George had told him some of our ideas about tanks, so the General directed most of his questions at me. By the time he had finished, it was time to go home. He said it was interesting, and thanked us, and that was that.

A few months later, General Conner sent word to me that he was going to Panama to command an infantry brigade. Would I like to go along with him as executive officer? When I told my commanding general about the opportunity, he countered that he could not spare me. I argued the point until the General said he would send my application on to the War Department even though he knew it would be disapproved. He was right. It was turned down.

IF MEADE was at times frustrating, it was also a school where I gained additional experience in handling men. At the beginning of my time there, the General gave me the job of coaching football. I was largely an ad hoc coach, cutting the suit to fit the cloth, and hardly a first-rate one. In only one tactic was I a confirmed practitioner: whenever I could find a good passer, I always tried to open up the game. But our teams did well through 1919, 1920 and 1921.

Barracks or not, Mamie, Icky and I had settled down to a fuller family life than we'd ever known. Icky, naturally, was in his element. For a little boy just getting interested in the outside world, few places could have been more exciting than Meade. The noisy tanks enthralled him. A football scrimmage was pure delight. And a parade with martial music set him aglow. I was inclined to display him and his talents at the slightest excuse, or without one, for that matter. In his company, I'm sure I strutted a bit, and Mamie was thoroughly happy that, once again, her two men were with her.

By now, I was entirely out of debt and I decided we could afford a maid to help Mamie. We hired a girl who seemed both pleasant and efficient. This began a chain of circumstances leading to a tragedy from which we never recovered.

We learned later that, just before we met her, the girl had suffered an attack of scarlet fever. Although her cure was quick and she showed no evidence of illness, the doctors finally concluded that she had brought the disease to the camp—and that our young son had contracted it from her.

We did everything possible to save him. The camp doctor brought in specialists from the nearby Johns Hopkins Medical School. During Icky's illness, the doctor did not allow me into his hospital room. But there was a porch on which I was allowed to sit and I could look into the room and wave to him. Occasionally, they would let me come to the door to speak to him. I haunted the halls of the hospital. Hour after hour, Mamie and I could only hope and pray. Within a week we lost our firstborn son.

I have never known such a blow. I didn't know what to do. I blamed myself because I had often taken his presence for granted, even though I was proud of him and of all the evidence that he was developing as a fine, normal boy.

Icky was completely devoted to soldiers. Not long after his arrival the men in my command had gotten together and bought him a tank uniform, including overcoat, overseas cap and all the rest. Every time they were out on a tank drill, one of them would ask Mamie's permission to take him along. With his death at the age of three a pall fell over the camp. When we started the long trip to Denver, to bury him with others of Mamie's family, the entire command turned out in respect to little Icky. For Mamie, the loss was heartbreaking, and her grief in turn would have broken the hardest heart.

This was the greatest disaster in my life. Even now as I write of it, the keenness of our loss comes back as fresh and terrible as it was in that long dark day soon after Christmas, 1920. In the months that followed, no matter what activities and preoccupations there were, we could never forget the death of our boy. My wife and I have arranged that when it comes our time to be laid away in our final resting place, we shall have him with us.

IV PANAMA AND BEYOND

A military graduate school

SOME TIME after my application for transfer to the Canal Zone had been disapproved, orders came out of the blue for me to proceed to that station. What had happened? Fox Conner had informed General Pershing, now the Chief of Staff, that he wanted me as his staff officer, and the red tape was torn to pieces. I was to arrive at Camp Gaillard by January of 1922.

Panama was not the best introduction to life outside the United States. The houses at the station were old, flimsy survivals of Canal construction days. They were infested with vermin and bats, and Mamie hated bats with a passion. Frequent thundershowers penetrated roofs and walls and made the house so damp it was like a Turkish bath after every storm.

Nevertheless, this tour of duty was one of the most constructive of my life, the reason being General Conner. Fox Conner was a tall easygoing Mississippian; he never put on airs of any kind, and he was as open and honest as any man I have known. One change in my attitude he accomplished quickly—with profound and endless results.

He discovered, with a casual question, that I had little or no interest left in military history. My aversion was a result of its treatment at West Point as an out-and-out memory course. In the case of the Battle of Gettysburg, for instance, each student was instructed to memorize the name of every brigadier in the opposing armies and to know exactly where his unit was stationed at every hour during the three-day battle. Little attempt was made to explain the meaning of the battle, or why it came about.

That same evening I found myself invited to General Conner's quarters. I saw that he had an extraordinary library, especially in military affairs.

"You might be interested in these," he said quietly, picking out two or three historical novels. I remember that one was *The Long Roll* by Mary Johnston, another *The Adventures of Brigadier Gerard* in the Napoleonic Wars. A third was *The Crisis* by the American Winston Churchill.

They were stirring stories and I liked them. "Wouldn't you like to know something of what the armies were actually doing during the period of those novels?" the General asked me when I returned them.

So I took home a few books on military history, and found myself becoming fascinated. But fascination wasn't enough for the General. After I read the first of these books, he questioned me closely about the decisions made. "What do you think would have been the outcome if this decision had been just the opposite? What were the alternatives?" And so I read Grant's and Sheridan's memoirs, and a good deal of John Codman Ropes on the Civil War. I read Clausewitz's *On War* three times. The General had me read Fremantle's account of the Battle of Gettysburg, as well as that of Haskell. As I began to absorb all this material, I became even more interested in our Civil War and we spent many hours analyzing its campaigns.

The best chance for such conversations was when we were out

on reconnaissance, which was a good deal of the time. In the tropics, the terrain changes rapidly. A trail made one year through the jungle can become completely overgrown by the time the dry season makes it passable again, or a landslide may efface all traces of it. So we were constantly out on our horses, laying out and charting routes over which troops and their pack trains could be rapidly moved in case of attack. We would make camp before dark, and then spend the long tropical evenings in talk around a campfire.

General Conner's interests were not limited to military affairs. He was something of a philosopher. It was he who first said to me, "Always take your job seriously, never yourself." He taught me that splendid line from the French, "All generalities are false, including this one." He would quote Shakespeare at length; he would discuss authors until then strange to me, like Plato, or the Roman historian Tacitus; and he would broaden bull sessions into general conversation about the long history of man, his ideas and his works.

It is clear now that life with General Conner was a sort of graduate school in military affairs and the humanities. It took years before I fully realized the value of what he had led me through. And then General Conner was gone. But in a lifetime of association with great and good men, he is one to whom I owe an incalculable debt.

As my education progressed, I found myself, in turn, educating a horse. Horses and mules were the standard transportation at Camp Gaillard. Shortly after I arrived, I went to the corral to select a mount from twenty or more horses. They had already been well picked over by officers who had arrived before me, and none of them was trained. One of the soldiers on duty, a man named Lopez, struck me as being intelligent and at home with animals, so I asked him to go with me as I walked among the horses. His quick replies to my questions so impressed me that I asked whether he would like to be my orderly. The broad smile that accompanied his "Sí, Señor Captain" made us friends at once.

I picked a big, coal-black gelding a bit over sixteen hands. He was splendid in the conformation of hindquarters, barrel and legs. But forward of the withers he was pure mule, with a short, thick neck and a large head. I decided that he was the best of the lot for use in the jungles.

Lopez beamed. He said that my selection was very fine and he asked whether he could select his own mount from among those allotted to enlisted men. I said yes, and from that moment Lopez and I and the two horses became a closely knit unit.

Although at first Blackie knew only two gaits, the walk and the extended gallop, he soon learned the slow and full trot, and the canter. I was so pleased that I began to teach him some tricks. He learned to kneel when I was ready to dismount. I taught him to follow me when I was on foot and to obey the word "Halt!" He would remain immovable until I called either "March!" or "Come!"

Blackie's complete obedience to command saved his life. One day the General, his aide, our two orderlies and I reached a deep ravine, filled with mud and muck, and obviously impassable. With Lopez and another man, I worked upstream until we reached a spot that looked suitable for crossing. I started slowly into the ravine and found to my horror that there was nothing underfoot but deep, muddy slush. As I felt Blackie go down, I threw my feet out of the stirrups and leaped backward to the bank. The horse, badly frightened, began thrashing around and sinking deeper and deeper.

I shouted, "Blackie, halt!" At first it didn't get through, but at the third repetition he suddenly stopped dead. Had he been a Thoroughbred he would have fought the mud until he smothered. Now he lay quietly while we tried to figure ways to get him to firm ground.

Each orderly had a stout piece of rope on his pommel. We got one of these around Blackie's neck and the other around the top of his saddle. Then Lopez and I, with two other horses, found a place where the ravine petered out. Crossing there, we rushed back to Blackie, had the ropes' ends thrown over to us and began to pull. He was still sinking, so I said, "Come, Blackie," repeating the command until he began to move again. In the fashion of a horse trying to swim, he leaned forward into the muck as our two horses pulled, and in half an hour we had him safely out. A proud animal, he looked sheepish when he turned his head and saw that he and all his accouterments were completely covered with black mud.

Blackie was not only proud, he was sensitive to applause. I taught him to go up a set of steps on a hillside, fifteen feet in height, and after turning around on a stone at the top, to make his way down. This was difficult; a horse doesn't like steep descents because he can't see his feet and is unsure of his footing. However, once he had mastered the trick, Blackie became the talk of the post, and I frequently had to take him to the steps to show him off for the General's visitors. Whenever he learned a stunt, he did it thereafter almost at his own volition, and, having completed it, would snap his ears forward and walk more like a conquering hero than just an ordinary GI horse.

In my experience with Blackie—and earlier with allegedly incompetent recruits at Camp Colt—is rooted my enduring conviction that far too often we write off a backward child as hopeless, a clumsy animal as worthless, a worn-out field as beyond restoration. This we do largely out of our own lack of willingness to prove that an animal can respond to training, that a field can regain its fertility, that a difficult boy can become a fine man.

The tutoring by Fox Conner and the rewards of working with Blackie were important to me, but the heart of my life was my family. Consequently, the most important event of my Panama assignment was the news that we were to have another child.

The baby was due in August. In the early summer, Mamie took a steamer to New Orleans and then went on to Denver. I followed later and was there in time for the birth, on August 3, 1923, of another boy.

Mamie stayed in Denver until John was a few months old and then returned to Panama. The most absorbing interest in our lives was his growth into a walking, talking, running-the-whole-household young fellow. While his arrival did not, of course, eliminate the grief we had felt since the death of our first son, he was precious in his own right. Living with a healthy, bouncing baby boy can take parents' minds off almost anything.

ONE OF General Conner's profound beliefs was that the world could not long avoid another major war. He thought it might have been possible to avert one, had the United States been part of the League of Nations. But with conditions as they were, he was certain that the Treaty of Versailles carried within it the seeds of another, larger conflagration. He urged me to be ready for it.

One of his suggestions was that I should try for an assignment under Colonel Marshall. He often said, "In the new war we will have to fight beside allies, and George Marshall knows more about the techniques of arranging allied commands than any man I know. He is nothing short of a genius." There was never an opportunity to serve under Marshall prior to World War II. Indeed, before then I met him only twice, each time only for a moment. But it was enough for me to notice that he had many of the characteristics of Fox Conner.

The friendship of that outstanding man, and the joy of life with Mamie and John, would have made a station far worse than Panama a happy place for me. Nevertheless, the news, via the military grapevine, that I would be transferred from Panama, was welcome. I could dream about the orders until they arrived. Then I came back to earth with a thump. I was ordered back to Meade— to help coach a football team.

The Generals: Pershing and MacArthur

THE WAR DEPARTMENT moves in mysterious ways its blunders to perform—this sentiment expressed my mood in the fall of 1924. Why I was moved thousands of miles to join three other officers in a football-coaching assignment is still a cosmic top-secret wonder to me. But at least it was temporary. My permanent orders were cut before the end of the season. I was ordered to Benning to command a battalion of tanks—the same old tanks I had commanded several years earlier—as soon as I had had a sixty-day leave with my family.

However, I thought it was high time I was getting to one of the established Army schools. I went to the Chief of Infantry and asked whether the orders could be changed, whether I could instead be sent to Infantry School at Benning. I should have known better: he refused even to listen to my arguments.

While I was on leave in Denver, a telegram arrived from Fox Conner, now serving as Deputy Chief of Staff to General Hines. It was cryptic in the extreme:

NO MATTER WHAT ORDERS YOU RECEIVE FROM THE WAR DE-
PARTMENT MAKE NO PROTEST ACCEPT THEM WITHOUT QUESTION

For several days I was in a quandary until new orders came. They would indeed have been difficult to accept had it not been for my faith in Fox Conner. I was detailed to recruiting duty in the state of Colorado.

To be assigned to the recruiting service in those days was felt to be a devastating rebuke. After my gloomy interview with the Chief of Infantry, I had reached the somber conclusion that he and I did not see eye to eye on my place in the military sphere. The new assignment confirmed me in this opinion.

The mystery was cleared up in a letter from General Conner, who had known of my disappointment at not getting into Infantry School. Since Benning was under the jurisdiction of the Chief of Infantry, he explained, and it was impossible for an Infantry officer to go to the school there except with the Chief's approval, he, General Conner, had arranged for my temporary transfer from the Infantry to the Adjutant General's office (which was in charge of recruiting). I would never have thought of so drastic a way of circumventing the Chief of Infantry!

Under Conner's novel arrangement, a final order came which said that I had been selected by the Adjutant General as one of his quota of officers to go to the Command and General Staff School at Fort Leavenworth. I was to arrive there in August 1925.

I was ready to fly—and needed no airplane!

To THE CYNIC, all this may seem proof of "It's not *what* you know, it's *who* you know." Certainly, had I been denied the good fortune of knowing Fox Conner, the course of my career might have been radically different. Because I *did* know him, I did go to Leavenworth and profited professionally. But on this business of who you know, a one-minute lecture to any young person who may read these words:

Always try to associate yourself closely with those who know more than you, who do better than you, who see more clearly than you. Don't be afraid to reach upward. The friendship might pay off at some unforeseen time, but that is only an accidental by-product. The important thing is that such associations will make you a better person.

I must admit that once my first exultation was over, I began to take a second look. To go to Command and General Staff School without the usual preparatory infantry instruction, at Fort Benning or elsewhere, was like being sent to college without a secondary-school education. It could put me in an awkward position with classmates at Leavenworth, a highly competitive school.

I wrote Fox Conner asking him what I could do to get myself prepared. In his reply, he said:

> You may not know it, but because of your three years' work in Panama, you are far better trained for Leavenworth than anybody I know. You will recall that . . . I required that you write a field order for the operation of the post, every day. . . . You became so well acquainted with the technics . . . of preparing plans and orders for operations . . . that they will be second nature to you. You will feel no sense of inferiority. . . .

This was encouraging but I thought it would be a good idea for me to learn what I could. I got copies of the Leavenworth problems and spent considerable time during the winter months solving them and checking my answers against the approved solutions. It was by no means a chore. Practical problems have always been my equivalent of crossword puzzles.

Spring passed quickly and Mamie and I began to pack. Once at Leavenworth, I found the school exhilarating. We were instructed under the "case" method. A pamphlet outlined a suppositious force, located in a particular spot, and gave indications of the enemy's strength and of the mission of the Blue Force, which the student always commanded. The student had first to make a decision on the action to be taken, after which he was given the correct decision and asked to give the proper plans and disposition to support it. Fox Conner had been right. He and I had done this kind of "war gaming" in Panama.

As time went on, it was easy to identify those who were studying too long at night and coming to classes without fresh minds and an optimistic outlook. I established a routine that limited my night study to two hours and a half—from seven to nine thirty—and Mamie saw that I got to bed by that time. This went on five nights a week. On Friday and Saturday nights we unwound at parties at the Officers Club or in friends' quarters.

In the class was a friend from 19th Infantry days, Leonard T. Gerow. We decided to study together. Plotting tactical situations on a map, one of us read out the instructions from the memorandum furnished, while the other marked the map. This saved precious hours, and our teamwork method was proved useful by the fact that we both graduated with high marks.

In the mid-1920s, the Leavenworth course was for one year only. In May 1926, orders arrived from the Chief of Infantry (I had been retransferred) to proceed to Fort Benning to take command of a battalion. About mid-August, Mamie and I set out in a new automobile for Georgia. The quarters assigned to us at Benning were the nicest we had yet enjoyed, and as soon as the August temperatures went down, we were glad to be there. But if Georgia's temperatures declined, mine didn't. A week after I reached Benning, I was told that I would have to coach the soldier football team.

Though working with soldiers was always fun, I was getting exceedingly weary of the football-coaching interludes that were continually being inserted into my career. I asked the executive officer of the post if I could decline the responsibilities of head coach, and take charge instead of the backfield and the offensive tactics.

This was agreed, and I began working under a Texan, Captain Barry. The material at hand was raw and our season was not one to divert attention from Notre Dame, Wisconsin or West Point. Fortunately, I didn't have to face another. In mid-December the War Department ordered me to Washington, D.C., for duty in the office of General Pershing.

GENERAL PERSHING, the famed "Black Jack" and leader of our AEF (American Expeditionary Forces) in World War I, was then head of the Battle Monuments Commission. This new agency was charged with building and beautifying the cemeteries where our war dead were gathered abroad, and with preparing a battlefield guide to American actions of the war. The guidebook writing was assigned to me.

I had been in the job hardly long enough to do any damage when I was selected as a student for the War College in Washington. To graduate from the War College had long been the ambition of almost every officer, and I was anxious to go. When I graduated the following June, a choice was offered me: Did I want to be assigned to the War Department General Staff, or go back to Battle Monuments? When I learned that to complete the guidebook I would have to go to France, my choice was easy.

This was my first chance to get to know a European country. In June 1928, I saw Paris for the first time. The job involved travel, all the way from the Vosges in southeast France to the English Channel, following the lines of trench warfare. In this way, I came to see the small towns of France and to meet the sound and friendly people working in the fields and along the roads.

I often stopped to join groups of roadworkers who were eating their lunch. When my chauffeur (who was my interpreter) and I asked if we could join them, they would offer something from their lunch boxes. In the trunk of the car we began to carry certain specialties I thought they might like—oranges or bananas or a can of artichokes. Once I had half a dozen cans of sardines and opened one as an hors d'oeuvre. They went down so swiftly and with such exclamations of delight that I opened up another. Six cans were finished off in about as many minutes.

Mamie and I had found an apartment in Paris, in the Auteuil area, overlooking the Seine and Pont Mirabeau. We became a sort of junior-size American Express for visiting Army friends and were drawn into their sight-seeing until we were looked on as authorities on what to see and what to avoid. Mamie was a specialist in shops, from the flea market to the *grands magasins,* and I tried to find spots that were different from anything the Americans were used to.

One such place was the Musée Grévin. A waxworks not quite as large as Madame Tussaud's in London, but far more gruesome, this museum of French historic characters was absorbing. I suppose I was still an unsophisticated Kansan at heart; at any rate, this place stayed in my memory as a unique Paris attraction. Twenty-five years later, after I had assumed Supreme Command of the NATO forces, I lunched with two members of the staff and lectured on the wonders of the Musée Grévin. They agreed to go. Afterward one asked the other disgustedly, "Do you *really* suppose this was the most exciting spot he could find when he was still in his thirties?"

In two tours with the American Battle Monuments Commission, I served under General Pershing for about a year and a half. I never got to know him well. He was rather reserved, even remote in manner, and he kept odd hours, often not coming to the office until one o'clock or later but staying until midnight. This must have played havoc with the social schedules of his direct subordinates. And he had one really deplorable habit: he was always late—up to an hour or more—for every engagement. When no one else was available, I acted as temporary aide and it was embarrassing to try to explain to the host why we were so late. The

General himself seemed to be oblivious to time and made no excuses.

In his later years, I would visit him in his rooms at Walter Reed Hospital. He grew weaker and weaker, but whenever he spoke from his hospital bed it was always as a senior commander. I had the impression that he was standing stiffly erect, Sam Browne belt and all. To all the veterans of World War I, General Pershing is the single hero and they remember him with respect and admiration, even if not affection. But as time goes on his place in history will probably not be as prominent as it might have been had he been more outgoing in personality. Early in life he had been the victim of a dreadful tragedy. His wife and two or three young children had been burned to death, in an Army post in Wyoming, I believe. Only one son, Warren, was left. He is a successful and respected man who, I understand, heads up a Wall Street firm.

When General Pershing died, in 1948, I went to Washington to be present at his funeral. This called for a long march from the Capitol to the cemetery at Arlington, and in the middle of the march rain began to pour down. The moment it started, cars were rushed to the head of the column to pick up the senior officers. I declined to get into the car. I was certainly not going to give an example of brass running from a rainstorm when all the marching men in the column had to take things as they came. Not in the last walk for General Pershing of the AEF.

WHEN we returned from France in 1929, it was my hope to go back to troop duty. But there was a new role ahead. In those days there were two assistants to the Secretary of War: one was Assistant Secretary of Air; the other, and senior, was the deputy of the Secretary of War himself. One of the senior man's principal duties was to study ways of mobilizing American industry in the event of another war. To this task I was now beckoned.

Two of us, ordinarily Colonel Wilkes of the Engineers and I, visited firms which had been making fuses, ammunition or truck bodies during World War I, to see whether they could suggest improvements for retooling rapidly in case of another war. It was difficult to arouse any interest at all. There was not going to be another war, they felt.

One of the principal questions we had to study was the organization of the government, and the War Department itself, for control of production. To find out about the experience of the War Industries Board of World War I, I went to its chief, Mr. Bernard Baruch, who was not only cooperative but anxious that all the complexities of conversion be understood. He believed that, immediately upon the outbreak of war, prices, wages, and costs of materials and services should be frozen, as a means of avoiding inflation. At the same time he advocated measures for eliminating black-marketing. I made his views part of the plans that I was charged with drawing up.

It was a long, irksome job. Many people in the War Department were flatly opposed to Mr. Baruch's ideas. High officials believed that a war should be conducted through the normal, peacetime agencies of government. They did not favor price controls. Cooperation between the Army and Navy departments would take care of the problem, they would say.

All our experience has shown that this was convenient reasoning, and foolishness. But our antagonists persisted, and whatever we accomplished toward industrial mobilization was done on our own and in a rather isolated atmosphere. Indeed, the Chief of Staff of the Army, General Charles P. Summerall, forbade any General Staff officer even to go into the office of the Assistant Secretary of War.

Finally, late in 1930, General Summerall was succeeded by General Douglas MacArthur. The new Chief of Staff was receptive to the ideas we had been advocating, discussed the whole concept with us and assured us of his friendly cooperation. So our work received new impetus and our morale a boost.

I now began a relationship that was not to end until December 1939. General MacArthur, it developed, needed a personal military assistant who could draft statements, reports and letters for his signature. He asked me to take the job. I moved over to his office in January 1933.

Douglas MacArthur, then fifty-three, was a forceful—some thought an overpowering—individual, blessed with a fast and facile mind, interested in both the military and political side of our government. Working with him added a dimension to my experience. On any subject he chose to discuss, his knowledge, always amazingly comprehensive, poured out in a torrent of words. "Discuss" is hardly the correct word; the General's conversations were usually monologues.

A colonel who had a fifteen-minute interview with him sat and listened, inserting an occasional yes or no, and when he left the office realized that he had forgotten to bring up the subject of his visit. Later, he encountered another officer whose appointment with MacArthur had immediately followed his, and who said, "You certainly made an impression on General MacArthur."

Bewildered, the Colonel asked, "What in the world do you mean?"

The other officer replied, "Why, the General told me that he had just had a tremendously interesting chat with you. He said that he always looks forward to your visits because you are a fascinating conversationalist from whom he learns a great deal!"

Unquestionably, the General's fluency and wealth of information came from his phenomenal memory, without parallel in my experience. Reading through a draft of a speech or a paper once, he could immediately repeat whole chunks of it verbatim. He had one habit that never ceased to startle me: he talked of himself in the third person— "So MacArthur went over to the Senator, and said, 'Senator . . .' " Although I had heard of this idiosyncrasy, the sensation was unusual.

In several respects, he was a rewarding man to work for. When he gave an assignment, he never asked any questions; he never cared what kind of hours were kept; his only requirement was that the work be done. The difficulty was that I soon found myself so busy that I was in the office until 7:30 or 7:45 every night. My hours, keeping pace with his, became picturesque. But if I needed a week's leave, all I had to do was tell him I was going away and he would make no objection.

In July 1932, an event had occurred which brought the General a measure of lasting unfavorable publicity. This was the veterans' "Bonus March." Almost a decade earlier, the Congress—buffeted on one side by veterans who wanted immediate bonuses and on the other by an administration opposed to them—attempted to please both by authorizing a liberal grant for World War I service, but postponing payment until 1945. This action pleased no one, least of all the veterans. Their claims had been recognized—but they could not collect on them for more than twenty years.

We were then in the depths of a depression. As times got hard, many veterans came to think that the deferred bonus was identical to a deposit in the bank. This oversimplification, without any legal base, became an intensely emotional idea at a time when millions of families were hard pressed to feed themselves or to meet the rent. Despite the fact that almost all citizens were affected by the national calamity, some veterans seemed to feel that they were entitled to special privileges. They marched to Washington to get the promised money.

All in all, I think there were eighteen or twenty thousand men. Some were encamped outside the town, across the Anacostia River; others had taken over abandoned buildings not far from the Capitol; others built shacks out of tin cans and old lumber and the like—anything to shelter them from the bad weather. Over outdoor fires, they cooked their scanty meals.

Thirty years before demonstrations became an accepted mode of protest, the bonus veterans were pioneering direct action against Federal legislative authority. Both sides in the dispute were neophytes in conducting or facing such protests. Restraint and a degree of good humor marked the veterans' attitude. Restraint and a decent sympathy marked the government's.

For many days nothing happened, but the time arrived when the government, because of building construction going on there, had to move the marchers from the vicinity of the Capitol. The veterans refused to move, and the police could not handle such numbers. Then the President called out regular troops.

When the order was announced, General MacArthur decided that he should go into active command in the field. I told him that the matter could easily become a riot and I thought it highly inappropriate for the Chief of Staff of the Army to be involved in it. The General disagreed, saying that it was a question of Federal authority in the District of Columbia. He ordered me to get into uniform. (In that administration, officers in Washington went to work in civilian clothes, because a military appearance around the nation's capital was held to be undesirable.)

I reported back at the hour fixed by the Chief and then, with his aide and a couple of others, we went out. One of the others was George Patton, then a major commanding a squadron of cavalry at Fort Myer.

The veterans made no more vigorous protest than a little cat-calling and jeering at the soldiers, who were only performing their duty as they edged the men away from the disputed area, guiding and nudging them slowly toward the Anacostia River and the bridge over it.

Instructions were then received from the Secretary of War, forbidding any troops to cross the bridge, on the other side of which was the largest encampment of veterans. General MacArthur did not hear the instructions. He said he was too busy and did not want to be bothered by people coming down pretending to bring orders. In any event, we marched the column right on across the bridge, halting the troops on the other side. Shortly afterward, the whole encampment of shacks and huts began burning. I know that no troops started the fire; they were too far away. Some of the veterans themselves must have started the blazes to show their displeasure.

The whole scene was pitiful. The veterans, whether or not their march was a mistake, were ragged, ill-fed, and felt themselves abused. The sight of the whole encampment in flames just added to the pity one had to feel for them. The troops were dismissed except for a small group that was left to prevent any veterans from returning to the city itself. But the whole action from beginning to end did nothing to alleviate the lot of the veterans or to enhance the reputation of the government and the Army. When General MacArthur started back to the War Department, I remarked that there would probably be reporters trying to see him, and suggested it would be the better part of wisdom to avoid them. The troop movement had not been a military idea really, but a political order, and I thought that only the political officials should talk to the press. He disagreed and saw the newspapermen that night.

I think this meeting led to the prevailing impression that General MacArthur himself had undertaken the move against the veterans. Popular impressions are hard to eradicate. I have read at least one account that called this one of the darkest blots on the MacArthur reputation. This, I feel, is unfortunate.

Ordinarily, General MacArthur would have been relieved as Chief of Staff in the fall of 1934, but because of reorganization in the War Department his tour was extended by one year. Toward the end of this year, a bill was passed in the Congress bestowing commonwealth status on the Philippine Islands for ten years. During this period the Philippine government, then headed by Manuel Quezon, would acquire increasing autonomy, as it prepared for independence in 1946.

The American decision was at that time unique. So far as I can recall, never before had a great power deliberately proposed independence at a fixed date for an occupied country except under the pressure of armed revolt.

This congressional action affected my own professional life. The wheel of fortune had made a full turn. In 1915 I was sure that the Philippines would be my first assignment. Now, Manila was to be my next destination. In the happenstance of Army life I had become associated with General MacArthur and the General was a natural candidate for a special role in the Islands.

OF ALL American names, after William Howard Taft's, MacArthur's carried weight to the point of veneration in the Philippines. His father, General Arthur MacArthur, our last military governor there, was a symbol of American might in battle and

American understanding around the conference table. The son, a general officer in our forces in the Islands before he became Chief of Staff, had won the confidence and admiration of Manuel Quezon, who now proposed that he become military adviser to the emerging nation, directing the design and buildup of its security forces. MacArthur accepted enthusiastically.

The General was very insistent that I go along with him. We had worked together for a long time, he said, and he didn't want to bring in somebody new. MacArthur even then was thought to be a mysterious, romantic figure far above the frailty of dependence on others, but this insistence, I now realize, showed that he was very like the rest of us. In the decades that followed, I came to understand this fully. Whatever our position, whatever the power we exercise under the weight of responsibility, we need familiar faces about us as much as we need expert opinion or wise counsel.

I did not succeed in getting from General MacArthur a fixed period for the assignment. One privilege he did permit, possibly realizing that a familiar face meant as much to me as to him I could pick one associate from the Regular Army to go along with us. I requested Major James Ord, whom I wanted not only for his quickness of mind and ability as a staff officer but because he was as much at home in Spanish—the principal language of the Philippines after Tagalog—as he was in English. Jimmy Ord was eager to go.

With MacArthur in the Philippines

AT THE very outset of our mission, MacArthur suffered two shocks. The first struck while we were still en route to the West Coast. One moment Douglas MacArthur was Chief of Staff of the United States Army, whose arrival in Manila would be dramatic testimony that our country considered Philippine independence and defense of prime importance. The next moment, after he tore open a telegram from Washington, he learned that he was now only a former Chief of Staff, and was reduced from four-star to two-star rank.

Firmly fixed in the General's mind had been the conviction that President Roosevelt had agreed to retain him in the top position until a month after his arrival in Manila. The prestige of those four stars in the eyes of the Filipinos would have been a certain help, he thought. He would be retiring as Chief of Staff to aid the new cause. Suddenly, out of the clear, to learn that a new COS had been appointed caused an explosive denunciation of F.D.R., politics, bad manners, bad judgment, broken promises, arrogance, unconstitutionality, insensitivity. Then he sent an eloquent telegram of congratulations to his successor.

In the long run, no harm may have been done to our mission, except for personal resentments. The second blow had a far more deeply personal effect on the General. It deprived him of a lifelong source of inspiration and strength, his mother.

The widow of General Arthur MacArthur was among the most remarkable of Army wives and mothers. All her life she had been with the Army and she was certain that her son was destined for greatness; she lived for him and his success. The General relied on her when the going was tough, and he shared with her the joys of achievement.

Shortly after we boarded the SS *President Harding*, she became ill. Not long after our arrival in Manila, she was dead. The loss affected the General's spirit for many months.

WE SETTLED temporarily in a Manila hotel. The Ords and their two children soon found a house, but because Mamie had decided to stay in Washington, so that John could finish the eighth grade, I continued to live in the hotel. They would join me when the term was over, and next year John would go to school in Baguio, in the mountains above Manila.

From the outset, the work was difficult. Trying to figure ways to provide a reasonable defense establishment once the Islands were on their own, we started to build little training stations in various sections of the Islands. We built more than ninety of these, with about two hundred conscripts in each. We soon saw that it would be necessary to have a small "air force"—if only to get to the training stations scattered over the archipelago.

Though we worked doggedly through 1936 and 1937, ours was a hopeless venture in a sense. The Philippine government simply could not afford to build real security from attack. We had to content ourselves with attempting to produce a military adequate to deal with domestic revolt and to slow up any aggressor until some friendly nation, presumably the United States, came to its aid. Among other things, we were encountering an example of the costs of independence that others have met more recently. Many Filipinos were concerned too much with the privileges of freedom and too little with its responsibilities. President Quezon understood this fully but he also insisted that national pride would demand some kind of military force.

Then came an incident that chilled the warm relationship Jimmy Ord and I had had with General MacArthur. The General thought that morale would be enhanced if the people of Manila could see something of their emerging army. He suggested bringing units from all over the Islands to a field near the city, and camping them there for three or four days. The city's population could visit them and it would all end with a big parade.

Jimmy and I told the General that this would take money that was desperately needed for more important purposes. But, following his order, we began to do the necessary staff work. Among other details, we had to arrange with island shipping firms to bring in the troops. It wasn't long until news of this reached President Quezon, who called me in and asked me what it was all about.

I was astonished. We had assumed that the project had first been agreed on between the President and General MacArthur. Now I said I thought we should not discuss it until I had seen the General. But Quezon was disturbed and said he would telephone him. When I returned to the office, the General was exceedingly unhappy with his entire staff. He said he had never meant us to proceed with preparations for the parade, only to make investigations. Now President Quezon was horrified that we were planning a costly national parade in the capital. Because General MacArthur denied he had given us an order—which was news to us—there was nothing to do except stop the proceedings. This misunderstanding caused considerable resentment, and never again were we on the same warm and cordial terms.

Not long after this, Jimmy Ord was killed in an airplane accident. From then on more of the planning and the responsibility fell on me, but without my friend all the zest was gone.

President Quezon asked for my advice more and more. This was partly because of the office hours General MacArthur liked to keep. He never reached his desk until eleven; after a late lunch hour, he went home again. This made it difficult to get in touch with him. My friendship with the President became close, and our conversations broader and deeper. Taxes, education, honesty in government, all sorts of subjects entered the discussions and seemed to enjoy them. Certainly I did.

From time to time I suffered attacks of a strange intestinal ailment. For a long while I was on a bland diet, but I gradually drifted back to old habits. As a result, I suffered at least two more attacks after the first serious one in 1936. When, twenty years later, I had an attack requiring surgery, the doctors had a name for it: ileitis.

In 1938 my family and I went back to the United States briefly. I wanted to ask the War Department for more help. I went to the Chief of Staff, General Malin Craig, and told him General MacArthur's view that a friendly Philippines, able to provide at least delaying action in the event of invasion, was vital to the United States. General Craig agreed and hitherto closed doors began to open.

It has to be remembered that the American Army itself was starved for appropriations at that time. There wasn't much it could do for the Philippines without undercutting U.S. preparedness. After begging or borrowing everything I could in the way of obsolete but still useful equipment from the signal, quartermaster, ordnance and medical groups, I went to Wichita and with the limited funds available bought several planes. I also visited the Winchester Repeating Arms Company in Connecticut. With what I had "liberated" and bought, I went back to Manila.

There was by now a general uneasiness about the possibility of war. It was almost universally conceded that a European war would rapidly become global, and apprehension grew sharply in the Philippines. General MacArthur did his best to allay fears, assuring the Filipinos, for example, that the Japanese were rational and that it would be to their disadvantage to attack. At the same time, he speeded up the military training program.

I became certain that the conflict General Conner had predicted fifteen years earlier was likely to break out. And so when Chamberlain declared a state of war between Great Britain and Germany, I went to General MacArthur at once. "General," I said, "in my opinion the United States cannot remain out of this war for long. I want to go home as soon as possible."

MacArthur said that I was making a mistake, and Quezon was emphatic that I should remain. But both finally accepted my decision and Quezon gave us a beautiful farewell luncheon in the Malacañan Palace before Mamie, young John and I departed by liner. We spent Christmas in Hawaii and New Year's Eve in San Francisco, in an extravagance of blaring horns and glitter that marked, though we didn't know it, the end of an era of peaceful family life together. Ahead for Mamie lay long and lonely months when both her son and her husband would be far off; and for me, years that would be thronged with challenges for which all my life I had been preparing.

The States again

MY ORDERS had been for Fort Lewis, Washington. I found myself instead on temporary planning duty under General John L. DeWitt in San Francisco. I was to work out schedules for shipping and housing and feeding National Guard and Regular troops for the entire West Coast, who were to be brought for emergency training to southern California. Meanwhile, Mamie and I had registered John, now seventeen, in the high school in Tacoma, believing we were to be on duty there. Fortunately, that was where my brother Ed lived, so we let John stay with him until we should be free to go to Fort Lewis.

The Fort Lewis assignment restored me to active duty with troops—the 15th Regiment of the 3rd Infantry Division—and confirmed my conviction that this was where I belonged. I made my desires for continued service with troops clear to every Army friend I met, particularly anyone from Washington who was involved in personnel decisions. A letter from Patton, saying that he expected to get one of the new armored divisions and would ask for me as a regimental commander, raised my hopes to outright elation.

On the last day of November, however, with Pearl Harbor twelve months and one week off, my active service with troops came to an end. Orders arrived detailing me to the General Staff Corps, assigned to duty as Chief of Staff, 3rd Division, Fort Lewis. I was back on the staff—but at least I wasn't in Washington, D.C. To that extent I felt lucky.

It was about this time that John told us he wanted to try for West Point. I thought it wise to point out the possible advantages of a civilian education. If he could develop as a lawyer, doctor or businessman, he could go as far as his character, abilities and ambitions could carry him. In the Army, no matter how able an officer might be, his promotion was governed strictly by the rule of seniority until he reached the grade of colonel. I added, however, that my own Army experience had been wonderfully interesting and had brought me into contact with men of ability, honor, and a sense of high dedication to their country. Happy in my work, I had long ago refused to bother my head about promotions and had remained untempted by generous business offers that had come my way.

A few days after this conversation, my brother Ed dropped in. Edgar's law business in Tacoma was thriving and, he told me, he had offered John a proposition: "If you'll go to college for four years, and then through three years of law, I'll pay your entire educational expenses. If you join my law firm, I'll pay you twice your military salary at any comparable stage in your career—until you're earning more. Then you're on your own."

Ed said to me rather ruefully, "You know, that young devil just looked me in the eye and said, 'Thanks, Uncle Ed. I appreciate your offer. But I've decided to try for West Point.' "

Later John told me his reasons. "When you talked about the satisfaction you had in an Army career, and your pride in being associated with men of character, my mind was made up. If I can say the same thing when I've finished my Army career, I'll care no more about promotions than you did."

However little I cared about promotions, several were coming up for me in rapid succession. When in March 1941 my duties at Fort Lewis were enlarged, as Chief of Staff to the IX Army Corps, I was promoted to temporary colonel. Only a few months later I was transferred to San Antonio—Mamie and I arrived there on our twenty-fifth anniversary—and by August I was Chief of Staff of the Third Army under General Walter Krueger.

General Krueger's command, which stretched from New Mexico to Florida, had a strength that could be mobilized of 240,000 officers and men. During August and September we concentrated these forces in Louisiana and undertook maneuvers against the Second Army, commanded by General Ben Lear. Old Louisiana hands warned us that ahead lay mud, mosquitoes and malaria. Their description was accurate—we had many problems—but the work was gripping.

The lack of practical experience was particularly evident. World War I staff men of all echelons above regimental commander had largely passed out of the service. The rest of us had to transform textbook doctrine into action. After each stage of the maneuvers, we tried to assemble the principal officers for a critique. In these chats we emphasized everything that went right: encouragement was essential to morale. At the same time, we had to uncover and highlight every mistake, every foul-up that in war could be death to a unit or an army.

My tent turned into something of a cracker-barrel corner where everyone in our army seemed to come for a serious discussion, a laugh, or a gripe. I never discouraged those who complained, for often they worked much better after they had unloaded their woes. I was also kept up-to-date with Army humor. This revolved largely around the simulations of reality in maneuvers. The granddaddy of them all, I think, was this one:

An umpire decided that a bridge had been destroyed by an enemy attack and flagged it accordingly. From then on, it was not to be used by men or vehicles. Shortly, a corporal brought his squad up to the bridge, looked at the flag, hesitated, then marched his men across. The umpire yelled at him, "Hey, don't you see that bridge is destroyed?"

The Corporal answered, "Of course I can see it's destroyed. Can't you see we're swimming?"

I passed that on in a letter to my friend and Leavenworth classmate, Leonard Gerow, now in the War Department. Then I said:

> Handling an Army staff that has had very little chance to whip itself together has its tough points—in spite of which I am having a good time. But I would like a command of my own.

When the maneuvers ended, I got, instead of a command, the star of a brigadier general.

While in Louisiana we heard how narrowly we had escaped a legislative failure: in Congress, the extension of Selective Service had been passed by a single vote. It was reported that one man, General George Marshall, was largely responsible for this victory, however slim. I still shudder to think how close we came to returning trained men home and closing down the reception centers for draftees, all within weeks of our entry into the most colossal war of all time.

After eating lunch on Sunday, December 7, my ambition was short-range. I wanted to capitalize on the afternoon lull and take a long nap. The nap did not last long. Orders that I was not to be awakened were ignored by my aide, who wisely decided that the attack on Pearl Harbor was adequate reason to interrupt my rest.

Five days later I was suddenly summoned to Washington by General Marshall for "emergency duty." The telephone message was only, "The Chief says for you to hop a plane and get up here right away." Mamie hurriedly packed a bag for me, and I took a train to Washington, where I reported to the Chief of Staff on December 14, 1941.

DURING the tumultuous months I spent in the War Department, in the Planning Section and later as Chief of Operations, I was with General Marshall every day. Realizing the burden he uncomplainingly carried, I soon conceived an unlimited admiration—and affection—for him. But George Marshall was rather a remote and austere person. He was one man who never, except on one unwary occasion, used my nickname, but addressed me always as "Eisenhower."

One day he gave me a bit of his philosophy on the subject of promotion. "The men who are going to get the promotions in this war," he said, "are the commanders in the field, not the staff officers who clutter up all the administrative machinery in the War Department."

It seemed to him that in World War I the staff had been favored ahead of the field commanders who carried the responsibility, and he planned to reverse the process. Then, possibly because he realized that I had been brought in from the field on his personal order, he turned to my case. "I know that you were recommended by one general for division command and by another for corps command," he said. "I'm glad they have that opinion of you, but you are going to stay right here and fill your position, and that's that! While this may seem a sacrifice to you, that's the way it must be."

The frustration I had felt in 1918 because of my failure to get overseas returned. By his words, I was condemned to a Washington desk for the duration. I impulsively broke out: "General, I'm interested in what you say, but I want you to know that I don't give a damn about your promotion plans as far as I'm concerned.

I came into this office from the field and I am trying to do my duty. I expect to do so as long as you want me here. If that locks me to a desk for the rest of the war, so be it!"

I got up and marched toward the door. When I reached it, something impelled me to turn around and grin a little sheepishly at my childishness. A tiny smile quirked the corner of his mouth as I turned to leave the office.

About three days later I was startled to find on my desk a copy of the General's recommendation to the President that I be promoted. As I read, I was even more amazed. He had told the President that, as his operations officer, I was not really a staff officer in the accepted sense. Under his direction, he said, all dispositions of Army forces on a global scale—including the Air Force—were my responsibility. I was his *subordinate commander*.

Had the years of indoctrinating myself on the inconsequential value of promotion as the measure of an Army man's worth influenced the way I had spoken to the General? Certainly, I had always known a wonderful freedom from awe in the presence of superior officers. But I often wonder whether without my outburst General Marshall would have had any greater interest in me than in any other relatively competent staff officer. In any case, I was now a major general.

General Marshall then asked me to draft a directive for a Commanding General for our forces in Europe. I did so. When he asked me to recommend a commander I proposed the Air Force's General McNarney. Instead, he sent me. The desk job in Washington was behind me. In London, commanding the European Theater of Operations, I was to be brought up close to the war.

What might be called my official reminiscences of World War II have been recorded in *Crusade in Europe*. But during the war there were incidents that provided a break in tension, some insight, or some amusement that I think I did not report. I am by no means going back to scan every line to see whether I have been guilty of duplication. Here I am telling stories principally for the pleasure of it, and it's fun just to wander with no worries about repetitions, or "literary criticism."

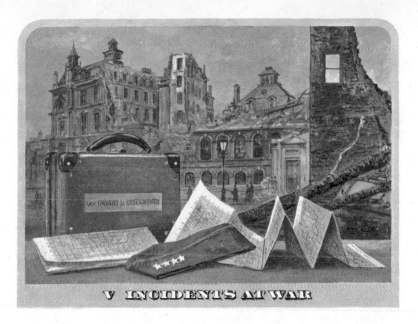

V INCIDENTS AT WAR

Lighting the Torch

WAR, AS SO many men have said, is the most stupid and tragic of human ventures. It is stupid because so few problems are enduringly solved, tragic because its cost in lives and spirit and treasure is seldom matched in the fruits of victory. Still, I never intend to join with those who damn all wars as crimes against humanity.

World War II, not sought by the people of the United States or its allies, was not, on their part, either stupid or in vain. Satisfaction, and memories precious beyond price, rewarded those who survived and who, in loyalty to country and to ideals, answered the attacks. But the loss of lives that might have been creatively lived scars the mind of the modern world.

In England, in July 1942, our future was murky and foreboding. Russia's Crimean fortress of Sevastopol had fallen to the Nazis, who could now plunge ahead into the Caucasus, to exploit their vast oil resources for further conquest. In Africa, the Nile delta was only a few hours from Rommel's advance Panzer units. Tobruk, symbol of British staunchness, had been lost again with all its men and guns.

It was decided that American forces should invade French North Africa, clean out resistance from Morocco to Tunisia, and then cooperate with the British under General Alexander, who would advance from the east, driving Rommel before them. Prime Minister Churchill thought that, because of difficulties between the British and French since France surrendered in 1940, this expedition should be as American in appearance as possible. At a London meeting of the Joint Chiefs of Staff, therefore, I was put in command of Operation TORCH.

After a preliminary survey of the problem, I concluded that we should make the landing in French North Africa so overwhelming in strength and so secretly prepared and executed that hopefully no bloodshed would ensue. TORCH, though, hardly began as a flaming success.

Throughout the war, I was always amazed that tens upon tens of thousands of tons of supply, from safety pins to tanks, reached their destination with dispatch. But through a crazy mixture of mistakes and oversights in the United States, the first materiel for the North African invasion arrived without one crate properly labeled. It was necessary to go through every package, item by item, before we could have the faintest idea what was on hand and what was missing.

For the drive on Algiers, all signal equipment for the *entire* task force had been put on one ship. When that vessel was shot up by an enemy ship, the task force was badly embarrassed. We rapidly learned to disperse specialized equipment.

More and more, I came to realize that brainpower is always in far shorter supply than manpower. The staff around me included intelligent officers who thought no problem beyond their ability to solve, no work load too heavy to endure. But such men became all too rare as the magnitude of our mission built up. Late in August, I wrote a classmate:

Solid, sound leadership, with inexhaustible nervous energy to spur on the efforts of lesser men, and ironclad determination to face discouragement . . . will always characterize the man who has a sure-enough, bang-up fighting unit. Added to this he must have a darned strong tinge of imagination—I am continuously astounded by the utter lack of imaginative thinking among so many of our people who have reputations for being really good officers. Finally, the man has to be able to forget himself and personal fortunes. I've relieved two seniors here because they got to worrying about "injustice," "unfairness," and "prestige."

Our landings in North Africa were fairly successful. Hoping to make the local French our allies again, we tried to persuade their commanders to sign an armistice. But they felt that honor required them to resist, unless authorized to quit by a direct representative of Marshal Pétain. Enter Admiral Darlan—and the start of one of the most discussed episodes in the six-month campaign.

A member of Pétain's cabinet, Admiral Darlan was taken as a political prisoner by our troops. Because he was one of the Vichy French and believed to have collaborated with the Nazis out of enmity to the British, I wanted nothing to do with him. But the local French military leaders insisted that only he could give them legal cover for a cease-fire. I was faced with my first "political" problem as a commander. If we were to go on and defeat the local French forces, we would also defeat our hope of making the French in Africa our allies—and that would hamper us in seizing Tunisia before the Axis forces. If, on the other hand, I dealt with Darlan, the public outcry could embarrass the British and American governments. To deal or not to deal . . .

In my offices in the dank and dripping tunnels of Gibraltar, my advisers and I discussed the question at length. Then I went off alone for an hour or so, and returned to announce the first major political decision I ever made:

The military advantages of an immediate cease-fire are so overwhelming that . . . I shall immediately recognize Darlan as the highest French authority in the region. He can act as the in-

terim head of such civil government as exists, on condition that
he carries out any orders I may issue.... I'll do my best to convince our governments ... that the decision was right. If they
find it necessary later to take action against this headquarters,
I'll make it clear that I alone am responsible.

The outcries came. Most of the time, I was too busy to worry
about them. But at the height of the furor about the "Darlan
deal," I did reflect uneasily that charges of incompetence as a
political man, a role for which I had little training and little liking, could end my career. The search for a scapegoat is the easiest
of all hunting expeditions. President Roosevelt and Prime Minister Churchill, however, both saw the situation clearly and each
effectively explained the circumstances to their countrymen.
Their support, and the fact that we simply went ahead with the
job at hand, meant that no heads would roll.

It didn't occur to me then that I would spend part of my life
after the war trying to sort out facts from hoked-up fiction. As
early warning that the printed word is not always the whole
truth, there was a story in *Yank*, the newspaper edited by and
for our troops, which purported to describe activities at my headquarters as we prepared for the African landings:

> The General, they say, was calm as a cucumber the whole
> time. He liked doing his own packing and hung up his own
> clothes. As for giving his batmen and orderlies an easy time,
> there wasn't much preparing involved in the General's favorite
> sandwich—raw beef with onions and plenty of pepper. One
> London newspaper said that General Eisenhower—a Texan
> and former cowboy himself when he worked his way through
> the University of Texas—even managed to indulge in a little of
> his favorite reading (wild West stories) while he was planning
> this vast campaign.

This may have been the origin of all the succeeding reports
that I never read anything but Westerns. If so, I wonder that the
other two bits of information were not as permanently incor-

porated into my public personality. Cartoons and sketches of the President devouring raw-meat sandwiches at his desk, or of Ike galloping on a cow pony around the White House lawn, would have provided a change of pace from the golf clubs with which I was usually armed.

THE WINTER of 1942-43 we worked harder than ever before. My headquarters was at Algiers. The battle line lay hundreds of miles to the east. Anxious to keep in touch with the front, I made frequent trips there, sometimes in a DC-3 but often, because of weather, by automobile—a long, tedious journey that took thirty-six hours. I became run-down and life was not improved by a murderous case of flu.

I was still carrying a high temperature when General Marshall visited the African front after the Casablanca conference of Allied leaders in 1943. He said he was worried about me. "You're trying to do too much. You're making too many trips to the front. You ought to depend more on reports." He looked at me rather fiercely. "You ought to have a man to be your eyes and ears."

The suggestion had appeal. It would have to be someone of ability, someone I could trust, someone of high enough rank to go into any headquarters. We began to go over names of officers who might fit. When he mentioned Bradley, I said, "Go no farther."

General Omar Bradley was not only a favorite classmate of mine at West Point, but a man I had admired throughout his military career. When he reached my headquarters, there began a close and enduring association that proved invaluable to me. Of all the ground commanders I have known, or even read about, I would put Omar Bradley in the highest classification. Patton, for instance, was a master of fast and overwhelming pursuit; headlong by nature, and fearlessly aggressive, he was the more colorful figure of the two. Bradley, however, was outstanding in every aspect of military command. As an attack leader and a defensive bulwark, I have yet to meet his equal.

He was not my "eyes and ears" for long. I needed his qualities so badly in command positions that I soon asked him to take over the II Corps. Later, of course, he became commander of the First Army, and in 1944, of the Twelfth Army group in Operation OVERLORD, the Allied invasion of northwestern Europe.

THE COMPLICATIONS of Allied command were intriguing. A small event that illustrated the difficulty of getting everybody agreed to launch any action was the campaign against a tiny island called Pantelleria, halfway between the northern tip of Tunisia and the island of Sicily. Said to be the Gibraltar of the central Mediterranean, it was heavily garrisoned by Italians, and thought by many to be unassailable.

There were other elements to consider, I thought. With the island's landing strip in possession of the enemy, our convoys, then going across from Africa to Sicily, were subject to strafing and dive-bomber attack; and we of course were denied the use of the field for our own operations. Believing that the Italian Army was sick of the war and that its morale was at a low ebb, I insisted on attempting the island's capture.

My immediate staff agreed. British ground commanders were doubtful. The attitude of Alexander and Montgomery was, "We must not risk a failure." I had to proceed cautiously to persuade my British associates that I was not going completely crazy.

We began full-scale bombardment of the island. To get a better picture, Admiral Andrew Cunningham and I went up with the bombarding fleet from Tunisia to simulate an attack. The reaction to this was so feeble that I said, "Andrew, if you and I got into a small boat, we could capture the place ourselves." When the attack was finally made, the men in our ships had not even completed getting into their landing craft when white flags began to appear.

Winston Churchill, by the way, was convinced that there were not more than three thousand Italians on the island. Our intelligence reports showed eleven thousand. He said, "If you'll give me a *centèsimo* for every soldier fewer than three thousand, I'll give you one for each man more than three thousand."

At the surrender on June 11, 1943, we got almost exactly eleven thousand. Winston paid off the debt, remarking in a note that at this rate he would buy all the Italians I could capture. I think the entire settlement came to about $1.60.

AFTER the Sicilian campaign and the landings in Italy, fighting went on during the winter, and we prepared to receive our political bosses. There was to be a conference at Cairo, followed by one with Marshal Stalin at Teheran; Stalin refused to go farther west. At Cairo, General Marshall told me to take two days off. I pleaded work, but he said, "Look, Eisenhower, just let someone else run that war up there for a couple of days. If your subordinates can't do it for you, you haven't organized them properly." So I used the two days to go up the Nile to the Valley of the Kings and to go to Jerusalem.

And when I got back to my headquarters, after the President had left the Teheran conference, I received a tattered piece of paper that, sealed in plastic, is one of my war souvenirs. At the bottom, General Marshall had written:

Cairo, Dec. 7, '43

Dear Eisenhower. I thought you might like to have this as a memento. It was written very hurriedly by me as the final meeting broke up yesterday, the President signing it immediately.

G.C.M.

And at the top of the paper, these few words:

From the President to Marshal Stalin
    The immediate appointment of General Eisenhower to command of Overlord operation has been decided upon

Roosevelt

Now events moved rapidly for me. After a last visit to the Italian Front and two visits with Mr. Churchill—one at Carthage, where he had a heavy cold, and another at Marrakesh, where he had pneumonia—I flew to Washington for two blessed weeks. There were conferences with the Chiefs of Staff, with the President, and a chance to see my family. Mamie and I had a secret meeting with John at West Point and I went to see my mother and brothers in Kansas.

The day before leaving, I had a long conversation with President Roosevelt, who was in bed with influenza. (At times, it must appear, the entire high command, civilian and military, was suffering from illness. Perhaps fatigue and responsibility were taking their toll.) We discussed the final division of Germany. I suggested that we avoid dividing Germany into zones and arrange for a military government under a coalition of the Western Allies and the Russians. I felt that any division of the country would make administration difficult. I also thought it would be far from certain that we could bring about the withdrawal of all Soviet troops when the time came for civilian authorities to take over.

The President made light of my fears. He had no doubt whatsoever about the eventual restoration of a satisfactory German government under the aegis of the occupying powers. What concerned him more than any relationships with the Soviets was that American troops should occupy Germany's northwestern rather than southwestern sector. He felt there was little in the southwest except "scenery," while the northwest contained the Ruhr's productivity. I repeated my opinion that if we divided the country into occupational zones we'd have trouble. He finally said that this was one point he had already decided.

Even though confined to bed, he was zestful and, as he had since our second meeting, called me Ike. He asked me whether I liked the new title, Supreme Commander, and I acknowledged that it had a ring of importance, something like Sultan. He bade me *adios*. It was our last meeting.

IT IS well for man to avoid superstitions, gossip, rumors and possible portents. If I had taken what greeted me on arrival in London on January 16, 1944, as a portent, I should have turned back. The fog was the worst I had ever encountered. Our automobile lights could not penetrate the heavy, yellowish curtain, so two or three men who were familiar with the area led the way to the hotel on foot. The next day my entire personal staff tried to get me to the new office. It was quite an experience. After reaching the address, two men got lost between the car and the front door. I was warned that near the door was an area-way into which anyone could fall. I called out that we would all stand still until one man made it to the door. He did, and by a dim glow from the interior we made our way inside 20 Grosvenor Square.

A genuinely auspicious sign was the presence of General Walter Bedell Smith to be my chief lieutenant during the intensely busy period of planning for Operation OVERLORD. I had communicated with General Patton and invited him to join us. But I told him that if he did so, his and Bradley's positions would be reversed, with Bradley commanding a group of armies and Patton a single one. He did not hesitate a second and I was happy to have him. After all, we had been friends for twenty-five years. There came a time when we needed all the friendship we could muster.

George Patton loved to shock people. Anything that popped into his mind came promptly out of his mouth. Not long after his arrival in England, he attended a meeting which he thought was off-the-record. He made a statement to the effect that after the war Britain and America would have to rule the world and other nations would have to conform. There was a newspaperman present and the story made vivid headlines.

All kinds of protests arose and General Marshall cabled to say I would have to decide this one on my own. I made up my mind to hang on to Patton, but to let him suffer for a week or so to impress upon him that he could not sound off this way and still be a worthwhile commander in a great Allied organization. George would sweat, I knew, because if there was one thing he wanted it was to continue in the war. So, after an interval, I sent for him, told him that I had decided to keep him on, but that he had to learn to keep his mouth shut on political matters.

Patton always lived at one extreme or another of the emotional spectrum. He was either laughing and full of enthusiasm, or filled with remorse and despondency. When I gave him the verdict, tears streamed down his face. He promised he would be a model of discretion and, in a gesture of almost little-boy contriteness, he put his head on my shoulder. This caused his helmet to fall off—a gleaming helmet I sometimes thought he wore to bed. As it rolled across the room, I prayed that no one would walk in on this ridiculous situation.

Without embarrassment, George picked up his helmet, adjusted it and saluted. "Sir, could I go back to my headquarters?"

"Yes," I said, "right after you have lunch with me."

Across the Channel

WE ALL think back to Sir Winston Churchill as a man who bespoke confidence. There can be no question but that his presence in the British Isles, a presence of the spirit as much as of the mind, is responsible for the fact that those Isles survive today, so that their phenomenally distinguished history reaches on through the present. But Winston was a human being and there were moments when none of us could be sure of success.

On my return to London in January 1944, the Prime Minister and I formed a habit of meeting at least twice a week. There was luncheon on Tuesday and dinner with the Chiefs of Staff and others on Friday. Occasionally, the dinner became a weekend at Chequers, the Prime Minister's country residence.

At these meetings, tension and anxiety were inescapable. Across the Channel, the Nazis had through four years been fortifying beaches and ports. These were supported by mobile reserves which could be rushed to any point we chose to assault, concentrating masses of armor and infantry against the relatively small numbers we could land by sea or air. Our lines of support, on the other hand, would be subject to fatal interruptions by stormy weather, by undersea attack, and, it was rumored, by assault from new projectiles whose range and speed would change the nature of war. For the sort of attack before us we had no precedent in history. OVERLORD was a singular military expedition and a fearsome risk.

In the early spring of 1944, the Prime Minister was not over-sold on its value. He felt that it would be far better to wait for more significant signs of German collapse. In the confines of an intimate meeting, he would say, "When I think of the beaches of Normandy choked with the flower of American and British youth, and when, in my mind's eye, I see the tides running red with their blood, I have my doubts . . . I have my doubts." But he would never show pessimism in public.

Bradley and I were convinced that we would not have un-usual losses. On the contrary, our confidence grew by leaps and

bounds. Our bombing operations were damaging German com-munications, cutting into their supplies of fuel, destroying both equipment and production capacity. Meanwhile, the Russians were making inroads on the Eastern Front, and there was little opportunity for Hitler to reinforce the west.

This optimism radiated. Winston said, "General, it is good for commanders to be optimistic, else they would never win a battle. I must say to you if by the time snow flies you have established your thirty-odd divisions, now in Britain, safely on the Normandy coast and have the port of Cherbourg firmly in your grasp, I will be the first to proclaim that this was a gigantic and wonderfully conducted military campaign." He added: "If by Christmas you have succeeded in liberating our beloved Paris, if she can by that time take her accustomed place as a center of western European culture and beauty, then I will proclaim that this operation is the most grandly conceived and best conducted known to the history of warfare."

I replied, "Mr. Prime Minister, we expect to be on the borders of Germany by Christmas, pounding away at her defenses. When that occurs, if Hitler has the slightest judgment or wisdom left, he will surrender unconditionally to avoid complete destruction of Germany." I smiled. "I bet General Montgomery five pounds that we would end the war in Europe by the end of 1944. I have no reason to want to hedge that bet."

The Prime Minister's mouth curved upward into a splendid smile. "My dear General, I pray you are right." Ultimately, we held two substantial command conferences to review our expectations for OVERLORD. At one of these there was assembled as much rank as may ever have been gathered for an operational briefing. Present were the King of England, his Prime Minister, several of the War Cabinet, all the British Chiefs of Staff, and all senior commanders of the proposed operation.

The meeting was also notable because of a statement by the Prime Minister. The presentations over, he said, "I am hardening toward this enterprise." The smell of victory was in the air.

EVEN before I was installed in London, the British had offered warm hospitality. In the spring of 1942, General Mark Clark and others had accompanied me on an inspection trip to Britain, and one Sunday afternoon we were given an opportunity to visit Windsor Castle. The Constable, Lord Wigram, was our host. The Royal Family knew of our visit, he told us, and to avoid any embarrassment to us they were remaining in their apartment for the afternoon. He could thus freely show us all the interesting places, including those which the Royal Family normally used for recreation on fair days.

Weeks later, I was fortunate enough to be presented to the King. When he recalled that some time back I had been to the castle, he laughed and said he had a story to tell me.

His promise to Lord Wigram that the Royal Family would remain inside during our visit had slipped the King's mind. The day had been sunny, so the entire family had decided to have tea in the garden. Sitting at the table, they glanced up the hill and saw, just over its crest, the bobbing heads of four men, one very tall—this would be General Clark—and one who was Lord Wigram. The King instantly remembered his promise. Should Lord Wigram get a glimpse of the Royal Family, the tour would be terminated and we might miss something the Constable wanted to show us. The King exclaimed, "This is terrible, we must not be seen." The question was: What to do?

The first thing they did was to jump quickly down on their hands and knees. This put them outside the line of vision of the party moving up the hill. The courtyard was surrounded by a stone wall; by keeping close to the ground, they could stay concealed until they reached the wall and in its shelter could go on toward their quarters. So the Royal Family of England crawled on hands and knees to the wall, made their way to the castle door and disappeared inside.

When the King told me this story, he laughed uproariously and I couldn't help joining him. "Your Majesty," I said, "if all Americans could hear that story just as you've told it, I can assure you that never again will a man be elected mayor of Chicago by running against the King of England."

At the same outdoor luncheon, George Patton was seated directly across from the King. The King asked him if he had ever shot anyone with the pistols he was wearing.

George said promptly, "Oh yes." But he added, "Really, not these pistols. These are the ones I carry socially. I carry my fighting pistols when I'm out on campaign."

"How many men have you killed in war?" asked the King.

Without batting an eye, George said, "Seven, Sir."

This was too much for me. "How many, General Patton?"

Instantly he replied, "Three, Sir."

"Well, George," I said, "I'll let you get away with that." George had often told me that during the Pershing expedition into

Mexico in 1916, he and a small cavalry patrol ran into a handful of Villa's brigands and in the melee he shot one of the enemy.

The King was popular with all the American forces, as were his Queen and his mother. He liked the simple life of a soldier and was perfectly at home with all of us. At the end of the war, he asked me to come to Buckingham Palace about teatime, mentioning that he wanted to see me privately for a few minutes in his office before we took tea with the Queen.

The reason for those few moments proved to be the presentation of one of the most prized decorations in Britain, the Order of Merit. As I recall, only twelve men in the services and twelve civilians can hold the Order at any one time. Having handed me the decoration, the King passed me a sealed letter, asking me not to read it until I'd left the palace. When I was free to open it, I found, to my amazement and pleasure, that he had written it in longhand. It was an expression of his and his people's gratitude for my war services. I have always held it as one of the most appreciated of all awards given me by any foreign government.

The privilege of command allowed me to meet kings, queens, presidents, ambassadors, and a rotund fellow named George Allen. We might never have met except for Mr. Allen's curious gift for prophecy.

George Allen had been made Chairman of the Prisoner of War Committee of the American Red Cross. A few days before I reached London, he was sent by the President on an inspection trip to the United Kingdom. In London a dinner was given in his honor by the American Ambassador, Mr. Winant. The Americans present were hungry for news and gossip from their nation's capital. George, a constant storyteller, gave them the latest servings of both, until someone said, "Who are the American generals likely to be prominent on this side of the water?"

Allen, who had no connection with the Army, stalled for time. Then he had an inspiration. His wife and Mamie had been friends in Washington in 1935, though he and I had never met. He suddenly remembered, from a newspaper account of the Louisiana maneuvers of 1941, that Colonel Eisenhower had earned a promotion to brigadier general. On the spur of the moment, he blurted, "Watch Eisenhower." Then, to demonstrate his knowledge further, he proceeded to enlarge on my personality.

Early the following morning, one of the guests called George and said, "Why didn't you tell us? Why were you so coy?"

Allen sleepily muttered, "Tell you what?"

"That Eisenhower was coming here in command?"

George was suddenly wide-awake. "Well, I would have been badly criticized if I had let it out before the General got here."

George saw only one way to save his reputation in official London circles. An old friend of his, Commander Harry Butcher, worked at headquarters, so he telephoned Butcher and told him the story. "Butch," he said, "I've just got to be seen with the General, otherwise people will call me the phony that I really am."

Butcher invited George to headquarters. He told me he had a friend there from Washington whose wife knew mine, and I might like to send a message back. He added quietly that his friend was in a bit of difficulty and perhaps I could help.

I agreed to see the friend and found a man of considerable avoirdupois, with a sparkle in his eye. He told me his story. "General," he continued, "I'm putting myself at your mercy. If I could just be *seen* coming out of your office with you, or if a little item could be put in the paper that Mr. Allen had called on the new commanding general, this would do the trick."

Mr. Allen's obvious distress, and his anxiety to avoid fame as a teller of fairy tales, made me laugh. "I'll tell you what we will do. I'll have Butcher arrange a luncheon at Claridge's with you on my right and a couple of military friends at the table."

His gratitude was overwhelming. Butcher arranged the luncheon and we all sat down together and had a wonderful time. It was one of the few times I dined in public during the war.

After that, George and I became friends. Now and then we would have a game of bridge. One evening we started out with only a single deck—for some reason it was difficult to keep two around my quarters—and in the first hand, George spoke up.

"Wait a minute, I have the joker. I need another card."

"Oh no you don't," I said. "That is the six of clubs. We lost the real six and you'll notice the markings in the corner."

George laid down his hand and said, "If the Commander in Chief of this armada, which is supposed to lick Hitler, cannot afford one complete set of cards, then I have grave doubts that more necessary items of equipment are adequate and ready."

"George," I said, "let me tell you this. We are not going to be playing games with the Nazis."

In the preparation of an immense military enterprise, the staggering multiplicity of decisions and details can tend to dwarf other things in life. But like all men in the services, I had personal concerns and worries, prides and fears, and a good thing, too—they helped save us from degenerating into one-track machines. With the awesome potential of D Day approaching, I found myself thinking like a father.

John's graduation from West Point was on June 6, which turned out to be the date of the invasion. General Marshall, characteristically thoughtful, directed that he be sent to London for a short leave before reporting to Fort Benning. As was to be expected, John wanted me to assign him to the troops right then, but he accepted my decision that he go along with the others of his class through the routine. We spent as much time together as possible during his limited leave.

After the landings on the morning of June 6, the battling stayed tough and constant for weeks until Bradley started a heavy attack, captured Saint-Lô, and about August broke through the left flank of the defending forces. For a while the front was quite fluid, and though the duties at headquarters were heavy, I managed to visit our forward units with some regularity.

General Wade H. Haislip, one of my oldest friends, was commanding the XV Corps and I determined to visit him. As I reached his headquarters about noon, he came out in a jeep to meet me. His greeting was almost surly:

"General, I think you should turn around and go right back. We've got Nazi artillery firing on our flank and we think there's a counterattack building up that just might overrun the area."

"Well, Ham," I said, "I'd like to see their attack. I'm confident you can handle it. Besides, I don't see you running."

"Of course we'll handle it!" he said. "But I don't want the Supreme Commander killed in my corps area."

I was sure there would be no quick overrunning of the positions, so I said I was going to stay for lunch, at least. That lunch was a comedy, served in double-quick time. Haislip ordered soup for me without waiting for the others to sit down, and he had the main course on the table before I was through with the first one. Just to plague him a little more I said, "Now look, Ham, I had no breakfast and I'm going to enjoy this. I won't be hurried."

He consented to my having thirty minutes for lunch. At thirty minutes plus one he took me for a ride, saying there was something interesting he wanted me to see. After a couple of minutes, I remarked, "Okay, Ham, I'm just smart enough to know this is the same road I came in on. What was it you wanted to show me?"

"I want to show you the shortest way out of this corps area!"

After the liberation of Paris, when officers came back from the front to my headquarters, I tried to treat them with more hospitality than that! Bradley came to my winter headquarters at Versailles and I wanted to give him a fine luncheon. The day before I had received a bushel of oysters, still in their shells. I told my mess sergeant, "This noon we'll have an oyster feast for General Bradley. Let's serve raw oysters, then oyster soup, and as an entree, fried oysters."

I was smiling in anticipation as we sat down at the table. When those beauties on the half shell came out, Brad looked up and said inoffensively, "I can't touch oysters."

I sent for the mess sergeant, whispered frantically, and dawdled over my raw oysters while he drummed up some kind of edible meat—Spam, if I'm not mistaken.

OF COURSE the war was not all oysters or bridge games. From the start of OVERLORD, we knew that we would win—knew it not factually, but with faith. Yet even when the Nazis' situation was hopeless, they could explode with bursts of deadliness. The Battle of the Bulge coincided with my advancement to five-star rank. It was a dangerous episode; but at Bastogne, the most publicized (but possibly not the most critical) of our stands against the German attack, thousands of encircled paratroopers held out and wrecked the Nazis' time schedule. On a smaller scale, Bastogne was repeated in scores of little places, hamlets and bridge crossings where handfuls of men might for hours hold up a Nazi column.

On December 22, 1944, our southern counterattack was launched and in my order of the day I wrote:

> The enemy is making his supreme effort. He is fighting savagely to take back all that you have won and is using every treacherous trick to deceive and kill. . . . In the face of your proven bravery and fortitude he will completely fail.

The enemy did fail. But to put it in those terms is to understate grievously what happened. These were the times when the grand strategy of high command became a soldiers' war of sheer courage. Our men responded gallantly. Along with the constant threat of sudden death, they overcame all that the elements could inflict on them—snow and ice, clammy fog and freezing rain—and all the pain of arduous marches and sleepless watches. They had left their wives and children, or set aside hopes of wives and children, and now they fought down their inclinations to rest tired bodies, to play it safe, to search out a hiding place.

In the light of their record, I am skeptical of those who criticize our young people today, and bemoan their alleged desertion of traditional American standards. Many things now going on disturb me because they seem senseless or graceless; but I believe that we can always rely on the willingness of Americans, including young ones, to endure greatly in their country's cause.

On May 7, 1945, a group of tired men met in my headquarters in Rheims. The moment was at hand. There had been long and tedious negotiations with German leaders, who were backing and filling, uncertain who was speaking for the deceased Hitler. When the signing of the surrender finally took place, my group went to bed to sleep the clock around. I waited up only long enough to call Omar Bradley. "Brad, I've got good news. Get the word around." And then I issued the climactic order of the war in Europe. "Make sure that all firing stops at midnight of the eighth."

London, Frankfurt, Berlin

FROM Pearl Harbor Sunday until the German capitulation forty-one months later, I had been under all the pressures for which I had been preparing myself through my entire career. However, the size of the job, and the number and uniqueness of the pressures, were unexpected, to say the least. Like so many other men and women who had been at war physically or emotionally, exhaustion rather than exultation was my first reaction to victory in Europe. As I write, two decades later, the days following the armistice are fuzzier in memory than any other period of World War II. I had been liberated too. In a deep sag of reaction, I luxuriated in freedom from decisions about the life and death of human beings.

In June, Winston Churchill invited me to come from my Frankfurt headquarters to Britain. I was to be made a Freeman of the City of London at a ceremony in the ancient Guildhall. The occasion would require a speech, the first formal address of any length that I had had to give. I labored at it mightily, going over and over it until I could say it without notes, but to fortify myself I wrote out on a small card the first words of each paragraph.

On the day of the ceremony my aides had to go to the Guildhall early. I was feeling confined, a little nervous, and thought I would spend half an hour alone in the park. I slipped out of the back door of the Dorchester Hotel, but as I crossed the street, a cabdriver put his head out the window and called, "Ike! Good old Ike!" He stopped and produced a piece of paper, which I signed. Then his passengers got out and asked me for autographs too. In moments, it seemed, a crowd of hundreds had gathered.

It was flattering, but it was becoming difficult to extricate my-self. As the crowd continued to grow, someone looked over from the hotel, saw the trouble I was in, and called for a squad of police. They formed a flying wedge, got in to me, and then got me out in time to meet my OVERLORD Deputy, Air Chief Marshal Arthur Tedder, with whom I proceeded to the boundary of the City, the old city of London. From there, in a horse-drawn car-riage, we were escorted through crowds to the historic Guildhall.

The outside of the hall was not imposing but the interior cer-tainly was. Before me was the Lord Mayor of London in cere-monial robes. The hall was jammed.

The sword I was to receive was not yet ready, so I was given, as a symbol, the Wellington Sword—a curved, oriental scimitar, encrusted with jewels. (The actual sword, bearing the Order of Merit insignia and other significant engravings, is now one of the prized possessions of my son, John, and will go down, I hope, from father to son as long as there are Eisenhower boys in my family.) Then the huge audience sat in absolute silence while I spoke. What I tried to express, in part, was that the honor was mingled with sadness—the sadness known to any man who re-ceives acclaim earned in the blood of his followers and the sacri-fices of his friends. The London papers later greeted the talk warmly—and even, in an excess of friendly misjudgment, boxed it on the front page with the Gettysburg Address.

After lunch at the Mansion House, across the street, Winston Churchill and I stood on a balcony, greeting a dense gathering in the square below.

"I've got just as much right to be down there yelling as you do," I said to the crowd. "You see, I'm a citizen of London now, too."

MY HEADQUARTERS was now absorbed in another unprecedented military move: transporting a million victorious combat veterans to the Pacific Front. Other veterans, many of them our recovered prisoners of war, were to be returned home. Inescapably, many of the men sent to the Pacific felt that an injustice was being done them. Dissatisfaction, contagious in an army fresh from battle with no enemy in its immediate front, could have produced wild disorder among less disciplined men. But somehow the turn-around was accomplished.

One way to speed up our veterans' return home from Europe occurred to me. Tens of thousands of men, ready for embarkation, were crowded into a camp near Le Havre. Every day they saw Liberty and Victory ships going home empty, while they had to wait for the relatively few troop-transport ships. Not realizing the impossibility of using cargo vessels because of the lack of sanitary facilities, etc., they were giving their officers a bad time.

One answer to the problem—if the soldiers were willing to put up with considerable inconvenience—was to double the passenger load of the transports by feeding and sleeping the men in shifts. To the thousands who had gathered to greet our party I said over the PA system, "Do you want to go back home comfortably—or would you rather double up and get home quickly?" Thunderous applause told me that a sticky situation had been resolved.

The time came for me to take a trip to the United States, to Washington, New York, West Point, Kansas City and Abilene. It turned out to be a far cry from the simple, secret visit I had earlier and naïvely planned. In the cities, I was amazed at the numbers of people who met us on the streets, and at the wild enthusiasm of their greeting. The trip to Washington was so overwhelming I thought everything to follow would be anticlimax. When we went to New York, however, the entire city seemed to be on hand. Hour upon hour, we traveled avenues jammed with people, while others hung out the windows of towering buildings.

Going back to Abilene was a visit to memories. My father was no longer there. When he died in 1942 the house had lost one of its commanding presences. However, the sight of my mother was one of the rewards of peace.

BACK in Frankfurt, the atmosphere was friendliness itself. There was a genuine welcome on the faces of the Germans. Whatever the postwar debates, it was easy to see that the population was relieved that the war was over and Hitler no more. American troops proved to be friendly ambassadors on the whole, free of ruthless vindictiveness or looting.

Between Frankfurt and the town where I lived was a little village with a school. As my car drove by, children of eight or ten would rush to the picket fence calling, "Heil, Ice-en-hower! Heil, Ice-en-hower!" It was ironic to realize that if they had said it a short time earlier, their families would have been executed.

In Frankfurt I had my final brush with George Patton's impulsiveness. At a press conference, something was said about the Allies' policy of denying former Nazis positions in the German government. Patton remarked that this was being overdone—and then had to add a suggestion that the Nazis were just another political party, like the Republicans and Democrats. Such a remark might have had its roots in traditional American readiness to let bygones be bygones, but George Patton was aware that a principal purpose of our occupation mission was to cleanse the Continent of Nazi control. His words could have been misinterpreted by those who wanted a soft policy toward Nazi leaders.

I ordered him to my headquarters and said, "The war's over and I don't want to hurt you—but I can't have you making such ridiculous statements. I'm giving you a new job. You'll be head of a study group to analyze the American war record in Europe and make conclusions on the major lessons of our campaigns."

Though disappointed to leave his Third Army, Patton gave his new job the same enthusiasm he gave to battle. From then on he had no occasion to meet the press and I had none to criticize him.

DEFEATED Germany was divided into four sectors, one each to be administered by the Soviets, the French, the British and ourselves. Periodically, the representatives of these countries—Marshal Zhukov, General Koenig, Field Marshal Montgomery and I—met in Berlin. In general, these meetings were friendly but at times there was acrimonious debate, when one of the Western Allies complained of Russian interference with their forces in Berlin, or they accused us of infractions of agreements.

Marshal Zhukov was rather standoffish with the other two representatives, but between him and me there was a degree of mutual understanding that permitted a frank exchange of views. We talked at length about the war. He was particularly interested in the logistic arrangements that had enabled the Allies to make rapid advances, such as our pipelines for gas and oil laid under the English Channel and across France, and our "Red Ball" truck lines, with one-way truck roads and three shifts of drivers to keep every vehicle on the road constantly. Later, in Moscow, he and Marshal Stalin made this sort of thing the subject of long conversations. Although the Russian scientific community had a pool of theoretical genius and engineering talent, the ingenuities of mass production were still a mystery to them.

So were the workings of our democratic institutions. In Berlin one day, Marshal Zhukov came to me scowling and spoke in abrupt terms about what he called a personal insult. One of our magazines had published a story about him alleging, among other things, that he was shorter than his wife.

I tried to convince him that while such errors were regrettable, they were not official and not meant to belittle him. He said they were deliberate insults and wanted to know how I was going to punish the journalists responsible.

My efforts to explain the workings of a free press were futile; had the matter not been serious, my failure would have been funny. I explained that one reason why my nation and I had fought in the war was to defend the right of free speech and of a free press.

The Marshal would not believe that such a thing could exist. He insisted, "If you were described like this by any publication in my country, I would see that it was eliminated immediately."

Zhukov had scant patience with political men. Once when I wanted to talk to him about a military matter and had not brought along my political adviser, I told him that he could have his present if he liked. "No," he replied, "if you're not going to have yours, I'm going to throw mine out." He turned to Andrei Vishinsky and said, "Get out, I don't want you here."

BACK IN THE SPRING of 1944, when we were preparing for the cross-Channel attack, most people believed that Germany would put up such a fight that it could not be overcome in less than two years. My estimate was too optimistic by four months. But it was satisfying to all field commanders that the surrender took place almost exactly eleven months from our landing in Normandy.

Then came the inevitable questions and arguments: Why was this done? Why didn't you do better? Our actions were not above criticism, and critique and analysis of history is surely of value. But at times, as the postmortems have gone on, it has looked as if we blundered throughout the campaign and were defeated.

The question with the longest life is why the Western Allies did not capture Berlin. It is heard repeatedly, sometimes in a context that implies a conspiracy to promote Soviet control of Eastern Europe.

No one has yet shown definitively why we should have captured Berlin. Indeed, considering the proximity of the Russian forces to that city as compared to our own when the final attacks were launched, no one has produced evidence of the feasibility of our capturing it before they did. If we had, we would not have gained much and we could have lost a great deal. The national zones of occupation in Germany had already been decided upon by our political chiefs. The orders I received for conducting the war were: You will land in Europe and, proceeding to Germany, will destroy Hitler and all his forces.

That we did. To then jeopardize thousands of Allied soldiers' lives in an onslaught on the Berlin bunkers would have been a sacrifice of men to gain a symbol.

On February 11, 1965, I wrote to Senator A. Willis Robertson of Virginia, who had asked for the bare facts. I told the Senator:

(a) The mission of the Allied forces was not the capture of localities but the destruction of Hitler's armed might.

(b) No matter what German areas might be captured, each nation was required, under the political agreement, to retire within the lines prescribed—long before the end of the war—by

Generalissimo Stalin, President Roosevelt and Prime Minister Churchill.

(c) When our final operational plans had been drawn up, approved, and issued to Bradley, Montgomery and Devers—in April 1945—the Western Allies had encircled the Ruhr, but their main body was two hundred miles from Berlin. The Russian front was thirty miles from Berlin and its spearheads were already west of the Oder River. Under these circumstances, our plans made no mention of Berlin. . . .

(d) My own headquarters had reported to our government in January that our advance in Germany would penetrate far deeper than the line which the political leaders had agreed upon as the eastern boundary for occupation by the Western Allies. Berlin was deep in the zone that was to be Russian. Our government decided that no change should be made in these boundaries.

(e) . . . During the Allied advance between the Rhine and the Elbe . . . Winston Churchill did suddenly suggest the possible political value of capturing Berlin. But the ground forces were accomplishing the prescribed objectives and to have changed these materially would have been difficult, and, in my opinion, absolutely unnecessary and unwise. It is not correct to say, as some suggested, that President Roosevelt *refused me permission* to take Berlin, but he was party to the earlier political decision that placed Berlin well beyond the Western Allies' sectors of occupation.

After I was transferred to the United States, General Lucius Clay became Commander in Chief of the American Zone. His masterful performance in that position has become history.

Lost in the Pentagon

THROUGH the many months of World War II in Europe, we had all heard about the wonders of the Pentagon. Every visitor arrived with at least one story about what had happened to someone lost in its labyrinth of corridors. One was told of an Army Air Corps captain who got so lost that when he finally arrived at the office he was looking for he had been promoted to full colonel. Suddenly, I was working there, and occasionally getting lost myself.

No personal enthusiasm marked my promotion to Chief of Staff, the highest military post a soldier in the United States Army can reach. The job ahead was not pleasant. The demobilization of a wartime army is a dreary business. The high morale that characterizes the healthy unit in campaigns deteriorates as the time nears for its dispersal. The citizen-soldier and his family want him at home, today, at once!

Long before the end of the war, General Marshall, recalling the frenzy of World War I's much simpler demobilization, had directed a commission of civilians and military men to prepare a charter for the orderly and speedy return home of our troops. Out of their studies came the point system—a table of credits earned by each soldier for his time of service, time in combat, wounds and disabilities, his age and family obligations. Every officer and man could easily figure out his own priority for discharge. I think there was general agreement that it was an equitable system. I know that when I first saw it I felt that here again was a striking example of General Marshall's foresight and wisdom.

On my return from Europe, my professional concerns were maintaining the peace we had won, ensuring the continued security of the United States, and demobilization. Washington seemed preoccupied with the present, with the widespread demand to "get the boys home." The past did get some attention: there was an obsession in both houses of the Congress to find a scapegoat for Pearl Harbor. But of the future, piled high with threats to our victory and our continuing security, there seemed to be little thought.

This was frightening to one who had seen Europe devastated from the Polish border to the Atlantic. Although the will to live was strong in those who had survived, the means to live had been so thoroughly disrupted that chaos was inevitable unless the Allied Armies in their occupied areas could provide a temporary framework of support. Without that framework, anarchy would engulf many of the liberated lands, and the next masters of

Europe could be either Communists or successors to the Nazis. To every rational American the Army's mission must have seemed obvious, but words of caution went unheard in early 1946.

Each month from V-J Day on, we had exceeded the established quota of soldiers to be returned to their families. By the end of 1945, the figure had reached five million, almost double the scheduled number. In part, this tremendous move was the result of a purely emotional surge in every echelon of command from the War Department down—a determination to get every possible man home by Christmas. Even as I sympathized with the deep-seated emotions, I knew that further yielding to them could produce the collapse of the demobilization system.

Only six weeks or so after taking over as Chief of Staff, I had to go before Congress, the principal target of those demanding instant demobilization, and explain all the facts. The Senators and Representatives were concerned by what seemed to be a wave of national hysteria. They were a difficult audience to face. All I could do was make a personal pledge that in each case where unusual hardship or any injustice was claimed, my staff would investigate and report to me. Returning to the Pentagon, I directed that the first thing every morning I wanted a digest of the pleas that had arrived the day before.

I read these every morning, on some days several hundred of them. The correspondence section of my office was enlarged, and working hours ran from seven in the morning until far into the night, weekends not excepted.

Inevitably, complaints continued that we were not moving fast enough. Not everyone was prepared to accept the fact that a globally dispersed army, stationed on all the continents and on islands from the Arctic to the edges of Antarctica, whose mobilization and transport had required years to effect, could not be returned home in a few months. To assure myself that there would be no slowing down, I insisted on daily reports of the movement of troops through the discharge pipelines.

In compiling these reports, we used the most modern statistical machines. However, the machines, perhaps feeling the pressures themselves, at times seemed confused by the data fed into them. Certainly the figures they turned out were confusing. Eventually, I ordered a hand count of every officer and man still in uniform. This old-fashioned census, laborious as it was, gave us our first accurate figures. We learned that our machines had been off by several hundred thousand men. Since then I've always mistrusted, a little, even the most handsome, most intricate and guaranteed computer.

By this time, a representative from every military service was before the Congress begging for a peacetime establishment that could meet our nation's new worldwide obligations. But the Congress was tired of wartime spending. Military appropriations were cut drastically. Even when I asked for money with which to salvage the Army's usable vehicles, scattered across the world and rusting away, my recommendations were ignored.

It was idle for the Joint Chiefs of Staff to warn that the defeat of Japan and Germany did not mean that peace and light were going to be order of the day for the coming years. This drastic retrenchment forced us to take nearly all elements of military strength from Korea. In my opinion, that unnecessary conflict was thereby encouraged.

AMONG all the skills with which a soldier these days must concern himself, not the least important is public relations—a phrase almost unknown to the Army until World War II. That ignorance—or negligence—may be one reason why at the end of every war the Army was a budgetary stepchild. Chiefs of Staff might argue that appropriations were inadequate, but they did it to their civilian superiors or to congressional committees. The general public, either as an interested audience or as a source of support, was largely ignored because of a long tradition, accepted by the Army, that soldiers should be seen but not heard.

George Marshall, who had a panoramic view of everything affecting the nation's defenses, saw that if there was to be an authentic partnership between civilians and troops in uniform, the public must be well informed about the Army's purposes and its need. He created a Bureau of Public Relations in the War Department, and assigned to it General Alexander Surles, one of the wisest soldiers I have known. Cynics describe P.R. as a maternity gown designed to hide the true figure of fact, and, if abused, it can be. Properly practiced, however, it is necessary in a republic where the citizens must know the truth.

My own relations with the press during the war had always been frank and cordial. Correspondents were scrupulously careful—when they understood the need for secrecy—not to compromise security; and the traffic in information was two-way. Because they reflected the reaction of civilians at home, and even of troops in combat, I learned much from them. After I had become Chief of Staff, when Aleck Surles retired, I appointed as P.R. officer Major General Floyd Parks, a man so sure that truth could be effective in the forming of sound public opinion that he was forthright to the point of bluntness. He was far more concerned with substance and accuracy than with phraseology or timing. It was only later, in the White House, that I understood how critical an ingredient timing is in the public's attention to news.

IN THE Pentagon, I encountered with full force a phenomenon of American public life—the total lack of privacy permitted a senior officer of government. I had to live with the knowledge that every phone call I made was monitored and possibly recorded in a stenographer's notebook; that every letter addressed to me, unless from my wife or a close relative or friend, was read by at least one member of the staff; that every word I wrote, even the scraps I rejected and tossed into the wastebasket, would be scrupulously filed away for eventual microfilming and scrutiny by students of history. I've heard this sort of life described as downright intolerable, but I was less troubled by it than some people, possibly because the Army way of life is an open society—the actions of officers often provide the principal topics of conversation among all ranks. Also, because I have always sought to develop a family feeling with my staff, I had the consolation that most of those intently watching me were friends.

Now and then, they went to remarkable lengths in their meticulous guard over me. Almost twenty years after the fact, for instance, I learned that the ribbons I had worn on my jacket one day had been a cause for alarm. When visiting a foreign embassy, I would wear the appropriate ribbon for the medal from that country's government. On a certain visit I had the wrong country—that is, the wrong ribbon—and the Pentagon was shaken to its foundations. In the matter of decorations, none are so sensitive as diplomats! Next morning, this memo was published:

. . . Hereafter when General Eisenhower's calendar indicates he is to call at a foreign embassy or to participate in any event in connection with a foreign dignitary, action will be instituted immediately to insure that he wears the proper ribbons. In order that all concerned display necessary initiative without prodding or last-minute apoplexy, the following measures will be taken:

1. When the engagement is made, Major Cannon will notify Major Schulz *immediately*.
2. Major Schulz will notify Sgt. Murray and is responsible that the ribbons worn by the General are proper and in order. *This will be done at once.*
3. Sgt. Murray will prepare the ribbons for General Eisenhower's blouse or jacket. *This will be done as rapidly as possible.*
4. Major Cannon will verify the propriety of ribbons.
5. Major Cannon will notify the undersigned when mission is accomplished.
6. Major Schulz will insure that Sgt. Moaney has ribbons and is informed as to when and where the General will require them.
7. If the General is required to be away on a trip and ribbons are necessary, either Sgt. Dry or Sgt. Murray will have required ribbons with them.

I should add that all five men involved survived the memorandum. The two majors became brigadier generals, and Robert L. Schulz has been my aide for twenty-one years. Sergeant William

Murray is retired from the Army and is now in hotel work in Washington. Sergeant John Moaney and I have been inseparable for almost a quarter of a century; in my daily life, he is just about the irreplaceable man. Sergeant Leonard Dry was Mamie's chauffeur at Columbia and in the White House; he has had the same job with Mrs. Kennedy and Mrs. Johnson.

MANY months before I left the Army I was approached by representatives of various publishing houses, each with a different reason for wanting to publish my memoirs of the war. To all these proposals I turned a deaf ear. For one thing, I was really tired; I wanted to loaf awhile and then try to find out what to do with the rest of my life. I had a notion I might settle down in the vicinity of some small college and make a connection that would bring me in touch with young people. I had a suspicion they could understand more about the world and its complexities than they were being taught.

Many of the publishing proposals were purely financial. I was not one to scorn money, but money alone had no temptation. Then Douglas M. Black of Doubleday and William Robinson of the New York *Herald Tribune* came to me with a different kind of argument. Historians, they said, use contemporary accounts as source material. Books about wars by authors who were not participants are frequently used as main sources. They reminded me of books on the African and European campaigns, written hurriedly so as not to "miss the market," some of them riddled with inaccuracies. Mr. Black and Mr. Robinson pointed out that since these errors were written during my lifetime and were not denied or corrected by me, the historians of the future must give them a high degree of credence. "You owe it to yourself and to history to tell the personal story of your European campaigns on a factual basis." This reasoning impressed me. I warned that there would be no sensationalism, and that my writings were unlikely to attract many readers. Mr. Black said: "All we want you to do is to tell your story, your way."

So on February 8, 1948, I started on a writing program, at a speed that a soldier would call a blitz. There was a great deal of material immediately at hand. I had years earlier formed a habit of dictating long memoranda for my files, with my opinions and conclusions on the principal developments of the past two to three months. In addition, I had throughout the war carried on an intermittent official correspondence with General Marshall, Prime Minister Churchill, Generals Bradley, Patton and Montgomery, and the Operations Division of the American War Department. These gave me a fairly complete record of events as I had seen them at the time.

I handed each chapter to my researcher as I wrote it. He then took it to the records to find documentation for every statement. After several drafts, the text went to experts who would come back with suggestions. Frequently I adopted some of these, but not if they seemed to change my meaning in the slightest degree. I tried to write as plainly and straightforwardly as possible. Just before starting the work I had reread Grant's memoirs, which I had always admired for their simplicity and lack of pretension. I refused superlatives or purple adjectives, and I would not indulge in the disparagement of others that had badly marred many military accounts.

In one way, this striving for plain objectivity caused me uneasiness. I constantly argued with my editors that the lack of drama and of criticism and argument would make the book banal and of little interest to the public. They assured me that this war book would be better received if it were factual and personal without any trace of theatrics. So the manuscript was finished, and in the fall of 1948 an ad hoc partnership of the *Herald Tribune* and Doubleday, in the persons of Mr. Robinson and Mr. Black, made an offer which I considered more than generous. I expressed again and again the fear that they would have an expensive white elephant on their hands. They smiled and said that, to the contrary, they were not sure they were treating me fairly. Both publishers and I later became warm friends.

The book sold unbelievably well. In the fall of 1966—eighteen years later—I asked Doubleday for a roundup of the story and was assured that the book had been a profitable venture on their part. At least 1,170,000 copies of *Crusade in Europe* were sold in the United States, and there were contracts for twenty-two foreign-language editions.

THINKING back on whatever happened to my privacy, I have to think of what happened to my politics. There were journalists who believed that I was a candidate for public office. All journalists know that political life can be rugged, yet they assume automatically that every man who has the chance wants to get into it. Among those pushing me toward office were people whose opinions I valued, mostly educators and writers who shared my convictions about the need for balance among the several branches of government. However, I was insistent in my belief that a man's military success was not, alone, important to the nation's peacetime progress.

I had other personal ambitions. Mamie and I had always agreed that as soon as I got out of the service we would go to that little college town, and probably buy a modest ranch. After I entered the office of Chief of Staff I received numerous offers to join either commercial or educational institutions. The commercial offers I could decline out of hand: I did not believe it fitting for a man who had been honored by his government with military responsibilities to profit financially for no reason other than that his name was widely known. Offers from the educational field were something else. I looked at those long and hard.

On the political side, pressures increased. Finally, I put my views before the public in a letter I sent to a newspaper publisher who wanted to enter my name in the New Hampshire presidential primary of March 1948. I worked over the draft of the letter carefully because I did not want to make it appear that I was arrogant or aloof—but I did want to make it definite that I was not going to get involved in politics.

I ended, in a model case of cracked crystal ball, "In any event, my decision to remove myself completely from the political scene is definite and positive."

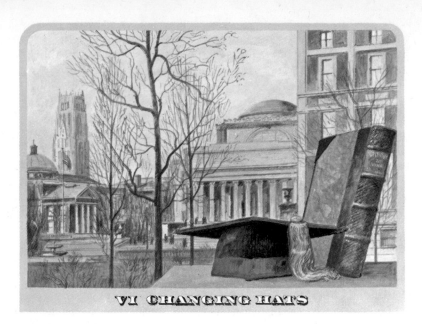

VI CHANGING HATS

Professor Ike

WHEN A COMMITTEE from the Board of Trustees of Columbia University asked me to become President of that great institution, I at first declined because I felt the post should go to a man who was not only a good executive but was known as a scholar. The committee was not discouraged. To all my hesitations, they countered that I had a broad experience in dealing with human beings and human problems; that I knew at first hand many areas of the earth and their peoples; that my interest in the training of young Americans offset my lack of formal preparation. They added that their invitation had the complete approval of Columbia's former President, Nicholas Murray Butler, that many-sided scholar who personified Columbia in the public eye.

My preference, as I've said, inclined me toward a small school in a rural setting. In such a place, where friendly ties with students and faculty could easily be developed, I hoped to share with them the lessons in hindsight from a reasonably full life. Such a role I would have loved and it would have been easy.

Columbia, on the other hand, was a formidable challenge. Located in the world's greatest city, it was an international mecca for students and scholars. Its twenty-six or so acres were a microcosm of the intellectual world. Famed philosophers, scientists, historians were familiar figures on the sidewalks. The students, who in the undergraduate and graduate schools numbered around thirty thousand, were variety itself, in race, dress, speech. In all this diversity, a single concern—the search for knowledge and its dissemination—gave Columbia homogeneity.

My difficulty in deciding was based on a natural fear that I could hardly hope to discharge responsibilities so different from all my own experience and in a place already so richly endowed with leadership in its deans and senior faculty. On the other hand, I saw in Columbia opportunities as rewarding as the environment might be strange and difficult. In the end, I decided that if the faculty could stand me, I could stand the job.

For more than half a century, Nicholas Murray Butler had been Columbia's chief, as scholar and builder, as spokesman and showpiece. My selection as President must have caused grumblings about the danger that a professional soldier might corrupt academic standards. But I soon learned that deep within the University structure my arrival had caused little stir at all.

On Friday evening, for example, Low Library, where the administrative offices were concentrated, closed its doors until Monday morning. For me, Saturday was just another day in the week, when I expected to put in at least a few hours at the desk. For the first few Saturdays I walked to the Library with a staff member who had the proper keys. One Saturday I attempted to penetrate the vastness of Low without my guide, only to be confronted by a campus policeman who refused me entrance.

"I'd like to get into the President's office," I said.

"There won't be anybody there," he said.

When I added that my name was Eisenhower, his firm stand

changed not an iota. Nor did it when I assured him that I was President of the University. At that point another policeman, who had apparently seen my picture in the paper, came along and vouched for me. The ivory towers of learning on Morningside Heights were guarded by more than venerable philosophers.

Late one evening I visited old East Hall, which housed the studios of the Fine Arts Department. I had heard about the work of one of the painters there and wanted to see it. During the visit, a watchman asked me to identify myself. When I said that I was President of the University, a look of vigorous disbelief crossed his face and he was prepared to order my instant departure when the artist came out of his studio and saved me.

Later I learned that the watchman had reported discovering in East Hall an elderly man who claimed to be President of Columbia but did not look it. The guard was accustomed to Nicholas Murray Butler, who looked the role to perfection.

WHEN I first saw our future residence at 60 Morningside Drive, I was a little disturbed by its mansionlike appearance. Mamie set to work to brighten it up, but I still needed a room in which I could flee grandeur. There was no attic, and the basement was beyond redemption. But on the roof, where a water tank had been, was a sort of penthouse. From it, on clear nights, you could see the lights of Long Island. Here we put furniture, dear from association but ineligible for the gracious rooms below. Here I could escape from the demands of official life and be myself.

Soon after we moved in, an artist, Thomas E. Stephens, began a portrait of Mamie. I was an interested spectator. After a sitting one day, he asked Mamie to go with him through the house to find a proper place to hang the portrait. When the two of them left, it occurred to me to use the paints remaining on his palette to try poking away on my own. The only subject I could think of was right before me—Mamie's unfinished portrait. Using a clean dustcloth tacked to a board as a canvas, I started out and kept going until the two explorers came back about forty-five minutes later. I displayed my version of Mamie, weird and wonderful to behold, and we all laughed heartily. But Tom Stephens urged me to keep trying.

A few days later a package arrived. Opening it, I found a present from Mr. Stephens: everything I could possibly need—except ability—to start painting. I looked upon it as a wonderful gesture and a sheer waste of money. But I left the open package in my room, and one day I took the plunge. In spite of my complete lack of talent, the attempt to paint was absorbing. I had a new hobby, and the penthouse retreat was an ideal studio.

The one thing I could do well from the beginning was to cover hands, clothes and floor with more paint than ever reached the canvas. After eighteen years, I am still messy. I still refuse to refer to my productions as paintings. They are daubs, born of my love of color and my pleasure in experimenting. I attempt only simple compositions, and I destroy two out of each three I start.

In the White House, in bad weather, painting was one way to survive away from the desk. In a little room on the second floor, paints and easel were ready to use. Often, going to lunch, I'd stop off for ten minutes to paint. In Gettysburg I've tried landscapes and still lifes, but with magnificent audacity, I have tried more portraits than anything else—I've also burned more.

THE FIRST member of the University family to greet Mamie and me when we arrived at 60 Morningside in May 1948 was David Syrett, the nine-year-old son of a faculty member. He was outfitted in cowboy togs. Meeting us at our new front door, he made a good picture for the waiting photographers. Better still, for us, the informality—and the age of the University's unofficial greeter—set the right tone. I think David was more interested in getting an autograph than anything else. Our picture made page one in many newspapers the following day, I am told.

Fifteen years later, when I was in New York for the 1963 Alexander Hamilton dinner, David appeared again. We were photographed, and several newspapers ran a then-and-now layout, one of them pointing out that young Syrett had developed much more than I had since our first meeting. He was preparing to do his graduate work in history at the University of London.

The years between the two meetings had been for both of us, I think, exciting, unexpected and rewarding. Young David Syrett, on that May day almost twenty years ago, crystallized for me the idea that humanity would be present among the humanities and sciences. In the middle of that great center of learning, one small boy had set himself a mission and wanted proof of its accomplishment. In his eager curiosity, forthright warmness and initiative, he got it. My autograph was an urban counterpart to the jackrabbit a country boy might have exhibited after a chase.

I arrived at Columbia determined to enjoy a firsthand association with the students. However, I had not fully realized the scope of my other duties and responsibilities. Supervising the management of a vast endowment that included one of the largest real estate empires in New York; satisfying the demand for speeches, alumni appearances, ceremonial functions; correcting an appalling deficit that threatened academic standards, salary scales and Columbia's traditional objective of excellence—all these soon sealed me off from communication with the young men and women. Students, the chief reason for a university's being, and for me the paramount appeal of campus life, were numerical figures on forms and unknown faces on campus. This became a source of vast annoyance to me.

In the Army, whenever I became fed up with meetings, protocol and paper work, I could rehabilitate myself by a visit with the troops. As a university president, perhaps less sure of myself, I did not at first permit myself as much freedom. I know now that I should have tossed the rules of academic propriety into the trash can, abandoning my office and its minutiae more frequently—if only by looking in over Lou Little's shoulder while he worked out with the squad, or advising married students on the GI bill how to decorate their apartments. As it was, I never succeeded in liberating myself from the traditional decorum and pomp of the university president's role.

But if learning to take a place in academic life was not simple, learning to like the people of Columbia was. Most of the men and women of the faculty and administration were brilliant in their talk, profound in their thoughts, and enthusiastic about the University. I conceived an instant liking for them and they immensely broadened my horizons. Among them I felt myself a student who learned more than I could hope to give in return.

THE COLUMBIA faculty, I believed, could extend the moral and intellectual strength of the University and serve the whole nation by taking the lead in studying the vast problems thrust upon us after World War II. Among these problems were: First, the mental and physical health of our young people, among far too many of whom weaknesses of mind and body had been revealed during the war years. Second, the aggressive demands of pressure groups and special interests in every area of our social and economic life; these contradicted the American tradition that no part of our country should prosper except as the whole prospered. And third, a sort of torpor about individual responsibility, a disbelief that an individual could accomplish much for the good of all. This seemed to suggest a disregard for the meaning of American citizenship, its obligations as well as its rights.

I saw on our faculty an immense pool of talent, scholarly and humane, which could propose solutions to such problems. With Dean Philip Young of the Graduate School of Business, I began to elaborate the idea of a truly national assembly where we could add to the University's resources other experts from every walk of life. Gathered together, free from telephone calls and urgent summonses to make instant decisions, they might examine the larger problems, and arrive at working conclusions.

Working toward this idea became an absorbing pursuit for me. Through most of 1949 I talked about it, wrote about it, thought about it incessantly. Till late in the year, I got no farther than a name—the American Assembly. Then Averell Harriman became interested. He offered the family home, Arden House, high on a ridge near the Hudson, as a site for the Assembly. Now known as the Harriman campus of Columbia University, this old mansion has witnessed scores of meetings concerned with almost every aspect of human society. Throughout the years, its influence has been far-reaching beyond my dreams. Much of the time I think its beginnings were my principal success as University President.

A project called the Conservation of Human Resources had its beginnings in my wartime realization that we had seriously neglected the preparation of our young people to be vigorous, productive members of society. This neglect was tragically tabulated in the armed forces rejection records. I suspected that a study of these records could produce guideposts for our future conduct as a nation. Dr. Eli Ginzberg, whose profound scholar-

ship did not blunt an almost boyish enthusiasm about any proposal for the betterment of human living, took over this project with a passion. The support I was able to produce in furthering his research and advancing his proposals is still one of my proudest memories.

The Institute for the Study of War and Peace, the new Engineering Center headed by Dean John Donning, the Citizenship Education Project, were innovations we worked out during my Columbia years. And there was one innovation that reflected a country boy's distaste for concrete and macadam.

Our "campus" had a factory-yard appearance that distressed me. Leaving my office in the Low Library on a hot day I looked down the long flight of stone steps, across 116th Street, crowded with parked cars and creeping traffic, over the dry gravel and the clay of tennis courts to Butler Library, grassless, treeless. This was the physical center and heart of the University. It should be a green oasis. In my mind's eye, I could see the hot and noisy street converted to lawn, with automobiles forever barred.

It was, I thought, an improvement that could be accomplished in a few months and at little expense. But settling one problem seemed to spawn two or three more. The project dragged on, and I was living in the White House, surrounded by lawn, before the dream became reality and 116th Street a pleasant mall.

From the alumni point of view, my largest contribution to Columbia's stature may well have been my first. Before my arrival, I had known only one of my future colleagues. Lou Little, who was football coach at Georgetown University back in the twenties when I was coaching an Army team, had for many years been a fixture at Columbia. On the eve of my departure from Washington for Columbia, he was offered the head coaching job at Yale. The alumni panicked. A group of them, headed by Bill Donovan of the OSS in World War II, and Frank Hogan, District Attorney of New York, escorted Lou to see me at Fort Myer. With no professional or financial arguments to offer, I was reduced to a personal appeal. "Lou, you cannot do this to me," I said. "You're one of the reasons I'm going to Columbia."

He seemed flustered, but recovered quickly, and we talked football, reminisced, discussed the state of the game. For once, all my years of coaching seemed to make sense. But I was uneasy about what Lou's decision would be until I heard that as soon as he'd arrived back in his hotel he had called his wife, Loretta, in New York and said: "Stop packing. We're not going!"

I am told that my triumph was cited by the Columbia alumni as proof that I had leadership potential. And there was, I think, a substantial academic by-product. Other universities, with more ready cash than Columbia had, were raiding the talent pool of Columbia's staff. Had Lou been lured to a rival campus, the University might have been hurt by a chain reaction of raids from other schools against which it had, until we could raise the salary levels, little protection except appeals to loyalty.

My life at the University, exhausting enough for a neophyte in education, was complicated by a presidential summons in the fall of 1948. I was asked to go to Washington regularly to serve as senior adviser to James Forrestal, Secretary of the new Defense Department, created in 1947 when the Congress passed an act unifying the armed services. At the same time—due to the illness of Admiral William Leahy—I would serve as informal chairman of the Joint Chiefs of Staff. I was assured that it was to be part-time duty, but it turned out to be no less than a major role in the reconstruction of the military establishment. Sometimes I was an umpire between disputing services—the new Defense Department was plagued with rivalries—and sometimes a hatchetman on what Fox Conner used to call Fool Schemes. Commuting between Washington and New York ate up a good many hours, and making half a dozen speeches a week for the University was something of a burden, but the two jobs were not incompatible, and much of the time they were inspiring and rewarding. As the several kinds of work extended through many months, however, my health was affected.

My real acquaintanceship with James Forrestal began when, as Chief of Staff of the Army, I met him during the war. Now I became one of his close associates. He was the first man in government who warned me that in his opinion our government was being quite unwary in its dealings with the Soviets. Since I had, because of personal experience, become increasingly sure that the Soviets would not look upon the United States as anything other than a potential enemy, I had a high regard for Mr. Forrestal's opinion. He served in his very important post with as great a degree of selflessness as almost anyone I could name.

In appearance, Mr. Forrestal was rather pugnacious. However, in carrying on the heavy responsibilities of the Secretary of Defense, he seemed cautious and hesitant. He'd get into difficulties when tough decisions were placed before him, and when his advisers engaged in controversies among themselves. At such times he would come to what seemed a definite conclusion, only to reopen the question later. When this happened more than once, I realized that he was a worrier; he allowed problems to stay with him after they had presumably been solved.

The most serious of these occasions that I recall was one on which the Navy and the Air Force took opposite sides on the question of developing the B-36 bomber. Hour after hour we listened to opposing arguments, and finally to the advice of our scientists to the effect that if the United States was to have, during the next few years, any intercontinental bombing plane we must build a number of B-36s. This seemingly persuaded Jim Forrestal and, with my strong concurrence, he gave the go-ahead signal.

But within minutes he was in my office. "You know, Ike," he said, "I think we'll have to go into this B-36 matter a little more deeply." I was shocked, and realized that either the man was losing his memory or was becoming too confused to concentrate.

As time went by, though I watched for confirmation of my fears, I concluded that it had been some temporary situation brought on by intense study and sleeplessness. However, two of the Secretary's civilian associates came to me one day to say that he was showing signs of a nervous breakdown and ought to take a short leave. I promised to do my best to get him to do so.

It wasn't easy. Finally, I met him head on about it. "Mr. Secretary," I said, "you showed a great deal of confidence in me by asking me to act as your personal adviser. Obviously, unless you can go away for a week or ten days without feeling the place will fall around your ears, you haven't that sort of confidence in me. I might as well give up and go back to New York."

To this he reacted earnestly. "Oh, by no means," he said. And he faithfully promised to go away that evening for a few days.

The following morning he was in his office as if nothing had happened. I chided him, and he seemed to have completely forgotten the conversation. I was now convinced that something was really wrong. I talked again with his civilian assistants.

Ever since the election of 1948, Mr. Forrestal had been quite unhappy. Because of his conviction that Defense, like the State Department, should be administered on behalf of the United States and without regard to party, he had, although a lifelong

Democrat, declined to participate in the campaign. According to him, this attitude had incurred the enmity of the White House staff, which was now "out to get him." Whether such concerns intensified his nervousness I cannot say, but I believe its basic cause was overwork and lack of cooperation, not only in the government at large but within the Defense Department itself.

In the early months of 1949 it became obvious that his condition was deteriorating rapidly. When he said he would have to resign if the difficulties he was having in the Department kept up, I did not discourage him. As much as I liked him and admired his good qualities, I came to believe that this would be the best thing he could do. About the first of March he submitted a letter of resignation to the President. His place was to be taken by Louis Johnson, a past commander of the American Legion and an Assistant Secretary of War under Franklin Roosevelt.

Now it appeared that I, too, had pushed myself too hard. On the evening of March 21, I was struck with an attack of a most distressing kind (one that foreshadowed the ileitis of 1956). While I lay stretched out in my Washington hotel room, Mr. Forrestal called. "Ike," he said, "I simply can't turn this job over to Louis Johnson. He knows nothing about the problems and things will go to pot. I'll have to withdraw my resignation."

I replied with all my strength, urging him not to do anything so foolish. I said it would have no effect in any event because the ceremony of transfer had been set up for that day and would be impossible to stop. He seemed to accept this counsel.

Afterward, I became so ill that I lost touch with events. For days my head was not off the pillow, and I was forbidden solid food and cigarettes, but I was too ill to miss either. Then I woke one morning and asked for a cigarette.

My physician, General Howard Snyder, was no fanatic about smoking. Still, he did insist that I should reduce my consumption to less than my customary four packs. Although I was still sick, my head was clear enough to ponder this advice. Cigarettes, I knew, were doing me no good, but I rebelled at the prospect of a life in which they would have to be rationed by the clock. Inevitably, when I had exhausted my day's quota, I would either have to suffer the agonies of deprivation or start again on the four-pack-a-day road. "I'll just have to quit," I said. And I did.

When I was well enough, I went to Florida for recuperation. There I heard that Jim Forrestal had been sent to Bethesda Naval Hospital in distressing mental shape. Not long afterward we learned of his death, apparently caused by a leap from the top floor of the hospital. It was a sad end to the man with the fighter's face, the lonely responsibility of establishing a vitally important new Cabinet post, and a limitless devotion to his country.

WHILE I was Chief of Staff, Mamie and I had frequently discussed the sort of home that would fit us best, if we ever got one. Now, after moving into Columbia, we started thinking again about a place of our own. I wanted an escape from concrete into the countryside. Mamie, who had spent a lifetime adjusting herself to other people's housing designs, or the lack of them, wanted a place that conformed to her notions of what a home should be. In the fall of 1950, we finally did something about it.

My wartime friend, George Allen, and his wife, Mary, had recently bought a farmhouse in the Gettysburg area, a mile or so south of the battlefield. They urged us to consider the same sort of move. Gettysburg is within easy traveling distance of Washington and New York; the idea was attractive. So one weekend we went with the Allens on a farm-hunting expedition. The most appealing property we saw was a farm of not quite 190 acres, the house dwarfed by a huge barn, at the end of a lane half a mile long. The buildings had seen better days. So had the soil. It would take work and money, but this was a chance, I thought, to prove that careful husbandry could restore land to its original fertility. The view of the mountains to the west was good. And Mamie had found the place she wanted.

To complete the story, I must move ahead in time. The ink was not long dry on the deed to our property when a message from President Truman ended our days at Columbia and sent us back to Europe. Our plans for a home were deferred once more.

Later, entering the White House in 1953, Mamie said, "I still have no home of my own." She made up her mind to start restoring the old farmhouse, come what may. I had an engineering survey made and found, much to her dismay, that most of the house was actually a log cabin with a brick veneer covering its walls. The logs were moldy and worm-eaten, about two hundred years old. There was nothing to do but tear the place down.

So anxious was Mamie to retain even a fragment of the original structure, that when she found one portion of the wall and a Dutch oven in which no logs had been used, she built a complete house around them. We built step by step, according to Mamie's ideas. When she occasionally forgot a detail or two, work would have to be redone. For example, when the walls were going up, we discovered that no plans had been made for central air conditioning, and the walls had to be torn down again so that air ducts could be installed. But the work was done well and the house did conform largely to her ideas.

Before work began, the builder, a friend of ours named Charlie Tompkins, asked me whether I wanted to use union labor or local labor, which was not unionized but which he considered competent. I told him that as President of the United States I would be dealing with unions and I thought it only proper to use union labor. When the house was finished, he showed me two sets of books—one of costs actually incurred and the other of what the cost would have been if we had used local labor. The additional expense was $65,000.

This involved much more than a mere difference in wages, of course. It was caused by the time spent in transporting laborers, in some instances from as far away as Washington, requiring us to pay for an eight-hour day in return for only four hours' work. Finally, when the bill was handed to us, it amounted to $215,000. This did include $45,000 for improvements other than to the house itself, but it was considerably more than we had thought of spending. We scraped the bottom of the barrel and Mamie drew on some money she had inherited, so that by mid-1955 we had a place we could call home, and it was paid for.

We have now lived there for more than eleven years, counting weekends during the latter part of my Presidency. While it is beautiful to us, we have, like other home builders, found things we would like to change. But we have learned to live with our mistakes. And we have learned, too, that one room can constitute a home. Our favorite at Gettysburg is a glassed-in porch where we spend hours from early breakfast to late evening. Facing east, with the morning sun brightening it, and in shadow through the heat of a summer day, the furnishings casual and designed for comfort, it provides an oasis of relaxation.

We were on our way to Denver for a Christmas visit with Mamie's folks when President Truman's call reached me. He said that he would like me to command the NATO forces then being assembled in Europe. He put it as a request, not an order, but he was the President of the United States and I had been a soldier all my life. I was one still. I told him I would report at any time he said. He said to go ahead with our leave in Denver, and that he would see me in Washington after our return.

I was reluctant to end my career at Columbia, but I felt that my enforced absence, at a time when important new projects were getting under way, would be harmful. I therefore told Fred Coykendall, Chairman of Columbia's Board of Trustees, that I would resign. After discussing it with his associates, he said that all were in favor of giving me an indefinite leave; only in the event that my absence was prolonged beyond two years or so would they consider my resignation. I accepted their decision gladly for it permitted me the hope of eventual return.

The SHAPE of things to come.

AT FOUR O'CLOCK in the morning, on Washington's Birthday, 1951, Mamie and I were roused from a sound sleep and debarked from the *Queen Elizabeth* to drink champagne toasts in a warehouse on the Cherbourg docks. Because this was the region where the Allied forces under my command had begun the liberation of

Europe, the ship was met by the mayor of the city, his council and a number of other officials.

The toasts were frequent, grandiose, and delivered in French. My replies were brief, for my French was halting, the sound approximately that of a Kansas threshing machine. For Mamie and me the greeting was especially charming, an auspicious start to our residence in France.

That winter, the world outlook was bleak for those of us who only five years before had fought a war to eradicate tyranny from the earth. It now seemed that, at any moment, the arrogance of Communist power might be converted into offensive action against the West. It had already exploded in the Far East, where the United Nations troops in Korea were suffering tragic reverses.

Few things were predictable about the supreme command of an enterprise that required wholehearted cooperation by twelve nations—nations whose territories were as small as tiny Luxembourg or as globe-spanning as the United States and Great Britain. We were attempting to forge a unified organization out of many peoples and personalities, many languages, diverse cultures, faiths and histories. Apprehensions about a potential aggressive move against the West provided the starting point for an alliance for survival. But we were not at war. The absence of an imminent threat meant the absence of strong motivation and we had no assurance that NATO could win its members' complete allegiance. A personal reconnaissance was my first job.

In eighteen days, and in bitter winter weather, I visited eleven European capitals. I was favorably impressed by the governments with which I conferred. Of course, each wanted more American strength in Europe than we then had, and I agreed to try to attain *temporary* reinforcement, but I pointed out that the United States would be providing a strong Navy and Air Force for the benefit of all and that we would always be one of the principal arsenals of democracy in the event of trouble. I told them that the thickly populated areas of Western Europe should be able to provide the vast bulk of the land forces needed, even if we had to provide a few divisions to give them confidence.

That period has long since elapsed. I believe, however, that we should keep in Europe, for the foreseeable future, a force of reasonable size—about the equivalent of two divisions. Their presence there would be clear evidence that in the event of general war, we would be in it from the beginning.

President Truman had suggested that at the end of the trip I should report my conclusions at an informal session with the Congress, and in a nationwide broadcast to the American people. Aboard the plane, I began to work on the two speeches; few have ever given me so much trouble. On one hand, I had to stress as forcefully as I could the weakness, almost defenselessness, of Western Europe against possible irruption from the East. On the other hand I had to stress just as forcefully the spiritual vigor of the European peoples, who, having labored with the help of the Marshall Plan* to repair the devastation of war, now found in the North Atlantic Treaty new hope.

The three principal points I wanted to make were: that the preservation of a free America required our participation in the defense of Western Europe; that success *was* attainable, given unity in spirit and action; and that our own major role should be as a storehouse of munitions and equipment, although initially a fairly heavy commitment of American troops would be required—something like six divisions. I told the Congress all this, as I had the President the day before. Then, in executive sessions, first of the Senate Foreign Relations Committee, and then of the House Armed Services and Foreign Relations committees, I was questioned almost to the point of cross-examination.

I came to realize that these representatives of the people were sharply divided about the Republic's role in world affairs. A hard core of extreme nationalists seemed to be echoing the isolationist philosophy of more than ten years earlier. Others were skeptical of our Allies' dependability and even their will to defend themselves. Still others felt our contribution should be limited to money and supplies. Fortunately many shared the conviction that

---

* Or European Recovery Plan—a postwar program of U.S. aid, initiated by General Marshall.

NATO as a collective defense could be a success. But I felt I had to make it clear in person, to those opposed, that by going to Europe we were only protecting our own frontier. The long-range bomber had moved America's frontier to the heart of Europe, as far as military effectiveness was concerned.

At that moment, the debate in Congress centered on two issues: the constitutional power of the President to deploy troops abroad in time of peace as he saw fit, without the approval of Congress; and the size of the forces that the United States should deploy in Europe. The President, a Democrat, favored a strong commitment of approximately six divisions, and it was natural to suppose that his party would follow his lead. Some Republicans also believed that the free world could exist only through effective cooperation among its principal nations. But an important element in the Republican party was opposed to the President on both points. I felt that before leaving for Europe I should see what I could do to smooth over the differences. I asked Senator Robert Taft for an appointment to discuss the NATO project.

We had a long talk. I think he may have been a bit suspicious of my motives—a good many persons had been urging me publicly to run for the Presidency. My first purpose was to be assured that when I got back to Europe, the United States government would be solid in support of NATO. If such assurance was forthcoming from the chief spokesman of what seemed to be the opposition, I then planned to issue a statement so strong that it would kill off any further speculation about me as a presidential candidate. On the NATO question I used all the persuasion I could, and our conversation was long and friendly; but Senator Taft refused to commit himself. This aroused my fears that isolationism was stronger in the Congress than I had suspected.

His refusal meant two big disappointments to me. I could not now feel the unity of my government behind me, and I had lost the chance to settle the political question once and for all. In the absence of the assurance I had been seeking, it would be silly to throw away whatever political influence I might possess that would help keep us on the right track.

To PRODUCE ALLIED COOPERATION in World War II was far easier than developing a military defense for NATO and peace. This was an enterprise without precedent. In wartime, neither Britain nor the United States ever held back in the hope that the other would perform the necessary but nasty chores. In time of peace, and in spite of common danger, the same desire to make maximum contributions did not always prevail. Draft laws, for example, required too short a tour of military service to allow the kind of technical training necessary with highly sophisticated modern weaponry. I went the rounds of NATO governments urging a two-year term of service, but it appeared that none would risk incurring political resentment in its own country.

NATO was, nevertheless, a necessary mechanism. The Marshall Plan had not yet reached full fruition—self-confidence was still lacking throughout Western Europe. One of NATO's greatest goals was to restore and sustain that confidence. Existing defense forces could not match, or even scratch, those of the Communist bloc. But the knowledge that a unified, progressive effort to generate strength was under way had an almost electrifying effect on European thinking.

Clearly each NATO country could not be expected to produce a rounded defense. It would be ridiculous, for instance, to ask the smaller nations to create their own nuclear capability. Our effort was to mobilize the troops and weapons most easily and effectively produced in each nation, and so lighten the burden on each.

As we studied how best to do this, the idea of a single operational command for NATO's defense forces was conceived. Under this plan, known as the European Defense Community, each unit of division strength would be homogeneous as to nationality, while the larger units, corps and armies, could contain within themselves units of different countries.

From the first, the small countries agreed with the idea. Originally, Mr. Churchill was opposed. And the plan, largely designed by the French, soon ran into opposition—from the French, worrying lest Germany become so powerful that it might dominate the Allied establishment. Mr. Churchill's reasons were less clear, for he had been himself a major influence in achieving a somewhat similar organization in World War II.

For many months, my staff worked hard with the military officials of all NATO countries to get the kind of organization and command system that would give no nation a position of overweening influence. At the same time, they worked to produce the maximum defensive force.

By May of 1952, all the governments, including France, had approved the plan. By now Greece and Turkey had joined the organization, and we were sure that within a few years West Germany would become a full-fledged member also, bringing the total number of powers to fifteen. In a year and a half we had surmounted the obstacles of nationalism, provincialism, and outright disbelief that the job could be done. These nations had proved unified in purpose and performance—in the planning councils, on the maneuver fields. NATO had become a vital, intercontinental institution, a historic fact. Whatever the future might hold, and whatever history might decide, I am glad this mighty force has existed.

With the work I had been sent to do largely accomplished, I felt I could be released from active duty. During 1951 tremendous demands had been put on me to get into politics. Men of every kind and from both parties had visited my headquarters, each with his own reasons for asserting that I owed it to the country to become a political candidate. With none of this did I agree. Nor did I believe that my visitors, despite their political acumen and experience, reflected majority opinion in either of the parties or in the country.

Until March 1952, I made no personal contribution to the issue other than the statement of Republican affiliation I had felt it necessary to make in January. This gave me a little peace of mind, for I was sure that the Taft forces within the Republican Party were strong enough to deny anyone else the nomination. In this belief I was steadfast until the New Hampshire primary, for which my name had been entered.

The day before it was held, I dictated a letter to Arthur

Summerfield, the Republican leader in Michigan, declining an invitation to visit that state before the national convention. He had asked me, along with other "candidates," to be seen and heard by the Republicans there. I explained that I could not accept because I was not a candidate. The following morning, reading the letter over, I added a postscript saying that before nightfall the New Hampshire voters might very well eliminate me from the possibility of candidacy anytime, anywhere.

They did not. For weeks thereafter I had to wrestle with the facts and arguments so often and so long presented. Finally, I came to the conclusion that, with numerous people I deeply respected stressing our country's need for a change in political control and domestic programs, I should return to the United States. I would abide by the decisions of my party and of the electorate if I were nominated.

We looked around us, said good-by to Europe, and turned toward home. Once again, Mamie and I began packing.

The Town and Dr. Moore

The Town and Dr. Moore

A condensation of the book by

Agatha Young

Illustrations by Bernie Fuchs

"Medicine's changing so fast these days, we have to look out the patient doesn't get lost," said aging Dr. Moore, who with his admirable but out-of-date private hospital served the medical needs of Haddon, Vermont.

"The trouble with Dr. Moore," said the bright young surgeon from New York, "is that he cares more about his patients' comfort and happiness than about an accurate diagnosis."

"A half-dead hospital is worse than none at all," said the local banker.

"We want the hospital just as it is," said Moore's pretty niece, May.

* * *

Touched off by a fatal accident, a crisis arose that affected the whole town. The dedicated Dr. Moore; his partner, fiery Dr. Perkins; and their beloved hospital were all called to account. People found they had strong views on the way the town's medical affairs were run, and they didn't hesitate to express them.

How the doctors and the women they love weather the storm, and how they and the town together solve the problem of modern medical care, make an enthralling story. Mrs. Young's Vermont townspeople are very real and recognizable, and the fright and illness and sorrow that Dr. Moore so gently helps them through are those of men and women everywhere.

Chapter 1

T HE CLOCK in the church steeple at the far end of the village slowly struck ten. The sound came softly through the window of the hospital room, muted by distance and by the golden haze of the September morning. Dr. Edward Moore pushed his stethoscope into the pocket of his tweed jacket and drew the bedclothes over the lifeless form of the old woman.

While he did so, a part of his mind was aware of sounds beyond the closed door of the room, familiar, well-loved sounds that meant the smooth running of his hospital. Someone passed in the corridor with light, hurrying steps. Someone else wheeled a cart on which utensils rattled. That would be Helen coming from the operating room—a better instrument nurse than a hospital this size had any right to expect. Farther off, he heard the loud voice of Dr. Perkins, the only other staff member of Haddon Hospital. Howard Perkins was one of those surgeons who come out of an operating room a trifle above themselves, not boisterous exactly but with their personalities enlarged. The hospital awoke to an intenser life whenever Perkins was within its walls.

Dr. Moore turned to a wizened old woman sitting beside the bed, who stared at him with bright, fearful eyes. He met the gaze pityingly. "Alice," he said, "your sister's troubles are over now."

At first she made no reply. Then, startlingly, she shrieked at him. "*No!*" Gnarled fingers came up over her face and she wept such a flood of tears that it was a marvel her dried-up body could produce them.

Moore put his hand on her shoulder, giving it a slight pressure, and gradually her tears ceased. He could see self-pity beginning to crowd out sorrow, and knew that old Alice had found a means of coping with her trouble.

"I ain't agoin' to live long, Doctor." She spoke as though that would serve the world right. Then in a kind of screech that made him shudder, "What am I goin' to do? You tell me that."

"We'll talk about it after you've had time to rest a little, Alice. I have to go now but I'll send someone to look after you." He left the room, shutting the door behind him.

Radio music and the rattle of dishes came faintly from the maternity ward as he passed. There was here in the hospital a life, a character, and after thirty years even a kind of maturity independent of him, its creator. Like a child grown up, he thought, but still financially dependent. Every year the hospital failed, by a slightly greater amount, to earn its way. Neither dredging in his own pocket nor increasing bank loans was any longer sufficient; a new approach to the question of money was essential.

Burdened by these gloomy thoughts, he arrived at the top of the massive staircase that had been the chief grandeur of this mansion before he converted it into a hospital. There his attention was caught by a worn place in the linoleum. It was the sort of thing the inspectors for the Hospital Accreditation Board fastened on. Frowning, Dr. Moore went on down the stairs.

The hospital had an elevator in the brick wing that had been built by Howard Perkins when he came here fifteen years ago. Because it was his fifty thousand dollars—or at least his wife's—that had paid for it, and because it contained the operating room, Perkins regarded the wing as his special province and he always used the elevator.

Moore used the staircase. Its solidity pleased him, for he was a big man, solidly built himself, his body not betraying his sixty-five years except in the stoop of his heavy shoulders. From halfway down the stairs he looked into the hall below where his elderly head nurse, Edna Judson, sat at a desk. At the sound of his step, her impassive face softened into an expression reserved only for him. Their relationship was a special one, based on years of regard and trust. Tall and thin, Edna had a Gothic look. The effect was increased by a monstrosity she wore on her head, a high white cap rising to a forward peak like a Punch's cap.

"Edna," Moore said, "Ila Henderson is gone. Will you go up to Alice?" The cap bent forward with a beaklike motion.

"How will she carry on in that tumbledown place all alone?"

"She's no worse off than lots of others in the back country. The neighbors can look after her for a while, poor old soul. I don't suppose there's any coffee in the kitchen, is there?"

"I've been keeping it hot for you."

"Fine." He crossed the hall to his office. In the doorway he paused, looking around the cramped little room, at the old desk littered with papers, at the black-framed license to practice medicine in Vermont, at the photograph of his wife on the bookcase. This looking was a sort of reaffirmation of himself, a habit with him whenever, as today, death had dealt him a defeat.

He let himself down heavily into his battered swivel chair and picked up the telephone. "Get me Nortons', will you please?" He was speaking to the central operator, exerting his self-assumed prerogative not to be bothered with numbers. Listening to the ring, he allowed himself a pleasing, mind's-eye view of Ianthe Norton's ample figure and intelligent brown eyes. At the sound of her voice, he said, "Ianthe? How is Nat today?"

He listened to her reply thoughtfully, nodding his thanks as Edna came in with a cup of coffee. "Perkins thought it looked like a fatty tumor, not a recurrence," he said into the telephone. "But we'll get a lab report in a couple of days. I'm going to New York tomorrow to look for a young surgeon to assist here and I'll get in touch with you when I get back. Don't let Nat worry. . . ."

Moore was searching his desk for a death certificate when the door was thrown open with some force. Dr. Perkins, a big man like Moore, filled the doorway. He looked angry, which was not unusual, and Moore's manner became placatingly mild.

"Hullo, Howard. Come in. I was just talking to Ianthe. I said Nat's growth was a fatty tumor."

"You know damn well it wasn't, and it's my guess Nat knows it too." Perkins dropped into a chair. "I came in to tell you the Bovie broke down this morning. I've been operating alone for more than a month while you've been trying to find a replacement for that worthless character that got sick, and now the electric cautery quits, so I have to tie off every blood vessel by hand. We've got to have a new Bovie, Ed."

"You couldn't see your way clear—"

"I could not. That fifty thousand—all the money Adele inherited—was to be all, remember? You've got to take drastic steps, Ed, or we're going down the drain."

"You know I'm planning to."

"Plans. You're a dreamer. You—"

There were quick footsteps outside, and Edna Judson looked in. "Dr. Perkins. Excuse me. The little Jones girl is hemorrhaging."

Perkins stood up. "All right, Edna. Get her into the operating room. Ether drip."

He turned to Moore and spoke pleasantly, as though there had been no loud words. "I'll handle the ether myself. I imagine you've got plenty to do before you go to New York tomorrow."

Left alone, Moore picked up some typewritten sheets with columns of figures on them. He studied them, frowning; accounts were not his strong point. After a while he reluctantly concluded that he would have to ask Stoner for another bank loan.

THE DOOR to Timothy Stoner's well-furnished office stood open. Seeing Moore approaching from the main part of the bank, Stoner, thin and bloodless-looking, came forward and held out his hand. "Sit down, Ed. What's on your mind?"

"One thing only," Moore said, and Stoner laughed. The quality of the laugh made Moore angry, though he tried to hide it. "My estimate was too optimistic when I asked for the last loan."

Stoner swung gently back and forth in his desk chair. The powerful dark-rimmed glasses he wore gave the look he kept on Moore a magnified intensity. "How much do you want?" he asked.

"I was thinking of five thousand—eight, maybe."

"Ed, I've been meaning to have a talk with you. Your loan here has been getting larger and larger, and your prospects of paying off are no better than when it started. Meanwhile your building and equipment are going steadily downhill, and you and Howard aren't getting any younger."

"Howard's only forty-eight."

Stoner waved his hand deprecatingly. "In view of these discouraging facts, why do you think this bank has been willing to keep on lending you money?"

"Because the hospital is an essential community service, damn it! It's the town hospital, and—"

"It's *your* hospital. You own it. However you administer it for the public good—and you do that—the fact remains it's *private*. Run—theoretically—for your own profit."

Moore smiled wryly. "Tim, you know the town wants the hospital and needs it."

"I don't like to say this, Ed, because you've done a fine job here, but that's precisely where, in my view, you're wrong. Thirty years ago Haddon did need a hospital. Now there's the Warwick Clinic, a modern two-hundred-bed one, only thirty miles away on good roads. Haddon doesn't need a hospital now."

"Timothy, you're absolutely wrong. This town—"

"Ed, wait till I finish. I happen to think this town would be better off with no hospital than one that's rapidly getting to be second-rate. But I won't argue about that now. Are you interested in the real reason the bank has been lending you money?"

Moore shrugged. "I suppose so."

"A good proportion of your cases are sent to you by the manufacturing plants at Silver Springs, aren't they?"

"Yes—mostly surgical."

"Now, Silver Springs is thirty-*eight* miles from Warwick, which is too far to transport most industrial accidents. But it's only eight to your hospital here. See what I'm getting at, Ed?"

"You're saying the Silver Springs plants need my hospital."

"And the plants bank with us and we want to keep them from moving to places where they can get better facilities, so . . ."

"So you lend me money to keep my hospital going because they need it and it's good business for you to keep them happy. Well . . ." Moore sat up straighter. "This bears out my conviction that the way to lick my financial problems would be to expand. Add more beds, a couple of well-trained young men—"

"Ed, listen to me, will you? Most of the employes now get all their own and their families' medical expenses paid. That costs a company around twenty-seven fifty per man per month, and the company has a very direct interest in how that money is spent. If the plants are going to rely on a hospital, they want it to be a good one, and not a privately owned one. Now, all five plants in Silver Springs have old, inadequate buildings, and it wouldn't take much to make them move elsewhere. I don't say hospital facilities would be the deciding factor, but they would be *a* factor. . . . See what I mean now?"

Moore grunted and shifted uneasily in his chair. Stoner pointed a long finger at him. "Now, look here, Ed. I'm being very frank with you because I've always liked you, though I think you've never believed it. You've served the town without self-interest and at considerable sacrifice to yourself. I wish I could make you see that I try to serve the town too. I love this town. I want to use my position here for what I sincerely believe to be its good."

Moore made another inarticulate sound that Stoner ignored.

"It's because of the town's pride in you that I ask you now to do a difficult thing. I want you to give up your hospital."

"That I absolutely refuse even to consider."

"Make way for a new one at Silver Springs."

"I've heard of no such project."

"Of course not. So far, it's only in my mind. You must admit that Silver Springs is the logical place for a hospital, and that there can't be two only eight miles apart. Also, my bank would participate in the financing of a new hospital and couldn't very well do that and keep up its loans to you."

Moore sat in stunned silence. Stoner went on, "Retire or stick to private practice. But make way for a new hospital."

"I'll be damned if I will!" Moore jumped up. "After thirty years of giving this town the best medical service it ever had, you've got the gall to tell me to shut my hospital and get out. Well, I won't do it. This town wants my hospital and trusts me. *They don't want* to go to a strange hospital, with strange doctors, at Warwick or Silver Springs or anywhere else. If the bank won't back me, I'll go to the people at Town Meeting—"

"The people didn't help you when you went to them for money thirty years ago. You had to use the money your wife left you."

"The town knows now what a hospital means to them."

"And I'll stand up and say that a half-dead hospital is worse than none. There are other ways of closing you up than by cutting off your loan. Part of your building isn't fireproof. With a new, safe hospital eight miles away, do you think the government inspectors would pass you? For now, I'll let you have your five thousand, and enough to keep you going until the other plan is fixed. After that I am, frankly, your enemy. I'm sorry, Ed—"

But Moore was making for the door, and when he went through it he slammed it behind him, hard. Because he was a peaceable man, whom anger physically upset, he stopped and leaned against the wall until the heavy thudding of his heart had lessened. Then he drew a long sigh and went resolutely on his way.

Chapter 2

THE PERSONNEL MANAGER of the Silver Springs Machine Tool Company thumped the folder on his desk. "You're entitled to honest sick leave, Jeb," he told the janitor. "But you've had more than anyone. You must be the laziest man we've ever employed."

The janitor blinked at him with stolid resentment. "Like I say to Doc Moore, 'Me back hurts,' and like Doc says to me, 'I think you're a liar, Jeb Truelove, but I can't prove it.' "

The incidence of headaches and backaches was high among employes for exactly that reason—nobody could prove they weren't real. The personnel manager regarded Jeb with profound dislike. "I'm warning you, that's all. Now get on back and at least pretend to do your work."

Jeb left the room and plodded, muttering, through a forest of noisy machines to a private lair he had built out of packing boxes. He should be attending to his first duty of the day, which was to run the flag out on the pole that projected from below a window on the top floor. Instead, he pawed around behind some mops and brooms and pulled out three cans of beer. He drank one can rather fast because he was stimulated by anger. Finding his wounded feelings unappeased, he opened the second. The third he put in his pocket and set out for the fifth floor.

The elevator went only to the third floor, and from there on Jeb had to force his paunchy body up the stairs. He did this slowly, with many grunts.

The top floor was stifling, and Jeb felt compelled to rest a bit before tackling the flag. Finding himself still at outs with the world, he decided to open the last can of beer.

EIGHT MILES AWAY, at that moment, Dr. Moore was preparing to leave for New York. He pulled his stethoscope out of his pocket and laid it on top of the bookcase beside the photograph of his wife. A short time after this picture was taken, Matilda Moore had been carried to her grave. Moore did not look at the picture now, but he felt its presence as a kind of warmth. He changed

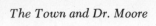

the baggy tweed jacket he wore on hospital rounds for a gray suit coat, picked up a shabby Gladstone bag and left the building.

Crossing the parking lot, he was joined by Dr. Perkins, on his way out of the emergency entrance in the wing. "Well, Ed," Perkins said in his big voice, "off on your wild goose chase, are you?"

"I'm hoping it won't prove that."

"Fairchild's reply to your letter sounded pretty vague."

"Still, he thought he might know someone. And I believe we'll find a better man this way than by advertising."

They came to a halt behind Moore's dusty red Jeep. Perkins said, "Well, good luck, Ed," and Moore said, "I'll be back as soon as I can, Howard."

He watched while Perkins drove past in his secondhand but impressive Cadillac. Then he started the Jeep and sent it expertly backward in a long curve.

JED DRAINED the last of the beer and slouched across to the window above the flagpole. He poked his head out, looking down on the shrubs around the main entrance five floors below. Then he picked up the flag and fastened it to the lanyards that would carry it along the pole. The ropes were about to break in two places—he should replace them now but it was too much trouble, so he tied a couple of knots in the weak spots, and pulled. The flag jerked out about four feet, then a knot caught and it would go no farther. He tried to haul it back in but the other knot caught.

He thought it over glumly, and decided he would have to sit on the windowsill, grab the flag and cut it loose. Feeling a little sick, he eased one leg over the sill. He got the flag in his fist, jerked it hard, lost his balance and fell.

The flag, before it tore loose, broke his fall a little. The tree he fell into broke it further. The manager's secretary, who was gazing out of the window, saw him hurtle down out of the tree, and screamed. The manager rushed out. Jeb was unconscious and obviously so badly injured that the manager, himself white and shaken, decided to leave him where he was until a doctor came.

In the hospital at Haddon, Edna answered the manager's call.

"Dr. Moore has gone to New York. . . . I'll call Dr. Perkins. Cover him with something but don't move him at all."

Adele Perkins answered Edna's call in that high, clear voice which always seemed to Edna so affected. The doctor had been home but had gone out on a call; she didn't know where.

Edna said to the operator, "Della, get me Dr. Ladd."

With the phone distantly ringing, Della said, "What is it, Miss Judson? Somebody took sick?"

"Accident out at Silver Springs. Man had a bad fall."

"Gee, and Dr. Ladd's not answering."

Now Edna was frightened, for she was facing a situation no one thought could happen—an emergency with no doctor available. She said, "Della? Call the state police and get them to head off Dr. Moore on his way to the airport. Then try that retired doctor, Harlan Greer. I know he doesn't have a Vermont license, but this is an emergency."

MOORE CROSSED the bridge over the Little Torrent. Looking at his watch, he decided that time was a little short for the regular road to the airport. There was an old logging track up the near side of the mountain, shorter and, in dry weather, passable for a Jeep. He therefore turned left instead of right. The state policeman waiting for him on the main road did not realize he had missed him until Moore had already parked at the airport.

EDNA, TIRED OUT, was about to have lunch in the nurses' dining room. Her mind was at rest for, though Della had been unable to reach Harlan Greer, by this time the state troopers would have located Dr. Moore. As she went to sit down beside the instrument nurse, she turned to look out of the window, and saw with mild interest that a light truck had pulled in and three men were taking something heavy out of the back. With a shock she saw that it was a man on a stretcher.

"Helen, they've got that accident case out there." The shrillness of her voice made the calm-faced nurse jump.

Helen joined her at the window. "Isn't Dr. Moore there?"

"No, he isn't. They must have missed him—I don't see how."

The two women faced each other in consternation and Helen said, "Edna, what are we going to do?"

Edna looked swiftly at her watch. "There's time to call the airport. We'll have to do the best we can until Dr. Moore gets here. Get the emergency room ready. . . ."

There is no sound in a hospital more ominous than that of some one running, which is why nurses almost never run. Edna ran, and Helen, pulling down her operating-room cap, followed her.

THE MOUNTAIN AIRPORT was small and windblown and the plane, an ancient DC-3, had a weight holding down its tail. One of the two airport attendants stood by this weight, ready to unfasten it, while the other helped the last of the passengers to board. Moore parked the Jeep, snatched his bag and ran. As he passed the office he heard the telephone ringing.

The young man by the steps said, "Hi, Doc. Just made it."

"Hullo, Henry. Your phone's ringing in there."

"They'll have to wait. Have a good trip, now."

Moore sank into his seat and the plane began to roll away.

Henry dogtrotted back to answer the still-ringing phone. A minute later he came out of the office again. "Emergency for Dr. Moore," he said. "I wonder should I have called the plane back?"

The other attendant said, "Naw. There's other doctors."

AT THE HOSPITAL Edna and Helen were bent over Jeb Truelove's unconscious form. Helen was holding an oxygen mask over his lacerated face. Edna removed a stethoscope from his shattered chest.

"I still get a faint heartbeat. I don't think there's anything more we can do until the doctor from Warwick gets here."

Helen looked down at Jeb. "I wish they'd taken him straight to Warwick. What are we to do if he starts to go, Edna?"

"I don't know. I've been trying to think. . . ." Edna tried the stethoscope again and Helen watched her lips as she counted the heartbeat. They moved and stopped, and moved again. They stopped. Seconds passed and they did not move. Slowly Edna straightened up. "He's gone."

They stood looking at each other. After a moment Helen remembered to turn off the oxygen.

Dr. Moore stumbled out of the plane into the humid New York afternoon and took a taxi into the city. At his hotel an irritable clerk slapped down a key and turned him over to a bellboy.

As he followed the bellboy to his room, he reflected that his presence here had less effect than a tossed pebble on a lake. It added nothing, took nothing away. It was a disconcerting feeling, and he wondered how it would seem to practice medicine in a place where most of your patients were strangers. It came to him that practicing in a community like Haddon might have values he had not fully appreciated. He would certainly feel seriously handicapped without a knowledge of the economic and emotional problems of his patients, a knowledge that the city man must in most cases do without. Stack up on the other side of the scales the city man's hospital and research facilities; association with men who were leaders in their fields; even ease of transportation. Sum it up by saying that the city man tended to treat the disease, not the patient, while the country doctor treated the patient and did the best he could about the disease. An oversimplification, of course, and country medicine was changing fast. Perhaps, in time, a better balance might be struck.

Now he must take steps to accomplish what he had come for. When the bellboy had departed, Moore dialed the office number of a former medical-school classmate, Dr. Adam Fairchild. Dr. Fairchild, it seemed, was occupied with a patient and could not be disturbed. Dr. Moore said he would call later.

Taking from his bag a small bottle of Scotch, he poured himself a modest drink and stood at the window, looking out over the city. Suddenly, astonishingly, it dawned on him that, for the first time since he could remember, he had nothing whatsoever to do. And then he made the second discovery: that he was very tired. He walked heavily across the room and sat on the bed and thought about the weariness that had overtaken him. Years of driving himself too far. A little bit of himself that each day had not rested adding itself to the leftover fatigues of all his former days. Slowly he took off his shoes. Then he stretched himself out on the bed and slept.

DR. MOORE awoke with a start. It was ten minutes to five. He lifted the telephone and dialed.

Dr. Fairchild had gone for the day. Moore looked at his watch again in disbelief. At this hour he himself would be in his Maple Street office, hoping to be finished in time to look in at the hospital and to cook a meal before evening office hours began at seven. Trying to keep his feelings out of his tone, he asked for Fairchild's home number. Was it an emergency? the voice asked crisply. Moore conceded that it was not. He asked what time Dr. Fairchild would be in his office in the morning.

The doctor would be operating from eight thirty on. He would be in the office at two thirty, but all his appointment time was filled. There might be something later in the week. . . . Moore hung up and swore with feeling. Then he lay back comfortably and marveled, and after a while he went to sleep again.

HE REACHED the hospital at seven thirty next morning. The huge lobby was still in semidarkness, and in the cathedral silence Moore's footsteps on the marble floor rang hollowly. At the far side of the lobby an elderly woman sat reading behind a counter. Moore walked toward her and she laid her book down, smiling.

"Good morning, Doctor. What can we do for you?"

So she knew by the look of him he was a doctor, did she? Amused, he said, "I want to talk to Dr. Adam Fairchild, or get a message to him. My name is Edward Moore."

"He's here, I know." She picked up a telephone. A moment later she reported: "He's up on the operating-room floor and he can't come to the phone. But he sent a message that he's awfully glad you're here and he'll send someone down."

Moore thanked her and moved away. He found a bench facing

the elevators where he could sit and watch the morning activity. An elevator door would clash open to let out tired-looking young doctors in rumpled white, their tour of night duty ended. Older doctors, coats stiff with starch, waited to be carried upward. Fresh student nurses appeared, wearing striped dresses.

Then a young doctor came briskly out, saw Moore and made directly for him. "Dr. Moore? I'm Dr. Kopf. Dr. Fairchild sent me down. He said to tell you he's awfully glad you're here. The op he's doing is an open-heart—pulmonary valvulotomy." A flush mounted the eager young face. "I'm scrubbing with him, sir."

"Congratulations, Doctor. First time?"

"First with him, sir; I'm mighty lucky. It's on closed-circuit television. He wondered if you'd like to watch it. And could you have dinner with him at the Union Club at seven thirty?"

"Glad to. Seven thirty would be fine."

The projection room was on the operating-room floor. Walking down the long corridor, Moore felt himself becoming again that young intern of long ago, felt again the wave of weakness that made even going to the OR floor an act requiring resolution. His dislike of surgery had been the strongest emotion of his young life. And in his day the odor of ether had clung to everything. Modern ventilation, he noticed, left no lingering smells.

An orderly passed them, trundling a cyclopropane apparatus on casters. OR nurses, who had always seemed to Moore a race apart, came and went in their wrinkled scrub smocks and round caps, their masks hanging loosely under their chins.

Then, at a bend in the corridor, all resemblance to a hospital vanished. "Lecture halls and the projection room, sir," Dr. Kopf explained, "where they hold Grand Rounds. I suppose in your day it really was Rounds—I mean, everybody trailed after the Chief from bed to bed."

"They did." This was, in his opinion, one of the few things done more humanely today. No victimizing of each charity patient, discussing him and his ailment as though he had no feelings.

The projection room was like a small theater, with steep tiers of seats and a huge screen that was, at the moment, blank.

There were other doctors present, and groups of student nurses.

"I'll leave you now. I have to scrub." Dr. Kopf smiled. It was a boyish smile that did disturbing things to Moore. Young lad, the best of life and medicine still ahead of him.

Moore held out his hand. "Good luck, Doctor."

While he sat waiting for the operation to begin, Moore's thoughts drifted, though he found he did not want them to, back to himself and Adam at young Kopf's age. It seemed inconceivable that they had ever looked so young, so filled with high resolve. He heard his name spoken softly. A nurse was holding out a note. *Keep an eye on my first assistant, whose name is David Armstrong. He may be the man you're looking for. Adam.*

He was thinking about the improbability of a first assistant to Adam Fairchild being willing to consider a country practice when a voice, loud and disembodied, startled him. "You are about to see a pulmonary valvulotomy to open the stenosed pulmonic valve. The patient is a twenty-six-year-old white male. For the past year he has had progressive dyspnea on exertion . . ."

Moore moved restlessly in his seat, irritated by the technical language. Why not say the young man suffered from shortness of breath because a heart valve was partly blocked and not letting enough blood go through to the lungs?

"The stenotic valve will be opened. . . ." The voice went on. All right, they're going to clean out the valve and take a feel around the inside of the heart.

The screen now came to life and he was looking at the figure of a young man sheeted to the waist. The body was fine, even beautiful, and Moore was moved by the admiration that the marvels of human anatomy never failed to arouse. The head was tipped back, a complex of hoses and dials strapped to the forehead, the anesthetized mind in abeyance, the body yielded up.

Four gowned surgeons now moved close around the table and one turned a capped and masked head upward to the camera. Not Adam, Moore thought. Perhaps the first assistant. The mask moved and the same voice, no longer disembodied, spoke: "The vein cutdown has been done. The patient will be kept on very

275

light anesthesia, which will be stopped while the pump takes over the function of the circulation. Pentothal and Demerol are put into the blood in the pump. As you can see, the patient's breathing is now being controlled by a respiratory cycler."

Moore sat forward with interest, for this was a mechanism he had never seen. There it was, a glass cylinder containing a bellows that was rising and collapsing rhythmically, pacing the lungs, monitoring the quantity of the air it gave them.

"Dr. Fairchild will use the approach to the heart through the sternum, instead of removing rib sections." The tallest of the four raised his head, and Moore found himself staring into the cold, pale eyes of Adam Fairchild—Adam, but a stranger.

The camera moved over to a screen on which a dot of light leaped up and down. "You see here the oscillograph measuring the patient's heartbeat," a new voice said. "Note that the beat is erratic. This screen and another, registering arterial pressure, will monitor the heart pump which you see here." A gloved hand rested on another outlandish piece of mechanism with dials and hoses. Then the camera swept back to the table.

The first voice said, "The incision has been made. In a moment the electric bone cutter will be used to divide the sternum. The sternum will be spread apart; the pericardium, the sac that encloses the heart, will be opened and sutured to the edges of the incision, exposing the heart."

The heart. He had never seen a living heart. Moore sat forward. He heard a snarling buzz and saw the flash of chrome in Fairchild's hand as the sternum was slit. Then there was an interval during which Moore watched the first assistant. He saw swift, sure motions of the gloved hands, which seemed to strive for efficiency rather than showiness. Then all four surgeons moved back, and Moore was looking down into the open chest.

He looked hungrily. He saw first the heart's motion. And he thought, It's not a beat. It's like the heave and roll of the sea. He watched the tremendous movement, rolling upward, bulging the network of veins on the outer surface of the heart, dying away, beginning once more. He saw the two great arteries curving upward, pulmonary and aorta. And he could see the damage to the pulmonary, the ballooning above the obstructed heart valve. Feeling weakened, Moore sat back. Whatever remained must be secondary to his first sight of a living heart.

An hour passed in minute preparation for detaching the pulmonary artery from the heart. Then Fairchild's voice broke in sharply, "Ready to go on the pump," and the operating room grew tense, filled with the quiet rustling sounds of many people moving with quick accuracy. Someone said, "Blood pressure, one hundred." Someone else said, "Ready to take off the arterial clamp." Fairchild said, "All ready? One, two, three—on." The pump took possession of the young man's bloodstream.

Fairchild was working fast now, repairing the valve. Moore could not see what he was doing. After a while Fairchild said, "We needn't detain the closed-circuit audience any longer. The patient is off the pump after being on it for thirty-eight minutes. The operation has disclosed that this young man had a slight arterial stenosis which, when I actually saw the heart and arteries, I was inclined to accept as the total problem. In other words, the damage was less than anticipated. Blood pressure, heartbeat and temperature are now all satisfactory. That is all."

The lights went up and Moore had that feeling of the shoddiness of the commonplace world that follows all good theater.

DR. DAVID ARMSTRONG entered the vast hall of the Union Club with an air of assurance he did not feel. It was not that the surroundings overawed him, for he had been here before with Fairchild. His uneasiness came from a feeling of inadequacy in his dealings with people, especially in unfamiliar situations. His effort to hide this produced a suggestion of the stuffed shirt which counted somewhat against him. He was bracing himself for the coming encounter when he saw Fairchild come in and greet a man who must be Moore, sitting in one of the armchairs.

For an instant Armstrong's mind played a trick on him and he saw, instead of Fairchild's thin, distinguished figure, a memory image of the older doctor's daughter Maryanne. Tall, with hair like a pale gold cloud, she had her father's remote eyes, but with a look of wanting something life had not given her. That look had vanished when she and David had been first engaged, and he had watched with anxiety its slow return. She had tried to explain to him what she felt, but their long talks ended in tears on her part and frustration on his. Once she had burst out, "You'll never make a good doctor unless you learn to *understand* people." He knew he didn't understand people. He saw no reason for a surgeon to try, especially as Fairchild, who was his model, did not.

When she broke off with him and became engaged to a surgical resident whose outgoing personality Armstrong greatly disliked, his feelings were too bruised to allow him to think clearly. It was not until this moment that he suddenly realized he had loved, not herself, but her father's daughter. The shock brought him back to the present, and he went to join the two older men.

Dr. Moore scrutinized him sharply through squinted, unexpectedly blue eyes, but the look was wholly friendly. Fairchild, assuming a role of benevolent goodwill, said, "Let's have our drinks at the table, shall we?" and walked to the elevator with a hand on Moore's shoulder.

Over the drinks Fairchild played the role of host easily and well. To David it seemed that he was not being patronizing toward his old friend only because he was too skillful, but that he had decided the gap between them had grown too great to be bridged by anything but the social amenities. That Moore was aware of Fairchild's attitude David felt more and more certain. He was given little opportunity to talk, and gradually he seemed to draw quietly away, glancing around the handsome room as though he were finding pleasure in it.

Fairchild interrupted his monologue to order the dinner, and was about to resume it when Moore said, "I want to tell you about my hospital." It was done so adroitly that David suppressed a smile, then found himself listening intently as Moore described the need there had been for a hospital in Haddon. " . . . So I went to the town and asked them to vote the money to build one. They turned me down."

Soup was brought, and Moore began to eat his quickly, as though, David thought, he never had time to eat any other way.

"Couldn't you have gotten federal aid?" Fairchild said.

"Not in those days. And not now, so long as I own it—"

"You mean you *own* the hospital?" David spoke with astonishment. "I didn't know there were any *private* ones left."

Moore nodded. "About a year after the town turned me down, my wife's father left her some money. My wife died shortly after. We had no children, so I took the money, about a hundred thousand dollars, and bought a big, old house and converted it. We're still there today. Fifteen years ago Dr. Perkins joined us from his surgical residency at a big Midwestern hospital. A better man than a country town has any cause to hope for. He put in fifty thousand and we built a new wing, with a good operating room. I took a four-months' course in anesthesiology—"

Fairchild made a startled gesture. "But, good Lord, Ed, anesthesiology's at least a two-year residency!"

"I know, I know—but we stick to simple techniques. Nitrous oxide, spinals, ether drip. We've never had any accidents."

The food was put in front of them. Moore ate his mechanically, then looked at his plate with pleased surprise. "We don't get this sort of food up our way."

Fairchild turned the talk to their student days. When David said, "I'd like to hear more about the hospital," Fairchild almost imperceptibly shook his head. He meant, it seemed clear enough, that David would be well advised to take no personal interest in the medical affairs of Haddon.

"You know, Adam," Moore said, "this trip has been a good thing. For the first time in years I've had time to think. Yesterday I got a bad jolt. It opened my eyes to the new demands on us. It's not just our town's needs I have to meet. People all around us want to use hospitals more than they did—farm people, and especially workers in unionized plants. I've been asleep and woken to find the hospital on the edge of a crisis."

Fairchild turned his pale eyes on Moore. "I don't see the problem, Ed. More patients, more money to expand your facilities."

"That's part of it, but not all, unfortunately. Sure I want to modernize, and I intend to." The blue eyes gave Dr. Armstrong a brief, intense glance; then he smiled, and the smile's quality increased David's liking for this man. "Not only the hospital, but my own thinking needs modernizing. However, there's a faction that thinks the hospital should be in a town in which manufacturing plants are practically the whole community. That would make it company-dominated, and—well, no need to go into all that. There appears also to be a feeling that the hospital shouldn't be privately owned."

"A-a-a-h." Fairchild drew the sound out. "And you wouldn't consent to its becoming a public hospital?"

"No, I wouldn't. It's become my life, and the town is proud of the hospital now. It will be even prouder in the future. I'm going to get young men in, a new medical generation." He turned to Armstrong. "It's not easy to give you a true picture. Why don't you come up and look us over? See the hospital and the town, go on some house calls with me. A hospital like ours is close to the life of the community in ways you probably couldn't imagine. And the pot of progress is getting ready to boil. A young man might have a lot of influence."

David nervously picked up his coffee cup and set it down again. "I assume Dr. Fairchild told you that I am looking for a post only for a year. I feel I lack clinical experience. I believe it's a weakness in a surgeon's education. I want a year of working in close touch with patients."

"I haven't had a chance to tell Dr. Moore anything about you," Fairchild said shortly, clearly disagreeing about a surgeon's need for clinical experience.

Moore faced Fairchild squarely. "I have an inducement to offer a young man you couldn't match, Adam. A young surgeon in a hospital like ours would have a chance to do major surgery on his own much sooner than he could hope to in the city." Moore now looked directly at David, the look producing in David a sense of involvement in the blueness and intensity of his eyes. "Why don't you just come up and take a look at us?"

Chapter 3

ON THE mountain airstrip rain had turned the runways dark and muted the colors of the surrounding hills. Moore left the plane and was greeted by the airport attendant, Henry.

"Hi, Doc." Then in a lowered voice he said, "I'm sorry about what happened. Maybe I should have called the plane back, but Miss Judson didn't say there weren't no other doctors."

"I don't understand, Henry. Edna Judson called you?"

"Gosh, don't you know? There was a man fell out of a window in Silver Springs, and they couldn't get a doctor. They took him to the hospital and he died. I guess Miss Judson done what she could. He'd have died anyway, most people say. . . ." But Moore was already inside the telephone booth calling Howard Perkins.

"Howard, I just got in. What's this about a man dying?"

"I didn't call you because there was nothing you could have done—it was just one of those unforeseeable things. And there's hell to pay. I went over every detail of what Edna did for the man, and I don't see what more she could have done. She's feeling pretty bad about it, but I'm certain the autopsy will show that ten doctors couldn't have saved him."

"That isn't the point, Howard. It shouldn't be possible—"

"What? Oh. No doctor available. You're right, of course. And the town's pretty wrought up. We are all three summoned to meet with the selectmen tomorrow night."

"That's inevitable. This is serious business, Howard."

"Are you telling me? Years of good doctoring for the damn town and something goes wrong and they're on our necks. I tell you I'm going to fight back."

Moore suddenly felt Howard Perkins to be an additional and very heavy burden. "Howard," he said, "there's a young fellow coming up to look us over tomorrow. A Dr. Armstrong."

"Couldn't have picked a worse time. Can't you head him off?"

"I don't think so. He'd hear about it anyway."

On the long drive home Moore tried to put the death out of his mind. He could not, and arrived on his doorstep worried and fretful. There he paused to arrange things in his mind. Lunch first, and then the office . . . He glanced at his watch. Patients would be waiting. He went on through to the kitchen where he fried three eggs and ate them rapidly. He was putting on his raincoat in the hall when he heard the back door open. His cleaning woman's voice called, "Is that you, Doctor?"

"Yes, Ellie," he said, then added, "Can you get the spare room into shape?"

"Sure. Why, sure I can. You goin' to have some company, Doc?"

"A young doctor from New York is coming to look us over. He might stay and practice here."

"A good thing, Doc. Since about that man what fell—"

Not wanting to discuss it, he let himself out of the house.

THE DOOR of the building on Maple Street where Moore had his office shut behind him with a familiar clash. He hurried down the hall and to his surprise saw that his office door was shut, with a small sign fastened to it. Then he remembered: he had put it there himself to say there would be no afternoon hours that day. Angry with himself for forgetting, and a little disturbed by it—was his whole organism perhaps just starting its decline?—he scooped up the mail and unlocked the door. He had just lowered himself into the chair in front of his rolltop desk when the telephone rang.

Ianthe Norton's deep voice never ceased to surprise and please him. "Ed, you *are* back. Have you time to talk?"

"Come on over now, if you want to," he said.

The sound of the Little Torrent River rushing past below his window, swollen with rain, was so loud that he did not hear Ianthe's step, and when she spoke she startled him. He whirled his chair around and saw her standing in the doorway, her tan raincoat hanging open. She had a fine carriage, and he admired it now as he rose to meet her. "Sit down, Ianthe."

For a moment they were silent, regarding each other with looks

that were oddly similar: direct, honest, experienced and sad. Then Ianthe said, "You told me once, Ed, that if Nathaniel's cancer reappeared in some other part of his body it would mean it had gone out of control."

"Yes, roughly so. We call it metastasis. It means that the cancer cells have traveled. It's not invariably hopeless. Let's say it's not good news."

"The cancer has appeared again, hasn't it, Ed?"

"The pathologist's report isn't back yet, Ianthe."

"But you don't have much doubt, do you?"

He saw that in spite of what her mind must have told her, she had been clinging to a thread of hope. He struggled with the problem, never resolved in all these years, of how to say there was no hope. Then he knew that his silence had told her. She began to breathe as if she could not draw enough air into her lungs, and he watched her grow rigid with the effort to control herself. Then something let go. Tears ran slowly down her face and she made no attempt to hide them. He put his handkerchief into her hand. She held it against her eyes and her whole body shook with one convulsive sob. Then she dropped her hands to her lap and once more gave him a direct look.

"Nat and I were never really close, Ed. That troubles me now. I love him, but not in the way he needs. The thing that's so tragic now is"—her hands clutched each other—"that he's lonely. I think he has been lonely all the years of our marriage. I want to make it up to him, Ed. . . ."

He said, "I wish I could help you, Ianthe."

Almost in a whisper she asked, "How long does he have, Ed?"

"It's not easy to say, at this point. Not more than a year, I should think. More likely less."

She picked up her handbag and rose, as though there were no time to lose. "I must get back to him."

"I'll drive you home. You don't want to meet anyone just now."

He put on his hat and raincoat. Ianthe was standing still, staring into space with wide eyes, and he knew that she was facing a full realization of life's cruelty.

"Nathaniel has had a good life, Ianthe."

She turned blank eyes on him, then walked quickly out. In the Jeep she sat in the numbed silence that he welcomed always as nature's anesthesia when grief becomes too great. He knew that her greatest difficulty was not in the shock of being told, but in the hours ahead when she would be alone with a clear mind.

He turned into the driveway between tall white gateposts topped by carved pineapples, and stopped at the side of the big house. A lilac, weighed down with moisture, brushed the top of the Jeep, and a shower of drops was released on them. He helped her to the ground. "Take one of Nat's sleeping pills tonight."

"If I did I might not hear him call. I'm not going to tell him I talked to you."

"I think that's wise. Phone me if you need anything, Ianthe."

As he drove away he thought how strongly habits of speech reflect what is normal in life. Nathaniel Norton, with vocal cords cut away, would never "call" again.

Dr. Moore hurtled the Jeep into the hospital parking lot and looked down the line of cars, hoping to see Howard Perkins' Cadillac. It was not there. Moore shied away from the uneasiness he always felt when Perkins was not where he might be expected to be. The plain fact was that he was drinking. Not that Moore had ever found him in a drunken state, or ever, in the operating room, noticed the slightest lessening of skill. But the unexplained absences, the bursts of temper, a look about the eyes, and the evasiveness of Adele, his wife, when Perkins could not be located, all spelled a problem Moore was reluctant to face.

In the gray light of the rainy afternoon the tall narrowness of the old hospital seemed to have taken on an aspiring look, along with its usual air of stoic and enduring dignity. Moore came here with a feeling of expansion and a warmth of satisfaction that his own home had not given him for some years. But the thought of what lay ahead of him cut his satisfaction short. First there was Edna. She had been left to cope alone with a responsibility that should not have been hers. She had done her best, but the man had died, and Moore knew she would be convinced that she was to blame. He hurried up the steps, deeply remorseful that he had left her so long without reassurance. She sat at her desk, looking as though life had at last dealt her a blow from which she could not recover.

Edna rose, disciplined as always, but he saw her trembling. "I did what I could, Dr. Moore."

He put his hand over hers and pressed it, but did not try to say anything. Later, as he was leaving the hospital, he heard her voice from somewhere upstairs. He paused and listened critically to its tone. It was quiet, but strong and steady; she was at least outwardly herself again, directing the hospital safely under his authority. Greatly relieved, he went on his way.

Moore parked the Jeep in the center of town and climbed a steep flight of wooden stairs that led up from the sidewalk between a dress shop and an appliance store. He knocked at a door on which a card read MAY TURNER. "May?" he called.

A light, breathy voice answered him. "Uncle Ed—come in."

He pushed the door open, frowning, for her cheerful voice was dear to him and he heard traces of pain in it. Crossing the sparsely furnished room, he bent over the couch where she was lying and kissed her cheek. "How are you?"

"All right."

"What have you got those shades down for? Let some light in." He pulled them up. "It's not good for you to be alone like this." He looked down at her, brooding, but enjoying her prettiness. She had long black hair, eyes of a deep, intense blue, and a translucent skin that was beginning to lose its rosy flush.

"Don't worry about me. I don't mind being laid up."

"That's just what worries me. Now let's have a look at those bruises." He pushed aside the quilt and bent over to study two angry-looking bruises across both thighs a little above the knees. "Still more pain in the right leg than the left?"

"Yes." She pulled herself up against the pillows. "But it's much better, Uncle Ed. Really it is."

He glanced at her keenly. There was a contradiction here that he did not understand—a normal desire to believe herself better, opposed to an odd reluctance to come out of the seclusion that her accident had brought about. He must try to bring these feelings of hers out into the open, he thought. He bent to examine her damaged legs, feeling first for the pulse of the artery below each instep. The pulse in the right foot he was almost certain was weaker than in the left. He felt above the bruise on her right thigh for the great femoral artery that carried blood into the leg; it was pulsing full and strong.

Sitting down, he studied her in silence, bothered by her mental state. Should he tell her he thought there was a blood clot in the artery under the bruise of her right thigh? Such a clot might form if the artery had been injured in the accident, and it would account for the lesser pulse below the bruise in that leg.

She was gazing at him. He must say something. "A young doctor's coming up tomorrow who will, I hope, decide to practice here a while. I want him to have a look at you."

"Oh no, please. I don't want him to. Really, it's better."

"I want you to see him," he said with firm authority.

"But why, Uncle Ed? I won't see him unless you tell me why."

He sighed. "I think perhaps all this pain is caused by a blood clot which is partially blocking the circulation in your right leg. Maybe it should be removed."

"Uncle Ed, I won't go to a hospital. I'd rather die."

"Now, now, May, calm down. If it is necessary, I won't press you until you yourself are ready." He reached for her hand. She was trembling and two tears slid down her cheeks. "May, my dear," he said with sudden urgency, "why don't you come and stay at my house? I don't like your being all alone here."

"I'd rather not, Uncle Ed. I'm twenty-five now and I want to look after myself."

"Well . . . I just hoped . . ." He rose to go, then bent to kiss her cheek. "You're all I have, you know."

He saw now on her face a look that he saw on other faces every day: the desire not to have the doctor's visit end, the fear of the return of anxiety. It always touched him, and he had developed a knack of seeming to give his patients all the time they wanted. It was often the best medicine he could provide.

May held out her hand to him. "Uncle Ed . . . About what happened after you left for New York . . . Everyone knows it wasn't your fault."

"Then everyone's wrong, May. All three doctors are to blame. Me, perhaps, more than the others." He gave her hand a slight pressure. "But don't you worry. Just take care of that leg."

It was about this matter, however, that he had at once to talk to Howard Perkins. He would just have time to stop at the Perkins' house on his way home for supper.

ADELE PERKINS was a slim, discontented-looking woman in her early forties with whom Moore never felt comfortable. She answered the door and said, "Come in. Howard's in the study."

Perkins was sitting at his desk, on which were a dismantled gun, some oily rags and a highball glass, nearly full. He rose when Moore came in.

"Hullo, Ed. Have a drink?" He moved over to a small bar in the corner and poured one. Moore took the drink and Perkins went back to his chair and picked up one of the gun parts.

"Did you come to talk about the selectmen or about Stoner at the bank? He told me about his talk with you. Ed, he's got you."

"What do you mean, he's got me? Who is he to say this town doesn't need a hospital?"

Perkins laughed. "Just your only source of money, that's all. And speaking of which, when the breakup comes let's not overlook the fifty thousand I anted in."

Moore looked at Perkins silently. Perkins went on, "All right. It's early to talk about that now. But, Ed, I have to assume that sooner or later it *will* be necessary to close the hospital. It'll be tough on you, but you don't *need* a hospital to keep on practicing. A surgeon can't function without one."

"What are you getting at, Howard?"

Perkins began to polish the gunstock. "I hate to tell you this, Ed, but there's a teaching job at Warwick Medical School—first-year surgery. Whoever gets it could continue doing surgery on the side. I'm going after it." He saw Moore start to speak, and went on quickly. "I know what you're thinking, Ed, but that business is so far back I don't believe it will count against me. And Adele would like it. She hates it here in Haddon."

"I hope you won't be precipitate, Howard. I intend to reorganize the hospital to meet the needs of the enlarged community. Somehow I'll find the money. And it's to your interest financially not to let the hospital fold."

Perkins looked thoughtful. "I'll do what I can to help you, Ed. I don't think this battle can be won, but I'll enjoy the fight. I just don't intend to go down in the crash."

"I really came to talk about this meeting with the selectmen."

"I thought you did. I wish you'd leave the so-and-sos to me."

"That's just what I don't think it would be wise to do."

Perkins laughed with one of those startling switches to affability that made him, in spite of other traits, so likable a person. "You're afraid I'll blast their tails off. All right you load and I'll back you. But if it comes to a real row, get out of my way. I'll do the infighting."

"That's fair enough." Moore finished his drink and stood up.

At the door Perkins said, "You're not tough enough, Ed."

Moore groaned and went out into the dusk, now clear, and promising frost. He wedged himself into the Jeep, remembering with wonder that this interminable day had begun in New York.

Chapter 4

D R. MOORE wandered slowly around Nathaniel Norton's sunny bedroom examining various objects. This was something he often did when visiting patients, to keep them from feeling scrutinized, but he felt that Norton, watching from his wing chair, knew quite well that it was a technique. Aware of the sardonic expression on his patient's bird-of-prey face, Moore sat down.

"You're pretty comfortable on the whole, aren't you, Nat?"

Norton's reply was a wheezing breath. It moved the gauze covering the tracheotomy opening that had been made in his neck when cancerous larynx and vocal cords had been removed. Moore decided to take the sound for assent.

"Nat, you should get out more. Go driving with Ianthe. Drive yourself, for that matter. No need to stay cooped up here."

Norton picked up a slate and wrote, in sprawling letters, DON'T WANT TO.

"Why don't you go down in the study, then? Get out of that damn bathrobe once in a while."

This time Norton wrote angrily, WHAT IS THE USE? Then, almost before Moore could read it, he jerked the slate back and added, LAB REPORT MUST BE BACK. WHAT IS IT!?

"Fatty tumor, like Howard told you," Moore said casually.

Norton wiped the slate and wrote No. He turned to meet Moore's eyes with a steady look in which there was none of his usual mockery. Moore saw hardihood in the brown eyes and, strangely, beauty. Deeply moved and feeling closer to Norton than he ever had, he was about to put a hand on Norton's shoulder when he saw that the old cantankerous self was back. The man had an air about him now—incredibly—of satisfaction.

Rebuffed, Moore stood there helplessly. Satisfaction for what, in Heaven's name? For being smart enough to catch me in a lie? Suddenly Moore was tired out, discouraged. He said, "I must go, Nat," and held out his hand. Norton half rose to take it. Then Moore went out of the room, leaving Norton tying his bathrobe around him with jerky, hostile motions.

DR. ARMSTRONG had hoped very much that Moore would not come to meet him. But when he stepped out on the breezy airstrip and saw a massive stoop-shouldered man coming toward him with a welcoming smile, he felt strangely reassured.

"Glad to see you, Doctor," and the large hand took his.

Waiting for Armstrong's bag to come off the plane, they exchanged small talk about the early fall coloring. Then, as Moore was about to start the Jeep, he said, "Something's happened in Haddon that I guess you'd better know about. As I told you, there are three doctors in town: Perkins, our surgeon, old Dr. Ladd and me—" And while the Jeep slued and bumped down the mountain road, Armstrong heard the story of that fatal day when no doctor could be reached and a man had died.

Finally Armstrong said, "I don't see why your telephone answering service couldn't find one of you."

"We don't have an answering service—or secretaries, or office nurses, for that matter."

"Then how . . . ?"

"Oh, Edna Judson, my head nurse at the hospital, looks after my telephone. Perkins and Ladd have their offices in their homes, so their wives take their calls. I imagine that a central answering service will be discussed tonight—the three selectmen who run the town are putting us on the carpet. Sorry this had to be your first night here. And that reminds me, I've got it fixed up at my house for you to stay. I've been looking forward to having you."

Armstrong answered him quickly. "I made a reservation at the hotel—the Republic House, is it? Thanks just the same." He was surprised to see disappointment in Moore's face.

They came now into a long, tree-shaded street of ample houses and Moore slowed the Jeep. "This is Haddon," he said. Ahead, the street divided around a green, and at the far end a church spire rose slim and white against the backdrop of a mountain.

Armstrong saw all this with pleasure while he listened to Moore, who was saying, "I'd appreciate it if you could find time to make a professional call on my niece while you're here. Her name's May Turner. Her father practiced medicine in southern Illinois. He died about three years ago; his wife—my sister—a few years earlier. May came here to Haddon and took a little apartment. Then she decided to train as a nurse at Warwick Clinic, though she's not temperamentally . . . Well, never mind that. Anyway, a couple of weeks ago she was alone in Emergency when an ambulance came in. She was standing back of it, helping, when the brakes let go on the sloping drive. She was pushed against the wall and injured above the knees on both legs."

"Fractures?"

"No, surprisingly. And the bruises are clearing up. But there's something wrong with the right leg. I suspect the femoral artery's damaged, maybe a thrombus partly blocking it. . . ."

"Have you had an arteriogram?"

"No, just the original X ray. There's something else. . . . Something happened to her during her training, some kind of shock, but I can't get her to talk about it. She was to leave Warwick for good the next day. Here we are, here's the Republic House. Do you mind if we wait a minute while I finish?"

They had stopped before a brick building with white columns and a porch. On the porch was a row of rocking chairs whose occupants, to Armstrong's discomfort, seemed greatly interested in the new arrival. He turned his back on them and listened to Moore. Finally he said, "I wouldn't care to attempt a diagnosis without an arteriogram."

"We can't do one in our hospital, and as things stand, you couldn't get her to go to Warwick. You'll examine her anyway, as a first step, won't you?"

"Of course. Do you have office hours in the afternoon, sir?"

"Yes, one thirty on. Good Lord, it's that now. I'll pick you up for dinner."

Armstrong was halfway out of the Jeep. "What did you say your niece's name is? And where do I find her?"

"May Turner." And Moore was suddenly cheerful as he pointed out where she lived.

On the steps of the Republic House, traveling bag in hand, Armstrong paused to watch Moore make a bold U-turn around a traffic stanchion that bore a sign saying NO U-TURNS. Smiling, he went on into the hotel.

MAPLE STREET and Main Street, meeting in the shape of an L, formed the business section of Haddon. This afternoon it was crowded with people shopping. Prosperity was in the air. Among the tightly packed cars nosed in to the curb scarcely one was more than five years old; the merchandise in the store windows looked expensive and citified.

Struck by the curious mixture of rural and sophisticated, Armstrong stopped to read the announcements on a bulletin board headed TOWN EVENTS. A bake sale by the ladies of the Congregational Church. A concert by the Haddon High School band. The arrival of the Bloodmobile on Thursday. . . . A country community in transition, he thought.

He arrived at the stairs that led to May Turner's apartment and took them in a rush until, halfway up, he heard music and slowed down to listen. The music was coming from a radio, and he recognized the closing bars of the César Franck Symphony in D Minor. He waited for the final note to fade; then he knocked on the varnished door.

A light voice answered him and he went in. May was on the couch by the window, and she smiled at him in the disarming way of those who expect every stranger to be friendly. He smiled too, and came into the room with sudden assurance. She made an attractive picture with the light on her dark hair, and the flowering plants on the windowsill beside her.

"I'm Dr. Armstrong, Miss Turner. Dr. Moore asked me to—"

"Yes, he told me you were coming." She seemed a little wary.

He would have liked to say something light to make her smile again, but nothing occurred to him. He brought a chair to the couch. "It was the bumper of the ambulance that struck you?"

"No, it was an old high ambulance with a folding step above the bumper."

"Then that's why you were injured above the knees and not below. I couldn't visualize it." In his most professional tone he said, "Let's have a look at the injury."

Without embarrassment, she exposed the bruises. She said, "They're better, really they are," and he heard, as Dr. Moore had, not her assurance but her anxiety.

His examination confirmed Moore's suspicion that a thrombus, or blood clot, was impeding the flow of blood to the lower part of the right leg. An arteriogram—a series of pictures made while a dye flowed through the artery—would show the size and location of the clot, after which its removal should not be difficult.

"This is nothing that can't be fixed up all right, with your co-operation. Now I want to give you a quick general check-over."

She was clutching the quilt, and her eyes were dark with fright—far more fright than was warranted, he felt. He examined her swiftly, with practiced care, then sat down by the couch. "You are pretty healthy, as far as I can see." He remembered that Moore had seemed to think she was using this accident as an escape from something. He studied her, seeking a clue to what it was. Finally he asked, "Why did you want to be a nurse?"

"I suppose because Father and Uncle Ed were doctors. I guess it wasn't a very good reason."

"When this leg's fixed up, you could go and finish training."

"Oh, *no!* I *couldn't* go on being a nurse. Before I got hurt it was all settled that I was to leave—"

"But why?"

"I don't want to talk about it. I don't want to see the inside of a hospital ever again." Abruptly she sat up and stared at him with wide, terrified eyes. "You and Uncle Ed are going to try to send me to a hospital, aren't you? I won't go. Not even to Uncle Ed's . . ." She covered her face and burst into tears.

He watched her in embarrassment. "I didn't mean to upset you. Can I get you something?"

She uncovered her face. Tears still filled her eyes, and her lashes were stuck together in points. She rubbed them with the sides of her fingers in a way that made her seem to him very young and vulnerable. "I'm sorry," she said. Then, "Oh—could you make us some coffee?"

Her tone was pleased and eager. Astonished by her sudden change of mood, he stared, then laughed. "Sure. Coming up."

While he assembled things on a tray, he thought about her. The blood clot must be removed as soon as possible, and any tendency on her part to use this injury as a means of withdrawing from life must be overridden. Moore's job.

They drank their coffee almost in silence. Yet, while they sat

there raising their cups from time to time, they seemed to be progressing toward a common feeling of ease and fellowship. Later, when he began gathering up the coffee things, he realized that they had dispensed with much that normally impedes the first stages of a friendship. He was surprised and pleased that something so uncharacteristic could happen to him.

"I'll report to Dr. Moore," he told her. "We must get you fixed up without any more delay."

She held out her hand. "Thank you for coming."

As he went down the stairs, he thought she knew quite well that he would like to be asked to come again, and that it was from an impulse of sheer mischief that she had not suggested it.

Chapter 5

I N HIS old-fashioned room at the Republic House, Armstrong was making himself ready to meet Dr. Moore for dinner, reviewing in his mind what he would say about May Turner. While he was trying to fit the plug of his electric razor into the ancient light fixture above the washbowl, an idea moved in.

"I'll be damned," he said, staring at his image in the glass and seeing instead May Turner's living room equipped with the paraphernalia of a doctors' telephone answering service. The equipment could be operated from her couch, and the feeling of being useful might help convince her that she must have the clot removed. In addition, a two-way radiotelephone could be installed between May's room and the doctors' cars. "Perfect!" he said, and turned on the razor.

He hurried through his dressing, then made for the lobby where Dr. Moore was waiting for him. "I'm sorry to be late, sir. I've been to see May Turner."

"Tell me about it while we eat. The meeting's at eight so we don't want to waste time."

The dining room was full, and Armstrong was aware that everyone was watching them. Probably the whole town knew about the meeting. He thought he would not like living so much in the public eye as a country doctor seemed to do.

When they were seated Moore said, "What about May?"

"It does look like a clot."

"You can open up the artery and take it out, I suppose?"

"Yes, and replace the artery where you go in, either with a plastic graft or one taken from a vein. I've done it with Fairchild."

"How long can we delay operating?"

"The sooner the better. She's in some pain and the leg isn't getting the circulation it should."

"Nevertheless, I'd like to postpone it as long as possible."

"Why?" Armstrong's opinion of Moore's professional skill was based not on what he had seen of Moore himself but on a deeply imbedded belief that country doctors were naturally inferior to city men. He never questioned this, but he was aware that he had spoken more peremptorily than a junior should to a senior, so he softened his question. "I'd be interested to know why, sir."

"Her nurse's training was, for whatever reason, a traumatic experience. She shouldn't have made herself stay with it so long. She has too much willpower for her emotional nature to support. If we were to force an operation on her in the state she's in, I think she might have a breakdown she'd never recover from. But I'm pretty sure that if she's left alone she'll recover her emotional balance in her own way."

"To me it seems that the better sequence would be to get her well physically first. Or put her in touch with a psychiatrist."

"That is financially out of reach for her or for me, and there isn't a psychiatrist nearer than Warwick. No, if you think postponing the operation for a year or a year and a half would be feasible, I believe that's what we should do."

Armstrong, realizing he had pressed his point as far as he could, now told Moore about his great idea. Moore was delighted.

"It would give her something to do," he said, "and be a real benefit to us. What do two-way radiophones cost, do you know?"

"A thousand dollars, maybe."

Moore's face clouded. "That's a lot of money. But maybe, the mood the selectmen are in, they'd agree to the town paying part. Now I can face them with a constructive idea. Good boy!"

The meal over, Moore pushed back his chair. "I've got a young fellow coming to cover for us during the meeting. His name is Ted Barlow, and he's doing his residency in medicine at Warwick. When he's through I hope he'll decide to settle here. Why don't you come to the office and meet him?"

Armstrong was about to stand up when Moore gestured him back. "Wait, those are the selectmen. Let them leave first."

Three men had risen from another table and were coming toward them. Two of them were short, wizened men with worn, bitter faces; their business suits seemed not quite right on them, as if only worn on important occasions. The third wore his clothes more naturally, and his thin face had the look of a sardonic eagle. Individually, these men gave the impression of finding life a hard and crusty business; collectively, they appeared tenacious and morally strong. They left Armstrong with an oddly satisfying conviction that, in this Vermont town, government of the people, by the people, and for the people had not perished.

In Moore's office three more men were waiting. Moore introduced the oldest first: Dr. Ladd, a tall, carefully dressed man in his eighties. The second was Dr. Perkins, who said "Hullo" abruptly and then turned angrily to Moore. "The more I think about this outrage, Ed, the madder I get. I'm going to ask those three where they think the town would be without us looking after their blasted little ills."

"We agreed you wouldn't take that tone, Howard. Remember?"

Armstrong tactfully moved out of hearing toward a young man who also stood apart. "Dr. Barlow? I'm David Armstrong."

They shook hands cordially. Barlow was clean-cut and studious-looking. Armstrong liked him on sight. When, a moment later, the three older doctors tramped heavily out, Barlow sang under his breath, *"Onward, Christian soldiers."* David laughed, then instantly felt guilty. "I hope they'll make out all right."

"Oh, they will, but it won't be pleasant." Barlow dropped into

Moore's swivel chair. "I hear you're considering practice here?"

"Considering, yes, but only for a year. Are you planning to practice in the country?"

"Yes. That's why I chose Warwick. I interned at Mass. General, but my wife and I didn't want to raise a family in the city on what I'd make starting out."

"I should think the city'd be better, from what I gather of fees here. Four dollars an office visit and five a house call. Right?"

"Right, but remember you're likely to have twenty or thirty patients a day. Vermont doctors pay more income tax than most others do. And all your expenses are less. You don't have to have a swank office, or dress as well, or drive so good a car. In fact, you'd better not. Another thing the doctor here has real influence in the town. How many city doctors have that?"

"None, I guess. But how can you do a good job medically on thirty patients a day?"

Barlow leaned forward earnestly. "You just have to figure out ways to spread yourself thinner. All the doctors in a town should form a clinic, buy equipment like X ray and fluoroscope in common, one office nurse, one billing system."

"Group medicine was a dirty word not so long ago."

"It's the only answer to the doctor shortage."

The telephone rang, startling them both. Armstrong listened to a woman's strident voice, and to Barlow explaining that if little Tom had eaten six doughnuts and a glass of chocolate milk, fried fish, fried potatoes and cold baked beans for supper, and then thrown them up, it was simply Nature taking her revenge. Hanging up, he said, "Country kids aren't what they used to be."

To KEEP the meeting unofficial, the selectmen had decided not to have it in the Town Hall, but in the room over Jake Miller's hardware store. The place was unfurnished except for a battered table and some wooden folding chairs. The selectman with the eagle face, Miller, sat at the table, with the others, Lund and Whittacker, to his left and right. Moore sat down facing them, and Perkins moved around restlessly, his hands in his pockets.

Ladd settled slowly into a chair by the wall, spread his delicate old hands on his knees and closed his eyes.

Miller began, "Well, I don't aim to mince words. On Wednesday, September twenty-third, the janitor of the Silver Springs Machine Tool Company fell off the flagpole outside a top-floor window. The manager phoned the hospital and got the head nurse, Edna Judson. Edna seems to have done all she could. I believe I speak for the three of us when I say we think no blame should attach to her. We're here to discuss one thing—why there weren't any doctors who could be reached when a man was dying, and what kind of guarantee you can give that the same thing won't happen again. You're the town doctors. The health of the community is in your hands—"

"What is this? Socialized medicine at the town level? Well, I'm not having any," Perkins said. "I've been here fifteen years, Ed Moore around thirty, Ladd . . ." he hesitated.

Dr. Ladd opened his eyes, said, "Never figured it up," and closed them again.

Perkins went on. "None of us has ever turned away a patient. Most of our days off we work. In all the time we've been here we've not one of us had a real vacation."

Moore looked up at him. "Howard, nobody's accusing us of not working hard enough."

"They take us for granted, have to be reminded what they're getting. None of us, including Dr. Ladd, who isn't young—"

"Eighty-four come March."

"—Has ever failed to answer a night call. We each take care of quite a few charity cases, and do it free because we don't have time to do the paper work to collect from the government. Now this thing happens when Ed is on his way to New York, Dr. Ladd was way off in the country and I had an emergency call. Did it ever happen before? Is it likely to again? No! And I refuse to be treated like a criminal because, unfortunately, it did happen once." Perkins pulled out a paper. "There's the autopsy report on Truelove. You won't understand the medical language, but it means no doctor on earth could have saved him."

There was a silence, then Miller said, "Dr. Moore, the town has always regarded you as head of medical concerns in Haddon. The feeling is that the doctors as a group are responsible." Moore gave him a swift, keen look, then bowed his head, listening passively. "Dr. Perkins says this man would have died anyway. That's beside the point. You *could* have been the cause of his death, because you have no system to prevent a situation like this. You've failed as doctors and you've failed the town."

From Dr. Ladd there came a sound, wordless, but full of hurt. Everyone turned to look at him. When he spoke his voice shook. "I don't know what this town has come to. . . . When I first came here to practice, people thought it was a privilege to have a doctor in the town. Now they think it's their right. They used to be grateful when you got to see them. Now they're indignant if you don't get there within the hour. I don't know as I like practicing medicine any more."

With an effort the old man rose and said loudly, "*I don't know as I like it.*" Then he turned his back on them and, heavy and slow but dogged with purpose, walked out the door.

For a long time no one spoke. Finally Miller said, in a voice from which the belligerence had gone, "The town has never interfered in medical matters before. But we've some suggestions to make, and we feel you doctors should take them seriously." The other selectmen nodded solemnly. Moore was faintly amused to see that they were embarrassed.

"The first suggestion is that you doctors make a general review of medical needs both here and in Silver Springs. And that you should consider the whole question of the hospital and its status. There's lots of feeling about this in the town. We suggest that after you've had time to think and talk, we meet informally and discuss it. Can you see your way to doing that?"

Moore said, "Yes, certainly." Perkins did not reply.

"And another thing. We want Haddon to have a health center, like other towns where all the doctors have offices together. The kind of equipment not one of you could afford alone. Then, even if Haddon should find itself without a hospital—"

Moore said, "It won't," and Perkins said, "Who's going to pay for this health center?"

"Popular subscription—a drive. We thought that Ianthe Norton might head it up. She's good at such things."

"Don't ask her just at present," Moore said.

"Nat kind of bad?" Moore nodded. "Sorry to hear it. Well . . . I guess that's all, unless you doctors got something to say."

Moore said, "We're setting up a telephone answering service for the doctors. That ought to include a two-way radio setup so we could receive calls in our cars."

"That's a good idea, isn't it?" and Miller turned left and right, and again two heads nodded like marionettes on strings.

"We thought the town might be willing to contribute to that."

"Might be. Yes, might be. Well, is this meeting ready to sugar off? Don't think we need to adjourn formally . . ."

IN MOORE'S OFFICE the young doctors pried the lids off paper cups of coffee from the dairy bar across the street. David took a cautious sip. "Do you know a girl named May Turner who was a student nurse at Warwick not so long ago?"

"Very pretty, and had an accident? Yes. Do you know her?"

"Well, not exactly. Dr. Moore asked me to have a look at her. It looks to me as though it's a thrombosis—partial occlusion of the artery. Should be taken out, but she seems to be in something of a mental state. Doesn't want the operation, doesn't want to get well. Moore thinks she may have had some sort of shock, and I thought you might be able to throw some light on it."

"Maybe I could." Barlow gazed thoughtfully into his coffee. "But I don't think it was any one thing. She just wasn't cut out to be a nurse, but she kept at it for over a year and then had a kind of breakdown. She didn't tell you about that?"

"No, she won't talk about her hospital experiences at all."

"I was in on it, as a matter of fact. She was on GYN-OB at the time. Somebody's baby died and she had to wash it, and I guess it was that on top of a lot of other things. She was found in the linen room having an attack of hysterical weeping. It was so bad the floor nurses couldn't cope. I went in and got her quieted down after a while, but I couldn't get her off my mind. She is damn pretty. I phoned Emily, my wife, and she came and took May home for dinner. After dinner she went to pieces again, but good. When I got home I gave her a shot. Next day I had a talk with Miss Terry, superintendent of nurses."

"Moore will be interested in all this. Go on—what happened?"

"Miss Terry said she had been worried about May and had tried to talk her into giving it all up, but May wouldn't. Miss Terry called her in again that day and told her she'd have to quit. Miss Terry liked her. We did too. The girl's got something."

"Do you think the accident had anything to do with her state of mind? Gave her a reason to quit other than failing at the job?"

"How can you know? I've never understood how the psychiatry lads feel so sure of themselves. My guess is it was a real accident, but that she hasn't got over the effects of forcing herself to do a job she was emotionally unsuited for. With that, and a feeling of having failed, she just doesn't feel up to tackling the world again. Listen . . . That must be Moore." Both doctors stood up.

Chapter 6

THE NEXT MORNING was clear and bright, a mountain morning, and as Armstrong walked beside Moore across the hospital parking lot, the sound of the church bell chiming the hour came through the thin air with perfect purity. Struck by the unusual beauty of its tone, Armstrong stood still to listen.

"A Revere bell," Moore said. "The town's very proud of it."

"No wonder. I never heard one like it."

They walked toward the hospital, Armstrong receiving his first impression of the old building's ugly dignity. That such a place could actually be a hospital came to him as a shock, and made him turn involuntarily toward Moore.

Moore seized his arm and held him back as a truck loaded

with apples, tomatoes and squash swerved in front of them. "Hi, Doc," the driver shouted. "You're doing good this year."

"Glad to hear it. Keep it up," Moore said. "This is Donation Day," he explained to Armstrong. "People give the hospital what they can. Some money, but mostly produce and merchandise."

"They give even though it's a privately owned hospital?"

"Yes, they know the hospital needs help, and they figure they stand to gain by keeping us going. The relationship between the doctors and a town like this is probably unlike anything in your experience. We serve the town, and so does the hospital, and the fact that it's privately owned doesn't make much difference."

They were going up the wooden front steps, and Armstrong tried to imagine himself working here, and failed. He saw the glow of pleasure on Moore's face, and realized with dismay how much his coming would mean to the older doctor. A little ashamed, he said, "How many beds do you have here, sir?"

"Thirty—plus five cradles. If you don't mind, I'll turn you over to our head nurse, Edna Judson, for the grand tour."

Edna acknowledged the introduction while Armstrong tried not to gaze too openly at her amazing cap.

"We're glad to see you here, Dr. Armstrong." He met the steady eyes and looked away. There had been other head nurses who had the power to make him feel like an intern again, but he had not expected to find one here. He discovered that he really wanted to see this hospital.

They went up the broad staircase, past three private rooms, past a cramped nursing station and a children's room. About one thing Armstrong was specially curious. "Have you many charity patients?"

"A few. But they don't stand out as they used to."

"Why is that?"

"Well, the patients from Silver Springs don't pay either. The company benefits usually cover medical costs for the employe and his family too. Then there are various government health programs, and Blue Cross and Blue Shield. Almost everyone nowadays has some of his expenses paid."

"I never thought of it in just that way before."

They moved on into the new wing, and she said, "Here is the operating room," and stepped back to let him enter alone.

The place seemed more up-to-date than the rest of the hospital, and his mind presented him with a quick picture of Perkins, assertive, dynamic. Armstrong began to make a mental inventory: operating table, old but serviceable; lights, good; anesthesia equipment, modern; the Bovie, the electric cautery that seals off small blood vessels, seemed to be the oldest piece of equipment in the room. As though the place were pulling at him, convincing him that he could work here (which he felt he could), he suddenly wanted to escape, as he had always wanted to escape commitments. He went out quickly.

From the next door Edna opened came a blast of radio music, talk and laughter. "The maternity ward," she said.

At sight of Edna Judson, the six young women sitting or lying on their beds let out a joyous shout. She said, "Now girls, behave yourselves. I've brought a visitor, Dr. Armstrong, to see you."

They were silent, smiling shyly. "Hi, Doc," one ventured.

He said "Hullo there," and to his exasperation felt his face grow red.

When they left, Edna was smiling. "Having a baby is the only vacation a lot of them ever get."

She led him to a large room on the floor below, where some women in smocks were taking inventory of mounds of produce. One woman came to greet them, and Edna introduced her as Ianthe Norton, chairman of the Donation Day volunteers. Armstrong liked the warm smile and her deep, gentle voice. She was saying, "People are sending us really useful things. Some years, Doctor, it's as though they were just cleaning out their attics. You should show him the cellar, Edna."

They went down precipitous steps into the cool cellar, and there was something that Armstrong, city-bred, had never encountered before: the wonderful aroma of hundreds of ripe apples. Baskets of them stood everywhere, red McIntoshes mostly, Edna told him, a whole winter's supply.

It was here that Dr. Moore found them. Smiling, he spoke quickly to Edna. "Mrs. Newberry's tumor isn't cancer, Edna. The report's on my desk. You might phone her. Have an apple, Doc?" And before Armstrong realized what was happening, a red apple came flying through the air and he caught it just in time.

They ate their apples, bending over to keep the juice from running down their chins. Moore said, "You wouldn't be doing this in a big city hospital, Dave."

"I sure wouldn't," Armstrong said, and laughed. The moment was a fine one, and it was important that it had happened, though he did not know why.

"Let's go into the X-ray room," Moore said, and led the way upstairs to what must once have been a pantry. "We can talk here without being interrupted." He hoisted himself onto the table.

David sat down on a white metal stool. "I'd like to ask," he said, "why, with your growing deficit, and with a hospital like Warwick so near, you feel it worthwhile to carry on here."

"Two main reasons," Moore answered with the affability that seemed to be his working attitude toward whatever faced him. "People here like to be taken care of by their own doctors. Warwick is 'closed staff,' so patients get turned over to doctors they don't know. A lot of them are upset by the impersonal atmosphere and the distance from home. I don't like it. An unhappy patient isn't easily cured."

David said, "The second reason?"

"Simply this. How are you going to get good doctors to practice in a town without a hospital? It's hard enough now. Close this one and Perkins would leave tomorrow. Ladd would stay, I'd stay, but only because we're too old not to. And another thing. The factories in Silver Springs that use this hospital are thirty-eight miles from Warwick. That's just too far."

"Then shouldn't you get someone permanent instead of me?"

"What I'd gain by your coming would be time. Your being here would convince the town and the Accreditation Board that I'm not letting the hospital go downhill. That will take the heat off and give me time to get new staff and work out the financial problems." Moore slid off the table. "I have an appointment. What are your plans, David?"

"I thought I might catch the two-o'clock plane to New York. I can take a taxi to the airport."

They went slowly toward the front door. Moore said, "I don't suppose you've made up your mind yet about coming here?"

"I'll let you know from New York. Promptly." They shook hands warmly. "It's been interesting being here. Thank you."

"It's been fine having you." Dr. Moore patted his shoulder. He looked tired, a trifle wistful, and the air seemed thick with his unspoken thoughts.

THE WOMAN behind the desk at the Republic House smiled at Dr. Armstrong because she liked him. "A message, Doctor. Mr. Stoner phoned from the bank. He is most anxious for you to lunch with him."

"I was planning to get the two-o'clock plane to New York."

"I can get you on the later one. You'll be in at eight."

David accepted and thanked her, wondering what the bank president wanted to say to him. He had heard about Stoner from Moore.

"Mr. Stoner said twelve thirty. Ah, here he is now."

The man who had entered the lobby was tall and thin, with sharp features and dark-rimmed glasses. As David advanced to meet him he received an impression of cold, shrewd intelligence. "Mr. Stoner? I'm Dr. Armstrong."

"Hullo, Doctor." Stoner closed a faintly moist hand over David's. "I heard you were here and hoped you could join us for lunch." He turned to a small man in his forties who had followed him in. "This is Mr. Whitall of the Public Health Service."

Whitall said, "Glad to meet you, Doctor," in a twanging voice, and Stoner steered them toward the dining room.

When they had ordered, Stoner said, "I don't mean to pry into personal matters, Doctor, but I should be interested to know why you are considering spending a year with us in Haddon."

David said cautiously, "For one thing, I'm deficient in clinical experience. I thought a year in a country town where the doctor-patient relationship is closer than in a city would be useful."

Stoner nodded. "I don't know whether you're aware of the great changes taking place in country medicine, but let me say, Haddon is not keeping up with the times. Mr. Whitall is naturally interested in our problems, especially that of the hospital."

Whitall said, "I am in charge of hospital area planning for the state, Doctor. I'll send you a copy of my report when it's ready."

Stoner cut in crisply, "The point is, the report will recommend abolishing Moore's hospital."

David, startled, said, "But how could you do that? It's Dr. Moore's personal property!"

Stoner was watching him keenly. "You saw, of course, that the building is not wholly fireproof?"

"But . . ." The wider implications of what had been said struck David and he was silent.

Stoner said, "The hospital has passed its usefulness. The town would be better off with no hospital than with one that is becoming second-rate. But you might like to hear the alternative plans. One would be to build a small, modern hospital here, to replace Moore's obsolete one. This would cost around six hundred thousand. The usual procedure in such a case is for the town to raise two thirds of the money and the federal government to contribute a third, in return for which certain controls are imposed."

"This is a practical and highly desirable form—"

"Mr. Whitall—please! Let me finish. I am against this plan, Doctor, only one of my reasons being that Haddon couldn't possibly raise such a sum. The other alternative is to have a hospital at Silver Springs. There would be no trouble with the financing, because the plants could be expected to contribute heavily. Also, this plan would have the bank's backing."

David pushed his plate away. The conversation was making him slightly sick. "And what becomes of Dr. Moore and his investment?" he said.

Stoner waved his hand and let it drop heavily to the table. "The purpose of telling you all this, Doctor, is that I presume you would be more likely to decide to come to Haddon if you thought the medical situation here were not completely static. And during your year with us you might be of considerable help and influence in establishing new medical standards for Haddon."

David said, speaking slowly, "I haven't made up my mind yet. I'm going back to New York this afternoon in any event."

MOORE, across the street, was at that moment walking in his office door. Eight patients were already waiting for him.

"With you in a minute," he said, and went into the inner office. Just then his telephone rang.

The voice was Helen's, from the hospital, and it was anxious. "Doctor, the examiners from the Accreditation Board are here."

"Oh, good Lord!"

"They're going into everything. Edna overheard them say the wiring for the X-ray is too near the wooden beams."

"They've passed that every other year."

"They want to talk to you, Dr. Moore. They said they'd meet you at the Republic House between five and six."

"All right. Thanks, Helen. Don't worry about it."

Moore put the telephone down, sighed deeply, and looked out into the waiting room. "Who's first?"

THE THREE EXAMINERS were seated at a table in the bar. They rose when Moore came in, and he shook hands all around. One of them, a man named Brown whom Moore considered the friendliest of the three, asked, "What will you have, Doc?"

"Bitter Lemon, I guess."

The laughter was loud. They had all had at least one drink before he came. The oldest man, named Zimback, said, "He's just trying to impress us," and they all laughed again.

The drink was brought. Moore said, "Well, did you find things about as usual?"

Zimback nodded. "It's well run, clean, needs quite a bit spent on plant and equipment."

"I hope you're giving me full accreditation again."

There was an uncomfortable silence. Brown asked, "How is your financing for the year ahead?"

"All right," Moore said. "I fixed it up with Stoner the other day." He had a strong impression they already knew this.

Brown leaned forward. "Is it true that Dr. Perkins is going to the Warwick Medical School?"

"How did you know about that?"

"It's our business to know. Obviously, a hospital without a surgeon couldn't be given even provisional accreditation."

"He told me he was going to apply. I don't know that he has."

"He has." Brown's tone was still friendly.

"But there must be others wanting the job."

"Dr. Greer for one."

"Harlan Greer—here in Haddon? Are you sure? He's a rich man and he's retired. It's hard to see why he'd want it."

Brown said, "Is that young New York surgeon coming here?"

"I don't know yet."

Brown signaled for the check. "We've got a long drive ahead of us. We'd better get going." They all rose, but Brown detained Moore until the others were out of earshot. "We're under pressure—I won't say from where—to make this report unfriendly to you. I don't like pressure, and I don't propose to be influenced by it. But I will say—you know it anyway—your hospital has several marks against it, and the uncertainty about Perkins is probably the worst. It would make an important difference if we knew this young surgeon was coming. Will you know soon?"

"I hope so. A week, maybe."

"Let me know, will you?"

"I'll let you know as soon as I do. And thanks."

From La Guardia David took a taxi to his small apartment on Seventy-sixth Street. He had expected to have to think things out, but his relief at being home, after the extraordinary pressures of Haddon, convinced him that New York was where he belonged. At least Haddon had served one good purpose: the unhappy affair of Maryanne had receded from his mind.

He thought about calling Fairchild, and decided the hour was too late. Then he found himself seriously considering putting in a call to May Turner, and was shocked by the fantasy of this idea. He set his alarm for six as usual, and went to bed.

Next morning at the hospital he dressed himself in smock and cap and was on his way to look up Fairchild's operating schedule when he met Fairchild himself.

Fairchild nodded gravely. "So you're back."

David fell into step beside him. "I got in too late last night to call you. What have we got this morning?"

Fairchild said, "A stenotic mitral first. Since you didn't tell me when you were coming back, I'm having Mike assist."

David, taken aback, did not reply. Mike Foley was chief surgical resident, the position David himself had held until June, when, his residency completed, he had entered Fairchild's office. He was also the man Maryanne was to marry. It came to David then that Fairchild had all along been angry and resentful at his plan to take a year's absence, and had characteristically waited to show it until a moment when he could cause extreme discomfort. He said now, "If you care to act as second assistant, you may, though for a mitral it's hardly necessary, of course."

Fairchild pushed open the door to the operating suite and went in. David hesitated for a fraction of a second, and then he slammed the door hard with his palm and followed.

Foley was already scrubbing. He saw David and said "Hi" loudly. David said "Hullo," and went to scrub in the next sink.

Fairchild said to Foley, "Dr. Armstrong is going to assist *you*." David was aware that Foley was expanding with satisfaction.

When the morning's operating was finished, David had time to think. He was amazed at his own thickheadedness in not realizing that by going to Haddon he had given Fairchild the opportunity he had been waiting for. Foley would finish his residency in June and marry Maryanne. What more appropriate than that he should step into David's place in Fairchild's office?

Usually Fairchild suggested that they lunch together, but today he had departed without saying anything, and David was eating by himself in the doctors' dining room. He came out of his thoughts abruptly to hear the paging system saying, "Dr. Armstrong, Dr. David Armstrong . . ."

It was a call from Moore. "Hullo. David, I don't suppose you've had time to think things out yet?"

Something in Moore's tone caught his attention. "Not yet. Is there a special reason why you'd like to know immediately?"

"Well . . . the inspectors from the Accreditation Board were here. It's going to be a near thing whether the hospital gets by. I gather your coming might make considerable difference."

"Oh Lord. I had about made up my mind not to, but since being back here . . . Will tomorrow be soon enough?"

"Yes, tomorrow will be all right. I hope very much your decision will be to come."

Thoughtfully, David went back to his cold lunch.

DAVID OCCUPIED a small office across from Fairchild's much larger one. It was there, in the afternoons, that they saw patients, the two working more or less together. This afternoon, however, Fairchild worked alone while David waited to be called. He saw three of his own patients; after that there was nothing to do.

A little after five he knocked on Fairchild's door. "I thought we should have a talk, Dr. Fairchild."

"I hardly think it's necessary. When a man has shown signs of being discontented, I would not want to hold him."

Strangely, this did not anger David. Instead, a feeling of emancipation took hold of him. Staring at Fairchild's pale, secretive eyes, he began to jingle coins in his pocket.

"Don't do that," Fairchild said sharply.

David smiled. "When would it be convenient for me to leave?"

The telephone rang and Fairchild answered without taking his eyes from David's face. After a moment, talking into the telephone, he picked up a pencil, pulled a scrap of paper toward him, and wrote on it. Still talking, he held the paper out to David. He had written in large letters, ANY TIME! David crumpled it, threw it in the scrap basket, and went out of the office.

Chapter 7

FOUR DAYS LATER David arrived at the Republic House and called Dr. Moore. "I'm here, sir. I just got in."

"Welcome to Haddon, Doc. We're going to work you to death. Have you applied for your Vermont license?"

"I wrote for it from New York."

"Good. It shouldn't take too long. I got an office for you near mine. I'll see you get an invitation to the Rotary lunch so you can get to know people."

David was about to protest, but thought better of it. He said, "I'll have to find a place to live, get a car . . ."

"I'd be glad to have you stay with me, but I suppose you'd feel more free on your own. Well, it's fine you're here, Dave."

It was five thirty. With some idea of finding a place to live, David wandered out onto the street. Almost at once he found himself watching a woman who was moving toward him with slim grace, her brown tweed coat open, her brown-gray hair blowing back from her face. Not a native, he thought. Though she greeted people with a quick nod, she seemed oddly aloof.

Conscious that he had been staring, he looked away, but a moment later a strong, clear voice said, "Aren't you Dr. Armstrong? I'm Adele Perkins, Howard Perkins' wife."

She held out a thin, tanned hand, and he felt nervous tension in the fingers closing lightly over his. There was sensitivity in her face. If she had an inner warmth it did not strike one.

He searched for something to say. The best he could manage was "I've been looking around. It's a pretty town."

"Yes, but it's becoming too self-conscious about it. Most of the fine old houses have been bought by outsiders with money who are set on preserving the Vermont 'atmosphere,' and the result is something completely phony. But enough of that. I'm on my way home. Come and have a cocktail with Howard and me."

"Thank you. That's most kind."

"Good. It isn't far." And she set out down the street that edged the village green, past beautiful houses with lights already showing above broad doorways.

David said cautiously, "But surely, you wouldn't rather live in the city than in such a lovely place as this?"

She made a swift half turn of her head toward him and spoke with a vehemence that startled him. "I hate it here."

He said, "Is it the town or the people that you don't like?"

"Oh, the people! The women especially. If you don't accept their standards, if you're more intellectually restless, or just more attractive—if you're different in any way at all, then they shut you out. I've been shut out, and once that happens the door is never, never opened."

David kept silent, hoping for a change of subject. Presently she said, "Here's where we turn—over this bridge." As they stepped on the planking of the old bridge she said, "Let's watch the water for a moment, shall we?" She leaned over the rail, and the breath of the river rose damp and chill around them. Then, with a quick movement, she drew back and faced him. "Dr. Armstrong, go away from this town. Leave it while you can. Don't stay in this dreadful place."

He attempted a light reply, and regretted it at once. "It sounds as though you should be the one to go away."

"I can't. Howard's in a trap here and so am I." She shivered. "I'm cold. Let's go on . . . There's just a hope . . . A teaching post will be open at the Warwick Medical School next fall . . . I don't dare let myself think about it . . ." After a few steps she said in an ordinary, casual tone, "That's our house facing the bridge."

She opened the front door and called, "Howard, I've brought Dr. Armstrong home for a drink." David could see into the living room where Dr. Perkins was sitting by the fire. He rose and came to meet them.

"Hullo, Doctor. Have a good flight up?" He spoke cordially, but the look he gave his wife made David think that unexpected guests were not usual in this house. "What's your drink? A martini for you, I suppose, Adele."

"If Mrs. Perkins is going to have a martini, I will too."

"Good." Perkins went to a table where glasses and bottles were set out. Adele threw herself into a chair opposite the one Perkins had been using, leaving David to pull one up for himself. With her long legs thrust out in front of her, she made a lovely picture, slim and graceful.

Perkins handed them each a glass, then took his own back to his chair. "What did you think of our hospital, Doctor? Not exactly what you're used to, I imagine."

"It seems to have the essentials. . . ."

"All the essentials but funds to run on." Adele sighed and gave Perkins a look of reproach. He smiled. "She hates talk about the hospital." Adele flushed, opened her mouth to speak and closed it again. This silent show of temper seemed to please Perkins, who watched it closely.

Absorbed in this byplay, David was unprepared for Perkins' next remark.

"I've a hysterectomy tomorrow. Perhaps you'd like to be there."

"Very much, if Dr. Moore has no plans for me."

"He won't have. He's giving the anesthetic."

He stood up and drained his glass. "Howard," said Adele in a tired voice, as though protest was useless. As Perkins went off to the table, she said quickly to David, "He'll be brilliant, you'll see. He always is when there's someone to watch him." And she looked at her husband with bright, hostile eyes.

Perkins was talking again. "Our surgical work is mostly with farm people and workers from the mills. You'll hear that I do more hysterectomies than any surgeon in the state, and it's true. This is why. Some farm woman comes to me with trouble with her uterus. I might be able to carry her along for years; but she'd have to keep doctoring and paying bills and probably not be able to do the work she should. So I take her uterus out and save her all that. Sound procedure, I think, though some don't agree with me. By the way, do you hunt, Doctor?"

David said vaguely, still watching Adele, "Hunt?"

"Deer season coming up."

"Oh, I see. No, I don't hunt."

A door slammed and a youth of about seventeen came in precipitately, saw the stranger, and stood there blinking awkwardly. He was tall and spindly as an undernourished weed. His blue jeans came to a point above his anklebones, and on his feet were dirty sneakers.

Adele said, in a voice too high and loud, "My son Howie, Dr. Armstrong, who, if you can believe it, is destined for the medical profession. I might add that he doesn't want to be a doctor."

Howie looked as though he had received a blow which made him shrink but caused him no surprise. Perkins, rattling ice in his glass, was staring at his son with cold contempt. Armstrong, embarrassed and angry with both Perkins and Adele, said the only thing he could think of. "I'm not at all familiar with hysterectomy procedures. I've only seen four—as an intern."

Both parents turned blank faces toward him, and from Howie he heard a sigh of relief. He plunged on. "I'll have a look at the *Atlas of Surgical Operations* tonight so I'll have an idea what you're doing. And now I must be getting on. . . ."

The front door was closed behind him almost before his back was turned, and he made his way toward the bridge feeling as though he were alone at the end of the earth.

As soon as the door shut behind Armstrong, Perkins snapped, "Why did you have to drag *him* here with you?"

"He's a stranger in town, for one thing. And he'll be working with you— Oh, *Howard.*" Perkins was pouring a drink again.

"Once and for all, will you keep out of my affairs?"

She stared at him a moment, then walked quickly to the kitchen. There she found Howie standing by the refrigerator, a glass of milk in one hand and two pieces of bread in the other.

"Howie, put that down. You'll have no appetite for dinner."

"I'd rather eat like this, Mom. I don't want to sit at the table and eat a regular dinner." His eyes shifted toward the living room where Perkins was.

"I said put it down—"

316

From the living room there was a sound of breaking glass, then they heard the slam of the front door. A car motor started into life. Adele threw herself into a chair and burst into tears.

With a convulsive movement Howie took a step toward her. He made an effort to speak, then flung his arms out in helpless desperation. Moving furtively, he opened the back door and slipped out into the night.

At seven o'clock the next morning Moore and Armstrong, both in scrub suits, sat drinking coffee in the nurses' dining room.

"See Perkins' car out there, David? A big black Cadillac."

David rose and went to the window. "There's a car down at the other end that might be it."

"Good." Moore straightened his shoulders as if in relief.

Edna Judson, also in scrub smock and cap, appeared in the doorway. "Excuse me, Doctors, we're ready when you are."

The two men followed her to the operating room where a woman wearing a crinkled hospital gown was lying on the wheeled cart. Moore smiled at her. "Hullo, Addie."

"Hullo, Dr. Moore." The voice was thickened by sedation.

"This is Dr. Armstrong, Addie, who's going to watch us and see we do right by you."

"Hullo, Doctor." Her hair was stringy, dried by too much sun and wind, her body thick and short. David could easily picture her lifting a full pitchfork of hay.

Moore spoke in an undertone to the green-gowned instrument nurse. "Perkins here, Helen?" and she answered, "Yes, sir."

"Addie, we've got to get you onto the table." Gently he put his arms under her, grunted and lifted her over. She lay there holding on to the sides of the table, her legs shaking.

"What kind of anesthetic do you want us to use, Addie?"

She stared up at him, saw he was joking and managed a weak smile. "Whatever you say."

"I always think a piece of lead pipe with some gauze around it is pretty good, don't you, Dr. Armstrong?"

Her smile grew firmer. "Go on now, Doc."

317

David picked up her chart: *Addison Day, age forty-three . . .* He saw that the anesthesia was to be spinal-block, and that in preparation she had been given Nembutal.

Moore came to the anesthetic table and began to prepare a spinal needle. "See many spinals these days, Doc?"

"Not many in my kind of surgery. They're used a lot in obstetrics, of course."

"They're popular in the country, for if a surgeon has to, he can pretty near do the whole show himself."

Suddenly Addie said loudly, "I feel fine. I think I'll go home," and everyone laughed.

Edna turned her on her side. Moore was swabbing the spot on her back where the needle would go in when Perkins came in wearing a scrub suit and cap. He looked sallow and lined and his eyes were bloodshot. "Aren't you ready yet?" he snapped.

Addie opened her eyes and giggled. "I'm going home."

Perkins looked down at her without expression and went out, saying sarcastically, "Take your time."

The spinal needle in his right hand, Moore was feeling the spaces between Addie's vertebrae with his left. Realizing that her time had come, she cried out in fright, "Edna, are you there?"

"I'm right beside you, dear. Now, arch your back."

"I can't do it like this," Dr. Moore said. "Can you sit her up?"

Edna held the back of Addie's head, pressing it down on her shoulder, and Addie put her arms around Edna's waist. And, unexpectedly, David was deeply moved. He had been a little taken aback by the informality of all that went on, but now he saw a quality here in this country operating room that was wholly new to him. Compassion, perhaps, and trust born of shared experience. The support given to the patient by such warmth and friendliness would, he thought, be possible only in a small community hospital like this.

Moore administered the spinal anesthetic. "That's it, Addie." He patted her back and laid her on the table.

A moment later Perkins was standing in the doorway of the scrub room, saying, "You better scrub, Dr. Armstrong."

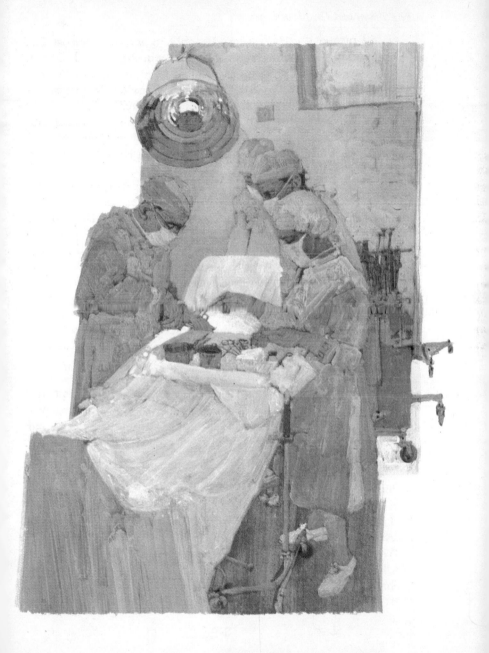

Startled, David said, "I won't be able to scrub with you, Dr. Perkins—my Vermont license hasn't come through."

"Look, I've done hysterectomies alone in my time, but I'm not doing this one. What do you think we hired you for?"

"Dr. Perkins, I'd be glad to assist. But my license—"

Moore had a protective hand on Addie's shoulder to keep her from being alarmed by their raised voices. "I thought you had one of the Warwick residents coming to assist, Howard."

"I called him off. Dr. Armstrong—get to the scrub room."

David, fighting down anger, looked toward Moore. "The law says, Dave, that you have to have a license except in an emergency. I guess we call this an emergency. Go along and scrub."

A few minutes later, the two surgeons stood at their appointed sides of the operating table. Armstrong began to swab the site of the abdominal incision.

Perkins was watching him closely. "Get a move on, Doc."

It was clear the moment Perkins began operating that he worked at a speed to which Armstrong was not accustomed, and with impressive sureness. Holding retractors and clamps, David had the feeling of being always just a little behind. Perkins was tying down on bleeders so fast that it was impossible to follow his motions, but the sutures were expertly knotted. Perkins said, "Self-retaining retractor, Helen," and received an instrument that held the incision open in a diamond shape, freeing the surgeon's hands to examine the uterus. It was unhealthy-looking and half again its normal size. "Nasty, isn't it? No question about its having to come out. Doctor!"

David started and met Perkins' challenging stare.

"Take over."

"What?"

"I said, take over. Take it out. Let's see what you can do."

"Are you asking me to finish the operation, Dr. Perkins?"

"Yes. Alone. Without assistance. You're a country doctor now."

Addie, aroused by the voices, was frightened into thick speech. "What's going on, Dr. Moore?"

"It's all right, Addie. They're just talking. Nothing to do with you." David saw him pick up a hypodermic, guessed he was going to give Addie an injection of Pentothal and was glad.

"Dr. Perkins, I've only seen four hysterectomies—when I was an intern. I told you that. I'm not competent."

"A country doctor has to do lots of things he isn't experienced in doing. You'd better find out what it feels like."

"Howard," Moore said, "you can't ask him to do that."

"I'm not going to walk out, Ed. I'll be watching every move. I just want to see what kind of a surgeon you got us."

What followed had the quality of a nightmare, but David became so absorbed in what he was doing that mostly he forgot Perkins. Step by step he repeated to himself what he remembered from his reading of the night before.

Slip a gauze sponge loosely into Douglas' pouch to keep any intestine from coming down into the operating field.

As though he had spoken aloud, Helen held out a sponge clamped in forceps.

Watch out with the Ochsner clamps. Don't point them downward for fear of damaging the ureters.

He hesitated over this, and when he directed the first clamp correctly, Perkins said, "Good."

David took no account of time, and again and again he stopped to figure out how some procedure could be done single-handed or with the help of Helen. At last the uterus came clear and was lifted out. He worked on, placing sutures with care, inspecting for bleeding, anchoring the bladder flap to the uterosacral ligaments. Perkins, to David's surprise, helped him with the closing, keeping to the assistant's side of the table, allowing him to work at his own pace. When they had finished, David nodded gravely to Helen and said, "Thank you," hoping she would realize how truly grateful he felt.

In the scrub room, pulling off his gown, he stood with his back to Perkins, too tired now to fan his anger into life. Perkins was the first to finish washing. With his hand on the door, he stood watching David for a minute. Then he said, "It took you damn near all day, but it was a good job, Doctor."

Chapter 8

D AVID HAD PLENTY to do while he waited for his license to
come. He rented an apartment, two rooms and a small
kitchen, over the shoe store on Maple Street; and he ordered some
furnishings from the furniture and undertaking establishment. He
also bought himself a small car. In every spare moment he studied, for he was appalled at the many things about general practice that he did not know.

This was brought home to him on his first house call with Dr.
Moore. The patient was a seven-year-old boy whose face and
chest were covered with sores. His condition looked serious to
David, though Moore seemed to be taking it lightly as he spoke
quietly to the boy's mother.

When they were driving away, David said, "What was your
diagnosis, sir?"

"What?"

"The skin eruption—what do you think is causing it?"

Moore stared at him, then burst into a shout of laughter.
"Haven't you ever seen chicken pox before?"

"No, as a matter of fact, I haven't."

Moore thought about this as they drove. Then he said slowly,
"I can see how that might happen. So much basic science a medical student has to learn today that there's not the time there was
for simple symptoms. And chicken pox isn't something that normally gets into a big city hospital."

"Just the same, it's pretty serious, my not knowing . . ."

"David, more than half the medicine I know, I learned after I
was in practice, largely from the older doctors. I imagine you've
picked up quite a bit from Fairchild, haven't you?"

"I have indeed."

"Same thing in general country practice, only more so, probably. Don't let it bother you, Dave."

One morning Dr. Moore asked David to go and see how old Alice Henderson was getting on since her sister died—not a professional call, he explained, but just to make sure she was all right. David drove out to the Henderson farm, overgrown now with weeds, the house unpainted and rotting. He gazed at the desolation with astonishment.

No one answered his knock, so he depressed the latch and went in. A peevish cry led him into a tiny bedroom where an old woman glared up at him with malignant eyes from her untidy bed. He controlled disgust, and told her who he was.

"Don't want you. Why didn't Moore come hisself?"

"Dr. Moore is very busy, Miss Henderson."

Her face was contorted with misery and helplessness, and he saw that she was crying. With parchment-colored hands she pulled the sheet against her open mouth.

"Are you all alone here?" he asked.

"Alone enough. Woman down the road comes and does for me, time her own chores is done."

"But wouldn't you rather be in a nice home with other people? Dr. Moore could fix it up for you."

"*You leave me be.*" It was a piercing shriek. The frail old body was shaking uncontrollably.

He waited until she had calmed down, then reached for her wrist to feel her pulse. It was light and uncertain. He laid her skinny arm back on the bed, frowning. There was no doubt in his mind that she should be moved out of here and into a hospital as fast as possible. He looked down at her and discovered that she had been watching him with animosity.

"You leave me be," she said. "Go away."

There was nothing in David's apartment but packing boxes from New York, for his furniture had not yet been delivered. On the way back to the Republic House he decided to stop there and see if he could find his record player. By the time he had located it and opened a carton of recordings, the floor was littered with packing material. Suddenly, to his surprise, someone

323

knocked on his door and he opened it to see Adele Perkins.

She said, "I heard you were moving in, so I thought I'd come and help. What a mess!"

"I was just going to clean up a little," he said untruthfully.

She was already picking crumpled paper off the floor. When her arms were full she dumped the load in the fireplace and turned to face him. "I didn't really come to help you unpack, and I'm in no mood to pretend I did." She held a match to the papers, which caught with a great burst of flame. "Here, collect some of the boards from the boxes and we'll have a good fire."

He pried some boards off the packing cases and laid them beside the hearth. She was sitting on the floor with her back against a box of books, and he let himself down beside her.

"It would shock the cackling old hens of this town to know that I was up here alone with you like this," she said. "The real reason I came is that Ianthe Norton's just been giving me a lecture in her irritatingly sweet way about my not having helped at the hospital on Donation Day."

"You mean you came here to defy her on principle."

He laughed and she joined in. "Yes, and all her kind. Come on, I feel reckless. Let's eat lunch here. I'll get some sandwiches from the dairy bar and you go to the liquor store—we want gin and vermouth for martinis. It will be fun."

Soon they were back, sitting side by side on the floor, eating their sandwiches. There was still some martini left in the pitcher and she held it toward him. "Let's finish this ice water."

He took a sip from his filled glass and set it down on the floor. She held hers and gazed in silence at the fire.

The room seemed to be growing darker. David looked at his watch. Two o'clock. Outside, black clouds scudded across the sky. He said, "It's going to rain." There was a sharp tapping on the windowpanes. Hail. The hail turned to rain. In the gray stillness of the room the fire seemed full of consequence.

Suddenly, fiercely, Adele leaned forward, pulled David toward her and kissed him. He held her by her arms, at first lightly, then with a fierce, hard grip. When at last he released her, she gave a little cry and pressed against him. His arms went around her and she moaned softly.

Then the telephone rang, shrill and nerve-shattering. He plunged across the room and picked it up off the floor. "Dr. Armstrong speaking." He sounded choked and unnatural.

"Oh, Doctor, I thought you might be there. This is Miss Judson. We've just admitted a patient, and Dr. Moore says could you get the work-up started? No special hurry. He'll be along as soon as office hours are over. And your license has finally come."

"Thank you. I'll be there in a few minutes."

He was wholly himself again. Adele called from the kitchen in her clear, high voice, "I'm making us some coffee." She too seemed to have returned to normal and, illogically, this made him a little resentful. He sat down on a packing case to wait—there would be no more close, unwise proximity on the floor. As he did so he realized with a shock the full enormity of what had almost happened. It was the most utterly witless thing he had ever done, or nearly done, in his life. What really disturbed him was that his self-discipline, so carefully built up, should vanish at the first writhing of desire. And not desire for this woman, merely desire.

Adele came back carrying two full cups, held one out to him and sat down on a packing case. In a barely audible voice she said, "I'm sorry. It's just that I need someone so much. But not that way. I need a friend, and I don't know how to go about it. Everything's a mess—my whole life." Her hand jerked, spilling coffee. He took the cup from her and she covered her face with her hands, crying in silent agony.

He said, as if to a patient, "Hadn't you better tell me about it?"

She drew in her breath. "Howard was drinking again last night. He got to yelling at Howie and when Howie didn't reply he hit him. He's never done that before. And instead of standing up to him, Howie just let him do it. Then he ran out of the house and never came back. He went up to Howard's cabin on the mountain, I suppose. He's often gone off in the woods, but never all night before. He's a queer boy. He wants to be a veterinarian, and his father despises him for it. He hates his home."

325

"Did he go to school today? Can you phone and find out?"

"Not without starting talk. If he doesn't show up after school, we'll have to do something. I don't know what. If people ever suspect that Howard's drinking, we'll be finished in Haddon."

"How did you happen to come here in the first place?"

She gave him a swift look and was silent. At last she said, "I might as well tell you if we're going to be friends. But nobody in Haddon knows except Dr. Moore and a retired surgeon named Harlan Greer. Howard was chief surgical resident at Midtown Central Hospital in Cleveland, and he was good. Dr. Greer was head of the department."

"The same Dr. Greer who lives in Haddon now?"

"The same. He thought highly of Howard's ability. I had inherited a little money from my parents, and we'd been married after he started his residency. One day Howard had an idea for improving a certain operation. He decided to practice until he had it perfected and then just do it someday when he was operating. He could have arranged with Pathology to let him experiment, but that way he couldn't have kept it secret, and he might have had to wait—he's very impatient. So one night he went down to the hospital morgue and tried it on a body. . . ."

"But that's against the law. Mandatory dismissal."

"Yes. Well, someone saw the light under the door."

"So he wasn't allowed to finish his residency."

"No. And he had no chance at all of working in a first-class hospital, so Greer got him taken on by Moore. Really, Howard bought his way in with what was left of the money I inherited."

"The new wing."

"Yes. And Haddon is a life sentence. Howard thinks we might escape, at least to Warwick. I don't believe it. I don't believe there's anything in life for us because of what he did. He was wonderful when we first were married—but then his career being wrecked, and now his disappointment in Howie . . . it's changed him so. . . . I feel so alone. You'll be my friend, won't you?"

"Of course, Adele."

She looked at him, her expression troubled, as though she

knew that his reply was perfunctory and that the friendship she wanted could not be had by asking for it. Then she rose. "I must go now. Thank you for listening, David."

When she had left, he hurried to the hospital.

It was several hours later that David went into Moore's office. They had returned from the hospital, and now the last patient had gone from the small surgery.

"I saw Miss Henderson, Dr. Moore. She's in a bad way, and I suggest she be got into the hospital quickly. She obviously has a lot of things wrong with her that tests would show up."

"I know pretty well what's wrong with her. She's old, and she's wearing out—heart, kidneys, everything. Just how worn-out doesn't matter, since there isn't much to do about it."

David jumped up and began to pace the narrow room. Moore, leaning back in his swivel chair, watched him. "Come and sit down, David. I know you don't like this way of doing things."

"No, I don't. It disturbs me very much."

"You're used to working in a big hospital, and it's natural for you to put a good deal of reliance on the hospital and its facilities. But to old Alice the hospital is where you go to die. The poor old thing would be terrified. It would be cruel, and all you'd gain would be a little detail about the extent to which her worn-out body had deteriorated."

"Didn't I hear that you had her sister in the hospital?"

"She developed pneumonia. I had no choice."

"I still don't think Alice should be left in that place."

"Then there's not much use my saying anything, is there?"

In the silence each gave the other a long, steady look. Then David rose and walked rapidly out of the office.

Anger, self-righteous and burning, propelled David along the street. He walked fast without the least idea where he was going, so that his arrival at the foot of the stairs to May Turner's apartment was, so far as he was aware, entirely unpremeditated.

He found May radiant. "Oh, David, come and see." She was

blushing, he thought, because of her unthinking eager use of his first name. It was charming.

"See what? Oh—the telephone-answering equipment."

She was patting, as though with affection, a box that had levers and buttons, and a telephone hanging from a hook.

"Does it really work?" It was, he thought, a silly thing to ask, but there was a feeling of being aware of each other on another level that made what they were saying of little importance.

"Of course it works. Imagine—when it's all installed I'll be able to talk to you in your car when you're *any*where. Come here and I'll show you." She made room for him to sit beside her on the couch, forgetting, in her excitement, to be careful. Pain contorted her face. He looked down at her seriously.

"I don't like it at all, May. You can't go on having pain like that. We've got to get you fixed up quickly."

"Don't let's talk about it now."

"All right. . . . Do you know how to work it?"

"Certainly I do. The man showed me."

The buttons were neatly labeled MOORE, PERKINS, LADD, ARM-STRONG. "Suppose someone calls me—what happens?"

"The button with your name lights up, something buzzes, and I pick up the phone. You've told me where you are, and then I call you and tell you whatever it is."

"But you can't call me in my car with that equipment."

"Not yet. We have to get permission to use a wavelength." She frowned. "Do you know it will cost nearly a thousand dollars just for the radio part I will have in this room?"

An unimaginable sum to her, obviously. "You know the town is going to pay half."

"Yes. But I hate Uncle Ed's having any more expense. David, you're going to help about the hospital, aren't you?"

"How do you mean?"

"Some people are saying that Uncle Ed's hospital is too old and run-down and that it should be closed!"

"It's old and run-down, all right. What I can't understand is why a man of his age should care. If there were a good modern hospital at Silver Springs, I should think he would welcome an excuse to close up."

"How can you be so insensitive? It's his lifework!"

"I'm not at all sure that so personal an attitude behind a hospital that is meant to serve the public is really wholesome."

"Then why did you come here?"

"I've just been wondering. The difference in point of view is so fundamental. To Dr. Moore, it seems, a patient's comfort and happiness come before an accurate diagnosis, before everything."

"Have you and Uncle Ed quarreled about this?"

"Not exactly, no. And May, I don't want to quarrel with you."

"But you don't even try to understand."

"To me it looks like a simple question of economics—Moore is going to run out of money and the bank won't give him any more. There couldn't be a drive for funds, as apparently there is to be for the Health Center, because it's a private hospital. And yet I gather public opinion is very much aroused."

"Public opinion runs a town like this. You'll see that at Town Meeting in February." Her head turned on the pillow.

"You're tired."

"Yes." Her prettiness seemed suddenly fragile.

"Please forgive me. I shouldn't have come, May, but I wanted to talk to you. I want to be friends."

"So do I!" She smiled.

IANTHE NORTON was in her kitchen when she heard a car brushing the branches of the lilac bush. She glanced at the clock, saw that it was almost eleven; then, at the sound of Moore's heavy footsteps, she smiled.

"I saw your light," he said. "I thought I'd stop by . . ."

"I'm glad you did, Ed. Hang up your coat, and I'll fry you some eggs. I'd like your company for a while. The house seems so empty now that Nat's upstairs all the time."

"I'll have to call May and tell her where I am. The answering service has just begun."

When he came back she was laying long strips of bacon in a

pan. Moore sat down and watched her with enjoyment. The warmth of the kitchen soothed him into a dreamy state. When Ianthe came to the table bringing eggs and bacon and coffee, he had to force his mind to take hold. "How is Nat, Ianthe?"

"There's been a change, Ed. Just the last two days. He's dulled and indifferent. He seems to have given up being himself. He sleeps a lot. What does this mean, Ed?"

"Maybe nothing. Anyone who's tired feels like that. I'll stop by in the morning and have a look at him."

Ianthe sighed. "Ed, I can't reconcile myself to this."

"I don't know how to help you, Ianthe. I wish I did. I felt that way when Matilda went. He isn't suffering physically. . . ."

"But, Ed . . ." She stopped. "It doesn't do any good to talk about it, I guess. How is your new young man working out?"

"Armstrong? He'll be all right, give him time. He's got a lot to learn and unlearn before he makes a good country doctor." He picked up his cup, frowning. "These new young men depend too much on laboratories and don't pay enough attention to the patient. That's a fault of city medicine. With changes coming as fast as they are, I'm afraid the patient as a person may get lost."

"Ed, there's talk around town that you might be going to give up the hospital. That isn't true, is it?"

"No!"

She considered this. "The trouble is money, isn't it?"

He rubbed his hand over his face. "I'm sure of enough money for close to a year. Stoner won't carry me beyond that."

"I don't like Tim Stoner and I never did."

"He's doing what he thinks is right. He thinks Haddon doesn't need a hospital, that there should be one at Silver Springs."

"Ed, no. We want *your* hospital."

"I'm not so sure people generally feel that way."

"How *can* you say that? Think of Donation Day."

"There's something else involved in all this—the trend toward government participation and control. People who believe in that want to destroy my hospital just because it's privately owned."

"A lot of people don't feel that way, Ed. The town should understand what the issue is. I can't do much as things are with Nat, but I can do something, and I will." Deep in thought, she smoothed the tablecloth with her hand. Moore was seized by an impulse to put his hand over hers. This so horrified him that he shoved his chair abruptly back from the table.

She looked up and smiled. "Ed, my father left me quite a bit of money. Nat never wanted us to use it, so it's still there. You can have it, and I don't care whether I get it back or not."

"Ianthe!"

"I mean it, Ed. It's about fifty thousand dollars."

"It's too great a risk. It's not a safe investment."

"I tell you, I don't care. That would help, wouldn't it?"

"Of course it would help, but, Ianthe, I can't . . ." Activated by emotion, he jumped to his feet.

Ianthe too rose. "Just go home and think about it, Ed." Suddenly he laughed. "By golly, you make a man feel good. Thanks for the eggs. I'll be in to see Nat in the morning."

As DAVID came down the front stairs of the hospital, Moore emerged from his office. "You're going to the Rotary lunch, aren't you? It's time to get going."

"I don't think I'll go. That's just not my line." It had not occurred to David to do anything with his Rotary invitations but throw them away.

"Now look here. I know you're not in a mood to take advice from me these days, but going to Rotary lunch is something that, in a small town, you have to do."

"Have to?"

Moore grinned. "You should—shouldn't he, Edna?"

"Yes, Doctor, you really should."

David, to whom the term Rotarian meant a special and unfamiliar type, saw the moment he and Moore entered the Republic House dining room that he was wrong. These men were no different from any cross section—average men with whom he could merge quite satisfactorily.

Perkins had saved a table. He gave David a slap on the back

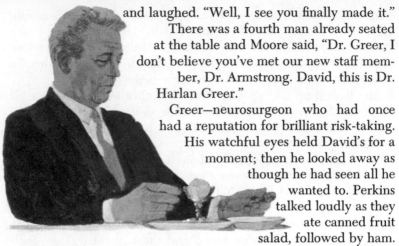

and laughed. "Well, I see you finally made it." There was a fourth man already seated at the table and Moore said, "Dr. Greer, I don't believe you've met our new staff member, Dr. Armstrong. David, this is Dr. Harlan Greer."

Greer—neurosurgeon who had once had a reputation for brilliant risk-taking. His watchful eyes held David's for a moment; then he looked away as though he had seen all he wanted to. Perkins talked loudly as they ate canned fruit salad, followed by ham.

David, not to seem wholly tongue-tied, said to Greer, "Are you practicing at all these days, sir?"

Greer's delicate hands cut his ham precisely. "No. Nowadays I write. And I think I will try my hand at teaching. There will be a post open at the Warwick Medical School—first-year surgery. I have applied for it, and"—Greer smiled at them all—"I rather think they will give it to me, don't you?"

Perkins laid down his knife and fork, his face expressionless. Moore hitched his chair forward sharply, but neither made any comment. A waitress put a dish of green ice cream in front of Perkins. He said, "*Ugh*," and pushed it away.

Moore touched David's arm. "Better listen to this," he said.

At the head table the president was standing with the gavel in his hand. "Folks . . . it isn't often the town gets a chance to welcome a new doctor. But we got one now. Dr. David Armstrong. Stand up, Doc."

There was a roar of applause and calls of "Welcome, Doc." Red in the face, David half rose and sat down again.

The gavel came down. "This is the *first* time Doc Armstrong's been to one of our meetings, though he's been invited before. I know, because I sent the two notices myself."

He was grinning, and all around men were beginning to laugh. David leaned over and said to Moore, "What's this about?"

"Wait and see."

The president went on, "You all know the rule—though maybe our new doc doesn't—about missing meetings. The fact is, our new doc gets the rabbit." He reached down behind the table and came up holding a cage. In it was a large brown rabbit.

Moore laughed at the desperation in David's face. "I got stuck with him myself, three times."

"This here is the Rotary rabbit. Name's Harry. When a man misses two lunches straight, he gets to keep Harry till the next meeting, to sort of remind him he'd better come. Come and get him, Doc. He's all yours for a week."

Greer said, "Don't look so serious, my boy. Smile." And David, wedging himself past chairs, heard Perkins say to Greer, "A good surgeon, but a bit of a stuffed shirt."

At the speaker's table he was handed the cage. The rabbit sat with ears laid back, eyes shut, a shred of lettuce hanging from his mouth. He had an air of raffishness, and David smiled; then, feeling fine, he laughed. "Hullo, Harry," he said. There was a great deal of noise, and in it all David was conscious only of good nature and friendliness as he returned to his table.

The gavel was pounding. A thickset man was standing to be recognized. David leaned toward Perkins. "Who's that?"

"Joe Zovick. Plumber. Belongs in the category of slob."

The president said, "All right, Joe."

"I been thinkin'," Zovick said loudly, "that since we got no special program today and since we got the doctors here—"

Moore said, "Good Lord" under his breath.

"—There's something the town's pretty much wrought up about. That's about the hospital. It's run-down, and it's broke, or so I hear. I hear Doc Moore's going to shut it up and quit—"

Moore said loudly, "I'm not shutting up, and I'm not quitting. And this isn't the place to discuss it."

"Sure it is. Whether Haddon has a hospital or not concerns us all. If Doc Moore won't discuss it, maybe Mr. Stoner will."

333

Stoner rose slowly and spoke without raising his voice. "Joe Zovick is wrong. The continuance or discontinuance of the hospital is no concern of the people at all." All over the room there was a murmur of dissent. "I will tell you why." His manner became sharp and incisive. "The hospital is private property. Dr. Moore owns it. The town has no voice whatsoever in what he does with it. Whether the private ownership of a hospital is desirable is another question. But—and in this I agree with Dr. Moore—this is not the place for such discussion."

Moore stood up so suddenly that David was taken by surprise. "Now *I've* got something to say." His voice was controlled and strong. "Tim Stoner is right. I do own the hospital, but only because, thirty years ago, the town didn't know it needed one. I don't profit by this ownership." There was a general laugh, and Moore smiled. "Now, I don't agree with Tim Stoner that it's nobody's business but mine whether I close the hospital or not. I have a proposition to make. I want to ask the Town Meeting in February if Haddon still wants a hospital. If the people do, I'll modernize and enlarge—"

Stoner's voice said a single sharp word: "How?"

David, watching Moore turn toward Stoner to reply, thought his eyes had never seemed so full of blueness and life. "I don't know how. I didn't know how I was going to start a hospital years ago, but I did it. If it turns out that the town wants a hospital, I give you my pledge to see that there is an adequate one. And to insure that I have an able successor."

During the outbreak of applause, Moore stood with his head bowed, and David thought that he was realizing that the applause might well be for him personally and nothing more. Zovick called, "And what about if the town don't want it, Doc?"

Moore drew a long breath. "In that case, I shall begin closing at once. You realize, of course, that Dr. Perkins, being a surgeon, could no longer practice here. I myself should retire."

As tumult broke out, David saw Perkins staring at Moore as though he had never quite seen him before. The room slowly quieted down. The president said, "Well, folks, that's the kind of personal ovation any man might be proud to get. I don't know's I ever heard anything like it before. But now time's getting on and we'll all have to get back to work. . . ."

Outside the door, Moore said, "Well, David. Office hours—remember? What are you going to do with that thing?"

David looked at the cage in his arms and his face grew red. "I almost forgot I had it. I'll take it to my room and be right over."

Chapter 9

OCTOBER FLAMED with colored leaves, and the wayside ferns made a bright filigree of golds and rusts. Then came a day of wind and driving rain, and after that the trees were bare, the air still and damp. Here the season seemed to pause before making the final change into winter.

As Moore turned the jeep into the Norton driveway, he was thinking that this was not unlike what had been going on in Nathaniel's dying body. The first struggle with his enemy had left him gaunt and wasted, but the sharp, sardonic mind had not suffered. Then the mind had changed subtly, softening in its relation to life. In this phase he seemed to be reviewing life much as he might turn the pages of a book that filled him with vague wonder, but did not truly concern him. This was the change that Ianthe had seen, and once established, it seemed as likely to continue indefinitely as the bleak fall weather. But Moore had begun to watch closely for signs of the coming end.

He knocked lightly on the kitchen door, thinking that if Ianthe had gone upstairs to be with Nathaniel, there was no need to call her down. She was looking worn and strained these days, and much more would be demanded of her before the end. When there was no reply, he turned the doorknob and went in. The big house seemed weary and sad as he went quietly upstairs.

The door of Norton's room was open, and from the hall he could see the high four-poster bed and Nat in his gray dressing gown lying there asleep. Nearby, in an armchair, Ianthe sat staring into space. She did not hear him there, and for a moment he stood looking at her face. Norton moved then and she looked up and saw him. "Come in, Ed. Nat, here's Ed to see you."

Nat slowly turned his head on the pillow and looked up at them with eyes softened by sleep, lips forming words that should have been "Hullo, Ed," but the only sound the breathy wheeze . . . and with that the sleep gone, and in the eyes the agony of remembering. . . . He groped on the bedside table for the slate, and they both leaned close to read, I DREAMED I HAD MY VOICE AGAIN.

Moore put his hand on Nat's shoulder. "Ianthe, I'm going to look Nat over now. Do you think you could give me a cup of coffee when I come down?"

"Of course, Ed."

The examination was careful, but it did not take long. The cancer cells had planted themselves in Nat's liver, forming masses which could be felt, and perhaps in his lungs and brain. Moore sat down on the foot of the bed, and for a moment they looked at each other in silence. Nat's gaze was steady.

Moore said, "Nat, I want you to go into the hospital now."

Nat's gaze did not shift but his eyes grew deep and sad, so that Moore knew he understood the full implications of this. He wrote, WOULD IT BE EASIER FOR IANTHE?

"Yes, Nat, it would."

Norton gave him a faint half smile, and Moore, suddenly unable to bear the resignation he saw in it, walked to the window. "I should think you might go as soon as possible, Nat. Why don't I phone Edna now and make sure she's got a room?"

He turned around. Nat nodded, his mouth pulled in tightly. There were tears in his eyes. Moore went quickly out.

He made his call, then went to the kitchen. Ianthe was not there, but the room was filled with the odor of fresh coffee, and cups were on the table. Thinking she might be in the garden, he went out and found her scattering pine needles on the flower beds for winter protection. She came toward him, pushing her hair out of her face, and suddenly his senses were overwhelmed and he had to grope like a schoolboy for something to say.

"Isn't it early to put on a winter mulch?"

"Yes, but I thought I'd better get it done . . ." She broke off as the shrubbery parted and a towheaded youth in a black leather jacket appeared. He carried the small, limp body of a fawn.

"Why, Howie Perkins!" Ianthe ran toward him.

"He's hurt, Mrs. Norton. I found him up on the mountain. Somebody shot him." His words tumbled out. "Dr. Moore, you'll do something, won't you?"

"Calm down, Howie. Take him into the barn. We'll have a look."

In the barn Howie laid the deer down, its dappled sides heaving. "Imagine anyone's shooting him, Dr. Moore. I didn't dare take him home because Dad would just call the game warden . . ."

"We'll have to report to the warden too, Howie. But I'm sure he wouldn't make you turn this little fellow loose in this condition. I'll ask him to let you take care of the deer through hunting season. If Mrs. Norton will let you keep him here, that is, which is quite a lot to ask."

"He can stay if you feed him, Howie."

"Oh, *gosh*, Mrs. Norton. Sure I'll do that."

"Here it is. Dog bite." Moore exposed some torn perforations in the deer's throat. "Went clean through." Moore had taken out of his bag disinfectant, gauze and a swab.

"Don't hurt him, Dr. Moore. Please don't hurt him. . . ."

"I can't help it, Howie." The deer jerked as Moore dressed the wound, then lay still.

When it was finished, Ianthe said, "Come in the house and get warm, Howie. I have a piece of chocolate cake."

"I just don't think I should leave him for a while, Mrs. Norton. He might get scared in a strange barn."

"All right. I'll bring you some cake."

As the kitchen door closed behind Moore and Ianthe, she said, "And that's the lad Perkins wants to make into a surgeon."

"He's certainly not cut out for it."

"But for all his nerves and anxieties he's got courage. You want a piece of cake too, Ed?"

"No, thanks. But I want to talk to you when you get back."

She gave him a look of alarm, but said nothing, only hurrying a little as she sliced the cake. He opened the door for her, thinking the screen door shouldn't be up this late in the year— thinking that one of these days soon he'd better take it down for her . . . and maybe look around for other chores to do. . . .

When she came back she sat by the kitchen table, the troubled, beautiful eyes watching him. He sighed and said, "Nat's trouble has come back again, Ianthe. I want him in the hospital."

Her breath came in quick, shallow gasps. "No, Ed, no. I can get a nurse to help if I have to. Let him stay in his own home."

"It wouldn't be wise. There's bound to be some suffering now, and if he's at the hospital we can minimize it."

She put her elbows on the table and her face in her hands.

Moore said, "Let's not wait, Ianthe. You get him ready and drive him to the hospital. I'll meet you there."

She moved toward the hall, and as she passed him he touched her shoulder gently. Then he let himself out and drove away.

Ianthe went upstairs, and at the doorway of her husband's room, she saw him bending over a bureau drawer, taking out a shirt. All her life she would never forget the way he looked then, his old gray robe hanging loose, one tassel on the floor.

"Oh, Nat . . ."

She went across the room to him. He put the shirt down and held her close. His cheek rested on her hair and his lips moved soundlessly. She felt him trembling.

After a moment he pushed her away and, keeping his face hidden from her, unfolded the shirt slowly and uncertainly. She said in a small, choked voice, "Let me help you, Nat." He shook his head and gave her a little smile, and she saw that he wanted to do it this last time himself. Down in the hall he put his arm around her, and they went out. It was he who was leading her.

Mr. Whitall, of the Public Health Service, looked appraisingly around the room next to Moore's that had become David's office. "You're fixed up fine in here. Everything new." He filled his pipe and tamped down the tobacco. "Quite a lot of noise the river makes. Bother you?"

"I don't even hear it any more."

Whitall fixed his eyes on David while he pulled out a kitchen match and struck it with his thumbnail. David said, "Did you want to see me about something special?"

"I've just come from an interview with Dr. Moore. I was trying to find out some minor facts about his hospital."

"Does the Public Health Service give this kind of detailed, personal attention to all small hospitals in the state?"

Whitall took a gurgling drag or two on his pipe. "By no means," he said. "I have a personal interest in this setup here. I want to make an important report. And I must say, though Moore answered my questions, he did it with nothing to spare."

"I don't think his attitude is hard to explain. He knows you think his hospital should be closed up. He doesn't agree."

"I'm surprised he's been able to keep it open as long as he has. Do you know, while I was talking to him a man came in for some antibiotic capsules. Moore shook a handful out of a bottle, put 'em in an envelope and handed 'em over. I happen to know those capsules cost twenty cents each. When the man had gone, I said, 'Are you *giving* him those?' He pretended he didn't hear me."

David looked at his watch. "Was there anything special?"

"Well . . . yes. As a matter of fact I thought we might have dinner together tonight—and sort of talk about things."

"I'm sorry, I have an engagement." To soften the baldness of the statement, he said, "A Dr. Barlow is coming from Warwick."

"I've wanted to talk to Barlow. May I join you?"

"His wife is coming. We're all going to a friend's for a picnic supper."

"Is the friend anyone I know?"

"I don't think you'd know her. Her name is May Turner."

"Oh, the one who runs the answering service. If it's just a picnic, I'm sure I could be included without inconvenience."

Whitall banged out his pipe in an ashtray with slow, heavy blows. David sighed with fortitude and reached for the telephone.

Dr. Barlow was already at May's apartment when they arrived. "My wife's in the kitchen," he said, receiving Whitall's handshake with blank neutrality. From her couch May said, "How do you do?" to his overelaborate greeting.

At a table in the corner Barlow began mixing drinks. "What will it be, Mr. Whitall?"

"Scotch, please."

"Dave, a martini—it's your night off. . . . Oh, here's Emily."

David turned to see a sturdy young woman with a pleasant, gravely intelligent face. Whitall was saying, "I'm very glad to meet you, little lady," and David found himself exchanging swift sidelong smiles with May. Because of Whitall's presence, these four comparative strangers had become at once a cohesive group, David reflected. He came out of his brief reverie to hear Whitall say to Barlow, "I tell you"—the pipe stabbed the air—"you doctors will have lost a lot of self-determination in ten years' time."

"How so?" Barlow sounded belligerent. "If you mean government controls, limiting our freedom of—"

"I don't mean anything of the sort," said Whitall pettishly. "I'm surprised at you. In one minute you're going to start talking about the 'creeping socialization of medicine.' "

"Well, that's exactly—"

"No, hear me out. Please. You younger men have been trained to use equipment for diagnosis and treatment that you can't possibly afford if you practice alone. So you form groups like this proposed Health Center, and all chip in and buy a fluoroscope and X-ray equipment. And sometimes you need equipment that's so expensive most small hospitals can't afford it. What I am getting at is that individual enterprise and charity have gone as far as they can in providing these things. The only way to advance from here on is by using federal grants."

Barlow waved his arms, then shoved his hands in his pockets as though to discipline himself. "Damn it, money means control. If the major share of 'health money' comes from government, then a bunch of bureaucrats will be telling me what to do. I don't like it and I won't have it. I'll work for my patients—"

"A large percent of whom, in ten years' time, will be paying you through government insurance. It's the wave of the future, Doctor. You— Oh, thank you, Mrs. Barlow. That looks delicious."

Whitall took the plate that Emily was holding out to him. "Did you know, Dr. Barlow, that federal grants now make up sixty-four percent of all medical research funds? And did you ever hear of research men being controlled or restricted in any way?"

"I can't answer that. I don't know."

David said, "I don't think I ever have—it's an interesting thought." He carried his plate to May's couch.

"David," she whispered, "do you agree with him?"

"So far, I do. But I haven't thought enough about the question of government in medicine. I guess I'm not alone in that."

Whitall was saying, "What you all don't see is that Moore's hospital couldn't survive under any circumstances. The town thinks it has a choice between having Moore's hospital and having none. That isn't the choice at all. Moore's hospital is dead, it's history. Don't you agree, Dr. Armstrong?"

"I don't know. I don't believe in private hospitals. Though there are good ones, as Moore's is. But with first-aid equipment in the Health Center, I can't see that a hospital is needed here."

"The town *has* a choice, but not the one it thinks it has. It's between no hospital at all or a good modern one enmeshed in a statewide plan. Now contrast Moore's old firetrap with a fine modern plant of colored tile and glass—"

"*Mr. Whitall!*" May brought both small fists down on the telephone box so hard that it jumped. "You're an outsider. You don't know how the town feels. We love Uncle Ed. We want his hospital just as it is. We don't want some agency telling us how to be sick according to a government plan. We want our *own* doctors and our *own* hospital, and we don't want any outsiders. Excuse me, but that's how we feel."

Whitall was red in the face, bewildered, and, David saw, hurt.

David held May's hand until she stopped trembling with anger. Presently he remarked that Mr. Stoner had assured him that the question of Haddon's having a new hospital was academic, since the contribution required by the town would be too great. The remark fell like a stone in the silence.

In a little while, subdued and moody, Whitall said a constrained good-by and left.

May pushed back her hair in a distracted way. "I suppose I shouldn't have said that to him, but he made me mad."

Barlow nodded. "There's nothing cockier than a little fellow with a government agency at his back."

Chapter 10

MOORE KNOCKED at the door of the Greer house, which he remembered from the days of the old doctor, Harlan Greer's father. It was opened by a squat man with a foreign air whom Moore had never seen before.

"I'm Dr. Moore. Is Dr. Greer in?"

"Ya, in study. He expect you, no?"

"He expect me, yes."

Moore was led through a room that he remembered as having faded wallpaper and a potbellied stove but that now had exposed beams in the low ceiling and an impressive fireplace. Then came a room that had once been the shed, then a very large room and Moore thought, The barn, by golly! and grinned at Greer who was getting up from a large desk by a big picture window.

"Hullo, Moore. Glad to see you. Fritz, another glass of sherry."

Moore sat down. "You've made a lot of changes. I remember helping your father hitch up in here one night when we were going to the same case. I didn't know how to hitch, and he thought that was disgraceful. He never really had any faith in me as a doctor after that. You've made the old place pretty comfortable."

"Yes. But it's finished now. And my book is finished. I find myself without any real occupation—and I don't like it."

"Is that why you're interested in teaching at Warwick?"

"Yes, I must keep active. Retirement bores me."

"Did you know that Howard Perkins has also applied?"

Greer put his sherry glass down carefully. "No, I didn't. You'd be in a bad spot if you lost him, wouldn't you?"

"I'm in a bad spot now."

"Just what did you want to say to me about this, Moore?"

"I doubt if anybody at Warwick knows about his early history, and they might not care if they did, but . . ."

"You're suggesting that if they did, it might prejudice them against him, and you wouldn't lose your surgeon?"

"Certainly not." Moore shifted angrily in his seat. "You were exceedingly kind to him once. I want to ask you, if you hear that old story coming out, to do what you can to put the lid on again."

Greer sighed. "You're a remarkable man, Ed. Any other man in your position would be likely to use any undercover methods to keep Perkins. Without him, your chances of saving your hospital are almost nil. Any chance of Armstrong's staying?"

"None at all. Let me ask you a question. Do you think there should be a hospital in Haddon?"

"On the whole, yes. At present we don't need one as much as Silver Springs, but this part of the state is growing fast. Soon there will be a large enough population to support a good one."

Moore gave Greer a sharp look and leaned forward. "All I need is money for repairs and some modernization, and there is the hospital that Haddon needs—or the start of it. I thought perhaps you'd be willing to put some money in and to associate yourself with the management of the hospital to any extent you cared to."

"How much money were you thinking of, Doctor?"

"Say a hundred and fifty thousand."

Moore waited, breathing heavily, while Greer sat tapping his fingers on his knees.

"There's a lot to be said against the continuance of your hospital. But putting it in shape, getting it ready for growth, would be a challenge. It interests me. But we're two old men. Let me think it over, will you?"

"Of course." Moore rose. "Your coming in would probably make all the difference in whether the hospital pulls through or not."

OUTSIDE NATHANIEL NORTON's hospital room Moore looked at his watch and saw himself doomed to dining on sandwiches—unless Edna was keeping some food warm for him. The thought cheered him, and he opened the door and went in.

Ianthe sat by the bed, lamplight shining on her hair. She smiled at Moore and he felt the beauty of the smile all through him. On the bed, Norton turned his head slowly; then his eyes went to Ianthe and the door.

"He wants to talk to you," she said. "I'll wait outside."

When she had gone, Norton began writing on his slate. Moore took note of how feeble he had grown. The effort to write seemed almost too much for him, and the letters, when he had finished, were half formed, wandering. HOSP—IT'S GOOD—THE FOOLS DON'T KNOW HOW GOOD. FIGHT THEM AND KEEP IT. KEEP THE GOVERN. OUT. IANTHE WANTS TO GIVE YOU MONEY. TAKE IT, ED.

Moore stood with the slate in his hands, too moved to speak. Then he realized that the groping skeleton hand was reaching out to take his and that the bony face was contorted in the only friendly smile he had ever seen there. A moment later Norton drifted off into apathy. Moore quietly left the room. Ianthe was waiting for him. "Ed, could you possibly come to the house for a few minutes after office hours?"

"I will. But you must go home now. Have you got your car?"

"No, I walked."

"I'll drive you back on my way to the office."

Good-by to Edna's hot food . . . He put his hand on Ianthe's arm and they went down the stairs together.

AT TEN O'CLOCK that night, after he had said good night to his last patient, Moore returned to the Norton house. Ianthe had made a fire in the study and set out a tray with glasses, ice and a bottle of Scotch. Moore poured himself a modest drink. "What's on your mind, Ianthe?"

"Ed, I realize that Nat's not suffering very much physically, but his mind is clear and he's suffering mentally."

"Nat's a brave man."

"I know, but it's cruel, Ed. I can't bear it. I can't bear it." The words were an agonized cry. She rose and went to the end of the room, standing with her back to him. After a moment she said in a more controlled voice, "It's the waiting that's so hard."

"I know." He went to stand beside her, and she brushed away her tears and looked up at him. He led her back to the fire.

"It's so strange, Ed. Nat and I are closer now than we've ever been. I feel that now he understands so much and he'd like to live to use this new understanding. It tortures him. Ed, I want you to fix it so he won't think any more. Can't you do that? So he won't be conscious . . . not for one minute from now until the end."

"Are you sure, Ianthe? You said you had a new understanding of each other. Are you sure you want to let that go?"

"We've had it, Ed, and from now on, as he grows sicker, it will only grow more dim. He knows that too."

"There are drugs—but do you know how *he* would feel?"

"Yes, I know. We haven't talked about it, but I know. Since he can't live he would like to go now. If he didn't have to think or feel any more, it would be like going. He's too proud to ask you, but I know he'd want you to, Ed."

After a moment he said, "You're sure?"

"Yes."

They were silent again. She put her hand over her eyes and he gazed at her sadly, feeling how alone she was, and feeling his own aloneness until these feelings mingled in a sadness that was not without its own comfort. After a while she reached out and put her hand on his sleeve. "Thank you, Ed."

"Ianthe, there's one thing more. There is risk in this. I'd give Nat morphine, but in the quantity I'd have to use, it would tend to repress respiration. It's a risk doctors often take when it's justified, as this is, but I want you to understand."

"I know it's a grave responsibility both for you and for me, Ed. I know it will be the end of his conscious life, and the real end of our life together." She went toward the door, and he followed her. "It will be the real ending of my life, too. I've struggled enough with all the cruelties and disappointments life brings.

345

I want in the future to live so quietly, so negatively, that I won't ever again feel anything very much."

He looked at her almost angrily and started to speak. His lips moved, but he said nothing, overwhelmed by the realization that the protest he wanted to make was personal. Then he went out to the Jeep. Snow had begun to fall and he stood for a moment, feeling its touch on his face, knowing that his life had changed in the last hour so that it would never be quite the same.

Day had barely come when David, driving back from a call, saw Howie Perkins trudging along, obviously intending to walk all the miles to Haddon. David hailed him. "Want a lift?"

"Well, sure, thanks." Howie scrambled in, all legs and arms.

"What are you doing way off here at this hour? Don't you have school today?"

"Yes, but gosh, there's lots of time."

His thin shoulders were hunched over and a tic in his eyelid flickered. David had a sudden, strong desire to shout at him to sit up straight and stop looking like a bent coat hanger.

"Do your parents know where you are?" He must have got up in the middle of the night to come this far.

"I guess not, maybe."

"Howie, you shouldn't worry them."

"They don't care."

"Don't you have any friends at school, Howie?"

"Oh, sure, yes, I guess I do all right."

A sidewise glance revealed the boy's misery under this questioning, and there came to David the certainty that the boy had been out all night in the cold, like an animal.

"Howie, what is it about the woods that you like so much?"

Silence. David was suddenly acutely aware of the isolation of youth. Aware also that his own tone had not been helpful.

"Howie, Dr. Moore told me I should carry snowshoes, just in case, and I don't know how to use them. Could you teach me?"

A look of blank surprise and then a dawning pleasure. "Why, sure, yes. I'd like to, Dr. Armstrong."

At the bridge Howie got out, stood hesitating, then said with a rush, "Dr. Armstrong—how do you get to be a veterinary?"

David laughed. "You go to a school, like a doctor. What gave you the idea you wanted to be a veterinarian, Howie?"

"Well, you see, I found this young deer that had been hurt . . ."

"I heard about that. How is he?"

"He got well, and then, after deer season, the game warden turned him loose. Now he's gone, I like to go and watch the deer in the evening or early morning when you can see them best. I'm sort of getting to know how deer think."

"But why spend your life with animals instead of people?"

"Animals are so easy to get along with. Everything is so simple between you and them."

"And it's not simple with people?"

"Well . . ."

"Don't answer if you don't want to. It wasn't a fair question. You better go get something to eat now."

"All right. Thanks for the lift." He walked toward the bridge.

David parked and went into the dairy bar. Moore was sitting at a corner table. David hesitated. The coolness between them had worn thin, largely because of Moore's failure to see it was there. He looked up then and beckoned. Suddenly David realized the wrongness of letting any estrangement come between them, and feeling freed of a burden, he sat down.

"Been out on an early one, Dave?"

"The Blake boy, out on the gulf road. Appendicitis, but it will keep, so I told them you'd be in touch. Dr. Moore, there is something I'd like to ask you about."

Moore looked up and smiled slightly. "Go ahead."

David lowered his voice. "I'm aware that Dr. Perkins now and then drinks a good deal . . ."

"Have you seen any sign of it in his operating?"

"No, I must say I haven't. His bad temper could come from other things."

"Like finding out that Greer wants—and will probably get—the teaching job at Warwick that Howard wants."

347

"I picked up Howie this morning on the gulf road. I got the impression he'd been out all night."

"Maybe at Howard's cabin up on Mount Adamant."

"He looked in a bad way, thin and nervous—obviously unhappy at home. It's not hard to imagine a tragedy building up. I was wondering if . . . you could help."

"I don't see how. I don't go along with the idea that an unhappy childhood is necessarily bad. If a young person has underlying strength of character, a maladjustment is as good equipment for success as I know. What time have you, Dave?"

"Just eight."

"And I wanted to get to the hospital early." Moore pushed his chair back. "By the way, our radio equipment has come. Leave your car at the garage and they'll hook it up. See you later."

EDNA JUDSON rose from her desk. "Good morning, Doctor. Mr. Brown of the Accreditation Board is in your office."

Brown was looking at the pictures in a medical journal with a layman's pleasurable horror. He put the journal down to rise and shake hands. "How are you, Doctor?"

"Sit down, won't you? What about your report?"

"You should get it today. Otherwise I wouldn't be here."

"What does it say?"

"Provisional accreditation."

For a moment Moore was silent. "That's quite a blow."

"There's not much else we could do. You're financed for less than a year. The tenure of your surgeons is uncertain, and with your equipment—frankly, you're lucky we didn't close you up."

"I've got an almost sure chance of getting enough money to put the hospital back in shape and do some building too."

"I wish I could say I'm glad, but the fact is private hospitals have seen their day. You now have funds. But how about staff? That may be your chief difficulty. Well, I've got to get going." He rose and held out his hand and Moore shook it.

When Brown had gone, Moore went out to the hall. "I'm going up to see Nat," he told Edna. "I'll need a hypo of morphine."

She looked at him anxiously. "Shall I give it to him, Doctor?"

"No, I'll do it."

"Ianthe's with him," she said.

"At this hour? I thought I'd be ahead of her."

"She's here all the time. I can't get her to rest."

Moore entered the room carrying a tray with hypodermic, bottles and cotton. Ianthe was sitting in the armchair. When she saw him she went to the side of the bed. Norton, opening his eyes, looked up at her. Moore knew without looking that Ianthe had put her hand in Nat's. He kept his eyes and his mind on what he was doing, giving them what privacy he could for this painful moment. He swabbed a spot on Nat's pitifully thin arm. And he knew by the way Nat braced himself for the needle that he had guessed. It was over quickly. Moore dropped the hypo on the tray, and went out without looking at them. He carried with him a feeling of their communication with each other and with himself. He did not realize that not a word had been spoken.

Chapter 11

ADELE LAY in her bed and stared at the dim oblong of the window. From the moment she awakened she had listened, though for what she did not know, for she heard nothing but Perkins' heavy breathing in the next bed. The night had a luminescence, not from the moon or the stars, but sourceless and disturbing. On such a night deer move out of the darkness of the woods, night birds fly low and small animals venture stealthily. Adele thought of Howie and how a night like this would stir him. She wondered if he might have gone to find his deer.

She pushed her legs over the side of the bed and let herself out into the hall. She opened the door to Howie's room. The bed was empty. Cold wind came through the open windows, billowing the curtains. She stood in the path of the wind until she was numb in body and mind.

She did not waken Perkins until she was back in her own bed. Then she said, "*Howard,*" sharply. He came awake like a doctor long accustomed to calls in the night and reached for the telephone. "It's not a call, Howard. Howie's gone again."

"You wake me up for that? He'll be back. He's done it before."

"Only once. But he must be made to stop doing it. He won't be any good at school tomorrow."

"I'll talk to him in the morning. What time is it?"

"Two thirty."

Perkins pushed himself down in bed with his back to her.

"Howard, I've been thinking . . . He's so unhappy all the time. Maybe, if it's what he wants so much, we *should* let him be a veterinarian. I'm convinced he'll never make a good doctor."

"I've told him, and I've told you—I won't discuss it."

Suddenly Adele burst into a storm of weeping.

Perkins said, "Oh, Lord!" under his breath and reached for the light. Then he sat on the edge of the bed, facing her. "Look, Adele. I'm not any prouder of him than you are, but I'll make something of him yet whether I get any help from you or not. Maybe if you'd stop nagging— Oh, forget it and get some sleep."

"You can't leave Howie out there in the night."

"What can I do about it? Do you want me to go rushing all over Vermont at two thirty in the morning?"

"You can *find him.* You know perfectly well where he is—at that cabin of yours."

He got out of bed and stood looking down at her. Then he turned away and started to put his clothes on.

LEAVING his headlights on, Perkins walked over to the cabin. He had little hope of finding Howie, but when he opened the door he saw the red glow of a dying fire on the stone hearth. He turned his flashlight toward the cot against the wall. Howie was sleeping there, the thin body seeming not so much relaxed as surrendered to exhaustion. The boy looked frail, almost ill. The paleness of his face was a shock, and there were marks of suffering on it that Perkins had not seen before. He backed away, having seen too much; and when he spoke there was none of the usual harshness in his tone. "Howie."

The boy slowly wakened and looked around. When he saw his father, his look of openness was replaced by a blank, defensive one. Suddenly this was unbearable to Perkins. He shouted, "You young fool, what do you think you're doing? Get up."

While Howie was dressing, Perkins extinguished the fire. Then he held the cabin door open. "Come on. Get going. I'm not going to hit you." Howie slunk past him and he slammed the door.

The car bumped and jolted down the rutty mountain road. Howie braced himself against the seat. They shot around a curve, and at the same instant a deer leaped in front of them. Howie cried out and Perkins braked hard. They hit the deer with a soft thud, but the force of it made the car shudder. There was a moment of frozen stillness. Perkins turned off the ignition.

"Well, we got him. We'll have to report to the game warden."

The headlights were full on the deer in a merciless white glare. The black hoofs of the front legs beat a rapid tattoo on the ground. The proud, beautiful head with its crown of antlers was lifted and blood gushed from the mouth. The hindquarters and the hind legs were motionless. "Back's broken," Perkins said.

Howie covered his face with his hands and moaned.

Perkins groped on the floor, and straightened up with a tire iron in his hand. "Howie, take this. Get out and kill him."

"I couldn't. Oh, Dad, I couldn't." Howie shrank away.

"Do you want to see him suffer? Do as I say."

"Can't we do something for him, Dad? Can't we help him?"

"I told you. His back's broken, you sniveling crybaby. I'll make a man of you if it kills you. This is only an animal. Do you hear me? Here, take this iron. Hit him on the forehead—hard."

Howie took the iron. Trembling all over, he got slowly out of the car and moved toward the deer; then with desperation he turned back to his father. "Dad . . ." He saw the implacable contempt in his father's face and dragged himself forward.

The deer, when it saw Howie, tossed its head high and beat its front legs wildly. Howie raised the iron slowly, then, with a sound that was both a cry and a moan, dropped it and scrambled up the steep bank. As Perkins shouted, "Come back here, you . . ." he fled into the woods.

Leaving the car, Perkins stood for a moment and listened to Howie crashing through the woods. Then he picked up the iron. With a swift, accurate motion he brought it down on the deer's skull. He dragged the body to the side of the road, got back into the car and sat looking toward the silent woods. Finally he turned the ignition key, and the engine started with a roar.

IANTHE WOKE EARLY and had at once a full recollection of the way Howie had come stumbling up onto the kitchen porch just before dawn: of his grief and exhaustion, of his tears as she held him in her arms. And she felt again her own shock at discovering what he had been forced to endure.

She wrapped herself in a warm robe, went downstairs to the telephone and got the Perkins' number. "Adele?"

"Yes." There was something anxious and guarded in the word.

"Adele, I thought I'd better tell you Howie's here with me."

There was a long silence before Adele said, "Thank you. Will you tell him to come home right away, please?"

"I think you'd better come here. Perhaps Howard, too."

"Why? Is Howie hurt? Isn't he all right?"

"Not hurt, he's upstairs sleeping. But I wouldn't say he was all right either. He came here in the middle of the night."

"Howard's already at the hospital. I'll come right over."

Half an hour later Adele was standing in the Nortons' study while Ianthe described the state in which Howie had arrived. "He was so upset it was hard to find out what had happened."

"Howard shouldn't have tried to make him kill the deer. But hitting it was an accident. Howie should be able to see that."

"I think perhaps he's been missing Spotty, his pet, more than any of us have realized. He kept talking about him, and at first I thought it was Spotty that something had happened to."

"It's not normal to be that fond of an animal."

"Perhaps not, but he seems like such a lonely boy, Adele."

"I wish you'd phoned us last night. We weren't really worried about his being safe. He knows how to take care of himself in the woods. But he shouldn't have come to you."

Her eyes were bright and hostile, and Ianthe thought, At least she loves him enough to be jealous. "Adele—I don't think an outsider should interfere between parents and child except in very exceptional cases. But I've grown exceedingly fond of Howie. Perhaps that doesn't give me a right to talk to his mother about him, but I have some things I want to say. Will you listen?"

Adele made a slight movement of her shoulders.

"He's desperately unhappy. Adele, he can't go on like this. I feel he's in a dangerously emotional state, and that he was before this deer episode. You must have felt it yourself."

Adele gave Ianthe a steady look, full of intelligence, that left Ianthe feeling that her past judgment of her had been superficial. She said, "We did so want—Howard especially—Howie to have the sort of career his father should have had. We thought he could do it if he'd only try. Perhaps we were wrong."

"Then couldn't you give him more freedom to be himself? I think he has it in him to develop into something very fine. Has he talked about being a veterinarian?"

"Not much. Howard is so against it he won't discuss it."

"You wouldn't reconsider, I suppose?"

"Perhaps we should. This deer business has been a sort of crisis. Howard was very troubled when he got home, though it was too late to talk. I'm sure he feels as I do that we can't go on this way. We'll talk tonight." She rose. "You've been kind, Ianthe. Howie can skip school and sleep it out. But when he wakes up, please tell him we won't scold him, and send him home."

"I'm not sure he'll go, Adele. He was so resentful toward his father last night, he said he'd never go home again."

Adele sat down on the edge of a chair. "But what . . ."

Ianthe said gently, "He could stay here awhile, Adele."

"And have all the old cats in town saying he ran away because we ill-treated him, and you were so sorry for him you took him in? Thank you, no. No indeed."

"I think you and Howard need a little time to think all this out by yourselves. You could say Howie's staying to keep me company for a week or two because, with Nat away, my house is very empty. That's true. I'd love to have him."

Adele walked to the window and stood there a long time in silence. When she turned around she seemed softened and, in some subtle way, younger. "I suppose everyone knows Howard and I haven't been getting on very well. The chief reason is Howie. We quarrel about him. We don't want to. I can see Howard hating it as much as I do—" She stopped, then said with emotion, "If Howard and I could just be alone for a little while . . . His disappointment in Howie has changed him so, and . . . lately I've been so worried about its effect on him. If we could be alone, he might be the sort of person he used to be and we could talk about things, and then I think it would be all right about Howie . . ." She put her hands over her eyes.

Ianthe went to stand in front of her, and Adele took away her hands and the two women looked at each other. Then Ianthe said, "I'll take good care of Howie, Adele."

Chapter 12

THE MORNING operating schedule consisted only of an uncomplicated tonsillectomy, but when Dr. Moore came downstairs after administering the anesthetic, Edna Judson thought he looked as tired as though this were the end and not the beginning of the day. That there was much to cause him uneasiness she knew. Whatever the outcome of the hospital's difficulties, there would be change. It would alter all their lives, and Dr. Moore's, perhaps, beyond his adaptability. She watched him through the window as he crossed the parking lot to his Jeep. He moved heavily, and she thought, We'll soon be old, both of us.

Quick steps on the stairs made her look up. It was Ianthe. "Edna, Nat suddenly looks different. Can you come?"

The two women went together to Norton's room. He lay straight and white and narrow, as he had now for many days. The only visible change was a slight translucence of the skin, a bluing of the lips. But Edna saw, with the eye of experience, something else which left no outward trace. Nathaniel Norton's body had quietly begun to relinquish its hold on life.

Edna's eyes met Ianthe's, and Ianthe knew. "Is Ed here?"

"He's gone to Warwick, Ianthe. I'll get Dr. Armstrong."

She found him studying a chart in the nursing station. "Doctor, Nathaniel Norton is going . . ."

David came, and watched for a moment the slow, erratic breaths. Then he pulled his stethoscope out of his pocket. "Mrs. Norton, will you leave the room now, please, for a little while?"

She answered slowly, "No, Doctor, but if you don't mind I would like you to leave."

He hesitated, and then very quickly went out into the hall.

In the room Ianthe slipped her arm under Nathaniel's shoulders, holding him close to her, feeling the faint stir of his breaths that now came so lightly. She put her hand under his motionless fingers and let it stay there quietly. It was like this that she felt his last breath. She knew when it came and that it was the last, and she held him as she had done before.

At last she groped for the push button at the head of the bed.

David saw the red light above the door go on. He went in and waited while Ianthe drew her arm gently from under Nathaniel's shoulders. Then he bent over the bed, using his stethoscope once more. "I'm sorry, Mrs. Norton . . ."

Ianthe went to one of the windows and stood there with her back to the room. When David was sure she was going to be all right, he said, "I'll ask Edna Judson to come. And I'll be in touch with Dr. Moore."

She said slowly, "Thank you, Doctor."

When Dr. Moore returned, afternoon office hours had begun. David hastily excused himself from the patient he was seeing, and stopped him outside the door to tell him about Norton. David thought how worn he looked, but how durable. In the language of the country, "seasoned timber." The strength he possessed had the rare quality of being communicable.

"Is Ianthe all right?" Moore asked.

"Yes. I was impressed by the way she stood up to it. I asked Miss Judson to look after her."

"Edna couldn't leave the hospital to go home with her. You should have taken her home." Moore spoke sharply. "I'd better see if she's all right. You'll have to handle those people in there." He jerked his head toward the waiting room.

But when Moore reached the Norton house, there were cars in the drive and two women were going up the walk carrying gifts of food. News travels fast in a small town, and the procession of friends and neighbors that follows any death had already begun. He drove back to the office.

After evening office hours he went over again. The cars had gone and light came from the study window, so he parked and let himself in.

Hearing him, Ianthe rose, dazed and uncertain, from her chair. "Oh, Ed, it's you."

He put his arm around her and she laid her head on his shoulder and wept. He held her until her tears lessened, then gave her his handkerchief and she wiped her eyes.

"I'm sorry I wasn't there, Ianthe."

"I'm sorry too, Ed."

"I'll make you coffee." He led her to the kitchen and put her into a chair by the table.

She laid her arms on the red-and-white cloth as though their weight were too much for her.

"I'm so tired, Ed."

"That's natural enough. I'm afraid you'll feel that way for some time. You must try and rest. Where's Howie?"

"I sent him up to bed. He's a dear boy, Ed—but I wanted to be alone. Do you realize it's been five years since Nat was first taken sick? I've forgotten what life was like before."

Moore looked moodily down at the percolator. Five years since the biopsy report from Warwick had lain on his desk; five years since he'd said, "We'll operate, Nat . . ."

He picked up the pot, carried it to the table and filled a cup for her, then one for himself.

She put her hand to her forehead. "I feel as though I'm so near to some great understanding of life, but I can't quite capture it. I think perhaps a person can only go through one experience of love with wholly pure emotions. After that, any emotion you feel for another person will be qualified by experience, because you've been through it before. Wasn't it that way with you, Ed, after Matilda died? Could you ever love anyone the same way again, or feel the same about anyone dying?"

"I don't know, Ianthe. I know I could still feel very deeply about someone, if not just in the way I did when I was young. Perhaps you're right. But don't close a door on life."

She laid her hand for an instant over his, then put both of hers around her coffee cup.

"It's late. You should be getting to bed, Ianthe." He drained his cup and stood up, and she stood too. For a moment neither moved, both reluctant to end this interlude, both knowing it was finished and that each must turn toward the future.

DAVID WALKED along the snowy village street, enjoying the feel of slush under his boots, for it signaled the season's change. The wind that blew on him was mild, and all along the street melting icicles dripped from the edges of the roofs. A man in a plaid shirt, carrying bunches of sap buckets in both hands, gave him a cheerful "Hi, Doc."

At a corner of the green he saw Ianthe Norton standing in front of a large cardboard thermometer with the words HADDON HEALTH CENTER at the top. She was raising the level of the "mercury" to the eight-thousand mark. The old house which would be converted to a health center had already been bought, showing, David thought, an optimism that seemed hardly warranted, for what doctors would there be to practice in it? Not Ladd, who refused to leave his office. And if the hospital went under, not Perkins or himself. Moore alone, or perhaps Ted Barlow . . .

David found May sitting up against her pillows, the accounts she was keeping for the health center spread out around her. "Oh, David," she said, "I'm so glad you've come."

"Give me those papers," he said gruffly. He piled them on a chair and sat on the couch beside her. "Now I want to talk to you. All this has been going on long enough."

"What has? What are you talking about? You look so angry."

"Angry!" He took her hand and held it in both of his.

She shook her head. "No, David, no."

"May, we've come to mean a lot to each other, haven't we?"

"Yes."

"Then, May, my darling . . . I love you. I want to marry you."

"Don't think I haven't thought about us. . . . David, you mustn't feel this way about me."

"But *why?* It makes no sense. We love each other. All you have to do is get that leg fixed up, so you can lead a normal life. Is that so much to do to make us both happy?"

"David, please don't ask me. I'm so afraid of an operation. I couldn't—I just couldn't go through with it."

"But there's nothing to be afraid of. It's not a difficult operation for a man trained in vascular surgery. . . . May, darling . . ." He put his arms around her and felt the tenseness of her body. "What kind of a married life could we have if you were an invalid?"

"David, I love you terribly, but I couldn't . . . I'm so afraid." And clinging to him, she burst into a storm of weeping. When the tears changed to exhausted sobs, he held her away from him.

"You have to choose, May. Do you want to lie here on this couch all your life, or lead a normal, happy life with me?"

For a long time she said nothing. Then he felt a shudder run through her. "Would *you* do the operation?" she whispered.

"A surgeon doesn't usually operate on someone close to him. I've been thinking we might take you to New York and have Fairchild do it. He's about the best there is."

"No, no. It has to be you, or I won't do it. And Uncle Ed to be the anesthetist. And our hospital here."

"Dr. Moore wouldn't want to. It would put too much strain on both of us. And this hospital hasn't the instruments—"

"I can't help it. I won't do it any other way."

"I'll see what Dr. Moore says, but I doubt if he'll . . ."

"And another thing, David. Don't rush me. I want to tell you myself when I'm ready. You'll do that for me, won't you?"

After a moment he nodded. Then he put his arms around her and kissed her.

AFTER evening office hours David met Moore in the surgery between their offices. He said, "May's consented to the operation."

Moore stared in astonishment. "You haven't been bringing pressure on her, have you? I don't want that."

"I've never understood why."

"Good Lord, I've tried to tell you. She's a strong-willed girl. She can force herself to do things that are hard for her. She drove herself to the edge of a breakdown, and she's not over it yet, by any means. Now you want to add the strain of an operation she's desperately afraid of. I won't be responsible if—"

"*I'll* be responsible."

"*You* will? She's my patient. I asked you for a consultation— nothing else. I didn't tell you to take over—you, an outsider."

"Dr. Moore—"

"May is my own flesh and blood—all of it that's left to me. She's like my daughter. I love her. . . . And now you tell me *you've* decided she's to have an operation. It's too much."

"Dr. Moore, May and I are going to be married. That's why she's decided to have the operation."

There was silence. Twice Moore's lips moved tremblingly, as though he were going to speak, and finally David said, "I'm sorry, sir. I know it's a blow to you."

"All right. . . . Maybe I should have seen it coming."

"There's something else. She's made it a condition that I operate and you give the anesthetic—here in this hospital."

A sound like a groan came from Dr. Moore.

"We can borrow the instruments. And she would feel much

safer with you giving the anesthetic. You could lessen her fear."

Dr. Moore breathed heavily. "I don't want to talk about it now. It's a blow, yes. I guess I'd better say good night." He walked out slowly, his big shoulders stooping.

Chapter 13

Dr. Moore stood with Ianthe before a fine old house the color of Jersey cream. From inside came sounds of carpenters pounding. "I can't say I like giving up my old office," he told her, "but it's a remarkable thing you're doing. I wish I knew how you got Tim Stoner to lend the money before the drive for funds had really started."

Ianthe laughed and led him into the house. He thought, She hasn't laughed like that since Nat . . .

"I'm sure he figures that if a fully equipped health center is in progress, people won't see so much need for your hospital and won't vote at Town Meeting to keep it. But they will."

"I'm not so sure of that as I was. I guess it's a sign of age, Ianthe, but I hate change. I hate this—" he gestured at the torn-apart interior of the old house. "I don't want to practice group medicine even in this modified form. Well, show me what you've cooked up for me here in the way of an office. I'll tell you right now I won't like it, but let's see it."

It was a cubbyhole—the best of the four, but a cubbyhole. The longest wall was not long enough, he saw, for his old rolltop desk. "All right," he said. "What next?"

"This is the reception room, and there'll be a desk in the hall for a receptionist."

"I wish May could be behind that desk instead of getting married. I don't like any part of this business, though I'm becoming used to the idea of her being in love with David. But I do not think she's ready for this operation. What's to be down these stairs? X-ray, is it? It all looks so different from the plans."

WHENEVER DAVID WAS ABLE, he took sandwiches and coffee to May's apartment and they ate lunch together. It was usually a gay hour. But one day he found her sad and thoughtful.

"I'm worried about Town Meeting, David. Can't you persuade Uncle Ed not to put the fate of the hospital up to the town?"

"I've tried, but he's been so sure the town would want him to keep it going. Lately, I've felt he's not so certain, but since this coolness between us we haven't talked much. Even if he weathers this crisis, he can't go on forever. He's sixty-five, isn't he? He should retire."

"Oh *no!*"

"He's been too busy to keep up with modern medicine as well as he should. He feels at a disadvantage, I think."

"I don't know that I like your revolution in rural medicine. We'll get better medicine, I suppose, but I'm not sure we're going to be happy about it. David, your year in Haddon is nearly half gone. Have you thought about what you're going to do?"

"Vascular surgery's the only thing I'm sure about. But it must be in a place where you'll be happy."

"With this new setup, couldn't we just stay here?"

"Unwise, I think. We'll talk about it. But there's something else we have to discuss now. If things do go against Dr. Moore at Town Meeting, he'll probably close up soon. So if you still insist on having your operation in his hospital, we should start making plans. First, an arteriogram at Warwick."

There was a moment's silence; then she said in a small voice, "All right, if you'll stay with me."

"I won't leave you a minute. Then I'll have to see about borrowing the instruments I'll need. What's the matter, dear?"

"Oh, David, I'm so frightened. Hold me tight. Promise you won't let anything happen to me. I love you so."

When David went back to his office he reluctantly put in a call for Adam Fairchild. Fairchild was not available, but his nurse thought she could get the hospital to lend the instruments without troubling him. "If you will tell me what you want, Doctor . . ."

He told her and thanked her with the warmth of his relief.

A FEW DAYS LATER, David found Helen unpacking the instruments in a back room. Dr. Perkins was watching. David never saw him without a tightening of the nerves, for Perkins' disposition was, to say the least, uncertain.

"Pretty gadgets you've got here, Doc." Perkins opened and closed an artery clamp. "Makes ours seem clumsy." He gave David a direct look that was both attention-compelling and amused, as though he knew something David didn't. "You'll need to modernize the OR equipment generally if you and May decide to stay on here. Perhaps it would help if we got together and made up a list of what you'll want."

Helen stopped gathering up wrappings and stared at him. Perkins grinned at her, then left without another word. Helen said, "Does that mean he's got the Warwick job?"

"Shush, he's coming back."

"I forgot to ask you, Dave," Perkins said. "Who're you going to have assist?"

"That's been bothering me. Someone from Warwick, I suppose, though I don't much like the idea of working with a stranger."

"Would I do?"

Startled, David stared at him. "Of course. Sure. I didn't feel I could ask you, but I'd be honored."

Perkins said, "I don't know a thing about vascular surgery. I'll find it interesting."

Between the two doctors there was suddenly an easiness that had never been there before. David said, "I'll show you the arteriograms and exactly what I'm going to do."

Helen watched them go off, her hand to her head as though this unusual atmosphere of amity had made her giddy.

THE NIGHT before Town Meeting there were few patients in the office, fewer than Moore could ever remember. It was as though people felt the old medical regime was already dead. When the last patient had gone, Moore went at once to Ianthe's house. She had never seen him in such a mood. He was restless, close to irritability, the humor and kindliness gone from his face.

"Ed," she said almost timidly as they sat in the study, "I think you need a drink."

"Need one! Well, all right."

He made no move to help her fix it, and when she came back he was angrily pacing the floor. He turned to face her. "The town's already made up its mind. It doesn't want a hospital."

"Ed, we can't possibly know until tomorrow."

"Tim Stoner's been at work, I'm sure of it. Telling people that a hospital at Silver Springs will attract more plants, which means more workers spending money in Haddon. Money's his argument. Why should people want my hospital when they'd be richer without it? I was a fool ever to think they would."

"Ed, you're worried and you're distorting things. Won't you come and sit down?"

He looked at her then, and she saw the suffering in his eyes.

"Ianthe, I'm going to retire."

"Oh, Ed, no."

"I've made up my mind. Soon as the meeting starts I'm going to get up and tell them I'm through. They can get on without me. And Howard will go to Warwick. At the end of his year David will leave. Then the damn town will be without any licensed doctors but Ladd, and they can see how they like that."

She rose and, taking him by the arm, led him to a chair. He dropped into it, letting his hands hang dejectedly between his knees. She saw that the anger had gone, leaving him with a look of bewilderment and uncertainty and very great fatigue. She said gently, "You've forgotten your drink, Ed."

He drank a little, then gazed into the fire, and she sat in her chair and studied him. Years of as selfless a life as a man can achieve . . . An old man now, or close to it, talking in bitterness about retirement, but without the money to make it possible. A few thousand, perhaps, from the sale of the hospital building and the vacant property beside it—both mortgaged, no doubt. His own house probably mortgaged too. Nothing more, and nothing to occupy a mind deprived of life's one dedication.

Tears came to her eyes and she rose and walked over to him

and laid her hand lightly on his shoulder. He looked up at her, and she saw that his face was calm. Then he took her hand and laid it against his cheek.

ON HIS WAY back from a late call, David stopped at the hospital. May was there now, preparatory to her operation the day after tomorrow. Quietly he opened the door of her room. "May?"

"Oh, David!" In the dim light he saw her holding up her arms to him and he went to the bed and put his arms around her.

"You should be sleeping, my dearest."

She laughed softly. "They gave me something to make me sleep, but I've been trying to stay awake, hoping you'd come." She paused. "I hope Town Meeting goes all right for Uncle Ed."

"Don't think about it now, dear. Go to sleep."

He held her close and she made a sound like a sleepy bird. He stroked her hair and then her cheek, and he found that her cheeks were wet with tears. "Don't cry, darling. There's just this one thing to get through, and then we'll be happy."

"I'm happy now, David. I'm frightened, but I'm happy."

"Don't be frightened. Everything is going to be all right."

"Stay with me. I'm only frightened when I'm all alone."

"I'll stay till you're asleep. Try to sleep now, May."

He straightened the covers over her. Then he brought a chair and sat beside the bed and held her hand.

PEOPLE WERE converging on the Town Hall. Inside the door Dr. Moore looked around him. The hall was already well filled. Howie Perkins approached him, and Moore thought how much stronger and happier he looked now that Howard was making an effort to understand him. His brief time with Ianthe had done much to restore harmony in the Perkins household; and Adele, too, seemed to have found a new serenity.

"Dr. Moore. Dad asked me to tell you he's got an emergency in the operating room and he and Dr. Armstrong will have to be late. He'll come as soon as he can."

Alarm seized Moore. "Do they need me for the anesthetic?"

"He says no, he's using a spinal and he's got Miss Judson on duty. I guess you'll sort of miss May Turner giving messages while she's in the hospital, won't you?"

"We'll miss her more than 'sort of,' but it won't be for long. Is Mrs. Norton here?" But he saw her then himself and made his way down the aisle to the vacant seat beside her that he knew was intended for him. He edged sidewise along the row, acknowledged her greeting, and sat lost in thought. There was comfort in knowing that Ianthe was beside him and that there was no need to talk. Up on the platform the three selectmen were already seated, and the moderator was leaning on the lectern.

Vaguely, Moore realized that the meeting was beginning. He heard fragments of speeches on street lighting, taxes, and the relocation of the dump. Then Ianthe touched his arm in an urgent way and he came out of his thoughts and sat up straight.

The moderator grasped the sides of the lectern and leaned forward. "The subject that will now be presented to this meeting cannot be decided by a vote. It will be put to you in the form of a question. Speeches for and against will be permitted. You will then be asked to express your opinion as though this were a vote. The expression of your views will be an important service to the town." He paused and looked down at Moore. "Before the question is put, I think you should hear from Dr. Moore."

Moore rose slowly and, smiling, looked all around the hall. He was about to begin when there was a stir at the back and he saw that Howard and David had come in. He waved to them; then strongly and with confidence he began to speak.

"A while back my hospital and myself were attacked publicly. I was told that my hospital had seen its day, that Haddon doesn't need a hospital any more. As you all know, my hospital is my own, except for a share in it that Dr. Perkins has. I can sell it, or I can close it up, or I can go on running it, provided I can afford to. What I do is my own business. Technically. Only I've never run it that way. I've tried to run it for the good of the town. Now, certain people want it closed, but I'm not sure they represent the real view of the town. If you, the people of Haddon, don't want my hospital any more, I'll close it. If you do want it, I'll find some way to bring it as near to good modern standards as I can. I want your thoughtful, honest opinion." He sat down.

There was an outbreak of excited talk. Someone shouted, "We want Doc Moore's hospital." Someone else called out, "No we don't. Shut up." The gavel was pounding. Moore saw Stoner on his feet, arm raised, waiting to be recognized.

The moderator said, "Just a moment, Tim. The question's not been put yet. The question is: Is it the intention of this meeting that there should be a hospital in Haddon? We aren't talking about Dr. Moore's now. Just, would the men and women of Haddon like a hospital here? All right, Tim."

"Mr. Chairman, ladies and gentlemen," Stoner began. "The question just put to this meeting is without meaning. There is no way that Haddon can have a hospital even if it wants one. Let me explain. There are two kinds of hospitals. The first, like Dr. Moore's, is privately owned. The second, called a voluntary hospital, is built partly with government funds, partly with money contributed by the town. Let me talk about Dr. Moore's hospital first. Dr. Moore and Dr. Perkins are fine men and outstanding physicians."

There was an outbreak of applause, and Stoner waited, smiling remotely, while it swelled and died.

"Dr. Moore has maintained his hospital in the best interest of the town, but with increasing difficulty. The bank has helped but, year by year, with costs rising, his deficit has grown. He lacks funds not only for running expenses, but also for modernizing his antiquated plant. And the bank has regretfully concluded that it can make no more money available. As to the voluntary hospital, I have found, with the help of Mr. Whitall of the Public Health Service, that to build and equip one of adequate size would cost in the neighborhood of six hundred thousand dollars. Of this the federal government might be expected to pay a third. That leaves four hundred thousand to be raised by the people of Haddon. Do I need to say that this sum is too large?"

Stoner paused and looked around the hall. There were shouts

of "No!" and the moderator pounded the lectern with his gavel.

Stoner went on. "But there is an alternative I think you would find acceptable. That is to have a hospital at Silver Springs. The plants there need something nearer than Warwick, and a hospital would draw in still more industry. Silver Springs is only eight miles from us and, moreover, we will have good first-aid equipment at the health center. The conclusion is absolutely clear. Haddon does not need a hospital, but Silver Springs does."

Stoner sat down. Someone behind Moore said, "Who's that just stood up in the back?" Moore turned to look just as the moderator said, "You want to address the meeting, Mr. Moriseau?"

The man introduced himself. "I am president of the Silver Springs Machine Tool Company, and also chairman of the community's Council on Industrial Health. We do, as Mr. Stoner said, need a hospital nearer than Warwick. In the past the plants have used Dr. Moore's hospital and, with the exception of a tragic incident last September, that arrangement has been wholly satisfactory. I must add, however, that the Council feels the hospital needs more beds and much new equipment; also that it is against our policy to give financial aid to a private institution. We were at first inclined to agree with Mr. Stoner that a hospital at Silver Springs would be the answer, but in some important ways it would not suit us. The responsibility for running such a hospital would fall to the Council, and this we are reluctant to undertake. Also, I doubt that a hospital dominated by the companies would adequately meet Haddon's needs. Recently the Council decided that if a voluntary hospital in Haddon became a possibility, the plants would contribute toward it the sum of two hundred thousand dollars."

Talk, loud and excited, broke out all over the hall. Ianthe leaned toward Moore. "Ed, what will this mean?"

He said, "I don't know," and shut his eyes. He felt Ianthe's hand resting on his arm and he leaned a little toward her. The gavel was pounding again. "The chair recognizes Dr. Harlan Greer." Moore forced his attention back to what was taking place.

Greer was standing, smiling thinly. "Before Dr. Moore came to Haddon, my father practiced medicine here. As a memorial to him I want to give a fund bearing his name to the proposed new voluntary hospital. The sum I have in mind is seventy-five thousand dollars." He raised a hand to quiet the beginning of applause. "I also want to add my word of tribute to the fine hospital that Dr. Moore has maintained in spite of so many difficulties for all these years."

There was tumult in the hall. The gavel pounded.

"It's getting late," the moderator said. "Let me put the original question: Do you think it desirable for the town of Haddon to have a hospital? . . . All those in favor signify by saying aye."

There was a roar of sound. Ianthe put her hand on Moore's.

"Contrary-minded?"

Moore could identify none of those who shouted "No."

"The ayes have it. Next question: Do you want Dr. Moore's hospital, if he can find a way to keep it going, or—"

Moore shouted, "I'll find a way," and there was a burst of applause, cut short by blows of the gavel.

"—Or . . . let me finish . . . do you want a new hospital, to which the people of the town would contribute a hundred and twenty-five thousand dollars? Those in favor of having Dr. Moore continue to run his hospital best he can, signify by saying—"

There was a roar of sound. Ianthe was saying, "Ed, that must be it . . . that must be it . . ." Tears came to her eyes.

"All those in favor of a voluntary hospital—"

Again the sound was very loud, but he couldn't tell . . .

The moderator couldn't either. "The result was not clear," he said. "We will have to have a standing vote. Those for Dr. Moore's hospital . . ."

Ianthe was standing. Moore looked around and shook his head. Then, "All those in favor of a voluntary hospital . . ." Without knowing it, Moore had Ianthe's hand once more.

"The voluntary hospital has it."

He turned to Ianthe and saw on her face so much pity and unhappiness that his lips began to shake. He tried to smile. Then he knotted his hands and stared in misery at the floor.

The gavel came down again. "Well, folks, I guess that about winds things up. If someone will move—"

"No, it doesn't wind things up." Perkins' voice was loud, and harsh with controlled anger. "It seems to me this town owes Ed Moore something for all the labor and expense . . ."

Moore said, "Oh Lord . . ."

"I don't mean he should be paid. All the money this town has couldn't pay for what he's done for it. I mean, give him an honor he deserves. Make him administrator of the new hospital."

There was a storm of shouts and clapping and foot stamping. Moore heard Ianthe saying, "*Yes, Ed. Yes.*" Then, still clapping, the selectmen got to their feet, and then all the people rose.

Perkins had not finished. "How about it, Moriseau—would the Council care to make that a condition of the gift?"

Moriseau replied, "Yes, we would indeed."

"Good. Greer, how about you?"

Greer nodded and said, "Yes, of course."

"Ed, maybe I should have consulted you first, but . . . how does the idea sit with you?"

Moore rose and said, "I'd have to think about it." He looked around him a little dazedly. "Thank you." Suddenly he smiled, said "Thank you" again with more emphasis, and sat down.

Chapter 14

THE OPERATING ROOM was ready, and the quiet there gave emphasis to faint sounds—the click of instruments being laid out, the hiss of oxygen, the creak of a rolling stand. On the table May lay in suspensive lethargy, her muscles held captive by sedatives, her eyes like dark openings into a troubled soul. Her loveliness had a lost, little-girl look that made Dr. Moore long to take her in his arms and comfort her. He spoke softly.

"Are you all right, my dear?"

She tilted her head back to look at him and managed a tremulous smile. "You look . . . so funny . . . in those clothes."

"Are you going to be a good girl now?"

She nodded and he saw that his words had made her ordeal seem so imminent that she could not bring herself to speak.

"There's nothing to it, May, nothing at all."

Edna, with a mask hanging under her chin, was busy with the mechanics of preparation. Helen stood at the foot of the operating table, laying out instruments in rows.

Moore sat at the other end of the table, in front of him the top of May's head, and to one side the anesthetic apparatus with its cylinders of oxygen and nitrous oxide. He picked up the black face mask. "Now, all you have to do is breathe."

She nodded, wetting her lips, her eyes wide and dark again.

The mask made a faint, sibilant sound as he lowered it to her face. He saw a tear on her lashes and bent to speak to her. "I'm right here, May. It's all right."

"Where's David?" her blurred voice asked.

"He'll be here soon. We'll all be with you, May."

The operating room grew quiet again. Moore glanced at the dials on the anesthetic apparatus, then up at the clock on the wall. The dials indicated a mixture of eighty percent nitrous oxide and twenty percent oxygen. The clock read seven forty.

Moore's right hand was still on the mask, the other on the black rebreathing bag. He held the mask close as May turned her head sharply. She drew her hand from under the sheet, groping desperately. Edna took the hand and held it between hers for a moment. "All right, May, it's all right."

Across May's chest Edna placed a low screen that would separate Moore from the operation. May's body, subdued now, was beyond her control, but her mind was still seeking escape. She made a guttural sound, startling in the quiet, then noises of urgent distress, words jumbled and run together. Moore, his hand shaking a little, pressed the mask closer. The babble changed to whimpering and died away.

He shut his eyes a moment, feeling the crisis in his own nerves. Then he made an adjustment in the anesthesia apparatus. The dials now showed an equal mixture of ether and nitrous oxide. He squeezed the bulb of the blood-pressure cuff, noted the healthy pressure, and made an entry on the chart. And he was thinking, Why am I uneasy?

He leaned over May's head and carefully pulled each eyelid back. The pupils were dilated and the eyes moved slightly. When the pupils shrank she would have gone beyond pain; she would be, in the language of the operating room, "ready."

The door of the scrub room opened and David looked in. "About ready, are you?" He sounded brisk and normal.

"I haven't got the tube in yet."

A nod of understanding. Then David came to the table and looked down at May. He was satisfying himself, as a doctor, of her condition, but the impersonal scrutiny began to soften, and Moore, seeing the change, felt something like jealousy of the young man with his life and his love before him.

David left and Edna came to stand near Moore. They both saw it—the outward swell of the rebreathing bag and its collapse, then no more movement. The bag hung limp, its sides caved in. The seconds passed beyond and way beyond the point at which she should have breathed, and still the bag hung motionless. Moore said, "It's her subconscious fighting us. I guess we'll have to help her . . ." He squeezed the bag, then released it. The sides swelled out, collapsed, and swelled again. "Good girl," he said.

After a few minutes Moore started to slip the intratracheal tube into May's throat. At the first touch her throat contracted, her chest heaved. He withdrew the tube and Edna said, "It's queer how they sometimes resist, even when they can't feel."

"That's her subconscious again. She's afraid of this operation and so she's fighting it." He thought, She faced this ordeal not with confidence but only with courage, and now her courage is vanquished by the ether. He bent over her again, feeling that they were as close in spirit as though she were his own child. This time the tube slipped in, and he fastened it with strips of adhesive across her face. Then Perkins and Armstrong came in, and the strange loveliness of his secret communication with May was destroyed. Gloved hands clasped like priests, they approached the table, Perkins taking his place on the assistant's side.

David pushed the sheet back to expose the injured leg. Edna set beside him a basin of disinfectant and a forceps with a gauze swab clamped in its jaws. As David reached for the forceps, Perkins said, "Here, that's my job today, David."

Perkins started swabbing the area where the incision would be made. "This makes me feel like an intern again." It was said with simple enjoyment, and David's mask moved with a smile.

The forceps that held the swab clattered into the basin. Edna brought a pan of brilliant red Merthiolate.

Perkins said to David, "You paint while I do a quick second scrub." One could tell even from the way David painted on Merthiolate what kind of surgeon he was. Slow and steady. None of Perkins' flashing brilliance, but everything he did backed up by solid knowledge.

Moore had little to do now but squeeze the rebreathing bag and keep on squeezing it. He took May's blood pressure and found that it had fallen, though not enough to cause concern. He tried her pulse and found that too within normal limits.

Then David was saying, "How do we stand?"

"Pulse one hundred, blood pressure one hundred over eighty."

Perkins came back and watched with interest as David, spray can in hand, sprayed the painted area with bacteriostatic adhesive.

David did a second scrub and returned. Helen held out a sheet of sterilized plastic and he spread it smoothly onto the adhesive. The plastic formed a tight, outer layer of skin that was completely sterile. Then came David's sharp "Are we ready?" and the flash of the scalpel as Helen pressed it on his palm . . .

Moore was thankful for the screen cutting off his view, because, even after all the years, the first sweep of the scalpel brought a wave of nausea. He stroked May's hair, the feel of it overwhelming him with tenderness. But a part of his mind still followed the operation. David and Perkins bending over the wound. The rasp of a hemostat biting closed a bleeder. The swift motions of David's hands with the black suture . . .

Moore pulled his mind away with a jerk. He checked pulse, respiration, blood pressure. Then he checked again, because . . .

"Dave, her pulse is weak, blood pressure eighty."

A slight, spasmodic tightening of David's shoulders. A swift glance from Perkins. "Watch her. Bring her pressure up if you can." The hypodermic needle exactly where Moore's hand went down to grasp it . . .

373

The surgeons not changing their pace or their concentration, but aware now of urgencies beyond their field. Then the snort of air in the blood-pressure cuff, the upward swing of the needle to one hundred. "It's coming up. She's all right, Dave."

David tipping back his head. Edna seeing and moving swiftly with a piece of gauze to wipe his forehead. Perkins pausing to say, "We're almost down to the artery."

Keeping close watch on May, Moore nevertheless knew that David and Perkins were working well in partnership. And keeping constant track of time, he was still startled when David spoke. "There it is. There's the artery." He was pointing with the tip of an instrument down into the wound.

Edna was at Moore's back with a riser in her hand. "Do you want to stand on this and have a look, Dr. Moore?"

Relinquishing the rebreathing bag to her, he stood and looked into the wound. There was the femoral artery in the channel it shares with the great femoral vein that returns blood to the heart. David's pointer was resting on a slight misshaping of the artery.

"There's the trouble, right in there. When we open it we'll find the clot that has hardened into fibrous tissue. We'll cut away all we can and put a plastic graft on the artery."

Speaking, Moore thought, as though this were a classroom, with that direct, pure, scientific interest characteristic of these younger men. Did he, at this moment, remember this was May?

Moore got off the riser and put his fingers on the carotid artery in May's neck, feeling the pulse—too thin and rapid, as though the anesthesia had not been able to conquer her fright.

David was saying, "All right. Metzenbaum scissors, please."

His fingertips still resting against the carotid artery, Moore suddenly felt nothing. He seized the stethoscope and pressed the disk hard against May's neck. The beat was faint even with the stethoscope. He felt a prickling in his finger ends.

"Pulse very weak."

The pulse far off, faint . . . *thump* . . . *thump* . . . so faint it might be only a projection of the will to hear . . . *thump* . . . Silence. . . .

One second more of desperate listening, and a voice, loud and not like his own, saying, *"I'm not getting any pulse."*

The clatter of a dropped instrument. He turned the oxygen to five, then to ten liters a minute and shut off the ether. He held the oxygen against her face and used the stethoscope again.

Silence, intense listening, and then he heard Perkins' urgent voice. "Ed, is it fibrillation or cardiac arrest?"

"Arrest."

"Then you're not getting anything at all?"

"No."

David's words were more a motion of the lips than sound, but the meaning was clear: Start the heart, by a shock, by a blow.

Perkins swept David aside. "I'll handle this."

The silence in the stethoscope filling the ears . . . Listening to it was making soundless Howard's violent jerking off of the sheet that covered her. Soundless too his call for epinephrine, but the glass cylinder with the long needle was going from Helen's hand to his. The driving of the needle between her ribs into the heart . . . Now the heart should beat. Moore bent over, forcing all the senses to listen for the beat, however faint. . . .

Silence, then Perkins' hands, one on top of the other to give him the strength of both arms, bringing them down together on the sternum bone to put pressure on the heart—bringing them down hard and lifting them again. . . . Perkins looked swiftly at the clock, a reminder that there are only a few minutes in which a stopped heart may be started again without causing permanent damage to the brain. How many minutes? Three? Not more. . . .

"Ed?"

"No beat yet, Howard."

The lifeless jerking of May's body under the blows becoming suddenly sickening. Then the two women saying together, "Three minutes." So they too knew about the time limit.

Then, many minutes later, Perkins breathing hard and leaning on the table edge. "That's all I can do. I'm sorry, Dave."

Slowly, Moore took the stethoscope out of his ears and laid it aside. Then he buried his face in his hands and thought, What could I have done? . . . I shouldn't have let David . . . but he was so sure . . . I don't know . . . I'm tired . . . May . . .

He felt a touch on his shoulder and looked up to see Edna.

"Edna, we're too old."

"Not yet, Dr. Moore."

He shook his head and turned away. After a while he reached to turn the oxygen off and found that Edna had already done so. He moved to take the mask off May's face and had to wait for the blurring of his sight to clear. He carefully removed the tube, then gently stroked her cheek as he had done hours ago to comfort her. Shakily, he picked up the chart, but though he looked at the clock intently, and repeated the time again and again, it was a little while before he grasped it clearly enough to make the final entry.

David was standing very still, as though he were beyond thought and almost beyond feeling. Then he walked unsteadily toward the scrub-room door.

"You'd better go to him, Ed." It was Perkins' voice. "Keep him in the scrub room until . . ." He glanced toward the table.

Moore found David hunched on a bench, his face in his hands. He did not look up when Moore sat down beside him. They sat there for some time, until Edna came and stood in the doorway. She nodded at Moore and went away. Moore laid his hand on David's shoulder. In a husky voice unlike his own, he said, "Come on now, David, we must go." They went out together through the empty operating room.

LATE THAT NIGHT David was sitting on the front steps of Moore's darkened house, waiting for the doctor's return. He had been sitting there a long time, thinking of May. The air was chill with the damp of a spring thaw, and his numb mind recorded sounds distantly—water running all around him, a car rattling over a covered bridge. Suddenly the arc of Moore's headlights swept over him. The Jeep halted and Moore got out.

"David, is that you?"

"Yes, sir. I wondered if I could talk to you a few minutes."

Moore led the way into the living room and turned on an overhead light. The light gave dreary emphasis to the shabby furnishings. Two chairs stood by the black hearth, one of dark and prickly plush, the other of cracked black leather. Moore stood defensively in front of the leather one and waved toward the other. "Sit down." Moore himself sat, and said, "Well, David?"

David gathered himself. "Dr. Moore, why did May die? What was the cause of her death?"

"That's not an easy question."

"Nevertheless, I can't live with myself until I've answered it. Did I overlook something? The electrocardiogram showed no heart problem. Why did she die?"

"You and Howard and I will have to find the answer as soon as we can. Tonight we can only guess. Operating-table deaths that can't be explained are rare—but it isn't always one cause. Sometimes it's an aggregation of seemingly trivial things."

"Do you think that may have been what happened here?"

"I just don't know. She was very afraid of the operation. Though fright isn't a recognized cause of death, perhaps someday science will find a reason why it's at least an important factor. I believe it is, and I think Perkins does. Tonight I'm willing to think that if she hadn't been so afraid she might not have died."

"Then, if that's true, I shouldn't have pressed her—oh God, you were right, I shouldn't have pressed her."

"We don't know that's true."

After that Moore was silent for so long that grief and the feeling of personal guilt overwhelmed David. He dragged his fingers across his face as though he could rake away all subterfuge and untruth. Moore saw the eyes, deep with earnestness and despair, and he was moved to relinquish a little of the harshness with which he had been protecting himself from his own sense of guilt.

"I saw her state of mind more clearly, I think, than you did," he said. "I let myself be pressured into your point of view. May was my patient. Fundamentally, the responsibility was mine."

"I knew she was afraid. I wanted her to be well. I didn't understand . . . I forced her . . ." David's voice caught in a sob. "I knew

377

this weakness in myself—that I don't understand how people feel—and yet I forced her . . ."

Moore rose and paced the floor, his face lined and sad. Before returning to his chair, he laid his hand on David's shoulder.

Presently David sighed. "There's something else on my mind. May and I never had time to make any decisions about our future. She wanted me to stay in Haddon. I didn't think it would be wise. I wish I'd told her we'd stay. Now I think I would like to, as a sort of memorial to her, if that meets with your approval."

"*My* approval!" Moore snapped in a sudden blaze of anger. "I'm on the shelf. I'm not to be a doctor any more. Administrator—what's that? I don't know anything about the kind of medicine that's practiced today; I'm finished."

With this outburst Moore plummeted to depths he had never in his life reached before. He rubbed his eyes and said unsteadily, "I'm sorry. This has been a terrible day for both of us."

"Dr. Moore, experience like yours—dear God, if I'd only listened to you about May. . . . That and your knowledge of the town is something none of us can ever hope to have. Haddon is lucky to have you, and the people know it."

"David, light the fire. I've just remembered something." Moore got up with sudden energy and went off toward the kitchen. When he returned, carrying a bottle of Scotch and two glasses, David was holding a match to a pile of firewood.

"I got this stuff when you first came to town, as a sort of welcome, but somehow we never got to it. Maybe now's a good time. Sit down." He gave a glass to David, but before picking up his own, he went around turning on lamps. Bleakness vanished, shabbiness became well-worn comfort, and as he came back to his chair, the leaping flames lit up a half smile on his face.

A moment of silence passed, but it was one of those silences that sometimes achieve more than words. Moore said, "Your staying here in Haddon would be a fine thing for the town, David, but wait a while, we'll talk about it later. I'd like to have you; that goes without saying."

"I lack the experience you have."

"What's experience without knowledge? Half of the diagnostic techniques used now weren't heard of when I left school. Advances are coming so fast that the day a doctor leaves school he starts to slip behind. And we can't afford to go back to school every few years. How is a busy doctor going to keep up?" Moore went on, "And a country doctor needs different preparation from a city doctor. Nothing, so far as I know, is being done about that."

David said thoughtfully, "I know that from my own experience. Maybe the new hospital might consider giving residencies in country medicine."

"I think one thing that's keeping young doctors from coming to the country is the variety of knowledge a rural doctor has to have. Maybe that sort of residency's something we should think about. Assuming any of us has time to think." And there appeared in Moore's sad face a gleam of the old, endearing humor.

Chapter 15

SUMMER WAS running out. It was six long months after that never-to-be-forgotten day when Dr. Moore had suddenly realized that the changes which had been churning up his life had stabilized and become the established order. He did not like it; he felt no ease in the pursuit of duties so different from the medical practice of thirty years, but he had to admit it was not wholly bad.

It had been decided that the old hospital was to function until one wing of the new one was ready. And in the meantime Moore had been permitted to keep his old office on Maple Street. The Health Center was now open, but the cell that was to have been his there was thought to be too small for the new hospital's administrator. It was occupied instead by Dr. Armstrong, now chief surgeon since Dr. Perkins had gone to Warwick. Ted Barlow used a smaller cell. In the smallest of all was a new assistant surgeon. The three serious young doctors in their white coats gave the Health Center the authentic atmosphere of a clinic, and if the patients felt timid, and missed Dr. Moore's shabby waiting room, they were correspondingly impressed.

In theory, Moore had ceased to practice medicine, and his new secretary spent a good deal of her time explaining this to former patients. Many of them, denied access to Moore in his office, went to his house. They would rap on his door at mealtimes, or wait for him to come home from his office, or telephone him late at night. Some of them he prescribed for, but they were those with the simpler ailments, such as any intern could have handled. The others he told—brusquely, to conceal his bitterness—that, like it or not, they must go to the Health Center.

About some things he was immovably stubborn. He would not allow the comforting clutter of his inner office to be altered. He would not give up the Jeep. And he still refused to put on a white coat, though he was now the only doctor not to do so.

Of the numerous unpleasant things that happened to Dr. Moore that summer, the one he considered the worst, though it was essentially trivial, was that he was forced to sit for his portrait. Brooding about how to distribute the blame for this, he thought that Ianthe had been largely at fault, along with that superannuated gadfly, Harlan Greer. Even Edna had been disloyally pleased with the idea.

Persuading Moore to sit for the portrait took all Ianthe's skill. He went through with the ordeal of two sittings, fidgeting and mumbling about the waste of time. After that he flatly refused to sit again, and the picture had to be finished from some snapshots that Ianthe found.

A women's committee, called the Haddon Hospital Auxiliary, arranged a ceremony to combine the unveiling of the portrait with the ground breaking for the new hospital. The whole town was invited. Ianthe said to Edna, "He'll simply hate it."

On the afternoon of the ceremony the sun shone brightly and all the flags in the town were out. Edna was in charge of flowers— "What do people think this is, my funeral?" Moore grumbled— and Ianthe, he found when he went to her house for refuge, was supplying trayloads of little cakes. She was putting them into her car as he parked the Jeep.

"You're not leaving yet, are you?" he asked her in alarm.

"Not for a while. I just thought I'd get this done. Shall we sit on the porch? It's such a nice day."

"I want to hide," he said, and, to her surprise, led the way not to the study but to the seldom used living room, a lovely, uncomfortable room furnished with gracefully insubstantial chairs and tables. He sat down, a little belligerently, at the end of a hard sofa and glowered, as though he had set himself to wait for this day to do its worst to him.

"Dear Ed—is all this really so difficult for you?"

"What do you think it's like to have your town behave as if you were dead—expecting me to go to my own funeral?"

"Aren't you being a little extravagant? You know they don't think of it that way."

She waited, hoping he would open his heart about what really troubled him. For she knew he was making this fuss to relieve feelings tortured by quite other matters.

Smartly, he hit the palm of his hand with his fist. "I tell you, everything I do these days is a mockery. Things would get along just as well if I weren't here at all. Those new doctors—you know not one of them has asked my advice about anything?"

"Ed, think back—when you first started to practice, didn't you, perhaps, pretend to be self-confident and assured to hide feelings that were really just the reverse? Did you go to Dr. Ladd for advice, though Ladd was older and knew the town?"

Moore laughed; then he looked interested and thoughtful, and her heart warmed to the fairness, the open honesty, of his mind.

"You know, Ianthe, I never thought about it that way before. But there wasn't the distance, medically speaking, between Ladd and myself that there is between me and these youngsters. The other day young Barlow used some words—I had to ask him what they meant. I suppose you might say that the older men, who don't know much about the science of medicine, tend to overestimate the value of the art. There isn't much we can do about guiding the younger generation. No, I think the best thing is for us to get out of the way. I shouldn't be in this job. The fact is I've outlived my usefulness."

"Oh no, Ed. I'm willing to grant that there's a great deal in what you've been saying, but not that there isn't a place for you in the medical life of Haddon. That's simply not true."

Moore drew a long, unsteady breath, and without taking his eyes off the point in space on which they were fixed, he laid his hand, palm up, on the sofa between them. She put hers into it. And as though he had not really expected this, he turned to face her and found that she was smiling. She leaned a little toward him, her fingers tightening on his. "Ed, I've been wondering . . ."

"What, my dear?"

He was leaning toward her, gripping her fingers tightly, a look of sympathy on his face. He felt a tremor go through her, and saw the blood come rushing into her face.

"I've been wondering . . ." her fingers tightened on his hand and she gave a gasp of resolution ". . . when you're going to get around to asking me to marry you."

He sat perfectly still and stared at her. Her cheeks were bright with color, and there were sparks of laughter in her eyes. A smile spread over his face, and she was laughing aloud. He laughed too, a roar of laughter. Then neither was laughing and they were gazing into each other's eyes, intently searching. He drew her slowly into his arms and kissed her. They did not move apart, but rested peacefully in each other's embrace while old and bitter wounds began wonderfully to heal.

In the silence a little gilt clock struck four clear notes. Ianthe disengaged herself gently. "The party. I have to go." But she didn't move at once.

Moore sat back in his corner of the sofa and watched her possessively. Suddenly the full force of his astonishment struck him. "I'll be darned," he exploded. They laughed, then laughed again because of their delight in laughter. She rose and he followed her to the door.

"You'd better tell me what time I have to show up."

"Five, I should think, dear. Not much after."

Her use of the small endearment pleased him inordinately. He started to hold the door open for her, let it shut again, and with determination took her in his arms once more.

Though he began to miss her the moment she was gone, he was not really lonely. The house was too full of her. He went from room to room, looking around him with as much interest as though he had never been here before, but actually seeing nothing at all. Emotions churned in him, some making him feel strong and confident of the future, but others—those that came from his desire to cherish Ianthe and to fill her life with happiness—making him feel timid and inadequate.

Finally he looked at his watch. It was already after five. He let himself out of the door. As he drove along, he found that he did not feel quite so intractably rebellious as he had. He swung the Jeep into the parking lot with a great exuberant swoop.

As he crossed the parking lot, looking up at the hideous pile of his beloved hospital so soon to be replaced by a modern blight, his mood sobered. His gaze shifted to the large tent in the weedy plot next door where the party was most audibly in progress. Shortly he would have to go there, receive a beribboned spade and "break ground" for the new hospital.

Moore mounted the steps to the open front door. Edna was not at her desk. He stood for a moment, missing her acutely. Then habit turned his steps toward his former office. It had become a common room for the staff doctors. The lone piece of his furnishings to survive was the glass-doored bookcase on which he had kept the photograph of his wife. On its shelves were piles of white coats neatly folded.

Moore stood in the middle of the room and let the change have its way with his feelings. The long past lay in shadows behind him, but on the horizon of the future the sky was bright. He had gone through a time of torment; but looking back on those distressful months it came to him that old age is like a birth into a world where the conditions of life are different but not necessarily distasteful. Regarding this new landscape, he perceived that there was work to be done here; and if his usefulness was not of the same order as in the past, it was usefulness nevertheless. There was progress here, and if he did not meet it with blind resistance, he might hope in a small way to influence its course.

Standing there in this changed, familiar place, he faced the future without resentment, but he paid the past the tribute of a sigh. On a sudden whim, he took off his jacket, then picked from the bookcase the largest of the starched white coats and shrugged his big shoulders into it. It was too small, but he could wear it.

When he went out into the hall, Edna was back at her desk, the absurd cap tipped forward as she bent over her work. No party for Edna. Since someone must stay by the patients, she would assume it should be herself. Seeing Dr. Moore, she rose and stood there as always, tall, Gothic, thin, a sentinel of time. She saw the white coat, and it seemed to Moore that the cap made the slightest nod of approval. For a moment the air between them was filled with wave on wave of regard and memory as their eyes held each other's gaze. Then with humor, finality, and with style, he put his hands behind his back and walked out of his hospital.

W. SONNTAG

AGATHA YOUNG

To gather authentic material for *The Town and Dr. Moore*, Agatha Young put on an operating gown, mask and cap, and stood on a stool behind the chief surgeon of a small Vermont hospital. She witnessed many operations, and also went on house calls with rural doctors. At first she thought of the book as a work of nonfiction, like her previous medical book, *Scalpel*. "But," she says, "I saw that you can tell a kind of truth in fiction that you can't in books of fact. You can also make your points more dramatically, and you reach a different readership."

Agatha Young was born Agnes Brooks in Cleveland, Ohio. After graduating from Dana Hall, Wellesley, Massachusetts, she studied art for a time, but gave it up in favor of stage costuming and design, becoming head of the department of costuming at Yale University Theatre. Her widely divergent fields of interest have led her to serve as a faculty member—departments of fine arts and adult education—at Western Reserve University, and as consultant to both the War Manpower Commission and the Retraining and Reemployment Administration during World War II.

Her early books, *Stage Costuming* and *Recurring Cycles in Fashion*, were published under her married name of Agnes Brooks Young. When she started writing fiction, she adopted the pen name Agatha Young. True to her conviction that you are only as good as your *next* book, she has already moved on to a new project: a trilogy, in novel form, showing the great sweep of medical advances from the Civil War to the present. To her delight, *The Town and Dr. Moore* is being read by hospital administrators and country doctors for the light it throws on their predicament. Says Dr. William H. Krause, chief of surgery at Windsor Hospital, Vermont—whom Mrs. Young observed in the operating room—"The book has held a mirror up to our problems, which are often too close for us to see."

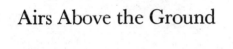

Airs Above the Ground

A unique suspense
story involving a
charming English trio,
a European circus
and the famous
white horses
of Vienna

Airs Above th

Ground

A condensation of the book by
Mary Stewart
Illustrations by Francis Marshall

*High in the Austrian Alps
an old piebald stallion executes one of
the incredible Lippizaner movements
called "airs above the ground,"
and one piece of a fascinating
puzzle falls into place.*

*For Vanessa March the puzzle
began in London when she saw
a newsreel picture of her husband,
traveling abroad, caught unawares
with a lovely, mysterious blonde.
Spurred by anger and curiosity,
she flew to Austria in search of
the errant Lewis and found herself
involved in a fantastic adventure.
Her companion, by chance,
was seventeen-year-old Timothy,
whose knowledge of the tradition
of the famous white horses of Vienna
made him a most useful ally.*

*"Airs Above the Ground" is a captivating
suspense story peopled with characters
who are seldom what they seem.
Set against the fairy-tale background
of a small European circus and an
ancient Alpine castle, the unexpected
twists of plot keep the reader
spellbound from start to finish.*

Chapter 1

CARMEL LACY is the silliest woman I know, which is saying a good deal. The only reason I was having tea with her in Harrods on a wet Thursday afternoon in August was that I had been so depressed when she called me that even tea with Carmel seemed preferable to sitting alone at home in a room still echoing with my quarrel with Lewis. That I had been entirely in the right while Lewis had been insufferably, immovably, furiously in the wrong was no particular satisfaction, since he was now in Stockholm and I was still here in London, when by rights we should have been lying on an Italian beach together, enjoying our first real holiday since our honeymoon two years ago. The fact that it had rained almost without ceasing ever since he had gone had done nothing to mitigate his offense; and when the weather reports said Stockholm was enjoying a permanent state of sunshine, it made me concentrate steadily on Lewis's sins and my own grievances.

"What are you scowling about?" asked Carmel Lacy.

"Was I? I'm sorry. I suppose I'm just depressed with the weather. Do go on. Did you decide to buy it in the end?"

"I haven't made up my mind. It's always so difficult . . ."

Her voice trailed away as she contemplated the plate of cakes, her hand poised between a meringue and an éclair.

And if you wait much longer, I thought, as she selected the éclair, it won't fit you anyway. But I didn't think it unkindly; plumpness suits Carmel, who is one of those women whose looks depend on the fair, soft coloring which seems to go on indestructibly into middle age.

She had been a friend of my mother's. The two girls lived near each other in Cheshire and had professional connections; for Carmel's father owned and trained racehorses, while my grandfather was a veterinary surgeon. My mother had married her father's young partner, and Carmel had married Graham Lacy, a wealthy, good-looking London banker. But Carmel's marriage had not worked out. To all appearances a soft maternal creature, she had a clinging possessiveness like warm treacle that threatened to drown her family. The elder girl had gone off defiantly to get a job in Canada. The second daughter had torn loose at nineteen and followed her air-force husband to Malta. The husband had gone next, leaving a positive embarrassment of riches in the way of evidence for the divorce. This left only seventeen-year-old Timothy, whom I remembered meeting round his grandfather's stables; a slight, darting, quicksilver boy with a habit of sulky silences forgivable in any child exposed to the full blast of his mother's devotion.

She was moaning comfortably over him. "I don't know what to do, he's being *so* difficult. Although his father really started it. You'd think he'd have the decency to keep out of Timmy's life, after what he did. But Timmy just *burst* it on me the other day that his father has been writing him quite regularly—imagine! And he wants him to go and see him in Vienna. He went there straightaway, you know, and Timmy's never seen him since. I never even knew they were writing. . . . And now this! Would you believe such a thing, Vanessa? *Would* you?"

I hesitated, then said, "I'm sorry, but it seems quite natural to me. You won't mean any the less to Timothy because he feels the need of his father."

"But to keep secrets from me, his mother . . . !" Her voice throbbed. "I feel it, Vanessa, *here*." She groped for where her heart presumably lay, failed to locate it, and, abandoning the gesture, poured herself another cup of tea.

Carmel's dramatics had dispelled any pity I might have felt for her and centered it firmly on Timothy. Wondering just where I came in, I said, "Most boys Timothy's age would grab at a chance to go to Austria. Why not just be sweet about it and let him go? Mummy used to say if you hang on to them too hard they'll only stay away, once they've managed to get free."

As soon as the words were out I was afraid I had cut rather near the bone. But I need not have worried. People like Carmel are impervious to criticism simply because they can never admit a fault in themselves; just as those people who complain of being unloved never pause to ask if they are in fact lovable.

Carmel said: "You haven't any children, of course. Doesn't Lewis want them?"

"Have a heart. We've only been married two years."

"Plenty of time to start one. Of course," said Carmel, "he's not at home much, is he?"

"What have our affairs got to do with this?" I asked sharply.

"Only that if you had children of your own you wouldn't be so gay and glib," she said.

"Timothy isn't a child anymore," I said. "Boys grow up, and you can't put fences round them." That I still spoke sharply was not entirely due to exasperation with Carmel; this futile conversation was reminding me of the fences that I myself had been trying to put round Lewis.

Suddenly Carmel spoke in quite a different tone: "As a matter of fact, Vanessa, I'm sure you're right. I *ought* to let him go. My own feelings hardly matter. After all, he has his own life to live." I waited. It was coming now, if I was any judge of the signs. "Vanessa, I do wonder if you could help me? You see, Timmy is such a *young* seventeen, and he's never been away from home before. I *can't* let him go alone. So I thought of you."

I stared at her. "Of me? I don't understand."

"Well, I knew you were to go on holiday with Lewis this month, and then he had to go on business instead." She couldn't quite repress a look of malicious curiosity. "But I did think, if you were joining him later, you and Timmy could travel together and it would solve everything."

"Carmel," I said, "I'd do it like a shot if I were going to Vienna, but we're going to Italy for our holiday, and besides—"

"But you could join him in Vienna first. It does seem the most marvelous piece of luck that he is in Austria. As soon as I knew, I rang you up."

"Carmel, Lewis is *not* in Austria. He's in Sweden on business for his chemical company."

"In Sweden? When did he leave Austria?"

"He's been in Sweden all along. He went on Sunday, and I heard from him on Monday." I didn't add that the only message in four days had been a very brief cable. Lewis was as capable as I was of holding tightly to a quarrel.

"But I swear it was Lewis. Molly Gregg was with me, and Angela Thripp, and they both said, 'Oh, that's Lewis March!' And it was."

I said: "I don't know what you're talking about."

"Well, yesterday." She sounded as if I were being as stupid as I had been over Timothy. "We were shopping, and there was an hour to Angy's train so we went to the news cinema, and there was a disaster or something—I don't remember much about it— in Austria, and Lewis was in it, as plain as plain. So I thought straightaway of you, because you might be going there too."

I must have been looking as stupid as she had implied. "You say you saw Lewis in a newsreel of something happening in Austria? You must be mistaken."

"I'm never mistaken," said Carmel simply.

"But he *can't* be—" I stopped. In Carmel's eyes I could see the little flicker of malicious curiosity again. I could hear Angela, Molly and Carmel twittering over it. . . . "Do you suppose they had a row? She hadn't the *faintest* idea where he was."

I glanced at my watch. "Well, I must be going. I wish I could help you, but if Lewis was in Austria, it was just a flying trip down from Stockholm. You wouldn't believe the way they push him about." I rose. "Thanks awfully for the tea, it was lovely seeing you. And I must say I'm intrigued about this newsreel. . . ." I hesitated, then said, I hoped casually: "Which cinema was it, did you say?"

"Leicester Square. And it was Lewis, it really was. We recognized him straightaway. You know the way he has."

"I know all the ways he has," I said, more dryly than I had meant to. "You really can't remember what was happening in the newsreel?"

She was busy applying lipstick. "Not really: I was talking to Molly until Lewis came on. Something about a circus, and a dead man . . . A fire, that was it, a fire." She examined her lips in the tiny mirror. "But it wasn't Lewis who was dead."

I didn't answer. If I had, I'd have said something I'd have been sorry for.

AT THE news theater I made my way to a seat. A travelogue was in progress, and it seemed a long time before the news came round: the latest from Africa, the Middle East . . .

All at once there it was. "Circus fire in Austrian village . . . elephant loose in the village street . . . province of Styria . . ." And pictures of the black and smoking aftermath in the gray of early morning, with police and gray-faced men huddled round whatever had been pulled from the wreck. There was the circus encampment with the big top in the background; behind it a glimpse of a pine-covered hill and the glint of a whitewashed church tower with an onion spire; and in the foreground a temporary billboard with circus announcements on it, a blurred photograph, some man's name, and something about *Eine absolute Star-Attraktion.* Someone shoved against it and it fell flat on the trampled grass, and there was Lewis. He had been standing in the shelter of the sign, staring at the burned-out ruins. He moved his head and I saw the expression on his face. He was angry. Quite plainly and simply angry. His anger was somehow incongruous and disturbing.

There was a girl beside him. A blonde; young and rather more than pretty in that small-featured, wide-eyed way that can be so devastating, and dressed in a dark raincoat with a high collar. She was pressed close to Lewis's side, as if for protection, and his arm was round her. She saw the cameras on them, and I watched her reach up and touch him, saying something, a quick whispered word that matched the intimate gesture.

Ninety-nine people out of a hundred, in that situation, would glance instinctively at the camera before either facing it self-consciously or turning out of its range. My husband didn't even look round. He turned quickly away and vanished into the crowd, the girl with him.

THE *Mirror* had it—a few lines under the headline, CIRCUS BLAZE RIDDLE:

> Austrian police are investigating a circus-wagon fire in which two men were burned to death on Sunday night. The circus was performing in a village near the city of Graz. . . .

Next morning I had a note from Lewis in his own handwriting, postmarked Stockholm. It read: "Have almost finished the job here; I'll cable when you can expect me. Love, Lewis."

That same morning I rang up Carmel Lacy.

"If you still want a courier for Timothy," I told her, "you've got one. You were right about Lewis; I've had a letter. He's in Austria, and he wants me to join him there at once."

Chapter 2

TIMOTHY LACY had grown into a tall boy, resembling neither parent, but with a strong look of his grandfather and a quick-moving, almost nervous manner which would weather with time into the same wiry, energetic toughness. He had gray-green eyes, a fair skin tending to freckles, and a lot of brown hair cut fashionably long. The expression he had worn ever since his mother officially handed him over at London Airport—much as she had handed over her spoiled spaniel in my father's office— had been reserved. To put it truthfully, he looked like a small boy in a fit of the sulks.

He was fumbling now with his seat belt, and it was obvious from his unaccustomed movements that he had never flown before; but I dared not offer to help. After Carmel's tearful—and very public—handing over of her baby, it would have seemed like tucking his bib round his neck. I said instead: "It was clever of you to get these seats in front of the wing. If there's no cloud we'll have a marvelous view."

He gave me a glance of dislike. The thick, silky hair made a wonderful ambush to glower through, and increased the resemblance to a spoiled but wary dog; and at that moment the Austrian Airlines Caravelle began to edge her screaming way forward over the concrete. He turned to the window.

The Caravelle paused, gathered herself, then surged into the air in that exciting lift that never fails to give me a thrill up the marrow of my spine. London fell away, the coast came up, receded, and the hazy silver-blue of the Channel spread out below.

"Angel's-eye view," I said. "We get a lot of privileges now that only the gods got before."

He still said nothing. I gave up, and opened a magazine. Lunch came, temptingly foreign, with *Apfelsaft*, red wine or champagne. The boy beside me was so pointedly refraining from comment on what must be an exciting experience for him that I felt a flicker of irritation pierce my preoccupation with the situation ahead of me.

The pretty stewardess wheeled a trolley up the aisle. "Would you care for cigarettes, madam? Perfume? Liquor?" I refused, and her eye went doubtfully to Timothy. "Cigarettes, sir?"

"Of course." He said it promptly, and rather too loudly, and I caught the edge of a glance at me. He made his choice, paid for them, tucked them into his airline flight bag and got out a paperback mystery. Silence descended again.

I said: "You know, I couldn't care less if you want to smoke all

397

day and all night till you die of six sorts of cancer all at once. Go ahead. As a matter of fact, the sooner the better. You have the worst manners of any young man I ever met."

He looked at me full for the first time, eyes and mouth startled open. I said: "I know you're perfectly capable of traveling alone, and that you'd prefer it. Well, so would I; but if I hadn't said I'd go with you, you'd never have got away. We're stuck with each other till you meet your father, so why not make the best of it?"

Timothy swallowed. "I—I'm sorry," he said.

"I didn't want to make you talk," I said, "but as a matter of fact, I always get nervous on takeoff, and if I chatter it takes my mind off it."

"I'm sorry," said Timothy again. He was scarlet now. "I hadn't realized you felt like that. I was so . . . it's all been so . . ." He stopped floundering, bit his lip, then said with devastating simplicity: "The cigarettes were for Daddy."

This had the effect of taking the wind right out of my sails. And he knew it. I could see the glint in the gray-green eyes. I said: "Timothy Lacy, you have all the makings of a dangerous young man. I'm not surprised your mother's afraid to let you out alone. Now tell me, do you prefer Timothy or Tim?"

"I'll settle for Tim, Mrs. March."

"Vanessa, please. And I'm twenty-four."

"Vanessa. That's an awfully pretty name. If you're going to be frightened when we land, Vanessa," he added kindly, "I'll hold your hand."

"Isn't she beautiful?" asked Timothy. Melting into relaxation, he had got to the stage of showing me photographs. This one was of a girl on a gray pony. It was an oldish print, and the girl, I was startled to see, was Carmel; nothing had led me to expect the enthusiasm with which he held out her photograph.

I asked lamely: "How old was she then?"

"Pretty old. About fifteen. You can tell by the tail."

"You can tell by the what?"

"The tail. Actually that pony's of the Welsh Starlight strain,

and they don't start to look old till they're dying on their feet."
Then he recollected himself. "Gosh, listen to me telling *you*, when you're practically a vet!"

"Not practically. I qualified before I was married."

"Did you ever practice?"

"Officially, only about six months; but you get a lot of practice as a student, especially your final year. You make your own diagnoses, use X rays, assist operations. I started work as Daddy's assistant; but then I met Lewis and got married."

"What exactly does he do, your husband?"

"He's employed by Pan-European Chemicals—P.E.C.—in the sales department. But he's planning to change over to another branch. His job takes him abroad so much that we hardly seem to have seen each other since we were married."

Timothy sat quiet for a moment, riffling through the remaining photographs; I saw they were mostly of horses. He seemed completely at ease now, as if I were his contemporary. Which, oddly enough, I felt myself to be, for now we had quarreled and made it up on equal terms, with a license to say what we felt.

He said suddenly: "I hate London. It was all right when Grandfather was alive, I went to his place a lot in the hols. But this summer it looked as if it was going to be London, and I felt I couldn't stick it. So I had to do something drastic—hadn't I?"

"Like harrying your poor mother into parting with you? I shouldn't worry; she'll survive it."

He gave me a quick, bright glance and seemed about to say something, but thought better of it. He said instead, "Are you interested in the Spanish Riding School? You know, the team of white Lippizaner stallions that give those performances of *haute école* to music? I've wanted to see them all my life."

I said: "I know of them, of course, but I can't say I know much about them. I'd love to see them. Are they in Vienna now?"

"They live in Vienna. The performances are put on in a marvelous building—the Riding Hall in the Hofburg. I hope my father will know a few of the right people, and get me in behind the scenes."

He was obviously talking about a subject of which he knew far more than he was bothering to impart. I asked, to keep him talking: "Why is it called the Spanish Riding School?"

"Because the Lippizaner stud was founded originally with Spanish horses. I think it's about the oldest breed of horse we've got—they go right back to the Roman cavalry horses in Spain being crossed with Arabians and so on, and they were the best war-horses in Europe in the Middle Ages. When the Austrian Stud was founded at Lippiza they bought Spanish stock for it."

"I see. Hence the name Lippizan. Didn't Austria give up Lippiza to Italy after the First War?"

He nodded. "It was a marvel the horses didn't disappear altogether when the Austrian Empire broke up. I suppose nobody then was much interested in a relic of, well, high life, but then they started giving public performances—they'd become state property, of course—and the Austrians are frantically proud of them. The stud had a pretty rough time at the end of the last war, too, when Vienna was bombarded. The director got the trained stallions out safely; then a string of mares, foals and stallions were rescued from Czechoslovakia by the Americans—an advance unit of General Patton's army. The herd had been driven north early in the war. Now they are resettled at Piber, in Styria, not far from Graz. What's the matter?"

"Nothing," I said, remembering the newsreel. "Go on."

"Well, the stallions are bred at Piber, and when they're four, the best of them go to Vienna to be trained. I suppose one of the things that makes the Lippizans' performance so exciting is it isn't even ordinary *haute école*; after all, you can see normal dressage anywhere at shows. . . . What's so beautiful is the way they've blended the dressage movements in to make the 'figure dances' like the School Quadrille, and then of course the 'airs above the ground.'"

"The what? Oh, you mean those marvelous leaps the horses do."

"Yes. They're as old as the hills, too. They were battle movements all the war-horses had to learn if they were to be any good —I mean, if you were using both hands for shield and sword, you had to have a horse that would jump to order in any direction. Half a minute—if you'd like to look at these . . ."

He bent to fish in his flight bag. We were coming down through cloud, steadily losing height, and people already were making preparations for landing. But even the novelties of flying seemed lost on Timothy now.

He straightened up, slightly flushed, eagerly producing an illustrated book.

"See, here are the different figures." He spread the book open on my knees. "All the stallions can learn to do the ordinary movements, but only the best of them go on to the actual leaps. There, see? That one is doing the *levade;* it looks like rearing, but it's a terrific effort to hold. If somebody took a swipe at you in battle, your horse was supposed to get between you and him."

"Well, I hope it had armor, that's all," I said. "These are lovely, Tim. Oh, he's a beauty, isn't he? Look at those wise eyes!"

"That's Pluto Theodorosta," said Timothy. "He was the absolute tops, I believe; he died just recently. Look, this is Neapolitano Petra doing the *courbette,* the most difficult leap of all. There's a story that they were going to present him to some Eastern potentate, but his rider killed him and then shot himself, so they wouldn't be parted."

"Good heavens. Is it true?"

"I wouldn't be surprised: you know how you can get to feel about a horse. . . . And when you've worked as these men do, every day with a horse for—oh, Lord, twenty years, perhaps . . ."

"I believe you. Where do they get such unusual names, Tim?"

"They all come from six original stallions. The first name comes from the stallion and the second from the dam."

I said, with genuine respect: "You seem to know an awful lot about them."

He hesitated, then said flatly: "I'm going to get a job there if they'll have me. That's why I came." He had pushed the thick hair back and was half turned to face me, no longer sullenly ambushed but still defensive. The seat belt holding him down helped the impression of something trapped. "That's not all," he said. "It's—I thought it would be all right, but now it's come to the point, I'm beginning to wonder . . . Have you booked a room at a hotel?"

Something in his expression worried me. "Yes," I said. "At the Hotel am Stephansplatz, opposite St. Stephen's Cathedral. Why? Would you like to go there before you meet your father?"

"Yes, if you don't mind. And I'd better tell you—" He swallowed, and the action seemed to use the muscles of his whole body.

"Tim," I said, "relax! Things can't be as bad as that. What have you done? Forgotten to tell your father which day you're coming?"

"It's worse than that. He's not even expecting me. He didn't ask me to come at all. I made it all up, to get away. In fact," said Timothy desperately, "he hasn't written to me since he left. Not once. Oh"—at something which must have showed in my face— "I didn't mind, really. I mean, if he didn't want to, well, it was up to him, wasn't it? You're not to think I told all those lies to Mummy because I felt he should have written. I only did it so that I could get away."

He finished the terrible little confession on a note of apology. It was all I could do not to state loudly just what I thought of his parents. "In other words," I said, "you're running away. Well, we'll have to think this out. How are you off for money?"

"I've got about twenty pounds. I took it from my savings account. I stole it, in a way, because I was supposed to leave it till my eighteenth birthday."

I said: "Well, we'll go to my hotel and ring your father up. I expect he'll come for you."

"If he's home. But it's August; he may be away on holiday."

"Timothy Lacy! Are you trying to tell me you've lied to your poor mother and gone blinding off into the blue without having the foggiest idea where your father even *is?*"

There was a rather loaded silence. He must have misunderstood my half of it, for he said quickly: "Don't think I'll be a nuisance to you. If I can't get hold of Daddy I'll take a room at the hotel till Monday. You don't need to bother about me at all. When's your husband joining you?"

"I don't quite know."

Another pause. The gray-green eyes widened. "*Vanessa March!*" It was a wickedly perfect imitation of the tone I had used to him, and it crumbled the last barriers of status between us. "Are you trying to tell me that you've lied to my poor mother and gone blinding off into the blue without having the foggiest idea where your husband even *is?*"

I nodded. We met one another's eyes. Unnoticed, the Caravelle touched down. Babel rose round us as people hunted for coats and hand baggage.

Timothy pulled himself together. "The orphans of the storm," he said. "Never mind, Vanessa, I'll look after you."

Chapter 3

As it turned out, Timothy's father proved easy to locate: he was in the telephone book. "If Lewis is as easy to find," I said, "our troubles will be over by dinnertime. Well, go ahead and phone. The girl at the switchboard speaks English."

"Oh, I took German in school. As a matter of fact I'm panting to try it."

He grinned and lifted the receiver. I went into the bathroom and shut the door.

Under the circumstances it seemed a remarkably short conversation. When I went in again he was leaning on the windowsill, watching the crowds outside St. Stephen's Cathedral. He said, without looking round: "He wasn't annoyed."

I opened a suitcase and began to lift my things out. "Good. Is he coming for you, or will you get a taxi?"

"He was just going out, as a matter of fact," said Tim. "He's going to a concert with his fiancée."

I shook out a dress rather carefully and hung it away. "I suppose you didn't know about her?"

"I told you he never wrote. She's Viennese; her name's Christl. I told him you were here. He said he couldn't get out of the concert, but would we meet them at eleven for supper in the Blue Bar at Sacher's."

He had turned back now from the window and was watching me. His face gave no clue to what he was thinking.

"My dear," I said, "do you mind about Christl?"

"To be quite honest, I don't know. My mother's going to marry again too."

I couldn't think what to say. I just stood there probably looking as stupid as I felt; I was beginning to find that I very much cared what happened to Timothy. I said finally, "I suppose your father won't have had time to make arrangements for you?"

"Well," said Timothy, "he didn't say anything about my joining him; but he took my coming to Vienna in his stride. In fact, he seems sure he can get me a job. He said something about a holiday to start with, and was I all right for cash."

"I like the sound of that last bit," I said. "Well, you'll get things fixed up when you see him tonight. He'll probably want you to move in there tomorrow."

"That's just what I wouldn't bet on," said Timothy. "I think it is the last thing he wants. Actually, I got the impression that he has someone living with him already." Unexpectedly, Tim laughed. "Poor father! I've put him in a spot, haven't I? Well, I'd better see if I can book a room." He crossed to the telephone.

There must be easier ways of growing up, I thought, than tearing loose from apron strings and then being thrown into the cold by your father, with a few coins flung after you. It was surprising how normal and nice Tim appeared to be.

"Number 216, one floor up," he said, putting down the receiver. "That's me settled. Now, what about you? Are you going to do your telephoning, or get something to eat first? I don't know about you, but I'm starving."

I glanced up. "You're being very tactful. You must be wondering like mad what I'm playing at."

He grinned. "Well, I'm not in a position to criticize."

I sat down in one of the armchairs. "I'd like to tell somebody. It's a bit sordid. I daresay it happens every day, only I thought it wouldn't ever happen to me. We were going away this month on our first real holiday since we were married. P.E.C. slave-drives Lewis and when we got married he said he'd change his job, only it would take time to train his successor. It was Lewis who suggested giving the job up, not me. You see, we both want a family, and, the way things are now, it wouldn't be fair. . . ."

Tim didn't say anything. He was back at the window, apparently tracing out with his eye, stone by stone, the massive facade of St. Stephen's.

"Well"—I tried to stop sounding defensive—"Lewis told me he was leaving the sales department in mid-August, and we would go just where I wanted for a whole month. Then, just before we were to go, they asked him to take on one more assignment; they couldn't be sure how long it would take. We had our tickets; I was even packed."

"What a rotten thing," said Timothy to St. Stephen's.

"That's what I thought. But Lewis said this was something that had come out of his last assignment and he had to do it himself. So I went all feminine and threw one of those classic scenes, 'You think more of your rotten job than of me'—that sort of thing. And I've always *despised* women who did that."

"Anybody would have been upset," said Timothy.

"Lewis was furious, too, at the change of plan; but he said there was no alternative. So I said well, why couldn't he take me with him for a change? When he said he couldn't, I really blew up, and we had a dreadful row. I said the most awful things, Tim."

Tim, perched now on the arm of a chair, looked at me with youthful gravity. "And now you're just torturing yourself all the time because you've hurt his feelings?"

"Lewis," I said, forgetting momentarily whom I was talking to, "is selfish, obstinate and arrogant, and has no feelings of any kind whatsoever."

"But if he doesn't want you to join him, why did you come, especially if you're still so furious with him?"

I looked down at my hands, clasped tightly on my knee. "Because I think he's with a woman, and I'm so unhappy I've got to do something. That's why I came."

"Please don't be unhappy, Vanessa." He was as awkward with his comfort as any man is at any age, but touchingly kind. "I'm sure you'll find there's nothing in it."

"When you get married, Tim"—I managed a smile at him—"never part on a quarrel. Lewis went storming out, and then, when he got to the door, he stopped and came back to me. I wasn't even looking at him. He kissed me good-by and went." I looked at Tim somberly. "It only came to me afterward, but it was the way a man would act if he knew he was going to do something dangerous, and didn't want to part like that."

He stared at me. "What sort of danger could he be in?"

Then I told him all about the newsreel, and when I had finished he was quiet for a minute or two. Then he pushed the hair back from his forehead with a gesture I was beginning to recognize as a signal of decision.

"Well, it will be dead easy to locate that circus. There are hardly any traveling circuses left these days, and everyone in Austria probably knows where this one is. Shall we start with the hall porter right now?"

I stood up. "No, we'll eat first. Then when we feel a bit stronger, I'll tackle The Case of the Vanishing Husband, and you can take on The Father and the Fräulein."

"We'll both tackle them both." He uncoiled his length from the arm of the chair and stood up. He looked down at me, suddenly shy. "I was an awful ass this morning. I—I'm terribly glad we came together after all."

"That makes two of us," I said, reaching in the wardrobe for my coat. "Let's go out and eat."

AFTER DINNER, the hall porter identified the circus immediately as the Circus Wagner, and the village where the accident had taken place as Oberhausen, in the hilly region west of the main road from Vienna to Graz and the Yugoslav border.

"There's nothing to this detective business," said Timothy, relaying this information. My own German is sketchy, but Tim's, though slow and liberally laced with pantomime, seemed to get results.

"Ask him about the fire," I said.

The fire? Ah, that had been a terrible thing! A living wagon burned in the night, and two men with it. One of them was the horsekeeper. The hall porter had known him. A good man, but he drank, you understand. . . . No doubt he had been drunk when the accident happened, knocked over a lamp. . . . The only reason they had kept him on, poor old Franzl, was that he was some relation of Herr Wagner himself, and then he was such a very good man with horses.

"And the other man?"

But here the hall porter's information ran out abruptly. It was no one belonging to the circus. There were even rumors that it had not been an accident, that the men had been murdered because of being involved in some crime; but anyone who had known old Franzl would realize that such an idea was absurd.

"Ask him if he's ever heard of a man called Lewis March."

"Never," said the hall porter briefly. He smiled deprecatingly. "It is over, you understand. The newspapers lose interest . . ."

A few more questions, and we had gathered all we needed to know. Two days ago the circus had still been in Oberhausen, detained there by the police; its next stop was to have been Hohenwald. There was an excellent small *Gasthof* in Oberhausen itself, the Edelweiss.

"Gosh," said Timothy as we left the hotel again, "I've always wanted to see the inside of a circus. If Father and Christl won't have me, I'll come with you. I really don't feel you ought to be allowed to go all that way on your own."

"I'll hold you to that. And now, if we're to get to Sacher's in time, we'd better get a move on. Can you really eat another meal? I thought you were a bit rash with that *Hühnerleberrisotto* at the Deutsches Haus."

"Good Lord, that was hours ago!" Timothy had quite recovered

his cheerfulness. He charged along the crowded pavement, examining the contents of every shopwindow with interest and enthusiasm. "What is this Sacher's anyway? It sounds a bit dull. Will there be music?"

"I've heard it's terribly glamorous, actually—typical of Old Vienna; all gilt and red brocade. The hotel was started by Madame Sacher in the nineteenth century, and everyone who comes to Vienna goes there at least once."

Sacher's was all I had imagined, with brilliantly lit scarlet and gold drawing rooms, oils in heavy frames, mahogany and flowers, and a last-century atmosphere of comfortable leisure. The Blue Bar turned out to be a smallish, intimate cave, lined with blue brocade and lit with such discretion that one almost needed a flashlight to find one's drink.

To my surprise, I liked Christl. She was a plump and pretty young blonde, and looked as if she would be more at home in the kitchen putting together an omelette for Graham than sitting in the Blue Bar having a champagne cocktail. Graham Lacy was still recognizably the man I remembered, with years and weight added. He was in love with the girl, and he made it plain. He also (though to do him justice he tried not to) made it plain that Timothy's appearance in Vienna at this moment was, to say the least, inopportune. By the time he shepherded us into the dining room for supper I saw with misgiving that the sullen look was back on Timothy's face.

Christl was watching Tim, too, and I saw the exact moment at which she set herself deliberately to charm him. It was beautifully done, and not too difficult, since she was not much older than he was and had in full measure that warm, easy Viennese charm which "sings the song you want to hear." Tim was soon looking entertained and flattered, and his father was able to devote himself to me. Clearly he was curious to know how Carmel had managed to involve me in her affairs.

"Oh, I'm just on holiday," I said. "My husband was called away to Stockholm just as we were setting off for a holiday in southern Austria, so I came on here myself. He'll be joining me soon, in Graz. I'm going down there tomorrow. It was pure luck that Carmel discovered I would be heading this way at the same time as Timothy."

"Ah, yes," said Graham; and then, to his son: "And what are your plans, Tim?"

Tim had been listening to my string of lies with no betraying gleam of surprise; but now, faced either with confessing that he had come expecting his father to take him in, or inventing a spur-of-the-moment story, he was dumb.

I opened my mouth to say something, but Christl rushed into the pause. "Well, of course, he has come to see Vienna! What else? Timmee, I wish I could show Vienna to you myself! All the places the tourists visit, the Hofburg, Schönbrunn, the Prater, Kahlenberg, and then all the places that the Viennese themselves go to! But I cannot. I am going out of Vienna tomorrow. It is many months since I have seen my parents, and they have been pressing me."

"But—" began Graham Lacy.

She touched his hand and he stopped obediently, but the look of surprise on his face was a dead giveaway. Obviously she intended to clear out of Graham's apartment so that he would be free—indeed, obliged—to do the right thing by his son.

"Well . . ." Graham cleared his throat. "Tomorrow's Sunday, so I've a free day. What do you say, old man—shall I come along about eleven and collect you and your stuff?"

Timothy's glance went from one to the other; he had seen as much as I had. He was a little flushed but he said composedly enough: "That's terribly nice of you, Daddy, but I won't descend on you just yet. I'd actually planned to go south with Vanessa tomorrow."

If Graham or Christl felt relief, they did not show it. Graham said: "It's very nice of Vanessa to ask you, but if she and her husband are off on a tour, they'll hardly want—"

"Lewis won't be able to join me for a day or two. I'd love to have Tim with me," I said quickly.

"I shan't land myself on them," said Timothy cheerfully. "I'd been planning to see the Lippizaner stud at Piber, in Styria, so if Vanessa wants company it'll be killing two birds with one stone. If you don't mind being called a bird in public, Vanessa?"

"Delighted," I said.

"Then," said young Mr. Lacy calmly, "that's settled."

We settled down to drink our coffee with a distinct air of relaxation and relief all round. When we left the dining room Timothy and his father vanished in perfect amity in the direction of the cloakroom, and when they returned I could see from Tim's expression of satisfaction that Graham had come through handsomely with funds.

"Well," said Graham as we bade each other good night, "I hope you enjoy yourselves. And let me know when you're coming back to Vienna, Timmy. If only you'd let me know this time . . ."

He added awkwardly, "I'm afraid this has been a rather odd welcome."

Timothy said: "I'll remember next time. And thanks for tonight, it's been smashing."

They drove off and Timothy and I turned to walk back to our hotel. "She's a nice girl, Tim," I said.

"I know that. I did mind at first. I couldn't help it. But I don't now, not a bit." He had a look I had not seen in him before, buoyant and clear and free. "After all," he said, "he's got a perfect right to his own life, hasn't he? You can't hang on to people forever. You've got to let them go."

"Of course," I said.

Chapter 4

TIMOTHY and I left Vienna in a hired Volkswagen the next day, making our way out through the mercifully thin Sunday traffic to the Wiener Neustadt road, with Timothy at the wheel. Not much to my surprise—I had long since ceased to underrate Timothy—he turned out to be a good driver, so that I was able to relax and think about what lay ahead of me. It was a beautiful day, and as we ran southwest from Vienna we soon found ourselves in a rolling landscape of forested slopes, green pastures and romantic crags girdled by silver streams and crowned with castles.

We ate at the Semmering Pass—a resort which, at three thousand feet, had air so dizzyingly clear as to make Timothy extra ravenous even by his standards. After lunch we descended through more beautiful country till, beyond Bruck, we left the main road and turned up a river valley. The road began to run through meadows, rich, sunlit, peaceful. Behind them rose the hills, their green curves framed by the pines which flowed downhill in every fold and crevice of the slopes.

The first thing I saw, as we ran into the village of Oberhausen, was the Circus Wagner itself, in a field to the right of the road:

a collection of tents, wagons and caravans grouped round the big top. Timothy slowed as we both craned to see. "Well," he said, "they're still here. That's something, anyway. What do we do first?"

"Let's find the Edelweiss and get ourselves settled."

The village street closed in. At length we emerged into an open square where seats were set under trees round a cobbled space. Timothy drew carefully in to the side and stopped in the shade of a plane tree. "Gosh, do you see that *Konditorei*, the baker's shop?" he said. "I could do with some of those cakes, couldn't you? Let's buy some later."

He chattered on, pleasantly excited. But for me the pretty village, with its lively Sunday crowds, had become a shadowy background for one person. I had seen Lewis's blonde.

She had paused in the square to speak to an old woman in black, and in the flesh she was prettier even than in the newsreel. She had a slender young figure, fair hair tied neatly in a ponytail, and she was charmingly dressed in the traditional white blouse, blue dirndl and apron. She looked about eighteen. As I watched she had bade a laughing good-by to the old woman and came straight toward the car.

"Tim," I said softly, "that blonde in the blue dirndl—that's the girl I saw in the newsreel. Try to see where she goes."

She passed the car without a glance, Tim watching her in the rearview mirror. After a pause he said: "I can't see her anymore. Shall I follow her? She was heading down the way we came."

"Would you?"

"Sure thing." He was already half out of the car. "I've always fancied myself in the James Bond line. Who hasn't?"

The door slammed behind him, and I watched in the mirror until he, in his turn, was lost to view. I felt myself trembling a little as my eyes reluctantly yet feverishly searched the crowds. This confirmation was a profoundly disconcerting experience. The sight of Lewis and the girl in the dark cinema had been like a distant, unreal dream. Here was the reality of Oberhausen, the circus and the girl herself. And next, Lewis . . . ?

"I told you I'd found my vocation." It was Tim, back at the car. He folded his length beside me into the driving seat. "I shadowed your subject with great skill, and she went straight to the circus. I think she must belong there, because she went round toward the caravans. And I've got news for you: they're leaving tomorrow. Last performance tonight, at eight o'clock."

We reached the Edelweiss, a long, low house on the edge of the village, with window boxes full of flowers, and a shingle roof where doves sunned themselves. A few people sat at tables under chestnut trees outside.

Timothy and I were offered adjacent rooms giving on a wide veranda at the back of the house. The small spotless rooms, with solid pine furniture and scrubbed floors, were very quiet.

I unpacked quickly. When I was ready, I pushed the long windows wide and went out onto the low veranda. Timothy came out onto his own section of veranda. He looked alert and excited.

"I thought I heard you. Have you decided what to do next?"

"Actually, I haven't. I can't get over seeing that girl. It was a bit of a facer, like seeing a ghost."

"You mean you didn't really believe in her till now? I know what you mean," added Timothy surprisingly. "I felt a bit the same about Christl. But I don't know why you're worrying." He hesitated, then abandoned finesse. "Dash it, she may be pretty, but you're *beautiful*. Didn't anyone ever tell you?"

Now and again, people had; but I had never been so touched. I said: "Thank you; but it's not just that side of it that's worrying me. Now I'm not so much wondering how to find him as what in the world to say to him when I do." I straightened up with what might pass for decision. "Well, the circus is the obvious lead. Let's have a meal and then walk down there."

Tim eyed me. "If this is the last performance, they'll start the pull-down the minute it's over, and be clear of the place by morning. Shall I go along there now and see about tickets?"

I laughed. "I see. Well, why not? But if you do track down the subject, you won't do anything rash, will you?"

"The soul of discretion," he promised.

413

THE SHADOWS OF THE chestnuts lay lightly across the café tables outside the Edelweiss, and a warm breeze fluttered the red-checked cloths. I sipped my vermouth, my eyes fixed on the street up which presently, I was sure, Lewis must come. But when Timothy reappeared, coming at high speed, I was startled to see whom he had with him. Not Lewis but Lewis's blonde.

Next moment they were standing beside the table and Timothy was performing introductions. "Vanessa, this is Annalisa Wagner. She belongs to the circus. You remember we saw a circus the other side of the village? Miss Wagner, this is Mrs.—" Too late, he saw the pitfall. He stopped dead.

I said, watching the girl: "I am Vanessa March."

"How do you do, Mrs. March?" There was no flicker of expression outside the normal noncommittal politeness. She had, I noticed sourly, a charming voice, and her English was excellent.

"Won't you join us for a drink, Miss Wagner?"

"Why, thank you. If you would please call me Annalisa? But coffee, please. We circus people drink very little. It's something that doesn't pay."

Timothy lifted a hand to the passing waitress, who responded immediately—an unusual circumstance in any country, but in Austria (I had already discovered) a miracle. He and the girl sat down, Timothy subtly telegraphing, "Over to you."

Seen at close range, she was still very pretty, in an ash-blonde way quite different from Christl's. Rather than in a kitchen, she would seem in place among those slim, tough beauties who win Olympic medals for skating or slalom. I said, "Your name's Wagner; the circus must belong to your family?"

"To my father. Timothy says that you will see it tonight?"

"Yes, since you're leaving. We don't want to miss you."

She nodded. "We move on tonight. We have already been here too long." I waited, but she didn't pursue this. She asked: "You are keen on circuses?"

"I love the horses," I said. "Do you have many?"

"Not many, we are a small circus. But with us the horses are the most important of all."

"They're Timothy's ruling passion."

She laughed. "I know. I found him down in the horse lines."

I said: "What good English you speak."

"My mother was English, and I still get plenty of practice, because a circus is a very mixed place. In ours, the clowns are French, the high-wire act is Hungarian, the trampolin artistes are Japanese, there's an American juggler and an English comic."

"Have you an act yourself?" I asked.

"Yes. I help my father with the liberty horses. But my own act is a riding one. I have a Lippizaner stallion—"

"A *trained* stallion? I didn't think they ever sold them." Timothy's interruption was robbed of rudeness by his excitement.

"He is trained, yes, but not at the school. My grandfather bought him as a four-year-old, and my uncle and I trained him."

She had soared, I could see, in Timothy's estimation. I realized that my own estimate of her had been right: a young woman who had the skill and strength to put a Lippizaner stallion through his paces was about as fragile as pressed steel. "Gosh!" said Timothy, glowing with admiration. "You're an *écuyère!*"

She smiled. "Oh, we don't do what you see in Vienna, I assure you! None of the 'airs above the ground' except the *levade*, and sometimes the *croupade* . . ." She turned to me. "This is a leap right off the ground where the horse keeps his legs tucked under him, and lands again on the same spot. We tried to teach him the *capriole*, where he leaps in a *croupade* and then kicks the back legs straight out, but this is very difficult, and he cannot do it very well. It is my fault, not his."

I half expected Timothy to contradict this; but he, too, was dedicated enough to know that it is never the horse's fault. She added: "He is one of the Maestoso line; Maestoso Leda. If he is good tonight I will try the *capriole*, especially for you."

Tim said, "I didn't see him with the other horses."

"You were at the wrong end of the stable." She dimpled at him charmingly. "Would you like to come round tonight after the show and see him? There will be time before we pull down."

"You bet I would!" Then, recollecting himself, "Vanessa?"

"I'd like to very much," I said. "How many horses have you?"

"Twenty-seven; and the ponies. We have twelve liberty horses. They perform in a group, under the direction of their trainer but without riders. There will be only ten of them fit to work tonight, but it is still very beautiful to watch."

"Is there something wrong with the others?" I asked.

"Last week, one of the wagons caught fire and some of the horses injured themselves, with fear, you understand." She added quietly: "There were two men in the wagon and they were burned to death."

"I'm so sorry. It must have been dreadful."

"It was a bad time for my father." The blue eyes lifted to mine. "The wagon belonged to Franzl Wagner, his cousin. I called him Uncle Franzl. He joined us when I was a little girl."

I forgot all my preconceived feelings about her in a genuine rush of sympathy. "My dear Annalisa, you must have had a terrible time."

"It is over," she said dismissively.

"And there was another man, you said?"

"He was nothing to do with the circus. He must have met Uncle Franzl somewhere, and gone back to his wagon for a drink. They pulled Uncle Franzl out, but he lived only a few minutes. They saved some of his things—the pictures and his flute and the parrot. Then when the wagon was nearly all burned they found the—the other one."

"I see." I was silent for a moment. Perhaps I ought not to press her, but the subject didn't appear to distress her unduly now. "But they did find out who the second man was?"

She nodded. "He was an Englishman named Paul Denver. He belonged to some British firm which has a branch in Vienna, something to do with farming. We think Uncle Franzl went out drinking and met this man, and they came back and perhaps they talked late, and drank a little more. . . . When people began shouting that there was someone else in the wagon, the other Englishman came and helped to pull him out. It turned out that he had come to Oberhausen to meet him."

It was Timothy who said: " 'The other Englishman'?"

"Yes. He works for the same firm. He had just arrived."

It was still Timothy who asked: "And when did he leave?"

"Leave?" said Annalisa. "He is still here. He—" She stopped and smiled and looked beyond me. "Why, here he is!"

A man had turned in from the street under the dappled shade of the chestnut trees. He paused there, looking toward our table. I was already half out of my chair, regardless of what Annalisa might think. And then the newcomer moved forward into the sunlight and I met, full on, his indifferent, unrecognizing eyes and slight look of surprise. I sank back into my chair.

"Lee," said Annalisa, "this is Vanessa March. Vanessa, Mr. Elliott. . . . And this is Tim Lacy."

I murmured something, and Mr. Elliott ordered a drink and then pulled up a chair next to mine.

"You must just have arrived here," he said, "or we'd have heard all about you. In a place this size every movement is reported."

I managed to pull myself out of the turmoil into which the appearance of "the other Englishman" had plunged me, and answered him civilly. "Yes, we've only been here an hour or so. We came from Vienna today by car."

"And what brings you to Oberhausen?"

"Oh," I said. "Actually, I was expecting to meet my husband in Graz, but after we got there we heard that he couldn't make it after all. So we thought we might as well see the countryside. We're staying here at the Edelweiss, and will go on to Piber to see the Lippizans in the morning. I'm putting in the time till I get a message from my husband."

Some fragment of what I was feeling must have shown through the careful social mask I had put on. He said, in a comforting tone, "I'm sure that will be soon."

I managed a creditably bright smile. "I hope so!"

He had taken a pipe out of his pocket and was lighting it. It made him look very British. Apart from this he might have been anybody, from anywhere. He was tall and toughly built, and when he moved it was with a kind of springy precision that

417

indicated strength and muscular control. His hair was brown, his eyes somewhere between blue and gray. His hands were good, but I could see a broken nail, and dirt ingrained in them as if he had been working at some dirty job. Perhaps he had been lending a hand around the circus. His clothes bore this out; they looked like cheap holiday clothes which had recently had rough wear. I said: "I understand from Fraülein Wagner that you're down here on business. What is your firm, Mr. Elliott?"

"Our Vienna connection is Kalkenbrunner Fertilizers."

"Do you know my husband's firm, Pan-European Chemicals?"

"Of course; though I can't for the moment recall any of the P.E.C. people. Is your husband in Vienna often?"

"I haven't the faintest idea," I said, with perfect truth, though not perhaps with perfect civility. I was feeling the strain. "Here's your drink. Have you been here ever since the accident?"

"Yes. Since my firm was willing to give me leave till things were cleared up, I stayed and gave a hand where it was needed." He smiled. "Not with the police inquiries, with the circus."

"You have been marvelous!" Annalisa gave him a glowing look. "Mrs. March, you've no idea . . . I told you we were a small circus, and this means that everybody has to work hard. I think we had not realized how much Uncle Franzl did. He was a wonderful rider, but would do no circus work—I mean, he would not work an act. He took charge of all the stable work, and he was also the doctor for the horses. I told you he trained Maestoso Leda and taught me my act. . . ."

It seemed to be some kind of release to her to talk, and we all listened quietly. Beside me, Mr. Elliott sat very still and relaxed, his eyes never leaving the girl.

"I remember when he joined us," she said. "It was ten years ago, and my grandfather was still alive. We were near Wels, and the Lippizans were staying in Wels at that time, so we went to see them. There was also a big horse fair in Wels, and my uncle Franzl happened to be there with a dealer he joined after he left a Czech circus where he had worked. I think before that he was in the army. He had not been close to the family, you understand. But he came to see my grandfather, and when we went north that night, into Bavaria, he went with us." She smiled. "Soon I even forgot that his name was not Wagner. My grandfather wished him to change it, and he did. . . . You can imagine what it has been like without him, with so many of the animals damaged. I've had to handle the horses, and Lee has helped me. It has not been easy."

"I'll say," said Mr. Elliott with feeling.

For the life of me I couldn't help glancing at his clothes. "So we are to understand that you've been grooming twenty-seven horses for a week, Mr. Elliott?"

He saw it and grinned. "I have indeed. The grooming's the easiest part of horse care, once you've discovered that the hair grows from bow to stern, and you have to brush that way; from the bite to the kick, you might say. Oh, it's been a most instructive week. I shall be sorry to leave." He glanced at his watch. "Annalisa, I really think we should be going. All those beautiful horses to get ready for the show."

"Goodness, yes!" She got to her feet. "We shall see you later?" She laughed unaffectedly. "I shall feel like a prima donna, with visitors after the show. I hope you enjoy it. *Kommst du*, Lee?"

They went.

Timothy said, "Do you feel all right? You look funny."

"Funny? How d'you mean?"

"Well, when he came, you went as white as a sheet. I suppose you were expecting your husband." I nodded. "So was I. When she said 'the other Englishman' was here, I thought we were home free."

"No. When she heard my name was March, she never reacted."

He frowned. "But why did you still think it could be Mr. March, when she said, 'Here he is'?"

"Listen, Tim—" I found I was clutching a fold of the tablecloth so tightly that my nails had gone through the thin material. "I— I've made a dreadful mistake. When I saw Mr. Elliott first, I thought for a moment that it *was* Lewis. When he came nearer, I saw I was wrong. Now do you see what I've done?"

"You mean this Elliott chap was the one you saw with Anna-lisa on the newsreel? That he's a sort of double of your husband? Gosh! So you've come all this way to Austria, and all the time he *is* in Stockholm, where he said he was?"

"Just exactly that," I said.

"It's . . . a bit complicated, isn't it?" he said. "What are you going to do?"

I said: "What would you do, chum?"

"Well, eat, to start with," said Timothy unhesitatingly, and looked round for the waitress.

Chapter 5

A s we sat down at the circus I saw that the place was half full of children. Most local people had already seen the show, so Herr Wagner had reduced prices for today, and the children from the area were perfectly happy to see the show again.

A dwarf in a baggy scarlet costume had sold us programs and ushered us into comfortable red plush armchairs at the ringside. The tent was not a big one, but floodlights threw so much brilliance into the ring that above them the top of the tent seemed a vast, floating darkness where, caught by a flicker of light, the high wire glittered like a thread. Then the big lights came on, a march blared out and the procession began.

For a small circus, the standard of performance was remarkable. In the Wild West act which followed the procession Anna-lisa appeared briefly as a cowgirl, riding a hideous spotted horse which looked as clumsy as a hippo and was as clever on its feet as a polo pony. Then came the English comic, and after this Herr Wagner with his liberty horses. These were beautiful; ten well-matched palominos with coats the color of raw silk, and manes and tails of creamy floss. They wheeled in under the lights, rearing one after the other in line so that the plumes and floss-silk manes tossed up like the crest of a breaking wave.

Timothy said in my ear: "Mr. Elliott did a good job of grooming on them. He's an odd sort of chap, didn't you think? You wouldn't expect a business executive to stay on here and do that sort of work. Bit of a mystery about it, I thought."

"Perhaps he's keen on Annalisa."

"He's too old—" indignantly.

"He's no older than Lewis. I don't see Mr. Elliott. Do you?"

"No," said Timothy. "He'll be out the back madly brushing Maestoso Leda from bow to stern."

The horses finished, and with a deafening crash of brass and a wild cheer the clowns came tumbling in, and Timothy and I, rocking with laughter, took a dive straight back into childhood. It was the old water act, and the wettest one I had ever seen, with a grand finale involving a very old elephant who routed the whole gaggle of clowns with a waterspouting act of its own.

After the clowns came a tightrope act and performing dogs. Then the trumpets brayed, the red curtains parted, and a white horse broke from the shadows and cantered into the limelight. On his back, looking prettier than ever and tough as a whiplash, was Annalisa in a hussar's uniform. The horse wore a magnificent bridle of scarlet, studded with gold, and his saddle glittered and flashed as if every jewel in the world were stitched to it.

"Oh, boy," said Tim reverently.

His eye was on the stallion, not the girl. It took great skill to put a horse through these dressage movements as Annalisa did, without any of her guidance being visible. She seemed simply to sit there, light and motionless, as the stallion went through his lovely ballet.

Prompted by Timothy's whisper, I recognized the slow, skimming Spanish Walk; the dancing fire of the standing trot, or *piaffe*; the shouldering-in, which takes the horse diagonally forward in an incredibly smooth movement; and then the "airs above the ground." The stallion wheeled to the center of the ring, snorted, laid back his ears, settled his hind hoofs, then lifted himself and his rider into a *levade*, the classic rearing pose. For two long bars of music he held it, then touched ground again for a moment, and—you could see the bunch and thrust of the

muscles—launched himself clean into the air. For one superb moment he was poised there, high in the air, dazzlingly white. One looked for his wings.

Then he was on the ground again, cantering round the ring, nodding and bowing his head to the applause. Then, still bowing and pawing the ground, he backed out of the ring and was lost in the darkness behind the curtain. I let out a long breath and smiled at Timothy. "What's the anticlimax?" I asked.

He looked at his program. "Oh, here's your 'absolute Star-Attraktion'—Sandor Balog—of Balog and Nagy. High wire."

"For goodness' sake. It always terrifies me."

"Me too," said Timothy happily, settling back as the high wire sprang into light and two men started their racing climb toward it. In the carefully wrought tensions of their act all other preoccupations fell away, and tomorrow—Lewis or no Lewis—could take care of itself.

WHEN WE CAME OUT of the tent, workmen were already un-
hooking its sides and rolling up the canvas. A tractor pulling a
large trailer churned its way slowly toward the gate. "The stables
are round this way," Tim said.

We dodged one of the trapeze artistes, looking graceful in
close-fitting black pants and sweater; and there in the door of a
caravan, silhouetted against the light, stood Annalisa.

"Tim, Mrs. March, is that you?" She ran down the steps. In
her dark blue pants and sweater she looked businesslike, but as
feminine as ever. "I'll take you to see the horses straightaway.
They're being bedded down now. Did you enjoy the show?"

"Very much indeed," I said. "Annalisa, you were marvelous."

"It was terrific!" Timothy chimed in with enthusiasm.

She glowed with unaffected pleasure. "It was a good evening;
I am glad. One cannot always be sure. I think, if there had been
more time to train him, Maestoso Leda could have been a very
good horse. Even in the Spanish Riding School, some of the stallions never get to do the leaps. Well, here we are. I brought some
pieces of carrot, if you would like to give them to him?"

In the long tent a few lights burned, showing up rows of horses'
rumps half hidden by their rugs, tails swishing lazily. There was
the sweet ammoniac smell of hay and horses, and the comfortable
sound of munching. From a corner in the shadows came a
whicker of greeting, and I saw the beautiful white head flung up
as the stallion looked round at Annalisa.

Shorn of his jeweled trappings and standing at ease, Maestoso
Leda was still beautiful. Seeing one of the famous Lippizans
now for the first time at close quarters, I was surprised to realize
how small he was, but stockily built, big barreled, big chested,
with the power in the haunches needed for spectacular leaps.
His head was narrow and sculptured, like a Greek relief.

He whickered again at the sight of the carrots. Annalisa and
Timothy fed him, and the two of them were soon busy, crooning
over him as they handled him. I watched for a little, then
wandered off to look at some of the others.

At the far end of the stable one or two horses were lying down.

I didn't wish to disturb them, but I talked to the ponies, mischievous shaggy little beasts, all wide-awake. In the stall next to the end stood another horse of much the same height and build as the Lippizan, but very different to look at. He was a piebald, with ugly markings, and he stood with his head drooping, mane and tail hanging limply. I thought at first it was the clever ugly horse that Annalisa had ridden in the rodeo, then saw that this one was older. As I watched, he lowered his head and blew sadly round the bottom of his dry water bucket. I spoke softly, then laid a hand on him and went in.

Annalisa saw me, and she and Tim came across. "Because we spend so much time with the king horse, you talk with the beggar? I am sorry there is no carrot left."

"I doubt if he would want it," I said. "He hasn't touched his feed. I wasn't being democratic; I thought he looked ill."

"He is still not eating? He has been like this all week. He was Uncle Franzl's horse. He used to say that he and poor old Piebald were two old men together." She bit her lip, watching the horse. "I think he is—what is the word?—weeping for my uncle."

"Fretting. That may be true, but I think there's something wrong physically too. The horse is in pain." I was examining him as I spoke. "He's wringing wet and his coat is as rough as a sack."

"Vanessa's a vet," Tim said.

Her eyes widened. "You? Are you? Oh, then—"

"Has the horse been working in the circus?" I asked.

She shook her head. "He is too old, I think more than twenty. Uncle Franzl had him in Czechoslovakia. He was a pet of Uncle Franzl's, or my father would not have kept him. They tried at first to use him—they had a liberty act then with mixed horses— but he was slow to learn, so he has done very little. We cannot afford to keep a horse that does not work. But now"— she looked distressed— "if he is ill . . . we are moving the horses in a few hours, and in three days we leave Austria. I am afraid of what my father will say."

Timothy said, watching me, "You've found something?"

I had indeed. Just above the knee on the off foreleg was a nasty swelling. I showed this to them, while the old horse stood with drooping head, turning once to nuzzle me as my fingers probed the leg. I asked Tim to hold his head. "It's a hematoma," I said, "a blood blister. He must have hurt himself during the fire. It wouldn't show for a day or two. But it must be dealt with now. It ought to be lanced and drained, and the leg stitched."

"Could you do it?"

I straightened up. "If you mean do I know how, yes, I do. But you should get a vet for him, Annalisa."

"On a Sunday night? At nearly midnight?"

Tim said: "Couldn't you, Vanessa?"

"Tim, I shouldn't. It's probably even illegal, without permits or something. Besides, I've no instruments."

"There are Uncle Franzl's things. They were saved. *Please*, Vanessa. If it is not legal, nobody need know!"

A voice spoke from the tent door. "If what is not legal?"

HERR WAGNER himself stood there, a thickset, powerful-looking man with a weather-beaten complexion, and brown eyes under fierce brows. He took in the scene with lively curiosity.

Behind him was a slim, wiry figure in black whom I recognized as the Star-Attraktion of the high wire, the Hungarian Sandor Balog. He had dark hair slicked back above a broad forehead, with thin black brows winged above tilted eyes so dark they were almost black, sharply carved nostrils and well-shaped lips. A disturbing face, perhaps a cruel one. He was looking not, as one might have expected, at the two strangers but with fixed intensity at Annalisa.

"Who are your friends, Licsl?" asked Herr Wagner. She introduced us, and Wagner said: "But what is not legal?"

Annalisa started to speak, then glanced at me: "You permit?" Turning back to her father, she plunged into a flood of German which, from her gestures, was the story of her acquaintance with us and the discovery of Piebald's injury. To all this the Hungarian paid little attention. He wandered into the next stall, where harnesses hung and trestles had saddles over them, and stood there idly fingering the bright jewelry on Maestoso Leda's saddle, still watching the girl.

She finished her story on a strong note of persuasion; but Herr Wagner, not much to my surprise, said in broadly accented English that his daughter was impulsive. He thanked me for my great kindness, but believed he must not trouble me.

"It's not that. But your own man would certainly come tonight. I'll telephone, if you like, from the Edelweiss . . ."

Herr Wagner didn't answer for a minute. He was examining the horse. "I am ashamed that this was not seen," he said. "But you understand, *gnädige Frau*, there has been so much . . . and always Franzl sees to this old horse himself. I will speak to Hans and Rudi. The boys perhaps were doing their regular horses, and this poor old one, he is missed."

He ran a caressing hand down the horse's neck, gave it a pat that had something valedictory about it, and straightened up.

"Well, it is late. You will have some coffee before you go, eh? My Liesl always makes the coffee at this hour."

"Thanks very much," I said, "but I'd better get back and call your vet. It's after midnight."

"I shall not trouble you to do that, *gnädige Frau*."

It was Timothy who understood before I did; who had seen the significance of that farewell caress and had added to it Annalisa's remark that they could not afford to keep a horse which did not work. He stiffened, still holding the headstall, and his free hand crept to the horse's nose, cupping round the soft muzzle in a protective gesture. Then he looked at me.

I said: "Herr Wagner, I'll operate now, if you'll let me. Once I've got the leg fixed you can move him to the train, and he'll be quite fit in three or four weeks."

"Please, Father," said the girl.

The Hungarian said nothing. He had Annalisa's saddle and cloth over his arm now, and was waiting to follow Herr Wagner out of the stable. Herr Wagner spread his hands wide in a gesture of deprecation. "But we cannot ask you—" he began.

Annalisa said suddenly: "No! It is I who ask! This was Uncle Franzl's horse, so now it is mine; he left me all his things—all that were saved—and old Piebald too. So if *I* ask Vanessa . . . and if he can go to the train . . . ?"

She finished on the note of pleading, but her father was laughing, his square brown face rayed with wrinkles.

"So—you see how she rules me, this child of mine? Always a reason she finds to have her way." He gave his great ringmaster's laugh, so that the sleeping horses stirred in their stalls, and the chains jingled and rang. "All right, all right, if you wish. What do you need, *gnädige Frau?*"

I told him, and added: "I wonder if someone could rig a better light down here?"

"Sandor, would you do this?" Herr Wagner said. "You know where to find the things you need. Just leave that saddle. Annalisa won't mind if it stays here for the night for once."

"I am taking it to my wagon to mend it. I see some of the stitching is loose."

Tim whispered in my ear: "Is this a bad operation?"

"Not at all. Have you ever seen this kind of thing before?"

"No, and I'm afraid I shan't be much help, but I'll do my best if you want."

"Thanks. I'd a lot sooner have you than the boyfriend."

"Him? You don't think he *is*, do you?"

I laughed. "No, only that he'd like to be. He doesn't look the type to run errands for girls otherwise. Why else did he come here? Just to carry her saddle for her?"

"He's going to stitch it up, too."

"Well, there you are," I said vaguely. Then I forgot about Sandor Balog. What mattered now was the horse.

ONCE HERR WAGNER had made up his mind to let me operate, he was helpfulness itself, and we had a surprise helper in the dwarf, who was the clown's butt in the opening act. His name was Elemer and, like Sandor, he was a Hungarian. Sandor brought an extension cord and tools, as requested, but restricted his help to lifting the dwarf to reach the light socket. When the light was rigged by the stall, the Star-Attraktion retired into the shadows while the dwarf bustled to help us.

Franzl's instrument case held everything I could want; and in a quarter of an hour the instruments were sterilized, and I had washed up and started work.

Herr Wagner stood near me, obviously constituting himself my assistant: even if he did not value the horse, he was too good a horseman to leave me unsupervised. I clipped the horse's leg, cleaned the area with alcohol and reached for the hypodermic. Tim stood by the animal's head and looked anxious. I gave him a reassuring grin. "I'm going to give him a local, Tim—procaine. He won't feel a thing, and twenty minutes from now he'll be doing a *capriole*. There; he never blinked, and that's the only prick he'll feel."

The beam of light was steady on the hematoma. "Scalpel, please," I said, reaching out a wet hand. Herr Wagner put the scalpel into it and I bent forward to cut.

You could almost feel the relief as the thing split and the pressure was lifted. "Forceps," I said, and Wagner handed them to me, following them with absorbent cotton. When the wound was clean, I dusted it generously with penicillin powder. I did six blanket sutures, sewed on the pad-bandage called a dolly, and the thing was done.

I smiled at Timothy. "Now, his antitetanus and penicillin shots and that will be that. Pull his mane across, will you, Tim? I'll put this in the neck. . . . There you are, old darling." I smoothed my hand down the drooping neck. "I think you'll live."

"Yes," said Herr Wagner, "thanks to you, he *will* live."

There was something in his voice that made it more than just a phrase. Timothy broke into a grin. Old Piebald rolled a big dark eye back at me and said nothing.

Tim, Sandor Balog and I sat in Annalisa's wagon while she made coffee. The wagon was rather attractive, with an authentic gypsy flavor. The stove burned bottled gas, but the lamp over it was an old storm lantern, and the little table was covered with a fringed red cloth for all the world like a gypsy's shawl. On a peg was the hussar's cap with its amethysts and diamonds and osprey plume. A wicker cage swung from a hook, shrouded with a green kerchief. Our voices roused the inmate to a sleepy croak, and I remembered Uncle Franzl's parrot.

I curved my hands round the hot cup Annalisa handed me. She put a dish on the table; flaky croissants, buns shining with sugared tops, and fresh sweet bread with new butter melting on it.

"*Götterdämmerung*," said Timothy reverently, if inappropriately. "Did you make them?"

She laughed. "No, no! They come from the village bakery. Lee brought them. He came down to the stables while Vanessa was busy with the horse. He only watched for a minute, then he went to get the bread, but he wouldn't stay for coffee."

Sandor said with a savage intensity that seemed out of place: "I don't know what he is doing here still. He did what he came for on Monday; why did he not go back?"

"Because I asked him to stay." Annalisa's voice was cold. "Why not? What objection have you, Sandor Balog?"

It was obvious that, whatever his objection was, it was a violent one, for the black eyes glittered, the nostrils flared like a horse's; he stirred his coffee in sullen silence.

"Personally," said Timothy, starting on his third bun with undiminished zeal, "I'd say Mr. Elliott had real executive sense, raiding a bakery in the middle of the night. Will you thank him for us if you see him again?"

"We shall be gone before he gets up. You might see him yourself—he has a room over the bakery."

"Gimme a bit, you greedy pig," said the parrot suddenly, directly over my head. I jumped and spilled coffee as the green kerchief, twitched aside by a powerful beak, came down over my head. "*Levez, levez*," said the parrot. "Shake a leg, Peter, *changez*, hup! *Gib mir was! Gib mir was!*"

Tim tore off a bit of bun. "All right, old chap, here."

"Put your comb up," said the parrot, accepting it.

"Keep your nose away from the bars, Tim," said Annalisa, laughing. "He's a terrible bird: a real *Weltbürger*, a cosmopolitan, and from all the worst places!"

Sandor, too, was laughing, and it transformed him. There was (I saw it sinkingly, because I liked Annalisa) a powerful animal attraction there. He draped the cage once more, and I said, "We must go; you have an early start. No, really, it was nothing, you're very welcome. . . ." This as she began again to thank me.

"If you come near us again," she said eagerly, "please come to see us. We go today to Hohenwald, and then to Zechstein."

Balog said, "I will see you to the gate." He produced a slim flashlight. "The ground is muddy and there is not much light. Please allow me."

"Thank you," I said. "*Auf Wiedersehen*, Annalisa."

"*Auf Wiedersehen*."

"*Merde, alors*," said the parrot, muffled.

Chapter 6

TIMOTHY and I walked through still, cold air toward the inn. A clock in the church tower struck two with a thin, acid sweetness. "You don't really think there could be anything between Balog and Annalisa, do you?" he asked.

"Not on her side, I'm sure. Anyway, you can leave Sandor safely to Herr Wagner and the parrot."

He chuckled. "I rather cared for the parrot. That's odd. I thought I saw Mr. Elliott over there, by those trees."

"Why not?" I said. "He's probably been down for some more buns for himself. Come along, Tim, I'm dropping."

But tired as I was, when I was ready for bed I found myself restless. I went out onto the veranda to look at the night. Timothy's window was open, but his light was out already. It was still and peaceful and very lovely.

I padded back, got into bed, tucked the eiderdown round me and wondered about Lewis. . . .

I don't think I was asleep, but I may have been floating into the edge of it because a tiny noise outside brought me awake with a start. I strained my ears. Nothing; but I was certain something—or someone—had moved out there.

Then a hand parted the curtains. He didn't make a sound, just slid between them like a ghost. He drew the long windows shut and stood there just inside them, quite still, listening.

I sat up in bed, pulling the puff round me. "All right, Mr. Elliott," I said. "I'm awake. What brings you this way? Couldn't you find Annalisa's wagon, or was Sandor standing guard?"

He came toward the bed, moving incredibly quietly, like a cat. "I think I'm in the right place."

"What makes you think that, Mr. Lee Elliott? What makes you think you have the faintest right to come wandering in here like a tomcat on the prowl and expect a welcome?"

"Oh, if we're talking about rights . . ." said Lewis, sitting down on the edge of the bed and taking off his shoes.

"AND NOW," I SAID, "supposing you start? What in the world are you doing here, and what's your connection with Annalisa?"

"How like a woman to start at the wrong end. I'll ask the questions. What are *you* doing here, and who is that boy?"

"It's Tim Lacy. Remember Carmel Lacy?"

"Ah, yes! That fair fat female. All soft and sweet, and full of icy drafts at the edges, like this feather thing on the bed. Must you have all of it, incidentally? I'm getting cold."

"Then you'd better get your clothes on. If Tim came in—"

"I suppose I'd better. A life of sin is beastly uncomfortable," said Lewis peacefully, sitting up and reaching for his trousers.

"Well, can't you tell me why we're having to lead it? When I saw you standing there this afternoon, I nearly yelled out."

"I know. That's why I gave you the high sign to say nothing. I must say you passed it off very well, though you looked as if you'd seen a ghost."

"It was the most unnerving thing that ever happened to me. For one dreadful moment, when you looked straight through me like that, I even wondered if I could have been mistaken. Those clothes were absolutely disgusting."

"Yes, weren't they." He sounded remarkably complacent. "So you honestly wondered whether you'd made a mistake. Well—damn, I can't find my sock—I hope I've convinced you now."

"Oh yes. It's you all right."

He grinned. "Well, so long as you're sure . . . Now, my darling Van, how did you find out I was here in Oberhausen?" I told him about the newsreel and the rest of it. He said, "I see. I saw the camera, but I was hoping I wasn't recognizable."

"It was fairly clear, I'm afraid. Does it matter?"

He didn't answer. "Do you know if it got on television?"

"I didn't see it, and I usually watch the news. Lewis, what *is* all this? Did you send that cable from Stockholm?"

"No."

"And I suppose someone posted your letter for you?"

"Yes."

"But—why Stockholm? Why not just Vienna?"

"I had to have somewhere clear away from where you and I were going. It wouldn't have been easy to keep you from coming if it had been more or less on the way."

"And you had to stall me off?"

"Yes."

I said miserably: "I've been so unhappy after what we'd said to each other that dreadful afternoon—"

"That's over. We'll not talk about that anymore."

"No, all right. I love you very much, Lewis."

He made the kind of noise a husband considers sufficient answer to that remark—a sort of comforting grunt—then reached for cigarette and lighter, and lay down beside me on the single bed. "Now, when you discovered I was in Austria instead of Stockholm, what did you think I was up to?"

"Well, Annalisa—she was on the film too, you know—"

"Was she? Yes, I see." He sounded rather pleased and blew a smoke ring. "Don't you trust me, then?"

"No."

"Fair enough," he said mildly, and a second smoke ring went through the first.

I shot up. *"Lewis!"*

"Keep your voice down, for pity's sake!" He reached a lazy arm and pulled me close. "I watched you operating tonight, Van."

"I know you did. I take it you brought the buns." I felt him laugh quietly to himself. "What's the joke?"

"Nothing. You do a nice job, Mrs. March."

"Poor old Piebald, he was Franzl's, and I've a feeling Annalisa will let him end his days in peace for her uncle's sake. Incidentally, I warn you you're about to lose her to Timothy."

"Half the rodeo act and all the clowns are in love with Annalisa, not to mention Balog and the dwarf. And if you say 'Are you?' I shall do you a violence."

"Are you?" He tightened his arm round me, and I snuggled my cheek into the crook of his shoulder. There was a long, comfortable silence. "As a matter of fact," I said, "I don't care anymore why you're here. You're here, that's all. Darling, can we have our holiday now? Have you finished what you were doing?"

"Almost. I report back to Vienna today, and that's probably it." He stabbed out his cigarette in the ashtray on the bedside table. "Listen, Van, dear, I ought not to tell you even now; but as things are I think I've got to. In any case I know by this time I can trust you with anything I've got; and besides, I will want your help. What I told you earlier this evening about my job in Oberhausen was true, as far as it went. Paul Denver and I worked for the same employer, and I came down here to meet him. I knew he was in touch with the circus, so as soon as I saw the fire in the circus field I went straight in. But Paul was dead.

"Now, my job at P.E.C. is genuine, but they let me do other jobs from time to time for another employer—I won't tell you who—under other names. Some—the jobs I wouldn't take you on— have been what you'd call cloak-and-dagger assignments."

"You mean Secret Service? *Lewis!* You're an *agent?*"

"As ever was." He turned his head sharply. "Darling, you're shivering! It's not dangerous. We don't all go roaring off in Aston-

Martins, loaded with guns and suicide pills—more likely a bowler hat and a briefcase and a roll of notes for bribing some informer. You've seen how dangerous this job is—grooming horses."

"But Paul Denver died."

"He died. But the police have found no evidence that it was anything but an accident. Franz had had a small fire in his wagon once before—and he was a drunk. Mind you, that made him the person for Paul to get next to if there was information to be got; but Paul wouldn't get so sozzled that a fire could break out round him. I've been trying to find evidence of foul play—which I can't. Paul had had a crack on the head, but the oil lamp had fallen, and that could have knocked him silly long enough to burn to death. Franz was able to speak—just. I imagine that if there'd been foul play he'd have tried to say so, but he didn't."

"I hadn't realized he was coherent."

"He was conscious, but I wouldn't say coherent, poor chap. All he did was rave about the horses—the Lippizan, mostly—and some precious Neapolitan saddle. We told him the horses were safe— the white stallion was out first, as a matter of fact—but he was still talking about the Lippizan when he died." He paused. "It was Annalisa he was trying to talk to. She was there all the time. . . . It's distressing to watch anyone die of burns, Van."

I knew he was trying to explain his swift intimacy with the girl. I said: "I understand. You're a comforting person to have around. Couldn't she make out what Franzl was saying?"

"Not really. She says none of the harness is valuable. So there's your mystery. Whatever Franzl had on his mind, it wasn't murder, and Paul's death looks like one of those accidents that cut right across the best-laid plans. What happened is this: Paul was in Czechoslovakia and came out ten days ago. He put in his report at Vienna Station—that's what we call our clearinghouse for eastern Europe—and went on leave here in Austria. But then the Department got a coded cable asking for me to go out immediately—no one else. Paul had made contact with the Circus Wagner, and I was to pick him up there as Lee Elliott. I'd worked with him under that name before. So I came."

"And you've no idea why he insisted on you?"

"The only clue I have is the circus contact: it's crossing into Yugoslavia in two days, and I speak pretty good Serbo-Croat. Whatever Paul was following up must be centered in the Circus Wagner—someone trying to get over the border—that's the obvious conclusion: a circus tends to have the freedom of borders, even Iron Curtain ones. But without a lead it's hopeless. I've hung around and fraternized and I've found nothing."

"Is there any chance they'll want you to stick with it—to cross the border?"

"I don't think so. But . . . well, I can't think why else Paul insisted on the Lee Elliott stuff if he hadn't expected to go on to Yugoslavia." He ruffled my hair. "Don't cross bridges, darling; it may not be necessary. But I knew Denver, and if he had something to tell me, it probably mattered. You'll have to forgive him for involving me; he had no idea I was quitting. I'm sorry."

"Don't. We've had all that. If it matters, it matters. The thing is, I may be able to help this time. I've got a good connection with the circus—I've a patient to see to."

"Well, then, do stick with the circus till it leaves Austria. I've got to go to Vienna; and in any case my reasons for sticking around with them are wearing a bit thin. If you and Timothy just happened to be traveling to Hohenwald, and if you felt you must look in on old Piebald . . . That's all; don't ask any specific questions, just look and listen backstage. I can feel in my bones there's something up; but they'll relax once they're rid of me. If you find anything that's out of pattern, *do nothing*. I don't want you to take any risks—stay with the circus until I get in touch with you, which will be by Tuesday night."

"All right. And you needn't keep reassuring me, I'm not a bit nervous, just happy." I moved my cheek against his shoulder.

"Hush a minute," he said. "I think I heard Tim move." From next door came a heavy creak as Tim presumably roused and turned over. We lay still, clasped closely. After a while there was silence again. He said very softly: "I ought to go. Damn."

"What about Timothy?"

436

"Leave it for the moment. We'll have to cook up some story for him—a special investigation for P.E.C. involving an insurance claim; something like that. When I get back I'll talk to him." He sat up. "Now, final arrangements. Today you'll be at Hohenwald. Try to ring me this evening. The number's Vienna 32-14-60. I won't write it down, I want you to remember it. Ask for Mr. Elliott. The next night you'll be at Zechstein; that's the takeoff point for the border. There's a hotel north of the village, an old converted castle. It's fascinating. Try and get a double room, in case I can join you as Mr. March. Now I really must go."

I got up and folded my dressing gown round me. Then I unlatched the windows and quietly pushed them open. The cold scents of the dawn came in as Lewis went past me like a shadow. When he paused at the veranda rail and turned back, I went out. I took him by the lapels of his jacket and held on to them tightly.

"Take care of yourself. Please take care of yourself," I said softly.

"Why, what's this?"

"I don't know. Just a feeling. Take care."

"Don't worry, I'll do that. Now get yourself to bed, and go to sleep." He kissed me, and suddenly I was alone. I thought I heard, over the rustling of the grass, a deeper rustling, and then it was gone.

I turned back from the veranda rail to see Timothy, in his pajamas, standing at his open window, staring at me.

For one long pulse of silence I could neither speak nor move. I suppose we stared at one another for a full half minute. It seemed like a year. I knew Tim had seen Lewis; but he was not to be told anything yet. There was only one thing to do: assume he had seen nothing, and hope he wouldn't dare broach the subject without my giving him a lead.

I said: "Hullo, couldn't you sleep?"

He came out and stood only a couple of feet away. There was no curiosity, or embarrassment, or even surprise in his face. He was going to play it exactly as he thought I wished.

I think it was his very lack of expression that decided me. Boys of seventeen ought not to be able to look like that. Whatever Carmel and Graham Lacy had done to Tim, I wasn't going to be responsible for adding another layer to that schooled indifference. Lewis would have to forgive me.

I took a breath and leaned back against the rail. "Well," I said lightly. "Now I suppose I'll have to confess I lied to you when I said Mr. Elliott was simply my husband's double."

His expression changed to one of relief and pleasure. "You mean that chap Elliott *is* your husband, himself? The newsreel was right?"

"Just that. As soon as I saw him I realized he didn't want to be made known—and then Annalisa said, 'This is Lee Elliott,' so I just shut up and said nothing."

"He's in disguise? Really? I said he was mysterious, didn't I?" He took a breath. "But why?"

"He didn't explain; only that there's something involved that his firm doesn't want made public. I'm not supposed to have told you who he was, so keep it dark."

"Okay. Good night."

"Good night." And I went back to my cold bed.

Chapter 7

NEXT MORNING, Tim stopped the car in front of the bakery and got out. "I'd like to get something to eat on the way. Come with me and help pick."

While he considered stacks of breads and cakes in the little window, I tried not to look at the side door, where a notice saying ZIMMER FREI might indicate that Lewis had already left.

"Vanessa, do look at the names of these things! *Sandgugelhupf!* How about a nice *Sandgugelhupf* each? Or a *Schokoladegugelhupf* and a *Polsterzipf?*"

"Good morning," said Lewis, just behind us. He had again moved very quietly. If it was getting to be a habit, I thought, it was a habit he could just get out of again. I didn't want to die of heart failure.

I said, "Good morning," wondering if I should tell him that Tim knew; but Timothy was already greeting him with aplomb almost as professional as his own, and it was too late.

"Oh, hullo, Mr. Elliott," Timothy said. "You haven't gone yet? I wondered if you'd leave when the circus did."

"Too early for me. The last wagons were due to go at five. I didn't hear them."

"You must be a very sound sleeper," said Timothy cheerfully. "I imagine there was a lot of coming and going in the village during the night, but perhaps it doesn't disturb you?"

"Thank you, no. I had an excellent night; far better than I had expected."

"Tim," I said quickly, "you'd better buy your buns. We really ought to be setting off."

"Okay," said Tim amiably, and vanished into the shop.

"That boy knows about us, Lewis," I said.

"Does he?" I was relieved to see that he looked, after the first frowning moment, no more than amused. "The little so-and-so, does he indeed?"

"I had to tell him. He saw you leaving last night. He thinks you're on some mysterious business mission for P.E.C. May I tell him you asked me to keep in touch with the circus?"

"I don't see why not. Tell him the P.E.C. may want more details about Denver's death. When do you go?"

"We're just setting off for Hohenwald, but Tim was afraid of starving on the way. Here he comes now."

When Timothy emerged from the shop with his arms alarmingly full of packages, Mr. Elliott was giving me directions for a pleasant day's drive, with a map drawn on the back of an old envelope.

"Well," I said, "we'll go. Have a good journey."

"And you," said Lewis. "Enjoy yourselves. . . . *Auf Wiedersehen,* and remember me to Annalisa."

As we drove off, Timothy said, "Was that a crack?"

I laughed. "No. In any case, you're a fine one to talk about making cracks. Timothy, Lewis knows."

Tim looked startled, then grinned. "You mean he knows *I* know?"

"Yes; all is in the clear, and thank goodness we can talk."

I explained to Timothy what Lewis had asked me to do, saying that his firm wanted to know if Paul could have incurred any enmities among the circus people which might have led to his death. "All he wants me to do," I said at length, "is to keep in touch. No questions are to be asked, or detective work done. Now, if you'd rather cut loose and go to Piber—"

"Gosh, no; I'd love to stay, if you're sure you can do with me."

"I'm beginning to think I can't do without you," I said.

THE VILLAGE of Hohenwald was little more than a cluster of houses set in smiling orchards and cornfields, with mountains lifting their stepped ramparts of pine forest beyond.

An arched stone bridge spanned a narrow mountain river and led into a cobbled square. The familiar circus posters were wrapped round trees and gateposts, and there was the Circus Wagner, settled in a field beside the river as if some genie's hand had picked it up complete and set it down again here, thirty miles away. It was midafternoon, and the first performance would not start till five; but already excited children were crowding round the gate where Elemer sat making them laugh. He gave us a wave of welcome.

We got beds at a small and scrupulously clean inn and walked back to the circus. Annalisa showed real pleasure in welcoming us; but I thought she looked pale. She was eager that I should take another look at the piebald while Tim watched the performance. "I am so grateful to you," she said. "He's a different horse already. He hardly limps at all."

In the stables, the liberty horses were being prepared for the show, their skins gleaming in the light. The Shetland ponies were beginning to fuss, nibbling one another's necks; while the Lippizan stood placidly in his stall, looking ancient and heavy with wisdom, a horse of white stone.

Opposite him the piebald stood with drooping head, but as I approached his eye rolled back and he moved an ear in greeting. The dolly was still in place and the swelling had vanished. I moved him back a pace in his stall and saw that he was putting the leg to the ground with more confidence already.

I straightened up as Elemer came by. "You know, a bit of gentle walking and grazing would do this old chap a world of good," I said. "Is there anywhere I could take him?"

"Of course," said the dwarf. "Behind this field there is a path up through the trees, and above, a meadow. You can leave him there till the pull-down. Wait a moment; I will get you a tether and a peg."

As I led the old horse gently up the mossy path, he lifted his head, and his ears pricked with the first sign of interest he had shown. We finally reached a long flat terrace of grass, walled on every side by dark firs, and Piebald shouldered his way past

441

me into the sunlight, dropped his head and began to graze. I drove the peg into the middle of the meadow, moved a little way off and sat down.

Faintly, from below the belt of pines, came the circus music. I sat listening, enjoying the last of the sunshine, while I contentedly watched the old stallion. There was an interval of silence from the circus; and then, quite distinctly in the still, clear air, I heard the fanfare and recognized it; it was the entrance of Annalisa and her white stallion. Old Piebald stopped grazing and lifted his head with his ears cocked, as one imagines a war-horse might at the sound of trumpets. Then the orchestra stole into the waltz from *Der Rosenkavalier*.

I settled back against one of the little haycocks and prepared to enjoy the concert; but something about the old horse caught my attention and I sat up to watch. He was standing with neck arched and ears pricked, in a sort of mimicry of the white stallion's proud posture. Then with a graceful, almost ceremonial movement a forefoot lifted, pointed, pawed twice at the soft ground; and slowly, bowing his head to his shadow on the turf, he began to dance. He was old and stiff and a bit lame still, but he moved to the music like a professional.

I watched him among the lengthening shadows of the lonely meadow, infinitely touched. I supposed all old circus horses felt this way when they heard the music of their youth; the bowing, ceremonious dance of the liberty horse was something which, once learned, could never be forgotten. But then I realized that this was not dancing as the palominos had danced; this was a version, stiff but true, of the severely disciplined figures of the Lippizaner: first the Spanish Walk; shouldering-in in a smooth skimming diagonal; then the difficult *pirouette*, bringing him round sharply to present him sideways to his audience. Then as I watched he broke into a form of the *piaffe*. It was a sick old horse's travesty of the standing trot which the Lippizan had performed with such precision and fire, but you could see it was a burning, live memory in him of the real thing. In the distance the music changed: the Lippizan down in the ring would be rising into the *levade*, the first of the "airs above the ground." And in the high Alpine meadow, with only me for audience, old Piebald settled his hind hoofs, arched his crest and tail and, lame forefoot clear of the ground, lifted into and held the same royal and beautiful *levade*.

This, it seemed, was enough. He came down to all four feet, shook his head, dropped his muzzle to the grass, and all at once was just an old, tired piebald horse grazing in a green meadow.

I WENT DOWN to the circus, found Tim, and told him I had something to show him during the evening performance. When we got up to the meadow it was dark, but the moon was coming up clear of the trees. The horse had moved on a little, still grazing quietly.

"Oh, you've got old Piebald here," said Timothy. "Why, he looks a different creature. He's eating like a horse, as they say."

"Exactly like a horse. Come over here and sit down. Listen how clearly you can hear the music for the second performance."

"That's the liberty act, isn't it? Now it'll be the clowns."

We waited, and finally I said softly: "Listen; those are the trumpets. Don't say a word, now. Keep still."

At first I thought it wasn't going to happen. The trumpets shivered the air, distant, silver, brave: the old horse grazed. An owl flew low across the field, silent, ghostly white in the moonlight. The horse lifted his head to watch it. The trumpets called on unheeded.

Then the waltz from *Der Rosenkavalier* wound its way up through the pines. Five bars, six bars—and then it happened. The old head lifted, the neck arched, the forefoot went out in that arrogant beautiful movement, and the piebald glided once more into his own private and ceremonious dance. Moonlight flooded the meadow, blanching all colors to its own ghostly silver. As the stallion rose in the last magnificent rear of the *levade* the moonlight poured over him, bleaching his hide so that for a few seconds he was a white horse dappled with shadows; a Lippizaner stallion of the oldest line in Europe.

Timothy turned and looked at me. "Am I right?" I asked.

He merely nodded. When he spoke, it was in a normal, even casual voice, but I knew he was moved. "The poor old chap," he said. Then his voice sharpened. "But, Vanessa! Why should they talk of getting rid of him? Nobody's given his age as a reason for putting him down; it's always been that the circus can't afford to keep a horse who does nothing. Annalisa said they'd tried him in the liberty routine and he was no use."

"If he was a trained dressage performer when they got him, he'd take badly to a new routine. Perhaps they *don't know* he's a trained performer. And I'm not sure we should tell them."

He turned to stare at me. "What do you mean?"

"I've been thinking," I said. "Annalisa told us that Franz Wagner joined the circus ten years ago, and brought this horse with him from a Czech circus. Why, if he brings a performing stallion with him (and goes on riding him in private, apparently), did he not cash in on such a big asset? There must have been something wrong. Lewis said to notice anything that's out of pattern. Tim, we should learn a bit more about old Franzl. He changed his name, remember?"

"So he did. And refused to work an act . . . appear in public."

I said slowly: "What if he'd stolen the horse from the circus he was in before? Annalisa's grandfather must have known about it, making him change his name and all that. If he'd done anything bad enough to lie low for, all these years, Paul Denver's connection with him might be—"

"Wels," said Timothy suddenly.

"I beg your pardon?"

"Annalisa said that when he joined the circus they were at a place called Wels, near the Bavarian border."

"That's right. And the circus was apparently pulling down when he joined them. If he was on the run, what better cover could he have? The circus crossing the border that very night . . ."

"The Spanish Riding School was in Wels till nineteen fifty-five."

"What would—" I stopped short and gaped at him. I said hoarsely: "It can't be, Tim. There'd have been a fuss—"

444

"There was. It's all coming clear now. Do you remember my showing you the photograph of Neapolitano Petra, and telling you he'd been killed? I was wrong. There was another story I'd read, and I'd got them muddled. He disappeared ten years ago, and one of the stablemen disappeared along with him."

There was a silence as we both turned to look at the old piebald grazing at the other side of the field.

"It would be easy enough to make piebald markings—hair dye, something of that sort," I said. "And *that* would account for the feel of that horse's coat! I noticed today it was still feeling rough and harsh even though the fever had gone. You know how brittle and hard hair feels when it's dyed often. I'd like to take a look at those black patches by daylight!"

"It fits, you know," said Timothy. "Just think how easily he could take the stallion out somehow, disguise him, and then simply melt into his uncle's circus. I can't help thinking it was a sort of revenge. The story said this stableman had worked his way up to junior *Bereiter*—that's a rider; but he was a bit wild, quarreled with the senior riders, and then got the idea that they had a grudge against him and he wasn't being given a chance. Then he *did* get his chance at a performance, turned up drunk, and was put right back to stable hand on the spot."

"Turned up drunk," I said softly. "Merciful heavens, it does fit. I suppose the Czech circus was a cover story. Of course, none of the books would mention the man's name?"

"No, but I think we can find out here and now. The Riding School Lippizans are all branded. There's a big *L* on the cheek for Lippizaner. If he was bred at the Austrian Stud, there'll be a crown and a *P* for Piber on the flank. And on the horse's side they do some sort of hieroglyphic which gives the breeding lines. If he's got all three brands, we can be sure we're right."

The moonlight threw our shadows long and black across the turf as we walked over to the grazing horse. He pushed his muzzle against my chest and Tim ran his hand quickly over the near cheek. His fingers hesitated, then slowly traced out the shape of a big *L*.

445

In silence, as he dropped his hand, I put mine on the horse's cheek. Ever so slightly ruffling the hair, I could feel the outline of the *L* for Lippizaner. On the flank was the crowned *P* for Piber. And on the ribs something that might be an *N* and a *P*. . . .

Neapolitano Petra blew gustily at the front of my dress, pulled his head away and took another mouthful of the dew-wet clover.

Timothy and I led the old Lippizan slowly down the dark path between the pines. Tim said: "I was just remembering the parrot. Those French commands he gave were the traditional Lippizaner ones. And 'Peter' could be Franzl's name for the horse."

We had reached the circus field. Excitement broke from Tim in a little laugh. "We're getting good and loaded with secrets. Do you suppose this one'll be any good to P.E.C.?"

"Heaven knows, but I can hardly wait to unload it on Lewis! It's no good ringing him up again tonight: I tried earlier, and they said he wouldn't be available. He's coming south as soon as he can, and then our troubles will be over."

Chapter 8

O N OUR arrival the following day at Zechstein the circus posters and the big top were already up. The village, with its pretty church and mill, lay in a wide valley where a river meandered lazily southward.

On its far side rose a steep mountainside, and perched on the outermost edge, like something straight out of a fairy tale, was a turreted castle, Schloss Zechstein. There was even a narrow stone bridge arching out of the forest to the castle gate, over a thin rope of white water smoking down below the walls.

When our little car roared its way up the winding road, we found the bridge to the castle gate. It led through an archway into a small cobbled courtyard. There was little sign that the place was a hotel. The hall had a flagstone floor and paneled walls, with an unlit green porcelain stove in one corner, and a heavy wooden table on which were bits of hotel paraphernalia. A man in shirtsleeves and green baize apron carried our luggage in and showed us where to register, then prepared to lead us to our rooms. There was a wide staircase, but when I started toward it he stopped me, saying with unconcealed pride: "This way, *gnädige Frau*. There is a lift."

I must have shown my surprise. He smiled. "One would not expect it, no. The Count has just put it in."

As he spoke he led us down a long, dim corridor into the north wing of the castle. I said: "The Count?"

"The Count and Countess still live here," the man explained. "They have their own rooms on the south side of the castle. I am afraid there is a little way to go down the passage here, toward the kitchens. Here is the lift." He stopped in front of a massive pine door with huge iron studs and hinges. Hidden in the stone to one side of it was an electric push button. The lift proved to be the self-service kind of which I am always stupidly terrified. But it took us safely to the third floor.

My room was on the main corridor, and included one of the turrets that gave the castle its fairy-tale appearance. There was also a narrow door which gave onto the battlements. Just as I had finished unpacking a tap on the door heralded Timothy. "This is smashing—but I must say it scares me a bit. Dare I ask for tea?"

"Yes—but heaven knows how. Perhaps if you look round you'll find a long embroidered tassel, and when you pull it you'll hear a bell clanging hollowly in some dark corridor a million miles away."

"There's a telephone by the bed," said Timothy.

"Good heavens, so there is. How disappointing. Well, go ahead and order. I want to look round outside this little door."

Going outside, I found that a narrow walk ran from my turret along the battlements above the sheer drop to the river. It ended at another turret at the southeast corner, in a narrow spiral of stone steps which corkscrewed up the outside wall. The roof was tiled with red, the castle walls were of honey-colored stone, and every spire was tipped with gold—here a globe, there a flying

447

swan, above my head a dragon. I leaned over the battlements, listening to the deep sound of the river far below.

Timothy said behind me: "What time do you expect Lewis?"

"They told me nothing when I phoned; but he did say he would come tonight for sure. I'm just hoping." I didn't add that I was praying too. It was still possible that he would have to follow the circus into Yugoslavia, and the prospect filled me with fears. "We'll go to the circus anyway."

We had decided that we would have to tell Herr Wagner and Annalisa what we had discovered, without waiting for Lewis. "Because after all," Timothy had said, "the circus crosses into Yugoslavia in the morning, and then Hungary; so if there's any question of returning the horse it'll have to be decided today."

"We can be down there well before the first show," I said now. "Listen, there's the tea coming. Let him in, Tim." I followed him back into the room. The servant with the green baize apron was carrying a tray.

"Thank you," I said. "Are you doing all the work today?"

"It feels like it, madam," he said, setting the tray down, "but this was almost a holiday for us. We've had a big party of Americans who left this morning, and now there is nobody but yourselves; many of our people are taking time off to see a circus in the village. I shall go myself at five o'clock, and then come back to let others go."

An exclamation from Timothy made me turn. He was standing beside the window, staring northward. "What in the world's that smoke? Is it a forest fire? Or are there houses up there—er—" This to the servant.

"My name is Josef, sir. No; that is just what we call *die Feuerspritze*, the fire engine. It is a little mountain train, built nearly a hundred years ago. It runs up on a small wheel that holds it, a cog, is that the word?"

"A pinion wheel and cogged rail," said Timothy. "We call it a rack railway."

Josef nodded. "It starts at Zweibrunn am See down in the valley, five or six kilometers from the village, and goes right up to the highest peak. There is a little *Gasthaus* up there—a place where you can have refreshments. You can see right across the mountains into Yugoslavia and Hungary. If you are going to be here a few days, madam, you must make this trip. The first train goes up at seven."

I said: "I should love to go up. Thank you, Josef."

As the door shut behind him I turned to see Timothy eyeing the tea tray with dismay. "Is that what they call tea? I'll nip along to my room and get some of the things I bought. You'd like some really nice *Gugelhupf*, wouldn't you?"

"I'd love it. Where is your room, anyway?"

"It's on the other side, down the corridor. It looks out over the courtyard, but you can see the mountaintops."

I sat down and began to pour tea.

SOMEWHAT to Tim's derision, I refused to go down in the lift with him but used the wide staircase, giving on every floor a magnificent view of the valley. Tim had already gone out to the car, but I turned down the dim corridor toward the kitchens. There was nobody in the hall, and at the first corner I hesitated. Just as I turned to go back, an old man in old-fashioned tweeds came into view. He saw me there and approached.

"Good afternoon. Is there anything I can do for you?" His English was slightly accented and his voice gentle. He had a thin face, and white hair worn rather long, and he walked stoopingly. He bent his head now in a courteous gesture, at once a nod and a slight bow. "I am Graf Zechstein."

I said: "Oh, thank you. I just wanted to ask Josef if I could stable a horse here for a night or two."

He showed no surprise. "If you wish to stable your horse, naturally there will be a place. I will tell Josef."

I thanked him and went out to where Tim waited with the car. "I saw the Count just now. He says we can house old Piebald in his stables, if Wagner decides to leave him with us. One thing has been occurring to me," I said. "If you're really serious about wanting a job at the Spanish Riding School, you could hardly

449

make a better start than by bringing home one of their long-lost stallions."

He grinned. "The thought had entered my mind."

"Then you are serious? Good for you. Well, in you get, then, let's be on our way. . . . I wonder if they've ever had a Lippizaner stallion stabled here before?"

" 'Airs above the ground,' " quoted Timothy, as we drove over the narrow bridge. "I bet the great Neapolitano Petra's never been stabled higher in his life. How is he going to get up here?"

"You're young and strong," I said cheerfully, "you're going to lead him."

"I had a feeling you had something like this in mind when you said you couldn't do without me. What a good thing I had that *Gugelhupf* for tea."

To OUR surprise Herr Wagner, whom we found in Annalisa's wagon, accepted our story immediately. "I believe you," he said, looking extremely worried. "I knew nothing; I never thought about Franzl's horse, why should I?" He paused, head bent, apparently studying the tabletop, then looked up and nodded slowly. "My father must have known. But he was a man who cared all for his family, and nothing for the law. Besides . . ." He shrugged. "In the circus we have people of all kinds. We live and let live. You understand?"

We assured him we did. He became practical then, and brisk. "There is only one thing to do now, and that is to return the horse where he belongs. But you can see my difficulty; tomorrow we cross the border and we do not return to Austria until the winter. So I do not know how this shall be done."

I said: "If you would trust Timothy and me with the horse, we would be delighted to do all that is required. And we will make it very clear that you knew nothing about it till we told you."

Herr Wagner's look of astonished delight did him great credit, and amid a torrent of mutual goodwill it was all arranged.

Annalisa had been listening in silence. Now her eyes lifted. She said quietly: "I knew about the horse."

Her father swung round. "*You knew?* From Franzl?"

"No. After Vanessa operated, Sunday night, I washed the instruments and put them away. I found . . . these." She lifted the instrument case from a bench and pulled out a drawer. In it was a bundle of newspaper clippings; I could see the name Neapolitano Petra and photographs, in different poses, of the great stallion. Annalisa spread them out on the table. The last was a yellowed photograph of the horse standing by a stable door beside a man in the uniform of the Spanish Riding School. Finally she laid on the table a brown tube labeled KOLOSTON. "It's hair dye," she said.

She turned to her father, her eyes filling with tears. "When poor Unclo Franzl was dying, he must have tried to tell me about the horse. He said 'Petra' over and over, and he spoke of Vienna and the Lippizan, but I thought he meant Maestoso Leda. '*Neapolitano Petra's Sattel,*' he said, and we thought he spoke of a Neapolitan saddle. But he meant we must take Neapolitano Petra back to Vienna, even his saddle and bridle, which came with him. It is the one I use for Maestoso Leda." Tears ran over her blackened lashes.

Her father patted her hand. "Do not trouble yourself, my Liesl; we make reparation now."

"The only thing that bothers me," I said, "is what we're going to do if they don't want him back at the school now."

Herr Wagner was on his feet. "They will take him. Their stallions live for thirty years, and when they die they are remembered. His name will still be on his stall, and fresh straw waiting."

Beaming, he took his leave. We went with Annalisa to the stable tent. Elemer was busy with the white stallion, while the pied horse she used for the rodeo was saddled and waiting, with Rudi at its head. Old Piebald flung his head up and whickered at the sight of me, and we went into the stall. "Elemer will help," Annalisa said. "Oh! The saddle!" She directed a flood of German at Elemer, and he and Timothy lifted the saddle off Annalisa's Lippizan. "We decorated it for the circus," said Annalisa. "All those jewels . . . If I had time to take them off—"

"Don't worry; I'll take them off and send them back."

"No, they're nothing but glass. Do as you wish with them; some of them are quite pretty." Then she said quickly: "There is the music. I must go. Good-by, good-by, and thank you." With a hand from Rudi she was up in the saddle, and the pied horse was gone through the curtains at the back of the big top.

Timothy, laden with the saddle, stood staring. Elemer said, "How will you take the horse?"

"We're staying up at the castle," I said. "Tim will lead him up there, and I will take the saddle up in the car."

"You will have a lot of work to make it plain again."

"Think nothing of it; I'll do it tonight. Look, are you sure she won't want the trimmings back? Some of them are awfully pretty. This one would look lovely on a dress—gold filigree, and sapphire bangles." I fingered the jewel; it was a big brooch, loosely stitched to the pommel, and flashed in the light as I touched it.

"Why don't you wear it, then? It will suit you." The dwarf produced a knife and cut the jewel from the pommel; he handed it to me with a little bow that was grotesque, and yet not comic at all. "Wear it and remember us all, *gnädige Frau.* It is a pretty thing, but your eyes make it look dim. I wish it could be real. Here is your bridle. Let Rudi put the saddle in the car for you." Then, taking my hand and kissing it—"*Küss die Hand, gnädige Frau—*" the ungainly little figure shambled out with his comic red costume flapping round the tiny legs.

I went to the car, got in, and was reaching for my handbag to get out the key when I realized that I had left the bag in Annalisa's wagon. Annoyed with myself, I got out and ran back to the wagon. The bag was just where I had left it, on the seat under the birdcage. The parrot, which was sulkily eating a tomato, cocked its head to one side and made some remark in German which sounded extremely rude. I said: "Get stuffed, mate," picked up the bag and ran down the wagon steps.

I collided with Sandor Balog. We were both moving fast, and I almost fell; his hands shot out and steadied me. They were remarkably strong and I cried out, not only with the start he had given me but with the pain of his grip. He gave me a queer look from those narrow black eyes, then took a swift step past me, peering up into the lighted doorway. "She's not in there," he said. "What were you doing?" His eye flicked down to my handbag. He was dressed ready for his act in a striking black costume, and had wrapped a long cloak round himself, in which he looked satanic.

I said: "What do you think I was doing? Stealing something?"

He turned back, looking a little at a loss. I got the impression that some urgent preoccupation had jerked him into speaking as he had done. "I'm sorry," he said. "I did not realize who it was. You . . . are differently dressed. We get many strangers who come round, and . . ." He shrugged.

I wondered why, if he had not at first recognized me, he had addressed me in English; but this was a question I did not particularly wish to explore. I said, pleasantly enough: "I shan't be seeing you again, so I'll say good night, and good luck."

But he didn't move. "Where did you get that?" He was looking at the jewel on my jacket.

"That's a souvenir off the Lippizan's saddle," I said abruptly, and headed for the gate. I thought for a moment that he was going to say something more, but he turned with a swirl of his black cloak and went rapidly the other way.

"Get stuffed, mate," the parrot said, and started to sing, in an unpleasant, wavering falsetto, "O, for the wings of a dove."

Chapter 9

I T WAS dusk when I returned to the castle, and here and there lights in the narrow windows pricked out, yellow in the gloom, and threw a pattern of light and shadow over the cobbled court.

As I mounted the steps, the Count came out. "Ah, Mrs. March," he greeted me, then stopped, looking past me at the car. "Did you not propose to stable a horse for the night?"

"Oh, yes; but he'll be brought up later."

"I see." His eye fell on the saddle. If he noticed the vulgarity of its tinseled trappings he made no sign. "Josef will carry your saddle in for you, but meantime you will want to see for yourself where we shall house your horse."

He turned away and crossed the courtyard toward the west side and what must be the storerooms and outbuildings of the castle: a line of small arches with heavy, studded doors. He pushed open a door which might have belonged to a young cathedral, and took down and lit a lantern. He went ahead of me, and in the wavering light the empty magnificence of the stables was impressive. Nothing, it seemed, had been too good for the Zechstein horses. The walls and partitions were paneled with inlaid oak, and the mangers were of marble. On the wall over each stall was carved a large shield surmounted by a crest and bearing Gothic lettering. I guessed that these were the names of the vanished horses.

In the stall at the end of the stables, the manger had been scoured out; beside it was a bale of straw. I had a strong feeling that it had not just been cleaned up for old Piebald, but was kept that way. A name, GRANE, was freshly painted on a carved shield above it, and the corn bin was comparatively new. "There is a peg for your bridle," said the Count. "Your man will doubtless put the lantern out when he has finished here." He hung it up, and led me back at a brisk pace to the castle. I hadn't the heart to say that I had decided to let Piebald graze outside that night.

As we came into the light, something about me caught his attention. Like Sandor, he was looking at the brooch on my lapel. "Forgive me, I was admiring your jewel. It is very pretty."

I laughed. "It's not really a jewel. It was given me by someone at the circus as a souvenir. It's only glass."

He peered more closely. "Perhaps, yes, perhaps it is, after all, not real. It looks familiar, like one in portraits of my great-grandmother. The jewel itself is in a museum in Munich."

Any wild thoughts I may have had of stolen treasure turning up as circus jewelry came to a speedy end.

There was a squat, dumpy woman at the desk in the hall now.

She had pendulous cheeks, and a little beak mouth pursed between them like an octopus between two stones. I took her to be the receptionist, but when she looked up I saw that her face, far from expressing the conventional welcome due a hotel guest, showed only cold surprise.

The Count said gently, "Ah, there you are, my dear."

"I've been to the kitchens. Were you looking for me?" This must be the Countess. She spoke, as her husband had, in English but her voice seemed to hold an undertone of exasperation.

She turned the exasperation on to me now. "How do you do? I hope you'll be comfortable here. I am afraid the service is not what it should be; it's very difficult now to get local help. Servants don't wish to stay in such an isolated spot."

I murmured something sympathetic, feeling uncomfortable and even irritated, as one always is in face of a determined grievance. I said: "Have you had any word yet from my husband, Countess?"

"No. But this has come for you." She handed a telegram across to me: VERY SORRY UNABLE JOIN YOU YET WILL GET IN TOUCH LOVE LEWIS.

My intense disappointment must have shown, for I saw the Countess's hard little eyes watching me curiously. I pulled myself together. "It's from my husband. What a pity: he can't join me. . . . Thank you very much. I think I'll go see if my young friend is on his way up with the horse."

As I turned to go the Count said to the Countess, "Did you say you were expecting another guest tonight?"

"Yes. Another Englishman. A Mr. Elliott."

By the mercy of heaven I had my back to them, for nothing could have hidden the surprise that must have shown on my face. I had quite forgotten that Lewis might still have to use his alias. As I reached the door, I heard her add: "He couldn't say what time he would get here. He thought it might be late."

IT DIDN'T take as long as I expected to cut the loosely sewn jewels off the saddle. I sat down on the bale of straw to do the job with a pair of nail scissors. The saddle, of soft pale leather,

had obviously been a good one originally, but now it showed signs of much mending. When I had finished, and dropped the glittering handful of glass into my pocket, I looked round for a peg. Shabby or no, I wasn't going to leave this saddle to the mercy of the rats I could already hear rustling in the stables.

The only peg that was big enough was broken, so I lifted the lid of the metal corn bin and put the saddle in it; Piebald would not need corn tonight. I put out the lantern and went to meet Timothy.

I went through the archway to the bridge and stopped there, leaning over the parapet. In the valley clusters of lights marked the outlying farms, and from beneath me came the trickling, splashing sound of the stream. I thought of Lewis. His use of the alias could only mean that he planned to see the circus people. And in twelve hours the circus would be out of the country. . . .

At that moment, faint and far away, I heard the slow clip-clop, clip-clop of a walking horse. I strolled down the road between the pines to wait for them.

The clip-clopping hoofs and a wandering knight in armor were all the scene needed, I thought, looking up at the castle turrets, dark and faintly lit against the stars. Then, when Timothy and the horse rounded the bend below me, it occurred to me that their mundane appearance was every bit as dramatic as any romantic legend: the old stallion, deposed, menial, debased by his ugly coat, was a sort of Frog Prince who might soon be back in his own royal palace.

As I called out, his head jerked up and his ears pricked forward sharply, so that for a moment he looked a young horse again. He quickened his pace and gave that lovely soft whickering through his nostrils. I remembered what Herr Wagner had said: "His name will still be on his stall, and fresh straw waiting." I hoped Herr Wagner was right.

Then the horse's muzzle had dropped softly into my hand and I was caressing his ears and telling Tim the arrangements—including those for Mr. Lee Elliott—for the coming night.

I didn't add what was very much in the forefront of my mind—

that if Tim and Lewis and I were the only occupants of the central part of the castle, Mr. Elliott would be able to prowl into my bedroom without any fear of discovery tonight.

I MUST HAVE BEEN asleep when at last he came; but when the door opened I was instantly awake. The room was dark; the heavy curtains, drawn close across the window and the turret embrasure, completely shut out the moonlight. I heard the door close softly behind him, then the creak of the boards as he approached the bed. I said sleepily: "Darling, over here," and turned, groping for the bedside light.

The sound stopped abruptly.

"Lewis?" I said. My hand had just found the switch.

A thin pencil of light from a small pocket flashlight shot and caught me full in the eyes. A swift whisper came: "Keep still. Take your hand off that switch." But even as he spoke I had pressed the switch and the light came on.

It wasn't Lewis. Standing about eight feet away from the foot of my bed was Sandor Balog.

"What are you doing here?" I said, in shock and fright.

Thrusting the flashlight back into his pocket, he stopped exactly where he was, no doubt sensing that if he moved a step fright would make me scream. "Keep quiet, will you, or—"

I said furiously: "Get out of my room immediately!" And I rolled over quickly to reach for the bedside telephone.

Now he did move. "Stop that, I tell you!" He wrenched my arm brutally aside and flung me bodily against the pillows.

I screamed Lewis's name with all my strength as I tried to throw myself out the farther side of the bed, away from Sandor; but he wrenched me back, and as I opened my mouth to scream again he hit me. The blow slammed me against the bedpost, and as my head was driven back he hit me again. In a daze of shock, fear and pain, I cringed against the pillows. When he saw that I was cowed and quiet he dropped my arm and moved away from me. I put both hands to my bruised face and tried to stop trembling.

"Look at me."

Slowly, I pulled away my hands and looked at him. He was standing now at the foot of the bed, but I knew that I was still within reach of that lightning athlete's pounce of his; and that, in any case, I couldn't hope to run out of range of the gun which he now held in his right hand.

He said: "You've just seen how much use it is to scream in a place like this. Anyway, there's only that boy here. He'll be sleeping like a baby, and if you *did* manage to wake him, madam, that would be too bad for him. Do you understand?"

I nodded. "What do you want?" My voice came out in a thin whisper, and he smiled. At the smile, anger stirred inside me, sending a flicker of warmth through the cold and the fear.

"You were expecting someone, weren't you?" The smile grew. "Did you think the husband had managed to get here after all?"

With his mention of Lewis, my immediate fears for myself fled and I began to think. So he knew Lewis was due, and that he had been delayed. . . . Without knowing anything further, I accepted Balog as the center of the circus mystery, the enemy in Lewis's shadowy assignment. My heart in my throat, I said, "How did you know my husband was expected?"

A quick shrug of the broad shoulders. His tight black trousers and black leather jacket looked as supple and sleek with muscle as the skin of a wild animal. "Some of the servants were at the performance; it was easy to talk to them afterward and find out who the guests were. In this part of the world it is not customary for hotels to lock their doors at night, so I walked in and looked at the register to find your room number—and to see if he had come." That grin again. "So don't try to frighten me by saying your husband will catch me here. Even if he did"—a brief gesture with the gun—"I could deal with him as easily as with you."

I said nothing. I was trying not to show my relief. It was apparent that he had not identified Lewis with Lee Elliott. In place of the bewildered tourist he presumably imagined my husband to be, Balog would be tangling with a professional at least twice as tough as himself. I said, "All right. What do you want?"

"The saddle," he said. "Elemer told me about the horse, and said you'd brought it up here too. Where is it?"

Suddenly I thought I understood, and it took all my self-control not to look toward the dressing-table drawer where I had put the jewels. "It's in the stables, of course," I said.

He said impatiently, "That's not true. I went there first, naturally. Did you bring it up here to tamper with it?"

"It *is* in the stables, in the corn bin. I didn't want the rats to damage it. I don't know what you want with it and I don't care." I pulled the bedclothes closer round me with what I hoped was a gesture of dismissive dignity. "And now will you please get out of here?"

But he didn't move. There was the familiar gesture with the pistol. "Get up and get dressed. You're coming with me."

I felt myself begin to tremble again. "Why don't you just go down there and take it and go away?"

"Do you think I'm going to leave you here to raise the alarm? Do as I say and get out of that bed." He gestured with the gun again, toward the side of the bed away from the telephone and the door.

There seemed to be nothing for it. Slowly I pushed back the bedclothes, got out and picked up my clothes. "I'll dress in the bathroom."

"You'll dress here."

Despising myself for the pleading note in my voice, I said: "All right, if you'll please look the other way."

"Don't be a fool. I'm not interested in you. All women are the same, they think you've got nothing else to think about."

I did the best I could on the principle that what we don't see isn't there: I turned my back on him as I got clumsily into slacks and a sweater. As I pulled on my shoes I summoned up courage to tackle him again. "And when you've got the saddle, what then?"

"Then we shall see."

I stood up. My fear had been so overpowering that I had not been able to think clearly. Now, faced with going out with this brute into the dark, my mind began to race, ticking the facts up and adding them as neatly as a cash register. Sandor's solicitude for the saddle (I had been right: he was not the type to run errands for Annalisa); the talk of loose stitching; and now, Sandor asking me if I had tampered with it. If he was a thief, where better could he hide jewels than among the tawdry glitter of circus trappings? How better could he get them out of the country?

So my interest in the horse had pushed me—right against Lewis's orders—into the middle of this dangerous affair. And that it was dangerous there could be no doubt. I would be alone with Sandor in the stables when he found the saddle stripped of its treasure; and he was, I felt sure, a man easily capable of murder.

Murder. . . On that thought, the last of the facts fell into place: Franzl's insistent mumble about something as trivial as a saddle implied that he was trying desperately to pass on the discovery for which he and Denver had been murdered. What had been worth two deaths to Sandor Balog then might be worth another now.

Well, no jewels were worth another death, and every minute of delay brought Lewis closer. I said quickly: "I know why you want this saddle. I know about the jewels you've stolen. Well, they're not my jewels, and I'm not going to risk anything for them. If I show you the saddle, it won't do you much good. I took the jewels off."

"You took the jewels off the saddle?" He was staring as if I had taken leave of my senses.

I swung round to the dressing table and got out the glittering stones, bundled in a clean handkerchief. "Here you are." I thrust the bundle at him. "Now get out."

Suddenly he gave a laugh of spontaneous amusement. He scooped three or four stones from the bundle and rolled them in his palm so that they glittered in the lamplight. "Oh, very fine, these crown jewels of yours!" Then suddenly the smile was gone and that white-toothed animal look was back. "Fool. Even if these were real, people in my country don't want jewels; they want dreams—beautiful dreams for the damned. You can always sell dreams." With a flick of the wrist he sent the stones flying. They

461

rolled away behind the curtains. "And now we go," he said.

He moved to the door and slanted his head, listening. Then he said softly: "Now, tidy the bed and pick up your nightdress and the jewels. The room must look as though you'd dressed and gone out of your own free will."

I obeyed; there was nothing else to do. After watching me for a moment, he pulled the door open quietly and listened intently for any sound in the corridor. I stooped as if to pick up the stones beyond the heavy curtains which masked the turret embrasure. Satisfied with my obedience, he wasn't watching me, but the corridor. I reached casually through the curtains. . . . He didn't turn. I slid silently back of them, and then I was fumbling at the catch of the little door that gave on the battlements. It opened without a sound, and I slipped out. I could hardly hope to have more than a few seconds' start—in fact, I think I hardly even hoped to escape this way, but my flight had been purely instinctive. There was nowhere else to go.

The moonlight was brilliant, merciless. It showed me my way clearly, but as clearly it showed my running form to Sandor. I felt terror between my shoulder blades as I ran headlong for the little door I had seen in the second tower. I seized the handle and pushed with all my strength. The door was locked.

I whirled, at bay. He was halfway along the battlements, and for one crazy moment I thought there was nowhere to go but straight up the steep slope of the tile roof. Then I saw the steps

twisting up the outside of the tower. I was flying up them and round the curved wall before he had reached the bottom step. I was winged by fear; and Sandor, athlete though he was, had put in two strenuous performances that night. I gained on him up that dreadful spiral. On the moonlit side it was easy. Even when we twisted back into the black shadows it seemed I couldn't put a foot wrong, though I heard him stumble and waste his breath in an ugly expletive, and once he paused, gasping, and called out a threat or command. And then the little staircase whipped round the last curve of the turret and shot me out onto the top of the castle.

I had a vague impression of slopes of tiles, gold-crowned pinnacles, turrets and chimney pots round the edge of the roof, and here and there great open chimneys. I ran for the nearest cover, a great stack of chimney pots, and swerved to avoid a broken one which was lying on the roof. He was near the head of the steps now; I could just see his head and shoulders. Instinctively, I stooped for the piece of chimney pot and with all my strength rolled it straight for the steps.

It hit the head of the steps with a clatter and hurtled straight over them and down. It must have caught his legs and swept his feet from under him, for his head and shoulders vanished with a crash, and I heard the flimsy iron railing creak as his body was thrown against it.

I had gained time, but I couldn't hope to dodge him for long. What I had to do, and fast, was to find a way down. Running as softly as I could, I dodged past two enormous chimneys and made for the battlements beyond. I hoped the northeast turret would have a stairway by which I might get down to find help. I was halfway along the hotel block when, fighting to control my breathing and to hear above my thudding heart, I risked a pause to listen. I heard him straightaway. He was casting about like a hound that has lost the scent.

I could imagine him, lithe and tough and black in his sleek animal's suit, peering among the angular shadows for a sight of me. I kept very still, and he took two slow steps forward and stopped again. I was pressing back into my corner, my hands digging into a crevice of the stone almost as if I could burrow my way into it. Under my rigid fingers a piece of mortar broke away and fell into my hand, silently. Imagining the sound that it might have made caused me a spasm of terror; but it also suggested something—an old trick, but worth trying. Cautiously, I eased myself away from the stone and, still hidden, lobbed the piece of mortar as far as I could back toward the south wing.

It fell with a crack and a slither, like a stone dislodged by someone's foot. I heard him whip round, and then the sound of his feet racing back the way he had come.

When I could no longer hear him I dodged north again, through the sharp moonlight and shadows, stumbling sometimes, until I came to the northeast turret. There was indeed a stairway; but it was in ruins, the first half dozen steps hanging, crumbling. Beside it, in the wall of the tower, was a heavy, iron-studded door with a big curved handle which I pushed. The door was immovable. I pushed and pulled, hardly believing that this miracle of escape was not after all going to work. Set in the stone beside the door was a bell push. I pressed it. It seemed the normal thing to do in this crazy night. But nothing happened.

For the first time it occurred to me seriously that perhaps I was not going to get away. Then, even as I stood there feeling my courage spill out of me, I remembered that I had seen a wide stone stairway leading down beside one of the towers at the main gateway on the west.

There was still no sign of Sandor. I slithered out of the shadow of the turret and dodged along the rooftops toward it. But when the head of it lay open in the moonlight, fifty yards ahead of me, I saw Sandor again. He had run right round the other wing of the castle, and was now heading for the opposite side of the gate. He had seen me, and I saw the gun flash into his hand; but I knew that here, over the main entrance, he wouldn't dare to shoot. I stopped dead, and as I did I saw that away below, down the hillside, there were the lights of a moving car.

It was silly, it was futile, but I screamed his name. *"Lewis,*

Lewis!" It came out only as a sort of sobbing gasp as Sandor
leaped down and came after me.

Almost immediately I realized that, even with the lead I had,
I couldn't hope to escape. I ran blindly back along the rooftop
maze of the north wing, round the turret where that nightmare
door stood in the shadows, fast shut—

It was wide open.

I was almost past it when I saw Sandor, now barely ten yards
behind me. I doubled like a hare and fell through the doorway. I
saw him shoot past me, taken completely by surprise.

I had expected a stairway inside the door. Instead, I found
myself sprawling on a level slippery floor; and then, as I put my
hands out to the wall, the door through which I had come slid
shut behind me, and a light came on. Then the floor dropped
frighteningly downward, like a stone. It was the lift. My half-
crazy action in pressing the bell push had summoned it and, as
I swung myself in, one of my hands must have caught the controls and sent it earthward.

Chapter 10

I WAS STILL sobbing for breath when the lift door opened and I
saw a large room, dimly lit by moonlight from spearhead
windows, empty and silent: a faint glint from ranks of bottles
showed me that this was the wine cellar.

Picking myself up from the floor, I turned to my left, which
must be toward the kitchens and stables, and groped my way
between the pillars to search for a way out. Somehow I must find
the courtyard and Lewis. If he were to meet Sandor, he would
be unsuspecting and, for all I knew, unarmed.

I came, finally, to a flight of stone steps and stumbled up. At its
top was the usual heavy door; but when I lifted the latch and
pushed, it opened smoothly and in silence. Cautiously I peered
out. . . . A corridor with flagged floor, dim lights; probably near
the kitchens. To the left it turned a corner; twenty yards to my

right it ended in a vaulted door. The bolts soon yielded and I was through. I shut it behind me and leaned back in the shadow, getting my bearings.

I had come out into the open coach house. In front of me loomed an ancient closed carriage; beside it was a limousine. I peered into the courtyard. It was empty, but at once I heard a car crossing the bridge. The lights speared through the archway and a big Mercedes came to a stop no more than a yard from the coach house.

The lights went off and Lewis got quietly out of the car and reached into the back seat for his bag. I breathed: "Lewis."

He did not appear to have heard me. As I nerved myself to go toward him in the open, he threw his bag back into the car, got into it himself and restarted it. The car, without lights, slid into the coach house. I remembered, then, his instinctive reaction to the newsreel camera. He was not giving anything away to a possible watcher. The car stopped by me; he got out and said softly: "Vanessa?"

Next moment I was in his arms, holding him tightly enough to strangle him, and able to say nothing but, "Oh, love, oh, love, oh, love." He held me close against him with one arm and patted me with his free hand, comforting me rather as one does a frightened horse. At last he disengaged himself gently and looked at me in the dim light.

"Well, here's a welcome!" Then in a suddenly edged whisper: "Your face. How did that happen?"

I had forgotten my bruised cheek. I put a hand to it. "That circus man . . . Sandor Balog . . . He's here, somewhere, and oh, Lewis—" My whisper cracked shamefully and I bit my lip and put my head down against him again.

He said: "My dear, it's all right now. I'm here. Just tell me about Balog." He sounded angry, but somehow not surprised.

I lifted my head. "You came back as Elliott because you knew about him?"

"Not about him, no. But I thought I'd have to follow the circus. Now things may break this side of the border. Van, tell me."

"I'll try, but he's somewhere here, Lewis. And he's got a gun."

"So have I," said my husband matter-of-factly, "and we'll see him before he sees us. What's behind that door?"

"A back passage, somewhere near the kitchens. I came up that way from the wine cellar."

"Come on then, back here behind the car. If he comes out that way now, we'll get him. And if he comes in through the arch we'll see him easily. Now, Van . . . ?"

Quickly I told him everything. "I think he's coming down by way of my room," I said. "The stones are there. He said they weren't valuable, but I think he was only trying to put me off. 'Dreams for the damned,' he said. 'You can always sell dreams.' But I don't see why he's still determined to get the saddle."

Lewis was holding me half absently, with his head bent, thinking. "'Dreams for the damned,'" he said. "I begin to see. . . . And he still wants the saddle, does he?" He lifted his head, and his whisper sounded jubilant. "I'll tell you later—but I think you've broken it wide open! Are the stables next door?"

"Yes. That's the connecting door. And there's a door off the courtyard."

"Right. I think you can take it he was telling the truth, and the jewels really are only stage props. But he still wants that saddle, which means he'll make straight for the stables. Did he have time to get down off the roof, pick up the saddle and get out before I arrived?"

"It seemed like years, but no, I'm sure he hasn't."

"Then he's still up there, or in the stables, waiting for me to go. In either case he'll have heard the car."

I could feel the calm, unhurried beat of his heart. It was something to be able to hand matters over to a professional. It was something that a sleek animal in black leather would find he had tangled not with stray English tourists but with Our Man in Vienna.

"I'll have to go into the castle by the front door," said Lewis. "He'll be waiting for that. Then I'll come straight back here by that back door of yours. May I leave you for two minutes?"

"Yes."

"That's my girl. Now, you'd better stay out here. What about that old carriage? Yes, in you go, and keep still."

"What are you going to do?"

"He'll get in touch with his bosses, and when he does I want to be there. So I think we'll let him take what he wants."

"You mean you're just going to let him go?"

His hand touched my bruised cheek very gently. "When I do lay hands on him, I promise you he'll never walk a high wire again. But this is a job."

"All right, Lewis. It's all right. But Lewis . . ."

"Yes?"

"Be—careful, won't you? He's dangerous."

Lewis laughed.

THE INSIDE of the old carriage was fusty and close, and curtains at the open windows shut out what little light there was. But though I could see nothing, I could hear; and almost immediately I heard the sound of stealthy footsteps in the courtyard and the quiet click of the stable latch.

Parting the folds of damp brocade, I saw a growing bar of light at the foot of the stable door. Sandor, flashlight in hand, approached it. There was a metallic clink as the corn-bin lid was lifted and closed. Then I heard shuffling sounds, and presently the sound of ripping cloth. He must be opening the thing up. Lewis was right; the jewels were worthless; there must be something else contained in the saddle, and sooner than carry away the whole clumsy burden Sandor was taking the time to remove whatever he had so carefully stitched into the padding.

Suddenly, I heard again the click of the stable latch, and steps approaching. Horrified, I heard Timothy's voice: "Why, Herr Balog! What are you doing here?" And then, sharply: "What on earth are you doing with that saddle?"

The rush of feet; the brief sound of a scuffle; a cry from Timothy. A thud, and then the sound of retreating, racing footsteps. I heard them cross the corner of the courtyard.

"Timothy!" Somehow I got the carriage door open and stumbled out. In a matter of seconds I was in the stables. Moonlight spilled mistily through the cobwebbed window, and beside the corn bin, near the wreck of the saddle, lay Timothy. I knelt beside him, and almost choked with thankfulness as he moved. He put a hand to his head and struggled up on one elbow. "Where did he hit you, Tim?" I said.

"My head . . . no, he missed. . . . My neck. Blast, it's sore, but I think it's all right. It was that swine Sandor, the—"

A voice came from the shadows behind us, and we both jumped. It was Lewis, looking for one fantastic second not like Lewis at all but like something as dangerous as Sandor himself. Almost before we had seen the gun in his hand it had vanished from sight again. "So you caught him at it, Tim," he said. "I've got to get after him. Did you see what he took?"

"Flat packets of some kind, about the size of those detergent samples they shove through your door." Timothy began to scramble to his feet. "He left one, anyway. I fell on it."

Lewis pounced on the thing. It was an oblong polyethylene package. He whipped a knife out and slit a corner. He sniffed, then shook a few grains of powder into the palm of his hand and tasted them.

"What is it?" asked Timothy.

Lewis didn't answer. He folded the cut corner down and thrust the package back into Tim's hands, saying abruptly: "Keep that safe; don't let anyone see it. Are you all right?"

"Yes, quite."

"Then stay with Vanessa."

He was gone. I heard the door of his car open and slam behind him as he got in. The engine raced to life. As it swung backward out of the coach house, I ran out into the courtyard. The car paused as Lewis leaned across and opened the door. "Yes?"

"I'm coming with you. Please. I won't get in your way."

He hesitated only fractionally. "All right, get in." As I scrambled in beside him Timothy pulled open the back door.

"Me, too. Please, Mr. March. Honestly, I could help."

Lewis laughed suddenly. "Come one, come all," he said cheer-fully. "All right, get in—but hurry." Before Timothy's door shut the Mercedes leapt forward like a bullet from a gun. The bridge boomed for a second beneath us and then, lights out, engine silken and quiet, we were running downhill under the tunnel of the dark pines. "I saw a parked jeep on my way up," said Lewis. "I bet it was his, but I don't suppose he's using lights either. See if you can see anything."

Timothy and I peered out through the black stems of the trees. Just as Lewis swung wide at a bend, I saw a flash of light a long way below. Tim and I exclaimed together: "There he is!" I added quickly: "It was just a flash, way down. It's gone again."

Timothy said: "Wasn't there a sort of woodsman's hut down there? When his lights flashed on, I thought I saw it in the beam."

"Yes, there was," said Lewis. "Damnation. A forest track goes off just beside that hut. He must have flashed his lights to see his way into it. A jeep would manage it easily, but whether this car can is another matter. Well, tell us what you were doing down in the stables, Tim."

"Some sort of cry woke me. I listened for a bit and didn't hear anything else, but I felt uneasy. So I opened my door and looked out into the corridor. I thought perhaps you had come, Mr. March. I went back into my own room. I was wide-awake by that time, so I went to the window and just stood looking out. . . . And then I saw someone dodging about among the battlements, so I shoved some clothes on and ran along to tell Vanessa. When I saw her room was empty and the door to the roof was open, I went out there, and just then you arrived. When you went into the castle, Balog ran down those steps into the courtyard and went into the stables."

"So," said Lewis dryly, "naturally you followed him."

"Well, naturally." Timothy sounded faintly surprised. "I thought it might have something to do with old Piebald. I went in very quietly and there was Sandor ripping the saddle to pieces. I asked him what he was up to and he went for me. I'm sorry if I've spoiled things."

"You've done plenty. It was a masterstroke, falling on that package. It's several hundred pounds' worth of cocaine, unless I'm much mistaken."

"Cocaine! Dope rings! Gosh!" Tim sounded vastly pleased. "And there were at least half a dozen packets!"

Lewis said, "I've a feeling that you two, with your long-lost Lippizan, have got a lead on a ring the police have been trying to break for quite some time. Hang on, here's the hut." The Mercedes rocked to a stop. A rutted track twisted upward and out of sight through a break in the trees. Lewis got out and examined it closely in the moonlight. A moment later he was back in his seat and the car was moving again. "He's making for the main road, thank God."

"He won't head back to the circus?"

"Not now that he knows your husband has arrived. He'll reckon that will be the first call the police will make after we alert them. Obviously, the circus will be stopped at the border and searched from stem to stern. Hold it! I see red lights."

The Mercedes slowed sharply to a crawl. The trees were sparse here and we could see down the next slope. The jeep's brake lights flashed again as Balog turned out onto a bridge at the foot of the hill.

Lewis said: "Let's see which way he turns. Left, for a bet. I don't think he'll risk going back through Zechstein."

"Yes," said Tim, craning. "He's turning left, away from the village. What d'you reckon he'll do?"

"What would you do, mate?" asked Lewis.

"Telephone the boss," said Tim promptly. "You can't tell me that blighter's anything but a second-class citizen. He won't be able to make his own decisions."

"You have the makings, Tim. That's just what I'm hoping—that our second-class citizen may give us a lead, if not to the boss in Vienna then to the local contact. He's got the stuff on him now— he may think he's got it all—and from the way he blazed his lights, he hasn't any idea we're after him so quickly. So we follow and watch."

"If I were him," Tim said, "I'd ditch the stuff, and fast."

"He well may. If he does, we may see him, with luck—and see who picks it up."

Tim was taking with remarkable ease Lewis's change from P.E.C. salesman to armed investigator. He leaned forward now and asked, "What sort of gun is it?"

"Beretta .32," said Lewis, and I heard Timothy give a sigh of pure happiness.

The car swept silently across the bridge and turned north into the main road. Lewis said: "We'll move up. Thank God for the moonlight."

The Mercedes seemed to leap forward. The road twisted between river and cliff. Now and again the black shadow of trees would sweep blindingly over the car; then the bright glare of moonlight seemed to expose us, like a fly crawling up a window. Once I glanced back. High, pale in the light, glimmered the Schloss Zechstein. The car snarled under a railway bridge and swept round a corner; and there was the fleeing shape of the jeep, mounting the crest of a long hill ahead of us. For a moment Sandor was exposed against the sky; and then he vanished.

"There's a stretch of wood a bit farther on," said Lewis. "He'll be well into that before we have to expose ourselves on the hilltop, even supposing he's watching for us. Get the map out, Van. How far is the next village? There's a flashlight in there."

I obeyed him. "There's a village called St. Johann, just beyond the wood. About two miles from here."

"Good. That may be it. There'll be a phone booth there."

Next moment we in our turn were sweeping over the crest of the hill and down into a dark tunnel of pines. The road slashed through the forest as straight as a ruler; at the far end we could see the village streetlamps.

I half expected Lewis to leave the car in the shelter of the wood and reconnoiter the telephone on foot; but he suddenly switched on the headlights, slowed, and took the village street at a reasonably decorous speed. It was very short. There was a little café, a well, a row of cypresses against the church wall, a big barn;

and then the glint of glass from the corner where the telephone booth stood. . . .

And in the shadow of the cypresses the jeep was parked.

With a snarl of our engine we were round the corner, up the hill past the barn, and running over a wooden bridge.

"He was there," said Timothy excitedly. "In the phone booth, just as you said."

Lewis didn't answer. He turned back the way we had come and then switched off the lights and the motor. The car coasted silently down the gentle slope back to the village. Then we were off the road and on the rough grass in the lee of the barn, facing the road but hidden from it. He spoke softly. "Keep down, both of you. I'm going out to see what he's up to."

He slid out of the car, shut the door very gently, and all in a moment was lost in the shadows of the building. I wound down my window to listen. Somewhere nearby cattle moved in a byre, and a cock crowed. I realized that the moonlight was fading toward the dawn.

Then shockingly loud in the still air came the sound of the jeep's engine. Timothy and I ducked down, and the jeep burst past within a few yards of us, still traveling north. I risked a look. He was using no lights.

Next moment the car door was pulled open and Lewis slid in beside me. Our engine sprang to life, and we were away on the track of the jeep. The speedometer swung hard to the right and held there. Timothy's head came between us. "You didn't see him hide the drugs in the old barn?"

"No. Nor did he hand them to a one-eyed Chinaman with a limp. He has his orders. So, you might say, have we ours."

"Orders?" It was the nearest Tim had come to a direct query about Lewis's activities.

Lewis said with a convincing sound of frankness, "I was speaking figuratively. I'm not a policeman, Tim; I just walked into this while engaged in an inquiry for my own firm. The common denominator of the two affairs is Paul Denver. He must have come across some clue to this business in Czechoslovakia, where the circus was recently. Franz Wagner must have found out about the stuff in the saddle and joined Balog's gang. Then, if Franz talked in his cups, Sandor would be frightened. He probably waited till Franz was drunk, then tackled Paul, pulled the lamp down and set the place alight. Sorry."

This as he swerved to avoid a fallen bough. "So don't go thinking we've any official standing; we haven't. But since I've got my own urgent private reasons for an interview with Herr Balog— I've done my best to legitimate us—I rang up Vienna from the Schloss Zechstein. I once got involved with an Interpol man there over a client who turned out to have a forged import license." The easy voice was convincing in its casualness. "This is Interpol's territory, of course, the narcotics branch. I rang him up and told him we might be on to the drug ring. The circus will be stopped at the border and the Graz police alerted."

"Then we'd better not lose him, had we?" Tim's voice was a touchingly faithful imitation of Lewis's cool tone, and I saw Lewis smile to himself. A sudden affection for them both caught at me chokingly.

"I want to get as close as I dare without frightening him. I know this part of the world fairly well, but keep me posted, will you, Van? When's the next turnoff?"

I crouched over the map. "The next proper turnoff's about four miles ahead, in a village called Zweibrunn am See. It branches to the left, but it seems to be a dead end, going up into the mountains."

"Zweibrunn am See?" said Timothy. "Josef told us about that, remember? He said it was where the rack railway started."

"Oh, yes, I remember. I think I can see it marked, like a fish's backbone. It goes up to nowhere, as far as I can see."

"The rack railway?" Lewis said. "I know where you mean, then. It goes to a restaurant on top of the mountain. It's two or three thousand feet up. I expect your road goes up to the same place. . . . Ah, thank God we're off that bit of road. If anything should be marked like a fish's backbone, that should."

We shot out of the deep shadow of the woods into the open

valley, and there was the jeep, a racing shadow, barely a quarter of a mile ahead.

"Won't he see us?" Tim's voice was quick with apprehension.

"I doubt it," said Lewis. "If he's expecting to be chased at all, he's expecting the police, and they'd be after him with all lights blazing."

"What are you going to do?"

"Heaven knows," said Lewis cheerfully, "play it as it comes."

"There's the village," I said quickly. "I see the church spire."

Next moment the jeep had vanished round the curve. "Hold on to your hats," said Lewis. "Now we close up."

Chapter 11

L EWIS was right. Sandor seemed not worried about being followed. As the jeep reached Zweibrunn am See we were barely two hundred yards behind him, but he gave no sign that he was aware of us. He swung left at the turnoff without a pause.

Seconds later we took the turn after him onto the narrow, steep and twisting road. Lewis made a sound of satisfaction. "This is a pushover. We've only to keep a couple of bends behind him and he hasn't a chance of knowing he's followed. . . . And there's no need to look for turnings. There'll be nothing going off this but a goat track. All we have to avoid is running slap into his rear bumper."

The road had already deteriorated into little more than a track with a gravel surface, twisting in and out of dense pine forest. Lewis drove with no diminution of speed, but it was not a road I would have cared to drive myself, even in broad daylight. As we raced and lurched upward, bend after bend, I could hear above us the intermittent splutter of the jeep's engine, the sound coming in sharp gusts as trees and rocks flashed between to cut it off. To Sandor the noise of our climb must seem like an echo of his own.

The Mercedes came to a rocking halt suddenly. Lewis said,

"The map, please." I handed it over and he studied it. "As I remembered. This road ends at a halt for the railway, about two thirds of the way up. The railway goes right on to the *Gasthaus*— the restaurant—on the summit; I suppose it tunnels some of the way." He started the car again. "Balog will have to leave the jeep at the end of the road. We'll stop while we're still under cover of his engine." He parked the car in the shadow of the trees, with her nose to the road, and gave us our orders in an urgent undertone:

"You'd better both come with me, only for heaven's sake keep quiet and under cover. Stay about twenty yards back and don't break cover until I give you the sign. I may need you, even if only as messengers. I'll leave the spare car key here."

At the foot of a tree lay a small flat stone. As Lewis thrust the spare key underneath it, Timothy said sharply: "He's stopped."

"Then come on," said Lewis and, swinging himself up the steep bank, vanished at a run through the trees toward the next curve of the road, seventy feet above.

We followed him over loose rock and through brambles, our progress covered by the splash of a small rivulet. We saw Lewis, above us, edging his way cautiously among the thinning trees in the half-light. Finally he paused and beckoned. As we scrambled to his level he reached an arm down, pulled me up and held me.

We were by a small building, perhaps a shelter for railwaymen or a storage place. Outside it the road petered out in a tangle of bushes and ragged saplings, and backed well into it I could dimly see the jeep.

Lewis said softly: "He's still alone, going up the railway to the restaurant. I'm going straight after him. Tim, you might immobilize that jeep and then come on after us. Vanessa, you stay with me."

"Whither thou goest, I will go. Excelsior," I said heroically, going after him up an easy path beside the railway.

The narrow tracks cut their way in a series of frighteningly steep slopes. Between the rails was the rackline, like a heavy cogwheel unrolled and laid flat—a fierce-looking toothed rail standing

477

well above the other two. A pinion or gear wheel on the engine meshed with the teeth of the rack for greater traction and controlled speed on the steep grades.

The trees soon gave way to the barer slopes of the high reaches of the mountain, but mist clung between the scattered pines. "Where did you see him?" I asked.

Lewis pointed above to where the line swooped in a lifting curve round a shoulder of white rock. "Just a glimpse there. He was going at top speed."

He himself was setting no mean pace, but making very little sound and prospecting carefully at the bends. As we toiled—at least, I toiled; Lewis seemed fresh as a daisy—the mist came down and we knew we could not be seen by our quarry.

Lewis said: "Our friends couldn't be better placed. This mountain is a clear signaling line across at least two borders. It'd be interesting to know what time the first train comes up."

"It's at seven. The porter told us—he thought we might like to take the trip." I added grimly: "It seems funny to think of coming here for pleasure."

He grinned. "You never know your luck."

I looked at Lewis. His response had seemed ironic; but I knew every tone of his voice—and he had meant it. For me the night had held terror, relief, and then a sort of keyed-up excitement. Drugged with this and buoyed up by the pleasure of Lewis's company, I had been floating in a kind of dream—apprehensive, yes, but no longer scared; for nothing could happen to me when he was there. But with him, I now realized, it was more positive than this. It was not simply that he wasn't prey to my kind of physical weakness and fear, or just that he was at the end of an exacting job. He was, quite positively, enjoying himself.

"Lewis," I said accusingly, "can you possibly be *wanting* some rough stuff?"

"Good heavens, no!" He said it lightly. It was a lie; he gave it away with the next sentence. "Is your face still sore?"

"My face? I suppose it is." I put a hand to the swollen cheek. "I was too busy to think about it. It must look awful!"

"Not from this side, beautiful. Praise be, the mist is clearing. There's a tunnel ahead."

Even as he spoke a freak current of air lifted the mist away. He pointed up the mountain, away from the railroad. "There, you see? It looks like a cave mouth. We'll take a chance and bypass it." So we scrambled on up with only a few trails of mist to blur our way, though the crest of the mountain remained lodged in cloud, mercifully blinding our quarry.

Just before that cloud swallowed us we saw Timothy, far below. He waved, and Lewis pointed higher up the mountain in a gesture which said, "Follow us." He said, "That's a good lad, Vanessa; his father must be a fool. What's he going to do?"

"He's talking of a job with the Spanish Riding School. He's hoping his father can help."

"I could probably help him there myself. I know a man— Watch that stone, it's loose."

"You know, I'm beginning to think you're quite handy to have around."

"Time alone will tell," he said, with a glance ahead through the mist. "We'll see what Tim says, anyway. But if I'd a son like that . . . Managing all right?"

"I'm with you, literally all along the line."

"So we can give it some thought when this job's over?"

"Why not? I daresay supply can meet demand, as the P.E.C. sales department would put it."

He reached a hand back to help me. "How my other department would put my doing a straight police job I hate to think; but I'm certain there'll turn out to be a security tie-up, with drugs going behind the Iron Curtain and Paul sending for me. But I think the Department will decide to let someone else cope with *that*. I'm quitting—and a man'll do anything when he's under notice."

At something in his tone I said quickly: "What d'you mean?"

"What I have to discuss with Sandor," said Lewis, "isn't exactly in the book."

"You mean your private reasons for catching up with him?"

"Exactly that. Any objections?"

"I can hardly wait."

"I always did say you weren't a nice girl. Now what I plan to do is to go straight in, if I can, and pick up Balog, his contact and the dope. The police might have got more information by just watching the *Gasthaus*, but Balog knows his cover's been blown, so we might as well muscle straight in and pick up the two of them before they clear out. When we get there, stay under cover till I give the word. If anything goes wrong, go downhill with Tim, get to the car, drive to the hotel and get them to telephone the police at Graz. Then get the local policeman and a few solid citizens and send them up here. But don't come back yourself." He smiled down at me. "Don't look like that; that's only if things go wrong, but they won't. . . . Now we'd better stop talking. Sound carries in mist, and it can't be far now."

"Look," I said.

Above us, and slightly to the left, nebulous and faint through the fog, like a strangled star, a light hung steady.

"Journey's end," said Lewis.

THE *Gasthaus* lay some twenty yards beyond the end of the railway. On one side lay a terrace edged with a low wall beyond which the cliff dropped sheer away; but on the side from which we approached, it was just a long, low, whitewashed building with shuttered windows, and a heavy door to the side of which were refuse bins and crates of empty bottles. Half of one shutter had been pushed back against the wall, and the window with it, perhaps so the light could guide Sandor.

There was a shed at the terminus of the railway, a squat oblong building which did duty as a station. We ran forward under cover of this, dodged in, and went to a window at the rear. From it we could look down on the *Gasthaus* kitchen, as well lighted as something on a stage.

Above a big stove hung a row of copper pans and a shelf of blue dishes. The end of a big scrubbed table jutted out near the window. On the wall beside the stove was an old-fashioned telephone, and near this Sandor Balog stood, talking hard to a stocky, heavy man who stood with his back to the window, an old bathrobe thrown over his pajamas. He was lifting a coffeepot off the stove and had paused to say something over his shoulder to Sandor.

All this I got in one swift impression, for in that moment Lewis, with a breathed "Stay here," had left my side. He ran in a curve toward the *Gasthaus*, keeping out of the direct line of vision, and in a few seconds, unnoticed, was backed up against the wall beside the open window from where, presumably, he could hear what was being said. I saw a gun appear in his hand.

A movement within the room caught my eye. The second man carried the coffeepot across to the table and poured coffee into two mugs. I saw the steam of it rising, and I still remember—overlaying even the apprehension of the moment—the glorious sudden pang of hunger caused by the sight.

Lewis drifted away from the window, along the wall, to try the door. But it was locked, and he drifted, ghostlike, back to the window. I was surprised they had overlooked that; but even as the thought crossed my mind Sandor said something, pointing, then put his mug down on the table, picked up the phone and said something into it. His host shrugged and went to the window to shut it. And Lewis, incredibly, put out a hand to hold the window and shutter tightly back against the outside wall.

The man yanked at the window. It jerked, and stuck. He pulled it again, and I could hear his irritable exclamation as it still stayed open. Then he leaned over the sill and reached out.

Lewis hit him hard over the head. The heavy body slumped across the sill, then slowly slipped back into the lighted room. Instantly Lewis was astride the sill, gun in hand.

At the same moment an upstairs light came on.

I left my hiding place and ran like a hare across the intervening space toward the kitchen window. Quick though Lewis had been, Sandor had had a moment's warning, for even as Lewis jumped for the sill Sandor slammed the receiver back and whirled round, reaching for his pocket.

But he never got his gun leveled. Lewis shot. He was content with shattering one of the blue dishes, but the shot froze Sandor where he stood. Then at a barked command he sent his gun skidding across the floor to Lewis's feet.

I heard Sandor say incredulously: "Lee Elliott! What in hell's name—"

Lewis cut across him. "Who is this man?"

"Why, Johann Becker, but what the devil—"

I said breathlessly from the window: "A light went on upstairs. Someone's awake."

Sandor's face, as he saw me, changed almost ludicrously. It held amazement, then calculation, then a kind of wary fury. "You? So you are responsible for this crazy nonsense? What's she been telling you?"

Lewis had neither moved nor turned at the sound of my voice. He said: "Come on in, Van. Pick up that gun, and don't get between me and Balog." Then to Sandor, curtly: "Who else is in the house?"

"Frau Becker, of course. If you'll listen to me, Elliott—"

"Keep back!" snapped Lewis. "It won't be a plate next time." As Sandor subsided, I slid quickly in through the window and stooped for the gun. "That's my girl," said Lewis, eyes and gun fixed on Sandor. "Have you ever handled one of those things?"

"No," I said.

"Then just keep it pointing away from me, will you?" he said mildly. "I want you to keep Frau Becker quiet with it."

Sandor said furiously: "What the hell is this about?"

Lewis said impatiently: "Cut that out. You know as well as I do why I'm here. You'll save yourself a lot of trouble if you'll tell me just where Becker and his wife come in—"

He got no further. The door of the room was flung open and in surged one of the most enormous women I have ever seen. She had on a vast pink flannel nightgown with a blue woolen wrapper over it, and her hair was in plaits down her back. The pistol shot and the sound of broken crockery must have made her think that her husband and his visitor were indulging in a drunken orgy, for she swept into that room like Hurricane Chloe, unhesitating, unafraid—and poker in hand.

I jumped to intercept her, thrusting the pistol at her much as David must have waved his little sling at Goliath. She took no notice of it at all. She lifted an arm the size of a ham to sweep me aside, and bore down on the men. And it wasn't the sight of her unconscious husband or the raging Sandor or even Lewis's pistol that brought her up, standing for one magnificent moment in front of the shelf.

"My dish! My beautiful dish!" It was only later that Lewis translated for me, but the source of her emotion was unmistakable. "You destroy my house! Burglar! Assassin!"

And, poker raised high, she bore down on Lewis.

I jumped for the woman's upraised arm and caught it, but in her attempt to wrench free she sent us both staggering across the room, and for a moment we reeled between Lewis and Sandor. Lewis leaped to one side to keep Sandor within range, but it was too late. Sandor went for Lewis's gun hand like a tiger to its kill, and the fight was on.

I didn't see the first stages of that fight; I was too busy with Frau Becker. For two or three sizzling minutes all I could hope for was to hold on madly to the hand which held the poker, and to prevent my own gun from going off as I was shaken about the room like a terrier hanging on to a maddened cow.

Then suddenly she folded up like a leaking grain sack and went down as if I had indeed shot her. By the mercy of heaven a chair was in the way, and into this we went, me on her ample lap. It was a rocking chair, and, tossing like a ship at sea, it shot screeching backward to fetch up against a wall just as a white-faced Timothy came hurtling through the window, tripped over the prostrate Becker, swept a mug off the table in falling, and landed on the floor in a pool of coffee.

The sight of a third assassin was too much even for Frau Becker. She opted out of the fight, sitting slumped in the rocking chair, wailing, while I picked myself up and Tim rolled off her husband and took the poker from her. Together we turned to watch the other hurricane that was sweeping the hapless kitchen.

Sandor was still hanging on to Lewis's gun hand, while Lewis fought grimly to free himself and regain control with the gun. For two horrible seconds Lewis was jammed, cursing, against the hot stove; then Sandor brought his wrist with a crack across the edge of the stove and Lewis's gun flew wide, to go skittering under the table. He kneed Sandor viciously in the groin and the locked bodies came with a backbreaking slam against the table's edge, while Tim's poker, missing them by inches, smashed down on the stove and sent the kettle flying.

"My kettle!" moaned Frau Becker, galvanized afresh.

"Tim! The other man!" I shrieked.

Becker was on his feet. Sandor gasped something and Becker lurched for the telephone.

Lewis said, "Stop him!" and somehow swung Sandor away from the table. One of Sandor's terrible steel hands was now at Lewis's throat. I could see the flesh bulge and darken under the fingers. Sweat was pouring off both men, and Sandor breathed as if his lungs were ruptured. Then instead of pulling away I saw Lewis close in. He had Sandor round the body and suddenly brought him slamming down across his knee in a backbreaker. Before Sandor could roll painfully free, Lewis had dragged him up again and I heard the sickening sound of bone on flesh as he hit him hard across the throat.

Becker was yanking at the telephone wires with all his strength. I yelled: "Stop!" and swung the gun toward him. He ignored me, and Tim jumped and struck him—just too late. The wires came away with a scattering of plaster, and poor Becker went down once more and lay still.

"My dish!" wailed Frau Becker. "My beautiful cups! Johann!"

The fight was over. Lewis was dragging Sandor to his feet. The latter still struggled, but it seemed to be without much hope of breaking the cruel grip that held him. Now step by sweating step he was forced toward the stove.

It was all over in seconds. I still hadn't grasped what Lewis was doing. I heard Sandor say, in a voice I didn't recognize:

"What do you want to know?" Then, quickly, on a sickening note of panic: "I'll tell you anything! What do you want?"

"It can wait," said Lewis.

And with the other's wrist in his grip, Lewis dragged him forward and began to force his hand over the stove. Timothy gasped, and I said: "Lewis! No!"

But we might as well not have been there. Slowly Lewis forced the hand downward. "It was this hand, I believe?" he said, and held it for a fraction of a second, no more, on the hot surface.

Sandor screamed. Lewis pulled him away, dumped him into the nearest chair and reached for the gun I was holding. But there was no need for it. The man stayed slumped in the chair, nursing his burned hand. "Keep your hands to yourself after this," said my husband thinly.

He stood there for a moment or two, surveying the unconscious Becker, the wrecked telephone, the woman snuffling in the rocking chair, Tim with his poker, and myself, probably as pale as he, shaken and staring. Tim recovered himself first. He went scrambling under the table for the Beretta.

"Good man," Lewis said. Then he smiled, pushing the hair out of his eyes, seeming suddenly human again. "Van, my darling, do you suppose there's any coffee left? Pour it, will you, while Tim and I tie these thugs up? Then they can tell us all the other things I want to know."

Chapter 12

TIMOTHY and I emerged from the *Gasthaus* at about half past four. It came as a surprise to realize that it was full light. Timothy was carrying Sandor's automatic, which he handled with what was to me a terrifying and admirable casualness. As we started downhill I said, "I hope you know about those things."

He grinned. "My grandfather had an old Luger from the First War. I used to go potting rabbits with it."

"You loathsome boy. I wouldn't have thought it of you."

"Oh," he said cheerfully, "I never got one. It's very difficult to pot rabbits with a Luger. As a matter of fact it's impossible. My hands so far are pretty clean of blood; but at this rate I have no idea whether they'll stay so or not. I say, that was some scrap up there, wasn't it? Why did Lewis burn Sandor's hand? To make him talk?"

"No, it was a private thing. Sandor hit me."

His eyes flew to my bruised face. "Oh . . . oh, I see." I could see that his admiration for Lewis had soared to the edge of idolatry. I thought with resignation that men seemed in some ways to pass their lives on an unregenerately primitive level. Well, I had had a fairly primitive reaction myself to my husband's eye-for-an-eye violence in the kitchen. That I was coldly ashamed of it now proved nothing.

"Whatever it was for," Tim said, "it did the trick. He couldn't wait to spill the beans. Did you understand any of it?"

"No," I said. Lewis's interrogation—since it included the Beckers had been in German. "Suppose you tell me now."

So, as we hurried downhill over wet, slippery grass and loose rock, he passed the main items on to me. The important thing from our point of view was that (as Lewis had overheard before he even entered the room) Sandor had cached the drugs in a tree on the section of railway that we had short-circuited. Becker had tried to shout Sandor into silence, but when he realized how much Lewis knew, the facts—and the names—began to emerge, perhaps in the hope of leniency if the trio turned state's evidence.

"Not everything came out," said Tim, "but then they're only messengers. Lewis says there'll be plenty to find when the police start to take the *Gasthaus* apart; and he overheard the number Sandor tried to call in Vienna, so Interpol can start moving there. I suppose if Sandor was passing the stuff along through Yugo-slavia into Hungary, Interpol could fix a trap up to catch the people at the other end, too. Or so Lewis thinks."

Something about his voice made me shoot a glance at him. Not quite authority, not quite patronage; but the unmistakable echo of that man-to-woman way even the nicest men adopt when they are letting a woman catch a glimpse of the Man's World. Timothy had joined the club.

I said, not irrelevantly: "He thinks a lot of you, too. Now, I hope we can find this tree where Sandor put the stuff."

"The stretch between the tunnels. A lonely, blasted pine. It's as good as a one-eyed Chinaman with a limp. Oh, we'll find it, don't you worry! There's the railway again now."

When we reached the cut I jumped down into it with a thump. Behind me Timothy slithered on the stones and almost lost his balance. "Watch it," I said. "Are you okay?"

"Yes, but I wish I had my boots. These shoes are murder on wet grass."

Once again we ran forward and down over the tufted Alpine grass until, in front of me, Timothy stopped. "There's no sign of the railway," he said. "D'you think we'd better go back and follow it down, instead of going cross-country?"

"Surely not. I don't see how we can have missed it. We're probably crossing the upper tunnel now. Wait a minute, Tim. Look up there ... that dead tree with the divided trunk. It's just the way he described it. Come on!"

The dead pine clung to the face of a low cliff some fifteen feet above the next loop of the railway, between the yawning openings of two tunnels. "Bang on," I said. "How's that for radar?"

"Vanessa March, dope hound," Timothy said. "Let's look."

We reached the little cliff and realized that it was not as easy as it had looked. A six-inch-wide track, presumably made by rather athletic goats, twisted its way down the railroad. One had to step off this track and, hanging tightly to the trunk of the dead tree, reach up to a hole quite far from the ground.

"Airs above the flaming ground," said Timothy. "I suppose it would be dead easy for Sandor. Well, you'd better let me have a go." He set his foot gingerly on one of the exposed roots of the tree while equally gingerly I slithered past him and edged my way down the goat track onto the railway. "I'll chuck the packages down to you if they're there," Tim said.

And they were. Tim, clinging like a monkey, managed to shove a hand into the hollow and gave a whoop of triumph. "I can feel them!" He sent the first one flying down to me. It was an oblong package with what felt like several smaller packets inside it, flat and neat and sealed in waterproof. A few hundred pounds' worth of dreams and death.

"Okay, next, please." Six more dropped down in turn.

"That's the lot," he said from above. "I'm coming down."

But as he eased his way off the tree roots, it happened: he missed his footing and hurtled down toward the railway track in a foot first fall. Next moment, with a sharp cry of pain, he was sprawling right there at my feet.

"Tim, are you hurt?" I went down on my knees beside him. He was making gasping sounds of pain, his body hunched tightly over his right foot.

"It's stuck. My foot . . . oh, God, it's broken or something."

"Here, let me see. Oh, Tim!"

The force of his fall had driven his foot hard into the little space underneath the center rail, and the sole of his shoe had jammed there, with the foot twisted at a horrible angle. I said, "I'll try to get it out." But wrestle as I would with it, it was fixed tight; and though Tim had now got control of himself, he was white with pain and I was afraid how much I might hurt him if I persisted. "We'll get the shoe undone," I said. "Then you can try to slip your foot out of it."

The laces were soaked and knotted tightly. I bit my lip and tackled them. I had no knife, and Tim's foot was swelling rapidly. After minutes of frantic wrestling and a broken fingernail I gave up. It would be impossible to get the shoe off without cutting the leather. Next I tried to scrape the gravel from under his foot, but here the rail ran over solid rock. There was nothing to be done, but the bitten-down pain in the boy's face terrified me.

It was Timothy who made the only possible suggestion.

"You'll have to go and get help. It's not so bad when we're not hacking at it, and if I turn myself like this . . . Yes, that's better. I'll be okay. Honestly."

He had dropped his pistol. I gave it to him. "All right. I'll be as quick as I can."

"Don't forget the dope. You'd better take the lot. I don't exactly fancy being stuck here with all that strewn round me, even if I do have a gun." He managed a smile. "Good luck."

"And to you." I picked up the packets and ran.

THE RAILWAYMEN'S hut and the jeep were exactly as we had left them. I ran on to the Mercedes, found the key and let myself into the car. I threw the dope onto the back seat, then started the engine and headed downhill. It was a far heavier car than I was used to driving, and the bends were sharp. I had to make a severe effort to suppress my feeling of hurry and concentrate on getting down this very unpleasant bit of road.

But at least it was daylight. I heard a cock crow not far off, and somewhere, nearer still, a train whistled. Smoke was rising from a farm chimney, and behind a thick belt of pines another column of smoke, black this time, spoke of some factory already at work. At the railway station, the train stood with its curious little tilted engine and its three carriages, waiting for the day. A man in dungarees was sweeping the platform by the miniature ticket office. There would certainly be a telephone here.

I stopped the car and hung out of the window. "Excuse me, do you speak English?"

He put a hand up to his ear and with maddening deliberation turned to lay aside his broom before he approached the car. Torn between the desire to drive straight away and waste no more time and the desire to get to the first available telephone as quickly as possible, I jumped out of the car and ran to meet him. "Excuse me, do you speak English?"

I think he said no. Then he started on a flood of totally unintelligible German, but I was no longer listening.

There were two sidings in the tiny station. In one of them stood the train; the other was empty. From it, a long shining section of track led up into the pinewoods; and beyond the first tree-clad foothill I saw the towering column of black smoke that I had thought came from a factory chimney. I remembered the engine's whistle I had heard three minutes ago.

I whirled on the little man and pointed up the track. "A train? A train?" He was elderly, with a drooping mustache and watery blue eyes. He stared at me with complete noncomprehension. I waved frantically again at the standing train, at the smoke, at the track, and pointed to my wrist. "First train, seven o'clock— *sieben Uhr* . . . train gone?"

He gestured toward a clock on the wall behind him; it said half past five. Then, pointing to the smoke on the mountain, he poured out another flood of German. But it wasn't necessary. I had seen that the black smoke was indeed marching slowly but inexorably up through the trees; and, clear above them, I saw an engine moving, pushing something that looked like a freight car. . . .

Beside me, the old man said: "*Gasthaus* . . . café," and pointed. I understood now. Josef had of course only mentioned the tourist trains, and the first one did indeed run at seven. No one had seen fit to mention that an engine took supplies up for the restaurant at half past five.

The telephone was not a bit of use now. The old man was still talking volubly as I said, "Thank you." I left him talking to the empty air. By the mercy of heaven there was room to turn. I swept the Mercedes round like a boomerang.

As I drove the car like a bomb up that horrible little road I tried desperately to recall the relationship between road and railway. As far as I could remember, there were only two places where they joined: a few bends above the station, the road ran along with the track for perhaps a hundred yards; the second place was at the end of the auto road. And that would be my last chance to stop the train.

I was past thinking, past reckoning what might happen if I miscalculated on these hairpin bends. I just drove on and up as fast as I dared. The fifth bend, slightly easier than the others, brought me to a long straightish sweep between trees. To my left, a cloud of black smoke puffed deliberately by. I put my foot down. Tree shadows accelerated across me in one long flickering blur. And then suddenly the rails swooped in from the left to join the road. For perhaps a hundred and thirty yards track and road ran side by side. The track here was empty, but black smoke hung in the boughs of the trees. I leaned as far out of my window as I could, straining to see forward up the railway before it curved away into the forest.

There was the square tail of the little engine with its hanging lamp, lit for the mountain mists, swinging like a small vanishing red eye into the trees beneath the black cloud of smoke. It was going slowly, the grade so steep that I could see the freight car beyond the engine. There were two men in the cabin, one leaning out to look forward up the track, the other uptilting what looked like a bottle of beer. I shoved my hand down on the horn and held it there.

I'll say this for the Mercedes; she had a horn like the crack of doom. Both men looked round, startled. I leaned out of my window and waved frantically, shouting the most appropriate German word I could think of: "*Achtung! Achtung!*" After a couple of seconds' agonizing pause one of them—the engineer—reached out a hand as if for the brake.

Another few yards and my road would bear me away from the railway again. I trod on my own brake and hung out, waving more frantically than ever.

The engineer found what he had been reaching for, and pulled. It was the whistle; it gave a long, friendly toot-toot. The other man lifted his beer bottle in a happy wave, the engine gave a last toot, and then the forest closed in behind it.

Why I didn't run the Mercedes off the road I shall never know. I just managed to wrench her nose round in time as the road bore away from the railway. I still had one chance, and through my exasperated fury I realized that it was a fairly strong one. The Mercedes would surely be more than capable of reaching the railwaymen's hut in time for me to stop the train. . . .

She had certainly better be. All that this last little effort had done was to make the train announce its coming to Timothy, and, however the boy had felt before, he would now know he was trapped up there with an engine mounting the hill toward him.

Mercifully, with every curve the grade eased and the bends grew wider. I have no idea at what speed I took the last six or seven stretches of that road, but the whole hillside seemed to reel past me in a long flickering blur of sun and shadow, and then suddenly I was round the last bend, and there was the hut and the shining stretch of track beside it.

The Mercedes zoomed along the last straight stretch like a homing bee and fetched up with shrieking tires within a yard of the hut. I jumped out and ran onto the railway track. I had done it! Below where I stood I saw the smoke, perhaps a quarter of a mile away, where the engine chugged its stolid, unexcited way up the track. They would not see me until they broke out of the trees some fifty yards away. I hoped they were keeping a sharp lookout forward. If I sounded the horn again? But I had seen how they reacted to that. Or if I had anything red to wave . . . Ah; the red rear lights on the Mercedes!

I ran back to the car. As I jumped in, the column of black smoke burst above the trees to my left and I saw the blunt nose of the freight car. I switched the lights full on and drove as hard as I could for the railway line. The tires lurched over the rail and the car stopped with her rear lights blazing a message to the approaching train. For good measure I jammed my hand down hard over the horn, while with my free hand I opened the off-side door. I would give them till twenty-five yards, and then I would be out of the car like a bolting rabbit.

Why had I thought the engine slow? It seemed to be roaring up the hill all of a sudden with the speed of a crack express. I could hear the panting of the little engine above the blare of my horn. Thirty-five yards. Thirty. I let go the horn and dived toward the open door. There was the clang of a bell, and a shrill furious whistle from the engine. I flung myself out of the door and ran clear, and with a horrible shriek of brakes, another toot and a flurry of angry shouts the train came to a standstill about seven yards behind the Mercedes.

The two men leaped down out of the cabin and advanced on me, the co-engineer still holding the beer bottle. A third man swung down—there had been a guard. They all started to shout in furious German—and I can think of no better language to be furious in. For a full half minute I stood there helpless before the storm.

At last there was a pause and I said desperately: "I'm sorry, but I had to do it. There's a boy on the line higher up. A—a *Junge*, on the *Eisenbahn*. I had to stop you."

The man with the beer bottle turned to the engineer. "*Was meint sie?*"

The driver snapped something at him and then said to me in a ghastly guttural, which at the moment I wouldn't have exchanged for a Gielgud rendering of Shakespeare: "Is that you crazy are? There is no young on the line. There is on the line an auto. And why? I ask why?"

"You speak English! Thank God! Listen, *mein Herr*, I'm sorry I had to stop the train—"

"*Ach*, yes, you have the train stopped, but this is a danger. This is what I will to the police tell. My brother, he is the police, he will of this to you speak. For this you must pay."

"I'll pay; but *listen*, please! I need help."

All of a sudden he was with me. His first reaction of shock and anger had ebbed, and let him see what must be showing clearly in my face: not only the swollen bruises, but the strain of the night and my terror for Timothy. Suddenly, in place of an angry beefy bully, I found myself confronted by a large man with kindly blue eyes who said: "There is trouble, yes? What trouble?"

"A young man fell on the railway up there. His leg is hurt." I pantomimed it. "He can't move."

"I understand. This young man, is he wide?"

"No, he's quite thin." I caught myself. "Is he *what?*"

"Wide. In German, *weit*. Is he wide from here?"

"Oh—is he *far*. Not very, only a little—more far, beyond the first tunnel." How did one pantomime a tunnel? Frantically I tried, and somehow he understood.

"You will show us. We shall now the auto off bring."

It didn't take those burly men long to shift the Mercedes. Then, almost as if I were a parcel, they heaved me up into the cab and with a horrifying eruption of black smoke and a shriek of cog-wheels the train resumed its ascent.

I suppose there is something in all of us which makes us want to drive an engine. Now that my apprehension had lifted, I enjoyed the ride; and indeed of all the engines I have ever seen this one was the most entertaining, possessing the almost forgotten charm of the nursery trains of childhood. The tank was squat and black, the smokestack enormous, and every available inch of the engine, it seemed, was festooned with tubes, wires and gadgets of unimaginable uses. The paint was green, the wheels scarlet, and the whole thing was smelly, dirty, diabolically noisy, and entirely charming.

We threaded our way along a curve of hill thick with gentians, and then ran between walls of rock until I saw, some yards ahead of us, the black mouth of the first tunnel.

The engineer made signs that I should keep back in the cabin. He could have spared himself the pains. I had ducked already. The tunnel looked not nearly big enough, but through it we went, with not more than a foot to spare. It was quite a long tunnel, and in the tight, heavy blackness the din was horrifying. I almost screamed at the engineer to go on as fast as he could out of this inferno of heat and blackness and shattering noise.

Then light was running through the filthy clouds of smoke; a bell clanged sharply; and I heard the sliding screech of brakes and the scream of steel on steel. The train stopped with a great puffing sigh.

I put a hand to the rail and vaulted down to the gravel. "Tim, Tim! Are you all right?"

When I ran up to him he was slowly uncurling himself from a desperately cramped position; and I realized he had tried to cram his long body down between the rack and one of the rails, hoping that if the worst happened and the train ran over him he might escape the wheels. That he could not have done so was quite obvious, and this he must have known. If he had been white before, he now looked like death itself; but as he pulled himself into a sitting position he managed a sort of smile. I knelt beside him. "I'm sorry; you must have heard it coming for miles. It was the best I could do."

"A bit . . . overdramatic, I'd say." He was making a magnificent effort to take it undramatically, but his voice was very shaky indeed. "I'll never laugh at a thriller again." He straightened up. "Actually, I'd say it was a pretty good 'best.' Transport and reinforcements for Lewis, all at one go."

The men had run up, and in a matter of seconds the engineer and guard had the laces cut from the now badly swollen foot and were beginning, very gently, to cut the leather of the shoe. One man went to the freight car and came back with a bottle of brandy which he presented to Timothy.

I said: "Go on, it's what you need; and for pity's sake don't drink it all. I could do with some myself."

And presently, as the brandy went round—the railwaymen had evidently felt the strain as much as Timothy and I—Tim's foot was drawn gently out of the wreck of his shoe, and willing hands half carried him to the waiting train. The freight car where they deposited us was stacked high with supplies, but there was room to sit on the floor.

"We will now," said the engineer to Timothy, "take you straight up to the *Gasthaus*. No doubt Frau Becker will attend to your foot, and Johann Becker will give you breakfast."

"If you have the money," said the guard sourly.

"That is no matter, I shall pay," said the engineer.

"What are they saying?" I asked, and Tim told me.

"Well, I wouldn't guarantee the breakfast," I said, "but I can't think of a better way to bring those thugs down to the village than in this freight car. And we've even provided the solid citizens Lewis asked for. Have you the German to explain to them that they're going to find Lewis, with the Beckers and another man at the other end of an automatic pistol, and that they must render him every assistance?"

"Okay, I can but try. I wish I knew the German for cocaine. . . . What's the matter?"

"The cocaine," I said blankly. "I left it in the car. And the key, too."

We stared at one another for a long moment of horror, then suddenly began to laugh, a weak, silly sort of laughter that turned to helpless giggles, while our three friends stood over us looking sympathetic.

"Well, I only hope," said Timothy at length, dabbing his eyes, "that you've got the English to explain to Lewis in."

And so it was that Lewis, holding Frau Becker, her husband and her husband's friend at the end of the Beretta, was relieved of his vigil not by the cold-eyed professionals he must have been expecting but by a peculiarly assorted gang of amateurs, two of whom were slightly hilarious, not to say light-headed, and all of whom smelled quite distinctly of Herr Becker's brandy.

It was some four hours later.

The cocaine had been recovered, our prisoners had been delivered to the properly cold-eyed professionals, and the battered Mercedes had brought us all to Schloss Zechstein, where Timothy's foot had been fixed up by a doctor who talked soothingly about sprains and a day in bed; and I had had a bath and was floating in a happy dream of relief and reaction while Lewis dragged off his battered clothes and fished in his case for a razor.

Then I remembered something. "Lee Elliott!" I said. "Did you register as Lee Elliott?"

"I didn't register. A female in the hall bleated something at me, but I just said 'Later' and pressed the lift button." He threw his sweater into a corner and started on his shirt buttons. "Come to think, the porter started in the other direction with my suitcase, but I took it from him and came along here."

"Lewis—no, just a minute, darling . . . *Hadn't* you better go down straightaway and get it cleared up?"

"I've done all the clearing up I'm doing for one day. It can wait till morning."

"Oh, darling, be serious, it *is* morning. If anyone came in—"

"They can't. The door's locked." He grinned at me and sent the shirt flying after the sweater. "If we need to reopen communications we can do so later—by telephone. First things first, my girl. I want a bath and a shave, and—didn't you hear what the doctor said? A day in bed is what we all need."

"You could be right," I said.

Epilogue

THE HALL was white and gold, like a ballroom. The huge crystal chandeliers glowed as ornaments in themselves rather than as lights, for September sunshine streamed in through the great windows. Where there should have been a polished dance floor there was a wide space of sawdust and tanbark. To begin with, it had been cleanly raked into a pattern of fine lines, but the hoofs had beaten it into surfy shapes as the white stallions performed their grave beautiful patterns to the music.

And now the music stopped. The five white horses filed out through the archway at the far end of the hall. The packed alcoves of people craned forward. Beside me Timothy was taut with excitement; and on my other side sat Lewis, sunburned, reading the program as if nothing mattered in the world but the fact that on this morning the great Neapolitano Petra was back at the Spanish Riding School, and the director himself was going to ride him, and all Vienna had come to see.

Beyond the archway a horse appeared, his rider sitting still as a statue. He paced forward slowly into the hall, ears alert, nostrils flared, his movements proud and cool and soberly controlled, and yet somehow filled with delight.

There was no hint of stiffness now; and the beat of the music hid the muffled thudding in the sand, so that the stallion seemed to skim as effortlessly as a swan in full sail. Light poured and splashed on the white coat where the last shadows of black had been bleached away, and his thick, silky mane and tail tossed like a flurry of snow.

The music changed; the director sat still; the old stallion snorted, mouthed the bit and lifted himself, rider and all, into the first of the "airs above the ground."

Then it was over, and he came soberly forward to the salute, ears moving to the applause. The rider took off his hat in the traditional salute to the Emperor's portrait, but somehow effacing himself and his skill, and presenting only the horse.

Old Piebald bent his head. He was facing us full on, six feet away, looking (you would have thought) straight at us; but this time there was no welcoming whicker, not even a gleam in the big dark eye that one could call recognition. The eyes, like the stallion's whole bearing, were absorbed, concentrated, inward, his entire being caught up again and contained in the old disciplines that fitted him as inevitably as his own skin.

He backed, turned, and went out on the ebb tide of applause. The lights dimmed, and the white horse dwindled down the corridor beyond the arch, to where his name was still above his stall, and fresh straw waiting.

MARY STEWART

W<small>HEN</small> Mary Stewart's first novel was accepted for publication in 1954, her publisher's only major query was about the name he assumed she had adopted as a pseudonym. "But my name *was* Mary Rainbow," the author replied. "If you don't like it I'll use my married name: Mary Stewart." And by that name she has become known as a most successful writer of suspense novels.

The daughter of a Church of England clergyman, Mrs. Stewart grew up in her father's parish in County Durham, and at eighteen went to Durham University where she studied English literature. During World War II she joined the English department as a lecturer.

Mrs. Stewart first met her husband, then a young Lecturer in Geology, on V-E night, and they were married three months later. Now head of the Geology department of Edinburgh University, he often takes research trips abroad, and Mrs. Stewart seizes every opportunity to accompany him. The vivid, exotic backgrounds of her novels are souvenirs of these journeys.

Her gift for description, coupled with her ability to tell a first-rate story, has been realized in such books as *Nine Coaches Waiting*, *The Ivy Tree*, *The Moon-Spinners* and *This Rough Magic*. Readers of her popular novels find that they become involved, as she does, in the attractive characters she creates. "I hate to leave the people at the end of a book," she confesses. This is one reason why she is thinking of taking Vanessa and Lewis, the principal characters in *Airs Above the Ground*, to the Middle East in a later novel. Her most recent novel is *The Gabriel Hounds*.